CHRONOS

EUROPEAN PERSPECTIVES

EUROPEAN PERSPECTIVES

A SERIES IN SOCIAL THOUGHT AND CULTURAL CRITICISM

Lawrence D. Kritzman, Editor

European Perspectives presents outstanding books by leading European thinkers. With both classic and contemporary works, the series aims to shape the major intellectual controversies of our day and to facilitate the tasks of historical understanding.

For a complete list of books in the series, see page 287.

FRANÇOIS HARTOG

CHRONOS

The West Confronts Time

TRANSLATED BY S. R. GILBERT

COLUMBIA UNIVERSITY PRESS

NEW YORK

Columbia University Press wishes to express its appreciation for assistance given by the government of France through the Ministère de la Culture in the preparation of this translation.

Columbia University Press
Publishers Since 1893
New York   Chichester, West Sussex
cup.columbia.edu
Chronos: L'occident aux prises avec le Temps by François Hartog
copyright © 2020 Editions Gallimard, Paris
Translation copyright © 2022 Columbia University Press
Paperback edition, 2024
All rights reserved

Library of Congress Cataloging-in-Publication Data
Names: Hartog, François, author.
Title: Chronos : the West confronts time / François Hartog ;
translated by S. R. Gilbert.
Description: New York : Columbia University Press, [2022] |
Series: European perspectives: a series in social thought and
cultural criticism | Includes bibliographical references and index.
Identifiers: LCCN 2021061936 (print) | LCCN 2021061937 (ebook) |
ISBN 9780231203128 (hardback) | ISBN 9780231203135 (pbk.) |
ISBN 9780231554886 (ebook)
Subjects: LCSH: Time—Philosophy. | Time—Religious
aspects—Christianity.
Classification: LCC HM656 .H36713 2022 (print) | LCC HM656 (ebook) |
DDC 304.2/3—dc23/eng/20220307
LC record available at https://lccn.loc.gov/2021061936
LC ebook record available at https://lccn.loc.gov/2021061937

Cover design: Milenda Nan Ok Lee
Cover image: Dirk Renckhoff / Alamy

Columbia University Press gratefully acknowledges the generous contribution to this book provided by the Florence Gould Foundation Endowment Fund for French Translation.

CONTENTS

To Readers of the English Edition   ix
Preface: The Undeducible Present   xvii

INTRODUCTION: FROM THE GREEKS TO THE CHRISTIANS   1

1   THE CHRISTIAN REGIME OF HISTORICITY: CHRONOS BETWEEN KAIROS AND KRISIS   10

2   THE CHRISTIAN ORDER OF TIME AND ITS SPREAD   49

3   NEGOTIATING WITH CHRONOS   83

4   DISSONANCES AND FISSURES   109

5   IN THE THRALL OF CHRONOS   139

6 CHRONOS DESTITUTED, CHRONOS RESTORED 183

CONCLUSION: THE ANTHROPOCENE AND HISTORY 226

Notes 239
Index 277

TO READERS OF THE ENGLISH EDITION

*C**HRONOS: THE** West Confronts Time* follows my book *Regimes of Historicity: Presentism and Experiences of Time* and offers a genealogy of Western time that begins earlier than did *Regimes* and continues to the COVID-19 pandemic. The goal of the earlier book was to try out the notion of the regime of historicity, demonstrating its heuristic potential to illuminate—or better illuminate—temporal crises, those moments Hannah Arendt called "gaps" in which temporal signposts vanished and disorientation set in. After serving as a trusty signpost, the past suddenly slipped into darkness. And inversely the future, up to then a surging engine, abruptly dodged out of view. When only the present seems to be available, when time has no reference point but itself, how is life or action thinkable? I proposed calling such a singular condition *presentism*. While the past had dominated the old regime of historicity, and the future had taken on the leading role under the new regime, during the presentist regime only the present remained. No one would claim that presentism swept into every locale and every social stratum overnight. But since the 1970s the presentist tendency has been buttressed in Europe by the digital revolution, by the increased role of finance in the economy, and more broadly by globalization. Capturing the texture of the present as accurately as possible was the explicit goal of the book, although the presentist present had only just begun.

In *Chronos* I again turn to the regime of historicity, and while my goal remains the same, my approach has changed. The inquiry now opens with Christian time—the Christian regime of historicity—presented as the beginning point of what eventually became Western time. Where did it come from? Who launched it? What initially drove it forward? My starting point has changed, yes, and my ending too: the beginning of the twenty-first century bears little resemblance to the end of the twentieth. Presentism has not gone away, but it is now thrown into question, and, to borrow the phrase of Dipesh Chakrabarty, a "planetary age" has upended all of our temporal preconceptions.[1]

* * *

This history begins in the Middle East, in ancient Palestine, centered on Jerusalem, with one book, the Bible—the matrix for the three revealed religions, the three "religions of the book," also known as the "Abrahamic religions." While I have traced only the Christian thread of what is a long and complicated history, it is clear that there would never have been a New Testament or a Christian time without the Jewish prophets and apocalyptists. No more than there would have been an Islamic time or a Koran without those earlier books and the various communities—Jewish, Christian, polytheistic—inhabiting seventh-century Arabia.

To characterize Christian time, the subject of chapter 1, I have borrowed and transformed three concepts used by the Greeks to apprehend time: *chronos*, or ordinary time; *kairos*, or opportunity, the decisive moment; and *krisis*, or the judgment that slices. Between the second and the tenth centuries, Christian time gradually assumed control over the Roman Occident, the kingdoms that came after, European space more generally, until, beginning in the sixteenth century, it colonized the rest of the world. One may speak of the Catholic and Protestant missionaries who brought Christ to new lands as "Christophores," but the same missions made them "Chronophores," as they brought the true time. Such a time comprised not just a daily discipline marked by prayers and divine offices as well as a calendar (originally liturgical), but a universal chronology and a theology of history too. To convert the world is to labor with the end of time in mind.

Addressing the wide range of times and calendars used by different communities, the first Greek chronographers and historians set to work to establish synchronisms by which they oriented themselves—battles separated by great distances occurred at the same time, the reign of this ruler overlapped with another at a far remove, and so on. Hence the prominent list of Olympic champions, an instrument for measuring time that permitted each city to find its own place. Since it was Panhellenic, it belonged to no one. But the Christians were compelled to go further. From synchronism they advanced to synchronization, enthroning Christ as the great synchronizer of all times, past and future. The Incarnation initiated a time unlike any other, radically new, and it would inform every time, whatever it was and wherever it held sway. Until the Judgment Day, just after the torments of the Apocalypse, this time will last. Incarnation and Judgment became the two limits set on the history of the world. How this Christian order of time borne by the apostolic and the Roman Catholic Church developed, spread, and imposed itself is the subject of chapters 2 and 3, beginning in Europe and occupying the length of the Middle Ages.

Still, doubts soon arose, and this providential temporal order was undermined by waves of skepticism. With the coming of modernity, time outstripped the bounds imposed by scripture. Long a subordinate, Chronos now stepped free of its bonds and seized its chance as a global sovereign. Did this spell the end for the times born of the biblical matrix, the often messianic and apocalyptic rhythms of Judaism, Islam, and Christianity? Those who hoped so and labored to that end included the French revolutionaries who drew up in 1793 a new, purely Republican calendar, part of a project to fashion a new time. As we know, they failed: calendars put up a fight. During this period, the three concepts that framed Christian time—chronos, kairos, krisis—were, despite answering to Chronos, present and active all along. That inversion is the subject of chapters 4 and 5. The title held by chronos time may have been supreme, but it was always *primus inter partes*. Of this the evidence leaves no room for doubt.

* * *

During the decades on either side of the turn of the twentieth century, a period when Chronos worked to extend its empire, time gave rise to lively debates. Dignitaries at a conference convened in Washington, D.C., in 1884 selected Greenwich as the prime meridian for a universal time, GMT, and for slicing the globe into twenty-four time zones. The procedure entailed protracted planning and many delays, and it met with resistance. All along the United States, Canada, and Great Britain shared the leading parts, while France was sidelined. When the meridian of Greenwich was named "synchronizer," the French, isolated, had no choice but to abandon "their" meridian, Paris. From that date forward, each nation would establish its own time: to each its own time, and a common time for all. In theory, any meridian could have served as the reference point, yet it so happened that the one selected, Greenwich, lay as the very heart of the dominant imperialist power of the day. Promoted as a monument of "modernity" and "utility," the universal mean time was unmistakably Western, Anglo-American even.

Those years also witnessed a burst of work on calendrical reforms in Europe, the United States, and elsewhere. The newly formed League of Nations embraced the project in the 1920s. As a complement to commerce and globalization, a "world calendar" would bring all calendars into agreement and contribute to world peace. Among those non-Western leaders who favored the idea was Mahatma Gandhi, just as he supported the idea of "a uniform coinage for all countries and a supplementary language—like Esperanto, for example—for all peoples."[2] In the end, unlike the effort to reform clock time, this calendrical reform failed. Why? Because calendars involve not only, not even mostly chronos time, but a mixture of chronos time and religious time. And on that occasion religious leaders made their opposition to the proposal known—the Vatican would not even discuss it. With the prospect of wandering Fridays, Saturdays, and Sundays, Easter sliding past April 21, the three religions of the book made a united front. To cite but a single example, in 1932 Joseph Hertz, chief rabbi of the

United Hebrew Congregations of the British Empire, launched a "Battle for the Sabbath"; he had spied on calendar reform the fingerprints of "American financial interests" and an attempt to "Americanize and mechanize life."[3] Facing such resistance, the various governments conceded. Hitler had just come to power; war seemed close at hand; no further talks were held. As we have since seen, capitalism managed to adapt.

Would it be fair to say that the America that inspired in Hertz visions of "mechanized life" (he was thinking of Fordism) was utterly dominated by chronos time? Did that time subsequently take power? In other words, did the empire of Chronos and the "American empire" march hand in hand? Any attempt to address these questions seriously would go far beyond the present contextual sketch. A few comments must suffice to show that in the United States Christian time, or more accurately the Christian regime of historicity, not only has survived—it is quite active today. When we consider the entirety of the score, we see that the melody line has never been interrupted; it has continued, gaining in volume. It would be a mistake to imagine that the religiosity that saturates political life is lip service to the founding fathers. Only in 1956 did Congress designate "In God we trust" the nation's official motto and order it printed on currency. President Jimmy Carter is a very pious Southern Baptist; George W. Bush, a born-again Christian, included in his first inaugural address a comment inspired by a psalm: "An angel still rides in the whirlwind and directs this storm."[4] This is quite close to messianism. And, lastly, Joe Biden is a practicing Catholic. More broadly, America's many evangelical churches have intended since the nineteenth century to revive the nation's Christianity, and they participate more in kairos time (which emphasizes a direct connection to God) than in chronos time. Many of those churches envision the Apocalypse on the horizon. Few would accuse the pastor Jerry Falwell (1933–2007), a famous televangelist who founded Moral Majority, of paying no attention to worldly time, let alone worldly satisfactions. Yet in 1999 he did not shrink from announcing the coming in less than ten years' time of the Antichrist—a Jew, according to Falwell.

In fact, a burst of apocalypticism has been noticeable in the early twenty-first century. The phenomenon is complex and anything but consistent. To get at its scale, its diverse constituents, the intensity of belief it inspires, a sophisticated comparative study is needed. Unlocking it means connecting it both to the crisis the Western world now faces, to varying degrees, as it looks into the future and to the consequential rise in the fortunes of the present—presentism, in my formulation. A darker future that seems to be growing downright menacing has precipitated a doubling down on the present. As one would expect, a crisis affecting modern time has cleared the way for apocalyptic upheavals. Added to the doubts assailing modern time and the closely related idea of progress come the dangers associated with global warming, whose granularity increases constantly. The final chapter addresses a double movement. With a present ever more presentist at its throat, Chronos stands poised to surrender its empire, even as the rise of the Anthropocene drags in a future, a great deal of future, an immense future amounting to millions of years. Once again Chronos encounters an empire, but this is not its own; this is a wholly new empire ruled by the Earth system.

Apocalypse has found an arena within this unlikely configuration, where one side offers a future on the point of vanishing while the other threatens us with the imminent sixth mass extinction. While the "traditional" apocalyptists perform their parts as they always have, the very word *apocalypse* has penetrated the glossary of culture workers: producers, directors, screenwriters, singers, authors. . . . So often the word feels like a synonym of *disaster*, yet the disaster films of today possess an added level of drama since instead of *a* disaster they depict *the* disaster to end all disasters, the one from which there is at last no escape. For a new ice age, see *The Day After Tomorrow* (2004). For a mutant named Apocalypse intent on eradicating the human race, see *X-Men: Apocalypse* (2016). You may also wish to consult, in the same key, maps of the United States that address the question, "How vulnerable is your state to the Zombie Apocalypse?" A related theme, explored by Cormac McCarthy in his famous novel-turned-film *The Road* (2006; 2009), is that of the day after, a world whose traversal reveals an endless disaster. All the Jewish and Christian Apocalypses halted on the threshold of the day after, beyond which lies the beginning of a time utterly other.

In closing, I would note that Western time has not been alone in grappling with the Apocalypse. All three religions of the book have addressed it. In the Koran, Allah is called the "Master of Judgment," and his Prophet is ordered to announce the "Signs of the Hour" that he sees coming. Most recently, Islamic State's mobilization of the Apocalypse entailed enormous bloodshed. When Abu Bakr al-Baghdadi abruptly imposed the law of God in Al-Sham, that is, the land of the end of times, he opened a new time, an apocalyptic present that turned away from the chronos time of the infidels and crusaders. Textbooks were recovered in 2017 when the Iraqi Army wrested Mosul back from the control of Islamic State. One contained an English lesson in which the word *time* was illustrated with a clock attached to a bomb.[5] The message was clear: time, specifically Western time, would not last much longer. Its sequel would be the endless present of the caliphate of Daesh. This scale model of the Apocalypse, this portable Apocalypse, is implemented by the "martyrs" at the moment they detonate the explosive belts they wear.

François Hartog
November 2021

TRANSLATOR'S NOTE

The author has chosen to preserve in the English edition the use of the term *Parousia*, in French "la Parousie." From the Greek παρουσία, meaning "presence," this is the term used in most European languages (German, Spanish, Polish, Catalan, Swedish, Slovenian, Italian, and so on) to express what is known in English, Welsh, and Irish alone as "the Second Coming."

PREFACE

The Undeducible Present

*To what use history? Only—
and it's a lot—to multiply ideas—
and not to keep us from seeing the original
present—undeducible.*

—Paul Valéry

CHRONOS—WHO OR what is it? The question is not new, yet it renews itself each time we reflect on the times in which we live—the present, our present. Yet instantly that warning arrives from Paul Valéry, who never missed an opportunity to lecture the historians who, alleging that they were practicing science, were in fact practicing literature. In his *Notebooks*, the record of the day's thoughts drawn up late at night, he often criticized the history that, looking backward, saw no further than from one day to the next. The lessons of history? Certainly not! Rather, a history "to multiply ideas," which is not bad at all—indeed, it is a great deal. Offering up ideas by multiplying points of view helps us to see that which we do not see, do not wish to see, are not able to see—that which blinds us, fascinates us, or terrifies us—in a word, the "undeducible" present.[1]

Still, is this a case of utter novelty? No, to the extent that it does not spring from nowhere and is not made of nothing: it is a social object with its own texture, a tapestry in which warp and weft interlace, fashioning distinctive hues and patterns. The texture of the present has fascinated me—an understatement—for many years. That interest inspired the reflections on time that I inaugurated with *Regimes of Historicity* and then extended in this new study. As always in my work, my path has amounted to a long detour.[2] That has meant setting out from the present and traveling deep into time, so as to return to the present somehow improved. On this occasion, we do not start from Odysseus's stinging encounter with historicity, the moment when he hears a Phaeacian bard praise "Odysseus" as though he had ceased to exist. Rather I shall begin by traveling toward the very beginnings of Christianity and even earlier still, to understand which revolution in time ushered in the minor apocalyptic sect that broke away from Judaism—a revolution precisely in the texture of time, through the establishment of an unprecedented present. Why begin one's journey from so distant a point? Because this new time left a lasting, possibly even permanent, mark on Western time. Because modern time, in every sense of the term, emerged from Christian time: from there it came, and from there it has moved on.

For humans, life has always meant experiencing time—an experience by turns intoxicating, painful, often tragic, and, finally, ineluctable. Confronting Chronos has always been, for each social group, routine—whether that meant trying to catch hold of it or flee from it. Trying to regulate it by cutting it up or measuring it has meant setting out to master it, wholly a matter of believing in it and convincing others to believe as well. Over the course of millennia many methods have been used, countless really: everyday stories, myths, religious formulations, as well as theological, philosophical, and political formulations, scientific theories, works of art, works of literature, of architecture, urban designs, the invention and fabrication of tools to measure time and to regulate the life of societies and individuals. Nothing truly human is foreign to time—nothing escapes from its grip, its domination.

Yet such a history, the most familiar—the one that humans have told themselves, the one they have claimed—is only partial. Forgotten or overlooked, Chronos extends far beyond human time or that world time that the moderns fashioned for their own use and gain, thinking that it might be reduced to a pure present, as with the ass's skin in Balzac's novel, a process that nearly amounts to destroying time. Since our recent arrival in a new era, known as the Anthropocene, our economy of time has been dislodged by a time both immensely old and quite new, that of the Earth. Those various strategies for dominating time that were developed and deployed over the centuries, the rhythm and rule of the history of the West initiated by the splitting of Chronos into natural time and human time—all now undone, ruined. How are we to come to terms with this unprecedented time, a time more "undeducible" than ever? We stand in need of a shift in perspective, a conversion really, but to what?

Chronos is the omnipresent, the inevitable, the ineluctable, "the child of the finite," to cite the final words of the great history of the philosophy of time, Krzysztof Pomian's *The Order of Time*.[3] But above all it is that which cannot be grasped: elusive Chronos. That is the label that appears, as soon as Chronos is mentioned, from the earliest Greek tales to today, including along the way the famous Augustinian paradox on time—so long as no one asks him what time is, he knows; as soon as the question is posed, he no longer knows.[4]

So it is that, in the early 1920s, a leading Swiss horological engineer, author of a work on electric clocks, feels obliged to write that time "cannot be defined in substance; it is, metaphysically speaking, as mysterious as matter and space."[5] This comment, surely not meant to stir up trouble, is but a reminder of a truism; the hatching of ever more precise clocks—evidently the writer's first priority—will not be affected. In *The Order of Time*, Pomian scrutinizes what he calls the "well-known polysemy" of the word "time." Also, due to the "fundamental presupposition" that there are "plural times," he advocates a "stratigraphical approach" to time.[6] Rather than bring us face to face with Chronos itself, such an approach illumines the paths and procedures by which others have pursued it.[7]

The Order of Time is also the title of a book by the physicist Carlo Rovelli, who readily addresses the "mystery" of time. Published in 2017 (English edition: 2018), that work opens by showing that the "growth" of our scientific knowledge has been accompanied by a "disintegration" of the notion of time; in the second part, Rovelli leads the reader toward the "world without time" of quantum gravity, while the third part is a return toward lost time, "the time that we are accustomed to." He concludes that "the mystery of time is ultimately, perhaps, more about ourselves than about the cosmos."[8] While I am not competent to offer any pronouncements on quantum gravity as a world without time, I have retained Rovelli's approach to the problem, for in his contribution to the endless debate over cosmic time versus psychological time—initiated by the Greeks and dramatized by Augustine—the physicist, our contemporary, thrusts us toward psychological time.[9] Rovelli even ends his book with a passage from Ecclesiastes evoking the approach of death.

* * *

In what follows, you will find neither a philosophy of Western time, nor a history of time from antiquity to the present, nor a catalogue of the technologies that made the measurement of time ever more precise. Such a catalogue, if one dared attempt it, might never end—and what would it tell us?[10] We would know more, but would our understanding be any better? Instead this survey of Chronos embarks with a question in hand and tracks a unifying thread. My previous books, themselves just so many freeze frames on temporal crises, posed the same question addressed here, an unsettled inquiry into the present time. What is that time? What is our relation to time? What is our "today"—few would be tempted to call it a "beautiful today"—made of? The thread unifying this work of conceptual history is the regime of historicity's radar, and the goal has always been to illumine temporal crises. In those moments shifting landmarks throw us off balance, and the articulations of past, present, and future come undone.

As always, it is the shift that interests me: temporal crises or "gaps," as Hannah Arendt called them. Think of those moments when something that was still there yesterday, which left a trace, slips into darkness and undoes itself, while at the same time something new, something unprecedented, seeks a voice, despite lacking (for now) the words it needs to shape itself. For a long time, I was haunted by that sentence from Michel de Certeau: "It might seem that an entire society expresses what it is in the process of fabricating through the representations of what it is in the process of losing."[11] And so, as always, we encounter that discrepancy, that lag between what we know and what we see. How are we to see something never before seen? How are we to say something that has never been said? How are we to offer a meaning that is not the "purer" meaning with which Stéphane Mallarmé sought to endow the words of the tribe, but a meaning that signifies something unprecedented? Valéry was posing, in his own way, the same question. But could it be that today the gap between what our societies are "in the process of losing" and what is coming into existence has become so vast that those societies no longer even know what to "build," let alone how? Or, more seriously, it may become impossible to build without making something utterly other. Valéry's "undeducible" would be intensified. This question, that of today, will accompany us throughout this inquiry, beginning with the Christian crisis of time and its resolution, continuing with the crises of modern time, and concluding with the contemporary crisis of time, that of the Anthropocene.

Thus the following pages do not all address time, and they do not address all of time. Rather, they constitute an essay that examines the order of times and the eras of time in what was becoming the Western world. Much as Buffon distinguished among the "epochs" of nature, one may distinguish among the epochs of time. And as we examine the transition from one to the next, we shall pass from how the Greeks understood Chronos to the Anthropocene, a time that eludes our grasp, maybe for now, maybe forever. We will dwell on the time of the Christians, a new order of time conceived and instituted by the early church.[12] Christianity opened a new era of time—for the faithful, it endures today. This unprecedented way of talking about the past, the present, and the future amounted to a specific regime of historicity committed to presentism: the present is the dominant category, specifically apocalyptic presentism. Even though there has been much flirting with apocalypse lately, Christian presentism was quite different from today's presentism, which has been with us for a half century. Why then, given that presentism allows for only a minimal chronos time, revive scenarios that, in one way or another, picture an ending that draws ever nearer?

What entitles me to open an inquiry on Christian time? After all, I am anything but an exegete, one who offers guidance and interpretations from within a canonical text. Nor am I a commentator, for that would mean thinking alongside and explaining those texts. I possess none of the authority that accompanies such titles. I am only a reader, posing as I read these documents a single question—what is the time that they weave? A common reader then, with a question.

I must thank those who were kind enough to read these pages, whose encouragement and advice over the past few years, as the book was gradually coming together, meant so much to me. My thanks to Olivier Bomsel, to Thomas Hirsch, to Christian Jambet, to Gérard Lenclud, who has acted as my first reader for a good many years now, to Olivier Mongin, to Robert Morrissey, to Guy Strouma. My thanks, too, to Dipesh Chakrabarty, my guide to the Anthropocene. With each of them I have spoken more than once. To Pierre Nora, in closing, I wish to convey gratitude and friendship. He published my first book, *The Mirror of Herodotus*, forty years ago, when I was a young member of the "Vernant gang," and he both encouraged me to persevere with this one and helped me bring it to a happy conclusion. I am aware of my debt to him. This book, finally, is dedicated to my granddaughter Georgia, born at the very moment when this study of Chronos, the ever elusive, was being completed. Maybe one day she will read it.

INTRODUCTION

From the Greeks to the Christians

For what is time?" Augustine's meditation, which opens with these words, is so often cited that it has become the emblematic reflection on time, effectively closing the book on the topic. "Who could find any quick or easy answer to that? Who could even grasp it in his thought clearly enough to put the matter into words? Yet is there anything to which we refer in conversation with more familiarity, any matter of more common experience, than time? . . . What, then, is time? If no one asks me, I know; if I want to explain it to someone who asks me, I do not know."[1] Could there be a more lucid presentation of the aporia that constitutes time? This is an aporia in the strictest sense—no road leads to it. Augustine's formulation of the question interests me more than his answer, namely, that time is the "distension" (*distensio*) of the spirit. For him, the issue is strictly the psychological conception of time, which he felt he might link to a quantified cosmological time. This meant rejecting Aristotle, for whom motion was the measure of time; Augustine believed that time itself, that ability to extend the mind, made measuring time possible. For Aristotle, by contrast, "we apprehend time only when we have marked motion, marking it by before and after; and it is only when we have perceived before and after in motion that we say that time has elapsed."[2]

As much as it is aporetic, the Greek word *Chronos* can refer to the site of a puzzlement or the moment of a revelatory quid pro quo. And we have both *Chronos*, whose etymology is unknown, and *Kronos*, the mythical figure. Kronos, the son of Uranus and Gaia, famously castrated his father (after his mother had told him to). Having thereby come to power, he wed Rhea, taking care to devour his children as soon as they were born to stave off the possibility one might topple him from power. The outcome of the story is well known. By subjecting Kronos to the same fate he had reserved for his father, Zeus came to rule over gods and humans. We find ourselves in the realm of myths of rulership, myths lacking any connection to time, or only a negative connection, inasmuch as swallowing one's children is the best way to arrest time. Yet a contamination between Kronos and Chronos has meant that Chronos, ordinary time, has long been seen as the devourer or the scyther, depicted as Saturn devouring his children or Father Time equipped with his scythe.[3]

The Greeks had more to say on the subject, and there was an entire mythology that cast Chronos as a primordial god at the origin of the cosmos. We find him in the Orphic theogonies. But, as Jean-Pierre Vernant pointed out, the time thereby sacralized is a time "that does not age," immortal and indestructible. A principle of unity and permanence, it functions as "the radical negation of human time," which is, by contrast, always unstable—erasing, sinking into oblivion, leading to death.[4] For Anaximander, a pre-Socratic philosopher active in Miletus in the sixth century BC, Chronos is not a god, yet there is an "order of time" (*taxis*) linked with justice. Tracing a line from creation to destruction "according to obligation," he declares that "beings . . . pay the penalty [*dikê*] and retribution [*tisis*] to each other for their injustice [*adikia*] according to the order of time."[5] Here we find the earliest indication of a cyclical time that renders a judgment. A link between time and justice would contribute, after many centuries, to the notion of history as the world's tribunal, though from Anaximander to Hegel extends the whole of Christianity's temporal mechanism, culminating in the Final Judgment.

DOUBLED CHRONOS

Such mythological configurations set out to capture Chronos by deploying a doubled time, combining an immortal, unchanging, atavistic time that encircles the universe with a transitory human time. While Aristotle formulates a definition that deviates from this, his teacher Plato acknowledges it in his definition of time as the "moving image of eternity." On one side we find the world of the immortal deities, while on the other is "our world," created by the demiurge working with the former as his model. But in his effort to improve the likeness, Plato ran into a paradox, the opposition between an immortal life and a created life. The best compromise is to think of time as a mobile image of eternity, its mobility due to a numerical advance. This leads to the birth of the sun, the moon, and the other heavenly bodies; all "have come into being to define and preserve the measures of time."[6]

Augustine draws on the elements of this Greek background that suit his argument: the doubling of time and the contrast between eternity and time. So, in order to get at time, he deploys a twofold strategy. As we have just recalled, he considers time—posing the question, "What is time?"—through a phenomenological approach. He also considers it by contrasting the eternity of God with human temporality, itself the outcome of Adam's sin and the sign of the resulting limits to humanity. The Fall is a fall in time.

"You are ever the same," says Augustine in his dialogue with God, "and your years fail not. Your years do not come and go. Our years pass and new ones arrive only so that all may come in turn, but your years stand all at once, because they are stable: there is no pushing out of vanishing years by those that are coming on, because with you none are transient. In our case, our years will be complete only when there are none left. Your years are a single day, and this day of yours is not a daily recurrence, but a simple 'Today,' because your Today does not give way to tomorrow, nor follow yesterday. Your Today is eternity."[7]

The Christian order of time owes everything to this handful of sentences. With God, the "I am that I am," we find eternity, an unending today or an absolute present, while with man it is quite the opposite—the years come and go, one on the heels of another, until all have been spent. The result is a near paradox: time exists only because it very nearly does not. Thus the past has ceased to be, the future has yet to be, and the present would, if always present, be eternity. Time is both destroyed and created by the same action. Only faith, which holds out the hope of returning to eternity's permanence, offers a refuge from the scattering across time, "where all," writes Augustine, "is confusion to me. In the most intimate depths of my soul my thoughts are torn to fragments by tempestuous changes."[8]

At the end of his long investigation into time and narrative, Paul Ricoeur, that acute reader of Augustine, acknowledges "the inscrutability of time." Is this, he wonders, an admission of defeat? No, rather an acknowledgment of the limitations of narrative, whose brief "consists less in resolving these aporias [of time] than in putting them to work, in making them productive." He continues, "This aporia springs forth at the moment when time, escaping any attempt to constitute it, reveals itself as belonging to a constituted order always already presupposed by the work of constitution. That is what is expressed by the word 'inscrutability.'"[9] All time thought is time narrated—that much he had shown. But narrative itself must encounter its own limitations. Ricoeur casts his thoughts back to the ending of Proust's book: "Nor is it an accident that *Remembrance of Things Past* ends with the words 'in the dimension of Time.' 'In' is no longer taken here in the ordinary sense of a location in some vast container, but in the sense . . . where time contains all things—including the narrative that tries to make sense of this."[10]

I shall preserve only the conclusion of Ricoeur's long meditation, a work that begins as a dialogue with Augustine and Aristotle and goes on by casting countless narrative nets in which the author hopes to trap Chronos, forcing a showdown. I shall not revisit the key moments of the battle, nor shall I discuss the outcome; I shall only note it. "Time seems to emerge victorious from the struggle, after having been held captive in the lines [or net] of the plot." And here, in pursuing the thought, Ricœur sets out his philosophical position: "It is good that it should be so. It ought not to be said that our eulogy to narrative unthinkingly has given life again to the claims of the constituting subject to master all meaning."[11] On that note ends philosophy's most sustained and powerful recent effort to investigate the ultimate "inscrutability" of Western time.

CHRONOS, KAIROS

Elusive and inscrutable, Chronos may escape, but simply pointing that out was never the plan. As our hasty survey has shown, humans labored incessantly, resorting to strategies simple and elaborate, to weave what they took to be the nets most likely to provide a glimpse of him, or at the least to negotiate a compromise with him. The Greeks also developed a strategy, that of doubling Chronos, that deserves attention since it will allow us to initiate the inquiry at the heart of this book. I have previously noted the doubling of time by contrasting an "unaging" time with the unstable time of mortals. Mediated by Plato and neo-Platonists, this is the backdrop against which Augustine develops his cogitations on time and eternity. But now we have a different strategy—the splitting of Chronos into chronos and kairos—with a more practical outcome due to its impact on our everyday chronos time and actions. For here is a remarkable invention: the Greeks were able to seize time by fabricating a net (to employ a venatic device) from the chronos and kairos pair. Kairos differed fundamentally from chronos, which is our measurable, flowing time; it opens on the instant, the unexpected, but also the opportunity to be seized, the crucial opening, the decisive moment. By bestowing a name on kairos we grant it a status, and we acknowledge that human time, which is to say that of well-regulated action, is a blend of chronos time and kairos time.

"The word *kairos* may refer to a crucial moment, a strategic location, or a vital part of the anatomy where a wound may prove lethal. Each of these involves a cleavage, a rupture in the continuity of space and time."[12] Poseidippos of Pella, in a well-known epigram, gives voice to Lysippos's sculptural embodiment of Kairos as a young man (ca. 330 BC):

> "Who and from where is the sculptor?" "From Sicyon." "And his name?" "Lysipposs." "And who are you?" "Kairos, the all-subduer."

"Why do you stand on tip-toe?" "I am always running." "Why do you have a pair of wings on your feet?" "I fly with the wind." "Why do you hold a razor in your right hand?" "As a sign to men that I am sharper than any sharp edge." "And why is your hair over your face?" "For the one who meets me to grasp at, by Zeus." "And why is the back of your head bald?" "Because none whom I have once raced by on my winged feet will now, though he wishes it, take hold of me from behind." "Why did the artist fashion you?" "For your sake, stranger, and he set me up in the portico as a lesson."[13]

No doubt to inspire the athletes who competed there, the statue was set at the entryway to the stadium at Olympia. It has vanished, but copies have survived. It should be noted that Kairos was never a leading deity, and few traces of his worship remain. The challenge of fashioning an allegory of Kairos, every bit as elusive as Chronos, was resolved by Lysippos with brio, and he endowed the young man with all the attributes of kairos: agility, liveliness, the opening for seizing him by the hair (which must not be missed), the razor blade.

While tragic heroes also encounter kairos, they invariably serve as counterexamples, missing every opportunity at the very instant they were certain they had triumphed. Here is a crisis that must end in failure, as is clear from the outset. One by one every escape route is sealed, decisions misfire, and every effort goes awry. Many end up blind. So it is that in Aeschylus's *Seven Against Thebes*, the city's ruler, Eteocles, declares early on, "He must speak home [*ta kairia*] that in the ship's prow watches the event and guides the rudder," meaning, his words must be in keeping with present circumstances. He thereupon commits his city to a perilous path that leads straight to disaster. Throughout the play, Thebes is compared to a ship, its ruler the pilot—who will succeed if he seizes opportunities and follows the correct route. The Messenger therefore enjoins Eteocles to act by seizing "quickest opportunity [*kairos*]." Later on, the Messenger repeats that it is up to the king to decide what efforts need to be made.[14]

The tragedies convey the feeling that escape is impossible, using the image of a net falling on the protagonists, encircling them, cutting them off. Time is the jailer, and it severs any links to the city's everyday time—no one will seize time in a net by getting a bead on good kairos. The brothers Eteocles and Polynices come to believe that "if Gods give ill, no man may shun their giving" when they prove unable to shake off the verdict of Zeus or the curse hurled at them by their father, Oedipus.[15] Broadly speaking, whoever lacks the ability to determine the right moment will never intervene effectively in the course of events. If they do manage to recover their sight, it is surely too late, and the battle has been lost.[16] Tragedies play out as explorations of a place without kairos time, a world where characters are always out of synch, their relation to time unsettled. And never can they return to a proper chronos time, that standard guide for regulated urban life, because their every attempt goes awry.

KRISIS

A third concept, krisis, should be added to the chronos-kairos pair. Although not in itself temporal, it affects time. *Krisis*, meaning judgment, comes from the verb *krinein*, meaning to separate, to slice, to select, to submit to adjudication. Here again, as perhaps with the etymologies of chronos and kairos, we encounter the action of cutting, which is transformed into, as it were, a shrinking of time, the genesis of a before and an after. In Thucydides, *krisis* means an adjudication, by extension a trial, as well as the peculiar judgment rendered by battle. The Persian wars, he notes, were soon decided: two land battles and two naval battles.[17] Krisis pertains less to the crisis itself, in our modern sense, than to a judgment and its consequences.[18] Kairos and krisis can be allied, then, through their connection to the notion of the decisive moment.

Krisis has been extensively explored by medical science. Physicians of the Hippocratic school speak of "the crisis of an illness when it increased, diminished, resolved into another illness, or ended."[19] The term applies to both the death and the recovery of a patient. Every decisive—or at least every significant—moment in the course of an illness is therefore a crisis. The medical arts are a discipline devoted to crisis. After a diagnosis comes a prognosis, pinpointing the rhythm of the crisis, which must include determining or recognizing the frequency of those climaxes (*akmê*) or "critical days." The practiced eye of the physician detects, beneath the seeming chaos of the sickness, an order of time.[20] This procedure renders an intervention possible, as the "suitable moments" (*kairoi*) are seized. At first sickness seems to belong to a time that eludes all pursuit, medical science involves drawing that time toward chronos time, plotting the regularity of critical days and making a timely (*en kairô*) intervention possible. To grasp the true time of the illness, the physician must possess a keen sense of how to combine the three concepts—chronos, kairos, and krisis. Chronos is both the beginning point and the terminus. As to kairos and krisis, these are the troops whose canny disposition can mean victory over the chaos of the illness, so long as it is inscribed in a well-regulated chronos time.

* * *

What was the goal of this introductory orientation? To confirm the general sense that Chronos always eludes capture, but also to add that the effort to capture it has never ceased, which has generally meant splitting it in two. For some this division has produced time and eternity—or sempiternity (*aiôn*)—and for others, chronos and kairos, time and the decisive moment. Krisis has now joined the second pair, as the third operative concept. The fields of medicine and of tragic drama discretely indicate how krisis, which belongs to the same semantic field as kairos, draws on both chronos and kairos. Another justification for going from chronos-kairos to the trio chronos-kairos-krisis is historical: as soon as we enter the universe of the Bible and the New Testament, Krisis becomes a central concept. And that is where we will now go, as Christian time becomes our first topic. Krisis advances to an eminent position, that of a final, incontrovertible judgment. Kairos, nearing Krisis, enters its sphere of influence, as it were, representing the decisive instant, Judgment Day. This trio will persist, but we shall see that the relations among its members will undergo a radical transformation. Outstripping Chronos, first Krisis then Kairos dominates the others, in keeping with the surging power of the Incarnation.

That Greek preamble made possible a description of Christian time—what is was made of, what its texture was, how its warp and weft interwove. The transit from one universe to the other took place at a very precise moment, when seventy-two scholars translated the Hebrew Bible into Greek. This momentous and quite contingent procedure opened a communications link between the two realms, the concepts that articulate time underwent a change, and soon a new net cast by the Christians will entangle Chronos—who will not soon break free. What will in due course become Europe's time, then the time of the Western world, long bore the marks of this Greek trio, chronos, kairos, krisis, perhaps until today. Here is a new age of Chronos, an unprecedented reckoning with it.

1

THE CHRISTIAN REGIME OF HISTORICITY

Chronos Between Kairos and Krisis

THIS WHOLE story is set in motion by the translation of the Bible into Greek. The Pentateuch was translated in Alexandria in the third century BC, and the remaining books were translated over the two centuries that followed.[1] In a letter to the Jewish high priest Eleazar in Jerusalem, King Ptolemy stated, "Since we desire to confer a favour not on these [i.e., the Jews of Egypt] only, but on all Jews throughout the world and on future generations, it is our will that your Law be translated from the Hebrew tongue in use among you into Greek, that so these writings also may find a place in our library with the other royal volumes." So he invited Eleazar to select six men from each of the tribes, sixty-two virtuous men in all, "well versed in the Law and able to translate, that we may discover wherein the more part agree; for the investigation concerns matters of more than ordinary import."[2] Originally intended for Alexandria's Jewish community, this translation was a crucial event, though not at the time. It became prominent only at the end of the first century BC, and Jewish communities never did discard their traditional texts.[3] For the first Christians, the Pentateuch represented the most sacred part of scripture.[4]

This procedure made possible what was to become Christian time. Without it, if each member of these communities had remained closeted in his language and her world, these conceptual transfers would not have taken place, and the history of the West would likely have been quite different. Indeed, to grasp time, to characterize times, the translators had recourse to the three Greek concepts *chronos, krisis, kairos.* Taken up and transposed in the New Testament, they would provide the armature for a new and unique way of thinking time.[5] Whoever shifts from the Greek world to that of the Bible is from the outset struck by the gap between the two. The Greek labels are indeed mobilized, but their content is quite different. Thinking about crisis is not the business of the physician, as it was in the Greek world, and no poet reflects on blindness in the Kairos of tragic heroes. Rather, it is once again the prophet and the apocalyptist, both bearers of the speech of God, who announce the times to come and the approach of Judgment Day (Krisis), which is, strictly speaking, the sword that will cleave. Kairos takes on the role of the blast of apocalypse. "This," Ezekiel intoned, "is the end for you [Israel]; I shall unleash my anger on you, and judge you as your conduct deserves and call you to account for all your loathsome practices."[6]

Bossuet will be quite clear in his *Sermon on Providence*: "In holy scripture, the Final Judgment is always represented by an act of separation. The evil shall be set aside; they shall be taken from among the just. . . . The reason is clear, since discrimination is a judge's main task and the essential quality of judgment, so much so that the grand day when the Son of God descends from the heavens shall be a day of universal discrimination. If the Day of Judgment will see the good separated from the sinners, then until that grand day they must live jumbled together."[7]

Yet the age that is coming, while routinely called the "Day of the Lord," is also known as *Kairos*.[8] Just as *kairos* indicates a rupture within continuity, *Krisis*, acting as judgment, cleaves. While krisis places the stress on the very act of judging, kairos focuses on the temporal rupture that accompanies it. To speak conventionally of the "day" (*hêmera*) of judgment is to insert it into ordinary time—yes, a day is coming—except that it will enjoy the distinction of being the final day (at least, of the ordinary chronos time) and the beginning of another time, specifically the time of kairos. More precisely, the change in time, which nearly amounts to its transformation, interferes with the very act of judging, which creates the change.

Should one then understand Kairos as a time of transition, an intermediary between the time of human beings and the eternity of God, who defines himself as "the one that is" ("I am who I am")? Yes, certainly—but one also finds that Kairos has, as it were, a wider scope. One might speak of a kairos "aura" extending toward the time preceding the Final Judgment. Because the very announcement of its imminence by the prophet, or better yet the apocalyptist, opens a particular time that is already somewhat different from the normal course of chronos time, the opening of that time known as kairos. Within the orbit of Krisis, Kairos gives a name to that unprecedented time that has already begun.

Krisis indicates the decisive rupture brought about by the Lord, seated on his throne; what follows is the unalterable punishment of sinners and the reward of the chosen. With the Day of Judgment, chronos time comes to its conclusion—it fractures—while another time begins, something quite different, a time of endless joy for those who have successfully passed the test of the final days. But announcing the Day of Judgment, whose rapid approach is indicated by those signs that the apocalyptist recognizes and records, itself transforms, at least qualitatively, the time that has gone before. Attached to those signs of an ending, revealed to those whom God chose, are the sketches or, rather, the splinters of kairos time. The mission of the prophet or the apocalyptist is precisely to reveal to his audience that the "times have (already) changed." They say, effectively, "You behave as if you were still living in chronos time, the time of your ordinary sins, or the time ruled by respect for the letter of the Law, even as a new time, that of Kairos, has begun and the Day of Judgment is coming."

Apocalyptic prophecies speak of an acceleration of time: God, "ruler of times (*chronous*) and moments (*kairous*)," of times and events, hastens times, will hasten times. Thus God reveals "the method of the times" to Baruch: "Lo! you have shown me the method of the times, and that which shall be after these *things*, and you have said unto me, that the retribution, which has been spoken of by you, shall come upon the nations." And he continued, "Therefore, behold! the days come, And the times shall hasten more than the former, And the seasons shall speed on more than those that are past, And the years shall pass more quickly than the present (years)."[9] As modern time sees an unprecedented acceleration, time replaces God as the engine driving a hastening felt by those who experience it as ever more rapid.

THE GOSPELS AND TIME

That is how the ancient prophets depicted Krisis and Kairos engaging with Chronos. Theirs was a Chronos buffeted by Kairos and inclined toward the Day of Judgment—eschatologized, apocalypsed, messianified—transformed and subjugated. We have left far behind the Greek dividing and doubling of time, source of chronos and kairos. Ecclesiastes, the most Hellenic book of the Bible, is just as distant—that dance of chronos with kairos generates no messianic power. No wonder Ernest Renan admired the book's author, whom he considered one of the "enlightened Jews, who were strangers to the ideas of resurrection and the judgement," thus "the modern Jew" par excellence.[10]

And when a little apocalyptic cult assembled, a handful of believers not yet ready to use the label "Christian," what did their earliest documents look like? How were they going to use Kairos and Krisis?[11] Between AD 70 and 90 the Greek documents called the Gospels were drawn up, contentious texts that urged readers to convert.[12] "Do you suppose," asked Jesus, "that I am here to bring peace on earth? No, I tell you, but rather division."[13] I am, said he, "a sign that is opposed."[14] And indeed he fought ceaselessly against every Jewish authority—those the evangelists called priests, high priests, scribes, lawyers, Pharisees, and even (in John) the Jews, all those for whom the Temple was both a religious and a political center. I shall not endeavor, after so many who have done so already, to sketch the life of Jesus, no matter how briefly. The task is beyond me. Instead I shall offer readings of these texts, so fundamental for the Western world, considering only the time that wove them. Against what temporal horizon do they unfold? What experience of time do they imply? Do they make allowances for what was called history, or do they see history as nothing but a chronicle of salvation?[15] Hans Blumenberg rightly observed, "Where the genuinely specific character of New Testament eschatology can be grasped, its untranslatability into any concept of history, however defined, is evident," while "after the Babylonian exile, the Jewish idea of the apocalypse was able to reduce the impact of disappointed historical expectations by means of a more and more richly elaborated speculative picture of the messianic future. 'Immediate expectation' destroys this relation to the future. The present is the last moment of decision for the approaching kingdom of God, and he who postpones conversion so as to put his affairs in order is already lost."[16]

First off, the four evangelists all presented Jesus as a messiah who felt time was running out.[17] "The time [*kairos*] is fulfilled, and the kingdom of God is close at hand. Convert [*Metanoêson*], and believe the gospel."[18] To convince those who would listen, he turned to speech (parables, debates with the Pharisees) and miracles (cures, resurrections, demonic exorcisms, and other signs). He behaved like one of the holy men (*theios anêr*) encountered in those messianic days, a category deemed charlatans by Lucian in the second century of the Christian era. But the powerful sense of urgency was new. All felt it: Jesus, who tells us more than once that his days on Earth are numbered; his disciples, who will soon have to do without him; his auditors (hoping for the restoration of the kingdom of Israel); and finally those determined to be rid of a rabble-rouser who shamelessly declares himself the son of God. Everything depended on the here and now, urgently.

PAST / PRESENT, OLD / NEW

In a world that treated tradition as the cardinal value, where piety meant observing the Law to the letter, particularly among the Pharisees, the "new covenant" heralded by Jesus amounted to a break. The relation between old and new, which had settled into a pattern among the peoples of the Mediterranean, was shattered. The order of time, of chronos, was inverted. And so it would remain.

Here was something at odds with the "normal" time of antiquity, a time of precedent, tradition, and ancestors, of imitation, destiny (*fatum*), and following the lead of history (*historia magistra*). At odds, too, with the Epicureans and the Stoics, who advocated savoring the present, that uniquely graspable time. Seers and oracles inspired by

Apollo enabled the ancients to plumb the realms of is, was, and will be. To possess such an all-encompassing vision is to exist amid all eternity.

The appearance of Christians brings with it novelty, and for the first time the new is awarded the laurels claimed by antiquity. The "new covenant" is meant to replace the Mosaic covenant, now cast as the old.[19] Likewise, the advent of a "New Testament" will transform the Bible into the "Old Testament." It is during the Last Supper that Jesus changes everything. Having broken the bread and offered thanks, he gives a cup of wine to his disciples, saying, "This cup is the new covenant in my blood, poured out for you."[20]

To the news that Jesus has concluded a new covenant with Israel is added, in the Letter to the Hebrews, the following comment: "By speaking of a *new* covenant, he implies that the first one is old. Anything old and ageing is ready to disappear."[21] After that first covenant, "sins" were committed, only to be redeemed by Jesus' death; as the "mediator of a new covenant," he sees to it that "those who have been called to an eternal inheritance may receive the promise." Immediately following those words is a quite legalistic note: "Now wherever a will is in question, the death of the testator must be established; a testament comes into effect only after a death, since it has no force while the testator is still alive."[22] A single Greek word, *diathekê*, means both covenant and testament, and the same is true in Hebrew. The passage clarifies the transition from covenant to testament, from the moment in which the covenant is sealed to the time that follows, forever marked by that seal—what is welcomed and transmitted is a memory. If the new covenant meant the "death" of Moses, that original covenanter, the "death" of Jesus Messiah, the (final) covenanter, turns a new covenant into a New Testament. The "New" reaches into the past to constitute the "Old"; it opens onto a new present. In keeping with his belief that "the letter kills but the Spirit gives life," Paul offers his version of this split: he will be the minister "of a new covenant, not of the letter but of the Spirit."[23] The letter is dead, a thing of the past surpassed, while in this fresh new age the spirit "gives life."

Such statements proclaim and demand a break with tradition. Consider how "Pharisees," "scribes," and "Jews" are challenged, first by Jesus, then by the apostles, particularly Paul. Yet the instigators of this rupture insist that they are the faithful, that they are the true traditionalists. By clinging to the letter of the law and losing sight of the spirit, those who declared themselves the law's guardians had betrayed it; they were deaf to the truths spoken by the law. Tradition informs the drafting of the Gospels, whose many citations from the prophets foretell the deeds of Jesus—what they wrote, he accomplishes. He may resemble a prophet, but he embodies something more, since "everything written about me in the Law of Moses, in the Prophets and in the Psalms, must be fulfilled."[24] A pair of assumptions undergirds this outright annexation: a repetition—better, a recapitulation—and a realization. The Bible story is one of repetitions, above all of failures to honor God.

Hence the reaction among the great exilic prophets, as the oracles of consolation responded to the oracles of destruction. The turning point was the destruction of Jerusalem in 587 BC. The army of Nebuchadnezzar sacked and burned the city, a foundational catastrophe that saw the temple razed and many of the city's inhabitants driven to Babylon.[25] But in 538, Cyrus, ruler of the Persians, commanded the rebuilding of the temple and the return of the exiles. Or such is the official version of the events as recorded by Ezra, though it is unlikely that things happened as he described.[26] What happened next, according to the Book of Daniel, drawn up between 167 and 164 BC, was the desecration of the temple by the Seleucid ruler Antiochus IV, framed as a reiteration of the catastrophe of 587. When the city was taken and the temple finally destroyed by the army of Titus in AD 70, that too amounted to a replay of previous disasters.[27] One might say that the entire history of the chosen—and rebellious—people was punctuated by echoes of the foundational breach of 587. The new covenant appears in the New Testament as a repetition of the original covenant, while going beyond it. Rather than abolishing the original, one might revive the passage from the Letter to the Hebrews and speak of its aging; the new covenant fully realizes the original, opening out that which was latent. Luke alludes to this doubling, for instance, when he presents Jesus's reply to the disciples' renewed questions about the coming of the kingdom of God.

"'As it was in Noah's day, so will it also be in the days of the Son of man. People were eating and drinking, marrying wives and husbands, until the day Noah went into the ark, and the Flood came and destroyed them all. It will be the same as it was in Lot's day . . . but the day Lot left Sodom, it rained fire and brimstone from heaven and destroyed them all. It will be the same when the Day of the Son of man is revealed.' "[28]

These dramatic scenes really and truly took place, yet we may think of them as rehearsals for that ultimate revelation: the apocalypse. Such a reading, this conceiving the past in terms of allegory or typology, was not pioneered by Christians, but it is they who make a system of it. Every item in the Bible can be passed through the mill of typology, and some have made the attempt. In its essence the idea is simple: every character, event, and action stands for itself even as it indicates, signifies, announces something other. It follows that John the Baptist must be understood in terms of Elijah, whose reappearance presages the coming of the Messiah. One of those associated with the final days, Elijah did indeed speak of the coming of John the Baptist. He possessed both an eschatological and a historical agency, having walked the Earth well before that. John the Baptist becomes both the new Elijah and the real Elijah or his full realization. His coming marks the advent of the final days: Jesus says, "Elijah has come already." As to Jesus, he is the new Adam, for just as the first man brought forth death, so with Jesus dying on the cross was death vanquished.

The labors of the first Christian chronologers bore fruit. Does reading the past *through* and *for* the present erase the past? It does not, though the present, the source of all meaning with which the past is imbued, clearly claims center stage. Jesus did say, "You search the scriptures . . . it is these that bear witness about me," yet the present relies on the past to justify its claims.[29] One sees this clearly in the confrontations with "Jews"—there was no question of blotting out the past. The church would never hear of shedding the Old Testament and its angry God, as Marcion proposed, so as to preserve only the New Testament and its God of love.[30] While the new will naturally take precedence—it is after all the endpoint of the old—the church will always insist on the links connecting the two testaments. Interpreting the past through typologies is in keeping with a prophetic reading; the words of the biblical prophets, mother's milk to the early disciples, turn out to be prophecies of Jesus. History is predictive, so long as one knows how to listen and see. The present is the key to grasping the past—more precisely, the events of the present reveal past events unrealized until then. Here we have, thanks to typology, the first instance of how time itself is temporalized. Four hundred thirty years elapsed, Paul tells us, between the promise made to Abraham and the advent of the Law, and Paul turns to the past to demonstrate that the Gospels apply to Nations.[31] Only the advent of Jesus and his teachings could fully reveal the potential latent in that past.

Such is the role assigned to the past in a prophetic economy of time that foregrounds the present. Yet chronology figures very little in the accounts of the evangelists, even as they present a Jesus going about his daily life in the present. Among them only Luke notes a few landmarks—a birth date, setting out into the world at thirty, and of course the climax at Easter. Otherwise what do we have? Some moving about between this place and that in Galilee and Judaea, with only the vaguest of sequential indications: "one Sabbath," "on another Sabbath," "afterward," "one day," "eight days later," "after that," "at the same time," and so on. These are nothing more than the means by which actions, scenes, and utterances (*logia*) are strung one after the other in a present that lacks all temporality, if not all time. The end of the story is known from the outset, conveyed first by things Jesus says, and if his listeners misunderstand then and there, the readers of the text certainly do not. Suspense holds no appeal for the evangelists, who are far more interested in underlining what is happening in the present, where the history of the world pivots. Any and all who hear the message will have to honor the example of the first disciples, rising that moment to follow the call. Does a crow worry about what it will eat tomorrow? Do the lilies of the field fret about what to wear? Those who have faith no longer worry about the future or the past. "Strive first for his kingdom. . . . Do not worry about tomorrow: tomorrow will take care of itself. Each day has enough trouble of its own."[32]

When a young man who wishes to follow Jesus asks for leave to bury his father before setting out, the brutal reply is "Leave the dead to bury their dead."[33] So much for the past. A clean slate it will be. The words Paul writes about himself—"forgetting all that lies behind me, and straining forward to what lies ahead"—sum up nicely the Christian way of being in time.[34] What lies ahead is not the future but rather the call to imitate Messiah Jesus in that new present opened up by the cross and the resurrection. The faithful must "watch," "hold fast," "walk," and "imitate." They must imitate Paul, who imitates Jesus.

THE APOCALYPTIC HORIZON

If the past is prologue, bearer of the new and realization of the ancient, what then of the future? In this new temporal economy, what place does the future occupy? Grasping it is inseparable from that apocalyptic horizon that informed the thinking of the first Christians, who created nothing new—even if this genre draws its name from John's Apocalypse.[35] The latter is in reality a hodgepodge, something the moderns use as a point of departure, for the text itself presents a defense and an illustration of a position that, compared to the "genre," is unique, extreme even.

PROPHETS AND APOCALYPTISTS

Apocalyptic writings first appeared among the Essenes and sectarians in Qumran, who produced an outpouring between the second century BC and the second century AD. Symptoms of troubled times and of abortive relations to time, these books posited a strict link between the time of the end and the end of times. The end was near, as signs foretold, and this will be the last of all endings. At this pivotal moment arrives the apocalyptist, whose visionary wisdom allows him, it seems, to speak about the present from a vantage point in the distant past, from which he sees what is to come. When forecasts of doom turned to account august figures from the biblical past, such as Enoch or Elijah, Daniel of course, even Abraham, rounding up the greatest of the prophets, they conveyed a Jewish resistance to Hellenism and the Roman supremacy that followed. Condemning those pagan powers, speaking of their imminent destruction, the apocalyptists spoke of the coming of a new kingdom without end. We find this apocalyptic dynamism in the Book of Daniel, the Fourth Book of Ezra, the Sibylline Oracles.

* * *

Among the many apocalyptic writings, the Book of Daniel occupies a central position, doubly central.[36] This is due to its canonical place in the Hebrew bible (which did not, to put it mildly, welcome texts of an apocalyptic sort) and its place in the Christian bible. But consider how its status differs. Jews place the book among the "Writings" (because when it was drawn up, the prophecy was considered closed), while Christians categorize it among the prophets (since it obviously heralded the coming of Jesus Messiah). The difference means everything. Among Jews, Daniel is the link between the catastrophes of 587 (King Nebuchadnezzar) and 168 (King Antiochus IV). The profanation of the temple by the Seleucid ruler was a replay of its first destruction commanded by the Babylonian ruler. Later, in AD 70, the destruction of the temple by Titus's forces will summon echoes of the earlier sacks. History comes to resemble a single catastrophe being repeated and repeated, sins and their punishment an endless loop.

The biblical Daniel was certainly less famous than Enoch or Elijah, yet he was respectable and presumably more responsive than they. We are told by the authors of the Book of Daniel that he is a young Jew living as a hostage in the court of the king of Babylon during the exile. To prove the superiority of Yahweh to all other gods, the book's first part emphasizes not the idea of a single god but the supremacy of this god as master of times (*chronous*) and seasons (*kairous*).[37] Such is the construction that must be placed on the king's dream. Daniel offers this answer, bestowed on him through faith in his God, after the magicians, the royal soothsayers, admit defeat. The king had seen an immense statue with head of gold, chest and arms of silver, stomach and thighs of bronze, legs of iron, and feet partly of iron and partly of clay. Then abruptly a stone broke away—not a hand had been laid on it—pulverizing the statue from head to toe. There will be, it meant, four kingdoms, from the Assyrians to the Greeks, who will be smashed by the stone, founding a fifth kingdom that will never end.[38] The notion of one empire being followed (*translatio*) by another was born here; it did not perish. We shall see that it was ceaselessly revived up to the modern era.

The thread of the narrative changes in the second part of the book. The focus shifts to the depravity of the present, the year 168 BC. If the present was to be addressed—a necessity—it would have to be placed in an apocalyptic context. For that, no more royal visions: now it is Daniel himself who experiences visions crying out for an oracle. Still in Babylon, he foresees the calamity and the retribution brought about through Antiochus Epiphanes. The fault is ours, he says, because we have "done wrong" and "have sinned" against the law of Moses.[39]

While history unreels an unchanging thread—the sins of the sons of Israel—God himself, that master of times and seasons, alternates between agents like Antiochus Epiphanes, whose deeds are calamitous, and those who offer brief respites, such as when Cyrus the Great ended the Babylonian captivity. One speaks of apocalypse rather than prophecy when evil seems to have exceeded all limits and the present spins out of control, leaving no alternative but to prepare for the last day, praying for its advent.

The Fourth Book of Ezra, evidently a later work than the Book of Daniel, extends the apocalyptic perspective of the earlier book.[40] Two crises—the abominations of Antiochus and the repercussions of the calamity of AD 70—are explicitly linked, as the reader is reminded that Ezra found himself in Babylon "in the thirtieth year after the ruin of the city."[41] Both Ezra and Daniel were men of the sixth century, both exiles, and the shadow of the calamity of 587, an event whose echoes and have never ceased to reverberate, extended to both. Ever since Babylon, the sequence of events leading to the Day of Judgment has been visible. That which God reveals to Ezra, commanding him to set it down in writing, wins him the title "scribe of the knowledge of the Highest."

Ezra begins with reflections on God's plan. Why would the Babylonians, he wonders, whose conduct fell far short of that of the Jews, be accorded might and glory? And a series of questions ensues, with answers from the angel specially dispatched, who sometimes declares that Ezra could not understand these matters since "they that dwell upon the earth may understand nothing but that which is upon the earth."[42] Next Ezra experiences a number of visions, which are interpreted by an angel expressly sent. Much as Daniel opposed the Greek beast whose eleventh—and cruelest—horn stood for Antiochus IV Epiphanes, profaner of the temple, so Ezra, calling Daniel his "brother," interprets the beast that takes the form of a many-winged eagle as the Roman Empire; the days of the empire are done, decrees God, and the time has come to "appear no more."[43]

Is the time that has already elapsed, asks Ezra, greater than that to come, or is it the reverse? The answer he receives takes the form of a parable, conveying that "the quantity which is past did more exceed."[44] With age, creation had lost its youthful vigor, or so the prophets of doom said. The angel drove the point further, announcing that one is weaker than those who went before, and those who follow will be weaker still.[45] And the Lord spoke, explaining that the duration of the world comprises no fewer than twelve parts, and ten have elapsed, leaving two.[46] The final ending will be announced by signs, some of which had already been revealed to Ezra. To a question regarding the timing of those signs, the following reply came: "Measure thou the time diligently in itself; and when thou seest part of the signs past, which I have told thee before, then shalt thou understand, that it is the very same time, wherein the Highest will begin to visit the world which he made."[47] The seeker may continue seeking, without fear of being contradicted, for the imminence of the final days shall be with us forever, the horizon may retreat. Only one ruler of the seasons is universally acknowledged: God. "He governeth the same [i.e., time], and such things as fall in their seasons."[48] So declared Ezra, echoing Daniel and indeed all the other texts in the Old Testament and the New.

The apocalyptist, in sum, sees what is about to happen; God shows him chronos time as it is overcome, as it were, by Kairos and Krisis. The seer's all-encompassing vision, much like the divine vision of the *tota simul* (all at once), differs from that eternity of the present which God views "all at once"—he sees all but as a series of bits, one vision leading to the next, through varying facets. And he must have an aide, one who will interpret his visions, which is generally an angel sent by God. The tale he then makes of it can only succumb to narrative and its diachronic way, one sentence after another, one scene leading to the next. To speak an all-encompassing vision can only take diachronic form if it is to reveal the (concluding) time of all sinners.

* * *

The end, meaning "the Day of Judgment," is announced, broadcast, approaching, even imminent.[49] In the Apocalypse of Weeks, as it is known, the patriarch Enoch presents the entire history of mankind divided into ten weeks, which will conclude with "the great eternal judgment": "the first heaven shall depart and pass away," upon which "there will be many weeks without number for ever, And all shall be in goodness and righteousness."[50] Such is the "course" of time, interrupted by the caesura of the Day of Judgment. The Book of Jubilees presents itself as a revelation offered to Moses of the "divisions of the times for the law and for the testimony, for the events of the years, for the weeks of their jubilees throughout all the years of eternity." To Moses on Mount Sinai, God shows "what (had happened) beforehand as well as what was to come." For everything, "from [the time of the first creation until] the time of the new creation," had been set down on the tables.[51] The Jubilees are a parallel Bible to which have been added all the dates, a universal chronology accompanied by a precise liturgical calendar; every significant date has a corresponding event to be commemorated. If the age of the world is 4,900 years, that gives 100 jubilees of 49 years' duration; the arrival in the Promised Land occurs during the fiftieth jubilee, at the midpoint of the world's span. "The divisions of days are ordained on the heavenly tablets the ordained, lest they [i.e., the children of Israel] forget the covenantal festivals and walk in the festivals of the nations, after their error and after their ignorance."[52]

Apocalyptists are ever alert to signs of the end; their visions usually lead them to those signs.[53] The more there are, the closer is the end, and the more urgent the task of interpretation and announcement to the few elect or to an entire community. Apocalyptic utterances forecast the end: just how long can this wicked world, in which the evil triumph, carry on? When will the Final Judgment come? But much as one stalks the end, calculating and recalculating its coming, it is not the final end. There is an after, complete with new skies and a new Earth—"a generation of righteousness arises."[54] Who shall cross over? How? All is hazy. The jubilees believe it will be "children," but which children? Enoch believes it will be the righteous, those "generations of righteousness." Less common are those, like Daniel or the author of the Apocalypse of Baruch, who assign a place to the resurrected elect.

Apocalyptic texts ape the pendulum of great oracles, swinging between prophecies of doom and of consolation.[55] After punishment comes pardon; if the covenant is forgotten and sin ensues, the covenant must be renewed and "Israel's survivors" exalted.[56] At the pivot of this pendulum is the catastrophe of 587 BC. Before exile came the prophecies of woe, and after exile Deutero-Isaiah provided prophecies of redemption. (One can also speak of the prophecies made during exile, found in Jeremiah and Ezekiel.) Such a narrative configuration leads to a unique temporality in which the prophet dwells less on what will happen than on the present situation. Only if the situation is misunderstood or misinterpreted by the powerful—the kings, in this case—will disaster ensue, loosing the fury of God and triggering Judgment Day.

"A sentinel of imminence" is what Charles Péguy called the prophet, explaining that his role "is not to imagine a future but to imagine the future as if it were already present."[57] The situation is not hopeless, but history might well call a halt, starting again only after a "slice of oblivion" had elapsed. To recycle a phrase of Paul Ricoeur's, prophets uniquely experience a "tragic of interruption."[58] The resumption is presented as something new: a new Earth, a new sky, a new covenant, another time. But much as novelty is prized in this context, it is something quite different from the novelty of modern times, as it lacks absolute novelty—it is neither astonishing, unprecedented, nor unheard of. On the contrary, this is a return to the inception, to the moment in the garden. This is why, as was the case with Enoch, the new generations will acquire the longevity of the ancients. The new is presented as repetition, but this is, as Ricoeur correctly noted, "creative repetition."[59]

A part of the prophetic moment, that great inaugural surge, the apocalyptic documents are focused on the negative portion of the story, that moment immediately preceding the collapse. All prophets start with an analysis of the present, but apocalyptists—uniquely—do not see a way out of the current crisis. They would rather hasten the end. Hence the obsession with calculating the remaining time, expecting that God will wish to speed things up, since he alone can. All these seers offer diagnoses of the present, but while prophets may play at politics, such things have been renounced by apocalyptists, who anyway have forgotten how. The Book of Daniel, drawn up during the crisis of 168–164 BC, does not incite revolt against Antiochus IV. Why bother?[60] If one is approaching the final crisis—Judgment Day—what is the use, ask the apocalyptists, of keeping a careful account of past crises, as the prophets do? Prophecy and apocalypse are two reactions to crisis, to a moment grasped, frozen, and reduced by the final conjunction of Kairos and Krisis.

THE NEW TESTAMENT AND THE APOCALYPTIC FUTURE

Now that we have surveyed the final boundary marker as sketched during those centuries of abounding apocalypse, let us consider what the earliest Christian writings have to say about the future. There is considerable overlap in both timing and genre. While some of the apocalyptic texts are earlier—Daniel, Enoch, the Jubilees—others date from the first century AD—Ezra and Baruch. Appearing after the destruction of the temple, such works were set down at roughly the same time as the New Testament. I do not mean to label as apocalyptic the whole of the New Testament, but a comparison may shed light on the temporal devices deployed by the evangelists, notably their words about times to come. The goal is contextualization not reduction.

All the synoptic Gospels—Mark, Matthew, and Luke—include an explicitly apocalyptic chapter in which the same scenario is presented, with many identical verses repeated in each.[61] The setting is Jerusalem, shortly in advance of the Passion, and Jesus is either in the temple or exiting it. When his disciples praise the building's massive architecture, Jesus evokes its destruction: "Not a single stone will be left on another which will not be pulled down." The reaction of the disciples is immediate: "Tell us, when will this be, and what will be the sign of your coming and of the end of the world?" Whether they date from ten or twenty years after the events of AD 70, by the time the Gospels were set down, the predicted destruction had come to pass.[62] Much like Daniel, Ezra, or Baruch, Jesus takes on the role of the apocalyptist, noting the classic omens presaging the end—blotting out of sun and moon, shooting stars, war, famine, and so on. Matthew even names Daniel, citing the "appalling abomination" standing in the holy place, the signal to flee without a moment's hesitation, without bearing anything away.[63] The watchwords are "Be ready!" and "Keep a look out!" The son of man will arrive, and with him the Final Judgment.

Besides this standard or "classic" apocalyptic format, the synoptic Gospels create another, a format unique to the followers of Jesus. One might say that there is room for a small apocalypse in the bosom of the large. The end is near, Jesus acknowledges, yet he insists that it has not yet come, that before it can arrive, false messiahs and false prophets will appear, his disciples will suffer persecutions, "will be beaten in synagogues," "will be hated by all on account of [his] name." To these events Mark and Matthew add that the end cannot come before the gospel has been preached throughout the world.[64] But this discourse is something original, meant not for the first disciples but for that second or third generation of Christians subject to tribulations, so that they may find solace in their faith. To treat evangelizing the world as a horizon is to open onto a history of salvation—a history seen as a history of salvation. The Acts of the Apostles, set down between AD 80 and 90, belong to the same movement. When Jesus, having risen again from death, speaks with his disciples, telling them one last time that the season and timing of the end cannot be foreseen, he adds, "You will receive the power of the Holy Spirit coming upon you, and you will be my witnesses both in Jerusalem and throughout Judaea and Samaria, and indeed to the ends of the earth."[65] And so one finds that there is space for a history, one that is to be conveyed by witnesses, and then the witnesses of witnesses. That linked series of witnesses will be the subject of *Ecclesiastical History*, a work by Eusebius of Caesarea (260–ca. 339) written early in the fourth century. And that new perspective, which grows out of the events at Pentecost, will be

THE CHRISTIAN REGIME OF HISTORICITY 27

adopted by the church, and it will come to serve as the foundation of the church's missionary activities.

But then the interlude concludes, and the question of timing is reclaimed by the major apocalyptic current, with the words, "Before this generation has passed away, all these things will take place. Heaven and earth will pass away, but my words will never pass away."[66] And the sense of an apocalyptic urgency takes over, with repeated declarations: "the hour has come," "that moment," "the time is near," and "the last hour" is imminent. Hand in hand, as it were, Krisis and Kairos are drawing near. And a more precise date is revealed: "There are some of those standing here will not taste death before they see the kingdom of God."[67] This sense of imminence is reinforced through allusions to the universally known story of Elijah's return. Lifted into Heaven, Elijah was to return shortly before the arrival of the messiah and hence Judgment Day. Typological readings of the Bible cast Elijah, whom the Gospels associated with John the Baptist, as the model for John. After all, the role of John must be likened to that of Elijah, so that the leading role of the former in an apocalyptic drama is unquestionable, and so that he too may announce the coming. He is "a voice of one crying in the desert, 'Prepare a way for the Lord, make his paths straight.'"[68] And so one must ask Jesus, "Are you the one who is to come?"[69] Yes, Jesus tells the disciples when they inquire about the return of Elijah, he will lead the way—adding, "Elijah has come already." He had come in the form of John the Baptist, no one had recognized him, and his head had been cut off. "The Son of man will suffer similarly at their hands."[70] If Elijah has "come already," then surely Jesus is the messiah who was to follow, and the teachings of John the Baptist, effectively encapsulated by the Gospels, lend further weight to the case for an apocalyptic Jesus: the end is nigh.

Whether in the synoptic Gospels or in the New Testament more generally, the life of Jesus belongs to chronos time but above all to kairos, that other time. "After John [the Baptist] had been arrested, Jesus went into Galilee, proclaiming the gospel from God and saying, 'The time is fulfilled, and the kingdom of God has drawn near. You must convert and believe in the gospel.'"[71]

Note that while the New English Bible and other translations give "The time has come," the Greek in fact offers something far stronger:

perplêrôtai ho kairos, "the Kairos is fulfilled, realized." The coming of Jesus Messiah coincides with the completion or the plenitude of time; the one expresses the other. Paul lays a heavy emphasis on this notion of plenitude, as will Augustine, who speaks of "plenitudo temporis." This is a trait of the new time inaugurated by Jesus, and it is the very reason for calling it *Kairos*. That fullness is the very incarnation of Kairos, for it is the expression of the decisive moment, the living sign of its imminence.

Imminence leads us to the Gospel according to John, which ends with a verse about John, "the disciple whom Jesus loved." This brief passage has been the subject of a great deal of attention, which began with the disciples themselves. When Peter, who was to be martyred, asked of his fate, then that of John, Jesus replied, "If I want him to stay behind till I come, what is that to you?" The disciples said to one another, "This disciple will not die." But the evangelist corrected them: "Jesus had not said to Peter, 'He will not die,' but, 'If I want him to stay behind till I come.' "[72] And indeed the two are different: the "till" sheds no light on the length of time.

Dates and durations—the apocalyptic prophets ceaselessly pursued them. When will the end come? Daniel, Ezra, and Baruch asked, "When? How much longer?" Beset by the same anxieties, the disciples asked, "Tell us, when will this be, and what will be the sign that all this is about to be accomplished?"[73] In every one of the synoptic Gospels, the answer came back the same, and it was quite precise: "As for that day and hour, nobody knows it, neither the angels of heaven, nor the Son, no one but the Father alone."[74] The church, addressing over the centuries every apocalyptic and millenarian movement, would never waver from that position; it could not. Those who did could only be heretics.

This yields an apocalyptic view both firmly maintained by the church and radically disapocalypsed. The Lord will indeed come, but "like a thief in the night," in Paul's words.[75] "Take care," Mark warns, "stay awake, because you never know when the time [*kairos*] will come."[76] Or one might say that this Kairos, this new sort of time born with the Incarnation, will last until the arrival of the Lord, until his unveiling. And here a definite split occurs between Kairos and Krisis. Because kairos time will end with the Apocalypse. Those who have dwelt only in chronos time, those who have not learned to inhabit kairos time (failing to "stay awake," they "fell asleep"), face eternal torments, while the elect, the people of Kairos, face a very different fate. So as to navigate the flux of kairos they set to work, at times giving their all. These are helmsmen determined to hasten to their anchorage, and having made contact with the favorable current, they cleave to it.

THE EPISTLES OF PAUL

The apocalyptic portions of the synoptic Gospels present Jesus as a prophet, an apocalyptist. He is more than that, naturally, since he is the one who has come and will come again, yet there is no mistaking that declarative element—everything follows from those utterances. While that apocalyptic element is not lost in the epistles of Paul, Jesus is no longer present, and we find ourselves in the realm of afterward. Paul is a Pharisee who began by persecuting Christians; he never was among the disciples, and the only title he claims is apostle ("messenger"): "Paul, a servant of Christ Jesus, called to be an apostle, set apart for the gospel that God had promised."[77] He believed that the death and resurrection of Jesus had put an end to the time of the prophets, those whose mission began and ended with the announcement of the coming of the Son of man, and that the time of the apostles had come, those charged with spreading the gospel, "the testimony of Jesus."[78]

How does Paul describe the texture of the new time he faces since turning away from "all that lies behind me, and straining forward to what lies ahead?"[79] He labels it, quite naturally, Kairos. As to his existence before being summoned to the faith of the Messiah, he summarizes it as follows: "Circumcised on the eighth day of my life, I am of the race of Israel, of the tribe of Benjamin, a Hebrew born of Hebrew parents. In the matter of the Law, I was a Pharisee; as for zeal, I was a persecutor of the Church; as for righteousness in the Law, I was faultless."[80] Now, though, he is running in a stadium, "racing toward the finishing-point to win the prize of God's heavenly call in Christ Jesus."[81] He hopes "somehow I may reach the goal of resurrection [*exanastasis*] from the dead."[82] His connection to time upended, Paul finds himself in the time of kairos, and through his life and writings he becomes one of the first and most zealous partisans of that Christian regime of historicity I have been defining. Embodying that temporality, he offers his own example to the communities he founds, warning them that there is not a moment to spare: "The night is far gone, day is near."[83] This forward impulse would not have tradition cast aside: tradition is enlivened ("the Spirit gives life") by the discovery that the Old Testament—Paul calls it "everything that was written earlier"—"was written for our instruction."[84]

"I will tell you a mystery," declares Paul to the people of Corinth. "We shall not all die, but we shall all be changed."[85] And in addressing the people of Thessalonica, he went into greater detail: "At the word of command, at the voice of the Archangel and the trumpet of God, the Lord himself will come down from heaven; those who have died in Christ will be the first to rise. Then we, the living who are left behind, will be snatched up in the clouds, together with them, to meet the Lord in the air, and so we shall be with the Lord for ever."[86] The end is quite near, as this thoroughly apocalyptic passage makes clear. Paul deployed all the tools and trappings of the genre. And when he wrote "we, the living," it resonated. Those words struck the recipients of his letter, and the shock waves spread. To say "we" is to say "you and I," so surely the final unveiling is near to hand. That is a first comment. Second, "we, the living who are left behind" marks a return to the idea of "remaining": those who have remained faithful. These are the saved whom the prophets reached out to time and again. Without them there would have been no renewing of the covenant, no rebuilding of Jerusalem. But the words of the prophets—"left behind"—yield to the words of the apostle—"we, the living"—for the saved are redeemed through their faith in the Messiah.[87] As to the end hastening toward us, when will it arrive? The question is unavoidable, and Paul does not ignore it, but he shakes it off: "About times and seasons, brothers and sisters, there is no need to write to you for you know very well that the Day of the Lord is going to come like a thief in the night."[88]

So often does the New Testament speak of a thief arriving in deepest night or the master returning unexpectedly that, rather than labor to determine the hour of the end, the faithful must learn perpetual vigilance. The advent of a Christly Kairos initiated the time of the end, but God alone tends to the end of times.

Paul shrewdly highlights the contrast between kairos time and chronos time. He repeats to the Romans, "You know the time [*Kairos*] has come," meaning that (*hoti*) "now is the moment for you to stop sleeping and wake up, for now our salvation is nearer than when we first began to believe. The night is far gone, day is near."[89] From that "now," the sense of imminence is palpable: kairos is translated into chronos. This means finding evocative equivalents—awakening, night, daylight, salvation drawing near like the dawn. Having described what the arrival of kairos time represents, Paul sets out to convey the very texture of kairos, which he calls several times "the kairos of now" (*ho nun kairos*). What time remains strikes him as "contracting." Paul uses the Greek verb *sustellein*, meaning "reducing sail," thus lifting, as one lifts a veil, shrinking. Kairos is lifted time, shrunken time.

The second trait of this new time is plenitude, seen already in the synoptic Gospels. "When the fullness of the time came [*to plêrôma tou chronou*], God sent his Son, born of a woman, born a subject of the Law."[90] The idea here is that the seasons had to be fully ripe for this shift from kairos time to chronos time. Paul tells us once again that Jesus was born of a woman, a subject of the Law, through participating fully in the time of men and Mosaic time. This plenitude means that the time of Jesus Messiah recapitulates all of time. "For the disposition of the fullness of time, to gather up everything [*anakephalaiôsasthai*] under Christ, as head, everything in the heavens and everything on earth."[91] All of Creation, through the Messiah, is undergone and united once more. "God wanted all fullness to be found in him and through him to reconcile all things to him, everything in heaven and everything on earth, by making peace through the blood of his cross."[92] If Adam's sin brought mortality, Jesus triumphed over it through his own death and resurrection. The first letter of Paul to the Corinthians calls out, "Death is swallowed up in victory. Death, where is your victory?"[93] Christly Kairos becomes the compressed time in which all history is resolved and recapitulated. Without a doubt, Adam is "the model [*tupos*] for the one who was to come."[94] The one opens and the other closes; the one proclaims and the other accomplishes. Whatever the contradictions, this is a dialogue. Thrust from kairos time, Adam tumbled into chronos time, dragging all mankind along with him; Jesus had entered chronos time of his own volition, only to reverse the course of events by broaching kairos time. This is that unprecedented moment Paul calls the *ho nun kairos*, the present kairos that is of the present. Only ignorance, blindness, or sensuality could prevent those who bore witness to that fullness of time from embracing it.

If he returns so often to certain tropes, it is because Paul had fully experienced this new time—a compressed time, a time of plenitude, of recapitulation—and wished to convey to his listeners what it means to be summoned to live in kairos time. This is how to understand those formulas found from Galatians to Colossians. At the moment you pass from the rule of the Law to that of faith, he says in Galatians, once you have been immersed in the Messiah, "there is no longer Jew or Greek, there is no longer slave or free, there is no longer male or female—for you are all one in Christ Jesus."[95] His preaching to the Colossians relies on nearly the same terms, after opening with the image of the old and new personae: "You have stripped off your old personality . . . and you have put on a new personality . . . there is no Greek or Jew, no circumcised and uncircumcised, no barbarian and Scythian, slave and free, but Christ is all and in all."[96] A clean sweep is made of those barriers between races, ranks, and sexes that will otherwise be deemed inviolable. By setting every person on the same footing, the advent of messianic time breathes the most striking, indeed the most scandalous words in the ears of Jew, Greek, and free person. But make no mistake: in most regards nothing will change. Such ideas are neither subversive nor revolutionary. Two schemes are clearly outlined in the directives Paul sent to the Ephesians: "Slaves, be obedient to your earthly masters, with respect and trembling in sincerity of heart, just as you are obedient to Christ; not only when you are under their eyes, as if to please human beings, but as slaves of Christ. . . . And masters, do the same for them, putting threats aside, aware that they and you have the same Master in heaven, and there is no favouritism with him."[97] All are equally "enslaved" to Jesus Messiah, a role embraced by Paul, himself a free citizen of Rome. Whether one is born master or slave, to live properly as *his* slaves, one behaves in accordance with one's station, honoring one's duties as master or slave.

In much the same way, one erects an alternative existence in this "compressed" time, as "those who have wives should live as having none, and those who mourn as not mourning; and those who rejoice as not rejoicing, those who buy as having nothing, and those who do business in the world as not doing so, for the present pattern of the world is passing away."[98] To conjoin a life in chronos time with one in kairos time, one adopts "as not" (*hôs mê*) as one's motto.[99]

It was long imagined that the time of the end would be brief, that above all one must live with an awareness of kairos, locus of the final presence (the Parousia) and Judgment Day. While the first letter to the Thessalonians, long held to be Paul's first apostolic letter, made this very clear, a second letter had a different intention. If the second borrowed from the apocalyptic discourse of the time, it also set out to dampen the end-times ardor the first letter ignited in Thessalonica. As important as the second letter has been in the development of Christian eschatology, it has been the subject of considerable exegetical inquiry. Did Paul write the letter? Does it recast or refute the positions taken in the first letter? To whom was the letter addressed—to the Thessalonians or to every first-century community of the faithful? When was it written? I shall not enter the lists on these issues, each of them valid in itself, as they are outside of both my topic and my competence.

For now it is enough to note that the letter was written between 80 and 100 after Christ—where and by whom are not known. Since Paul died in 67 or 68, the letter is referred to as Deutero-Pauline, possibly of the school of Paul. The many parallels found in the two letters to the Thessalonians only highlight the differences, including the discussion of the Parousia so central to the second letter.

In response to first letter's evocation of an imminent Parousia, here is a denial: that day has not come. "We beg you not to be too easily upset in mind or thrown into confusion by any manifestation of the Spirit or any statement or any letter claiming to come from us, to the effect that the Day of the Lord is already here."[100] Whomever the letter was sent to, it bespeaks a moment of apocalyptic ferment, rich in forged letters and false Messiahs.

Before one can speak of a Parousia, one must tabulate a number of signs and events, certain proof that the time had not yet come. Previously, that first letter had stipulated a short wait ("we, the living who are left behind, will be snatched up") between the "already" of the Resurrection and the "not yet" of the Parousia. But the second letter itemizes several intervening stages, all of them already mentioned by Paul, allegedly, during his earlier visit to Thessalonica. Paul did not invent these occurrences, which possess a strong apocalyptic flavor, though he did refashion them to address what some theologians have called "the delayed Parousia." As the gap between the "already" and the "not yet" seems to widen, the "kairos of now" swells. Chronos time is not to reclaim all this space, which must be staked out by kairos lest it suffocate. A destituted Chronos must never rise. The church's battle against Chronos, its will to dominance, is destined to continue to the modern era. This will entail, as we shall see, preserving the upper hand over Chronos even as negotiations descend into bitterness.

To fill this swollen Kairos, a series of familiar yet enigmatic figures arises. Among the antecedents current in sectarian circles were the "apostasy," the revelation of the "man of *anomia*," one whose transgression is so great that he passes for God and erects his statues in the temples, first of all that of Jerusalem.[101] The "abomination" Daniel denounced has reappeared, as has language resembling that used to deplore Antiochus's horrifying desecration of the Temple. But before the appearance of the apostate, there is one who must step aside—or is it something that must be set aside? "That which is holding him back" (*to katechon*) or "the one that holds him back" (*ho katechôn*)—strictly speaking, "that which holds back" or "that which delays"—must be neutralized. Paul prodded the Thessalonians, "Do you not remember my telling you about this when I was still with you? And you know, too, what is holding him back till he should appear at his appointed time."[102] And so he leaves it, and we are none the wiser. The "man of *anomia*" is not a creature of chronos time in any case; he belongs to a kairos time or, more accurately, to a counter-Kairos, an anti-Kairos.

In the second century Tertullian (ca. 160–220) inaugurated an interpretation, seconded by Carl Schmitt in the twentieth century, according to which *katechon* in the neuter referred to the Roman Empire and, in the masculine, to the emperor himself. The theologico-historical function of the empire, they wrote, and indeed the function of all powers, was the postponement of the end of time. Schmitt wrote, "'Empire' . . . meant the historical power to *restrain* the appearance of the Antichrist and the end of the present eon; it was a power that withholds (*qui tenet*), as the Apostle Paul said. . . . I do not believe that any historical concept other than *katechon* would have been possible for the original Christian faith. The belief that a restrainer holds back the end of the world provides the only bridge between the notion of an eschatological paralysis of all human events and a tremendous historical monolith like that of the Christian empire of the Germanic kings."[103] Here we have a plotted history of the period between the first century and the end of the Holy Roman Empire. More generally, the power postponing the Final Judgment—the *katechon*—will protect a space in which history can function. Turning to Paul, we note that he never attributes a "positive" function of the *katechon* and he says nothing on the subject of the Antichrist, a figure mentioned only by John.[104] Paul focuses on waiting for the coming of the Lord.

Other commentators underline the supreme role of God in regulating history and the seasons, reducing to insignificance the form or forms taken by the *katechon*, itself but a cunning means to the final realization of the divine plan. That plan ensures that all God's inventions, the persons and events, serve his design. Even under the sway of the *katechon*, the "mystery of wickedness [*anomia*]" is busy. The fullest extent of his evil power will be unfurled only once the *katechon* has been sidelined, only to be checked in turn by the coming of the Lord who "will destroy [him] with the breath of his mouth, annihilating him." And in that moment will be judged "those who do not believe the truth."[105] Once again we have the classical apocalyptic formulations. And having finished these, Paul returns to urging his listeners to thank the Lord. More than this we will never know.

THE APOCALYPSE OF JOHN

It would be unthinkable to conclude this overview of the age of apocalypses without exploring the work that lent the genre its name—the

Apocalypse of John. Invoked, inspected, and recast more often than any other work of the sort, Revelation inspired both towering hopes and rivers of blood over the years.[106] Millenarians seeking the heavenly Jerusalem with hearts fainting and exalted fed on John's promise of complete reversal, opening with a radically new time, a final farewell to chronos time. A deluge of commentaries and exegeses attests to a fascination that has never ceased to provoke questions, puzzlement, certainties—one misunderstanding after another. The Roman church and the Greek Orthodox took different stances, the first readily admitting the book to the canon, while the second waited many years. In the third century a disciple of Origen named Denys, bishop of Alexandria, reported, "Some of those who came before us rejected and excluded the book entirely, making a chapter-by-chapter investigation to show that the work is unintelligible, composed irrationally, and falsely attributed."[107] Then there is Eusebius of Caesarea, who played it safe by categorizing the Apocalypse of John as both an "acknowledged" book (he added, "if it seems right") and an "illegitimate" book (again adding "if it seems right").[108] As to Augustine, he found the book canonical but rather obscure.[109]

Some readers took chapter 20 and its announcement of a reign of one thousand years at face value, making this the most troublesome chapter.[110] In AD 156 "a certain Montanus proclaimed himself the incarnation of the Holy Spirit and unleashed an ecstatic and ascetic movement that feverishly awaited an *imminent millennium*. At any moment the New Jerusalem would descend from the heavens and come to rest in Phrygia."[111] Montanism will endure until the sixth century, defying the denunciations of several synods, and its conclusion is far from the end of millenarianism. Still, the Catholic Church had learned a lesson from that first experience and was determined to accomplish two goals: curbing and, possibly, preventing apocalyptic outbreaks while promoting Revelation as an inspired text.[112] This will mean exegetical labors paired with the most vigilant supervision of their application.

That Catholic exegesis has managed not to deny the future-oriented dimension of the book while emphasizing the centrality of Jesus, hence the present of the Paschal event. Jacob Taubes explained, "The nearness of the *coming* Christ changes into the nearness of the *present* redeemer."[113] And Elian Cuvillier writes, "The Apocalypse of John is less concerned with revealing the future or the end of times as an objective reality than with proclaiming the advent of this end in the event of Jesus, and with the attendant critique of the world of the present."[114] The advent of the end within the event of Jesus—this is precisely Kairos. As to the coming of Jesus Messiah, setting the book in the ritual celebration of the Eucharist maintains that not-yet-come quality, which is also somehow neutralized or defused. By suspending the Eucharist between the Last Supper (which it reenacts) and the Parousia (which it anticipates), outside of chronos time, past and future join or blend. For brief instants the faithful enter into the Christly Kairos. Being of the world and beyond the world, all the while remaining in the world is much like the "as though not" of Paul. When Jesus declares, "I am coming soon," the faithful reply, "Come!"[115] Situating the book in that fashion, as did the churches of Asia that first received the text, assigns it a symbolic place and a precise liturgical function—and eliminates all millennial potential. Within the *aura* of Kairos, all is (or should be) under control.

* * *

Having offered some general comments on how the book was put to use, now to consider the text proper, with special attention to how John of Patmos made use of times. His Apocalypse stands out among the New Testament books because on more than five hundred occasions it alludes to the Old Testament, an abundance far outstripping the others. The book also relies far more than did the synoptic Gospels and Paul's letters on apocalyptic materials—these have been mentioned, and much of the material is drawn from Daniel. In pursuit of his goal of making "A Revelation of Jesus Messiah" the first truly apocalyptic work—and also the last—John never shied away from abundance to the point of redundancy, verging into kitsch as he compiled all the apocalyptic writings to be had. The result both recapitulates and brings to fruition the genre; having fed on it, it goes beyond it and brings it to a close.

A series of visions came to Daniel during his time of exile in Babylon, and the angel Gabriel explained them to him. From his assumed standpoint in the sixth century BC, he foresaw the "appalling abomination" that would be wrought by Antiochus IV, who meant to change "the seasons [*kairous*] and the Law" by reenacting the destruction of 587.[116] Both eschatologically and chronologically, the abominable transgression would soon usher in the end of time, as Daniel proved by revisiting Jeremiah's seventy-year prophecy. Even how long the transgression would last had, mirabile dictu, been vouchsafed to the prophet: "a time, two times, and half a time."[117]

When John, who is living in exile on Patmos, receives from God a "revelation [*apokalupsis*] of Jesus," he rejects the apocalyptic practice of borrowing the name of a great biblical predecessor in order to speak in his own name, in his own moment, for his brothers. If earlier apocalyptists have been allowed to read a universal history inscribed since the beginning in the books of Heaven, this is not so with John, who puts all the familiar apocalyptic material to a new use. The history of Babylon no longer begins with the disaster of 587, nor is the city the one built by Nebuchadnezzar, where both Daniel and Ezra received their visions of the end. Christians have a new Babylon: Rome is "the mother of all the prostitutes and all the filthy practices on the earth."[118]

To claim the status of a prophet—"Blessed is anyone who reads the words of this prophecy, and blessed those who hear them, if they keep what is written in it, for the time is near"—John presents himself as a witness, for in addition to being a "slave" (*doulos*) of God, he is one who has seen and also heard.[119] "John testified to the Word of God and to the testimony of Jesus Christ, everything that he saw."[120] The prophecy offered by this witness is not a statement about what is to come; he offers instead a "revelation," disclosing the testimony of Jesus. This "of" functions as both an objective and a subjective genitive, since Jesus is both the revealed and the revealer, revealed as he presents himself to John and revealing to John the nature of the time of the end. In this context, "the testimony of Jesus is the spirit [*pneuma*] of prophecy."[121]

John did not wish to be called an apostle, as Paul did; he called himself a prophet. Consider his book's epilogue, where he repeats that the foregoing prophetic utterances admit of no alterations, whether additions or subtractions.[122] He was a witness and a scribe—like Daniel, he was commanded several times to record what he had seen and heard. But Daniel had been commanded to "keep the book sealed until the time of the End [*kairos*]," whereas John was told not to "seal up the words of the prophecies of this book, for the time [*kairos*] is close."[123] The divergence is deliberate, as John's right now confronts the future revealed to Daniel, the hostage in Babylon. Both could be said to intervene at a crucial moment: unsealing Daniel's visions during the crisis precipitated by Antiochus, four centuries after their self-professed date, meant that the end was near. Yet while Daniel felt obliged to turn to pseudepigraphy to gain a measure of distance from the present, John never felt the need. After all, he had received—so he claimed—testimony from Jesus, and to witness was to assume the role of prophet. This is enough. Jesus is even identified, in a notable passage, as "the one who attests these things" (*ho marturôn*): he will continue to offer testimony until Judgment Day.[124]

The word used by John for that time is *Kairos*, due "very soon" (*eggus*) as he announces in his first verse.[125] "That which is coming" will arrive "quickly" (*en tachei*), "swiftly," "shortly," and "unexpectedly" (since Jesus comes like a thief). Time is short, compressed, possibly accelerated. That same urgency encountered earlier can be seen here. And "swiftly" throbs the entire length of the book, conveyed by Jesus with his "I am coming soon," which he repeats thrice.[126] For "the hour [*hôra*] of his judgement has come," opening onto that decisive Kairos moment, a critical moment in the strict sense of the term; in that instant, time is split in two.[127] For Paul it was the Resurrection that gave birth to a messianic present that he called the "kairos of now," but for John only the second coming of Jesus will inaugurate the Kairos. This keeps him in line with the Jewish apocalyptic prophets, though his is a focus on the unique ending signaled by the event of Jesus on earth. And he resembles Daniel in insisting that one could not have Kairos without Krisis, the "judgment" and the "moment," two concepts that cleave. Just as Daniel had, John turned several times to the phrase "until the end of Kairos" (*sunteleia tou Kairos*).

The two occupy the same apocalyptic universe, by now familiar, divided in two by a temporal fracture. But if "the one who is coming" and "the one who (already) came" are one and the same, how can that be reconciled with the notion of a single, decisive apocalyptic moment? To accord to both events the same unique status is to recast the apocalyptic structure as a work in progress. Here is a contradiction: a unique event cannot happen twice. How can it recur both as Resurrection and as Parousia, that conclusive, complete manifestation of the Messiah? We have seen how Paul "expands" the Kairos, a time that in comparison to chronos time has duration. Yet the only thing of any importance to Paul is to live in chronos time "as if one did not," a life of watching, waiting, ever alert. This notion of Kairos was most fully worked out by Augustine, for whom it served as the main engine driving the trajectories of his two cities, propelling his universal history. The material city of man is enveloped in chronos time, while the spiritual city of God is infused with kairos time.

The Apocalypse of John resolves this problem by acting out the solution. When John is commanded to report "what he saw" (and heard), his response is not a treatise on apocalypse meant for future exegetes. Rather, a divine synchrony transforms into a diachronic series: John's affirmation of the bond between "Judgment" and "decisive moment" summons to his mind's eye a montage of possible forms the end will take. One event yields not a chronology—the seven seals, seven trumpets, seven angels, seven bowls are not seven disasters—but a multiplicity of views. Reporting what one saw leads one to blend past, present, and future. Visions beheld that have yet to occur meet the moment when John had the vision in the present as he narrates the whole—and blended into this are all the present moments in which the liturgy is read and celebrated. From the future to the perfect is a seamless transit. To proclaim the fall of Rome, future and ineluctable, an angel says, "Babylon has fallen, Babylon the Great has fallen," only for a second angel to say, in the future tense, a few lines later: "There will be mourning and weeping for her by the kings of the earth," which is followed by the present tense, and even the imperfect tense.[128]

It would be tempting to rant about stylistic gaucherie if mixing—better, systematically scrambling—these tenses were not in effect legitimated by how God presents himself. For does not John speak of God as he "who is, who was, and who is to come?"[129] This might be rendered more precisely as "he who is being, who was being, and who is coming." Present participles open a space for human duration, for God netted from the shore of chronos time. To say "God is" is to say "God is being here," and while it would be a mistake to speak of him as "he who will be," it is accurate to call him "the one who is coming." Just as Jesus is "the testifier," God is "he who is being" and "he who is coming." This form, the present progressive, inclines us to view the apocalypse as (if I may repeat myself) a work in progress, glimpsed in John's visions of things to come, which are reported as though the not-yet had already happened. After all, John tells us that Jesus himself reiterated that he was coming soon, so the not-yet is on the verge of being realized. Visionary experiences can shrink the gap between the Paschal event and the final event to almost nothing: they are seen as a single event, to which the liturgy of the Eucharist offers a first experience or an experience yet to come. Both John's vision and church ritual stand outside of time, the latter offering a glimpse of the end. Assembled to celebrate the wait before his coming, the faithful respond to Jesus's "I am coming soon" with "Come, Lord Jesus!"[130]

Dreaming of the end is unacceptable—it is to be lived. Here is a message both educational and exhortatory. At the beginning of the book, John castigates the seven Asian churches in a series of letters, singling out accommodation with the imperial cult as the worst of their compromises with the practices of civic life. Is not their true city elsewhere? Unlike the practices of the Jews, who are but a "gathering of Satan," the churches must be wary of any involvement in chronos time: his leitmotiv is "You must convert!" He reminds the church in Sardis, "Remember how you received and listened to the message. Hold on to that. Convert! If you do not wake up, I shall come to you like a thief in the night, and you will have no idea at what hour I shall come upon you."[131] Perpetually vigilant, poised to react with all one's being—such is life in the apocalyptic present.

THE KINGDOM OF A THOUSAND YEARS

If Revelation is meant to provide the faithful with a glimpse or a preview of fully realized Kairos, one faces an intractable, unavoidable question: Why the thousand years mentioned in John's chapter 20? Why draw into such close proximity the Paschal event and the final event, making of them virtually a single event, only to defer, abruptly, the latter event? Some commentators on Paul's second letter to the

Thessalonians have spoken of a delay of the Parousia. Could it be that John is acknowledging that delay?

John says, "I saw an angel come down from heaven" who bound Satan "for a thousand years . . . to make sure he would not lead the nations astray again until the thousand years were complete. At the end of that time, he must be released for a short while."[132] The interval permits several events to take place: a judgment and a first revolt by the faithful, who will share with Jesus Messiah the reign of a thousand years. At the end of that period, Satan will be unbound. He will once again lead astray all the nations of the world and assemble a redoubtable army—only to see it consumed by fire. This marks the final act of the devil, "hurled into the lake of fire and sulphur."[133] The dead will all be judged, and those whose names do not appear in the book will be cast into the lake of fire. That second death will be without remission. Without transition, John continued: "And I saw a new heaven and a new earth. . . . I saw the holy city, the new Jerusalem, coming down out of heaven."[134] As though by violence, we find ourselves treading in the zone following the final moment, a place devoid of sun, moon, day, or night, all of which are the stuff of chronos time and its landmarks. Kairos will occupy the eternity (*aiôn*) of God.

I shall not venture into the vast, inconclusive hermeneutical domain surrounding chapter 20. Yes, it gave rise to a number of millenarian movements, ranging from the quite "reasonable" to the outright raving. All sorts of reactions fed on what is, to put it mildly, a vague and allusive book far from anything else in the Bible, yet it could easily have produced bewilderment instead. Outlandish precision doubles the vagueness, as when John repeats five times that the reign will indeed last one thousand years—a minuteness common in apocalyptic writings. Shall we call that period chronos time or kairos time? Should we think of this is calendrical time or symbolic time? Is kairos not supposed to be far from quantifiable? Then why the number?

The number, reply certain exegetes, is itself a symbol. They point out that Adam dwelt in paradise for a thousand years before the Fall, so given the repeated depictions of Jesus as the new Adam, the number implies a return to a prelapsarian state. Others prefer to treat the chapter literally, with the thousand years to begin after the

Parousia. Those who value age have adopted this, the earliest known reading, which naturally inspired a range of millenarian communities.[135] A more cautious approach places the thousand years within human history proper; this is the reading adopted by, among others, some Protestants.[136] As soon as there is talk of setting this interim time or kingdom in a chronological horizon, one is obliged to launch an inquiry into the status of the time.

No such troubles crop up with the symbolic reading, which most Catholic exegetes in modern times have adopted. If the thousand years began with the first coming of Jesus, Revelation addresses, in reality, the time of the church—the present. And this is the surest means to draining Revelation of its apocalyptic content: drawing it nearer to the present. Even Augustine, who reacted to Revelation, as I have mentioned, with a certain bemusement, entertained no doubts on this head: "The Church even now is the kingdom of Christ."[137] The thousand years stand for the sixth and final stage of the world; John took the part for the whole, and he applied "thousand years" to the final moments of that stage, the present.[138] Every conceivable position, every possible amalgam, between the literal reading and the symbolic has been essayed—an inventory will stretch on endlessly, and the outcome will only confirm the ambiguous status of a time both kairos and chronos. And the questions will come: What are the proportions? What modalities are at work? Can one shift gradually from one to the other? Oil and water, the two readings are in theory hopelessly at odds, yet this is not apparent when one reads some of the interpretations.

Might we find some parallels—analogous, homologous—between the more puzzling passages of the second letter to the Thessalonians and those of John's chapter 20? The point is not to illuminate them, since the attempt would be both futile and naive; their mysteries have accounted for a good part of their lasting appeal over the centuries. But let us juxtapose the Pauline notion of the *katechon* and—another response to the "delayed Parousia"—John's thousand years. As close as we may be to the end, a number of events must happen before the Final Judgment. To be wholly in kairos time is to be already outside of history; but if the approaching end somehow belongs to two sorts of time, a space can be found for a human history, and for the church a raison d'être. "Convert!"

Ultimately John will maintain several theses. His declaration that the end is near echoes the other contributors to the New Testament. General assent also confirms the suggestion that the time of the end is a compressed span beginning with the Resurrection and ending with the Parousia and the Final Judgment. For God, endowed with a perspective both comprehensive and synchronic, one day is no different from a thousand years, and a thousand years flit by like a day, an outlook that justifies compressing the time between the rising of Jesus and his Parousia into a singularity. This offers yet another way of conceiving of a thousand years, as John's images and phrases multifariously imply. Yet his unique contribution is liturgical. Reading Revelation conveys to the faithful the experience of the coming moment—in a predictable, accelerated present. When Kairos rears up in this ritual outside of time, it sears your vision like the sweeping beam of a lighthouse. But, the service over, chronos recommences. Babylon "is fallen," "never to be seen again"—no doubt this will come to pass.[139] In the meanwhile, the pernicious city still stands, radiating threats and menaces, Nero looms on the horizon, and the lures of worldly compromise tempt no less than ever. Satan has not taken a holiday. One must be ever vigilant, march on, forgetting, like Paul, "all that lies behind ... and straining forward to what lies ahead"—a new present.[140]

A NEW REGIME OF HISTORICITY: THE CHRISTIAN REGIME

We have reviewed Christianity's earliest texts to address the question that inaugurated our study: Is there a Christian regime of historicity? The answer is "yes." What is it? A unique articulation of the Chronos-Kairos-Krisis trio. What is the texture of this new time? It is a presentism quite different from contemporary presentism, inasmuch as while its "now" is certainly valued, it is penetrated by or (better) shaped by the twin concepts of Kairos and Krisis. In addition, the present declares itself the "plenitude" of time. If the past matters, it is only by virtue of anticipating the present, because the proper direction is not from the past to the present but from the present to the past. We see this in the typological approach to reading and to understanding history:

Paul echoed Jesus when he declared that everything written earlier is written about us. And the future is contained within or inhaled by the new present destined to last until the Parousia or the Final Judgment.[141] Within this unprecedented economy of time, the field of experience may overlap with the horizon of expectations, providing a moment for learning to adapt to their inevitable divergence.

If the first Christians revive the structure of apocalypse, they are obliged to make deep changes as they seek to insert within it an astonishing sequence initiated by the appearance of a Messiah fated to come again. In the second century, when Justin Martyr spoke with a Jew named Trypho, he did not hesitate to speak of "two Parousias."[142] What followed was a necessary bricolage on the part of the authors of the New Testament, who wished to say something as yet unsaid, while employing words, images, mental frameworks, and beliefs created and deployed, above all, by apocalyptic Judaism. To return to the comment made by Michel de Certeau, which was cited in the preface, in order to say what they were "in the process of fabricating," the earliest Christians deployed the representation of what they were "in the process of losing." Thus, in order to address the end of times and the final judgment, they need to introduce quickly a distinction between the time of the ending, certainly initiated by the coming of Jesus Messiah, and the end of times, which pertained to God the Father alone. This opens, at a stroke, the question—one destined to remain open—of the status of this time, which is not supposed to last long, the chronos time that is temporary, intermediary, or even superfluous, from which little is expected.

For the apocalyptists, the Day of Judgment and the end of times coincide. The Greek concepts krisis and kairos enable them to name and think this conjunction. Apocalyptical writings are meditations on catastrophe, centering on that which occurred in 587 BC (the conquest of Jerusalem by Nebuchadnezzar and the exile of the Jews to Babylon), with its reprises in 167 and 63 BC, then again in AD 70 and 135. This series of disasters, which destroyed Jerusalem and emptied Judea, outlines the field of apocalypses, and over this long temporal arc is hung the great name of Babylon: from the Assyrian Babylon to the Roman Babylon, by way of that which Cyrus seized, itself foreshadowing the fall of the Roman Babylon. Because, as John in turn announces, "Babylon the Great has fallen."[143] But, as for the rest, the catastrophe of

587 was no longer the center, could no longer be the center. While all the terrifying phantasmagoria of the Judgment Day (Krisis) is preserved, the central event is the "unveiling" of Jesus. This last is a sign of the end, both that which offers the true meaning of the signs itemized in the Old Testament and that which effectively initiates the end in the present, ascertaining its existence in Chronos time. With he who is "the one who is to come" (the Coming) (Matt. 11:3), the apocalypse has already begun or is taking place. In other words, we have entered Kairos time, even though the Judgment Day has yet to occur. We shift thereby from a link between Krisis and Kairos to a sort of disjunction between the two. From that moment, the challenge will be to confront that gap, which is hard to imagine, a challenge to negotiate in one's daily life, and in perpetual need of reassessment. It will be, in a sense, the entire history of Christianity and, above all, the question of what Christianity can imagine as history.[144]

As for Paul, he offers a strong initial reply by originating the idea of a "kairos of now": the present is of kairos, and kairos is of the present. Drawing Kairos closer to the plenitude of time, Mark, for his own part, announces that with Jesus the "kairos is fulfilled."[145] Wholeness is one way to approach the nature of the kairos. When John sets himself in the context of ritual, he offers something practical: in the liturgical celebration the faithful can already experience the link between Kairos and Krisis. In these privileged (and repeatable) moments, experience and waiting coincide for them. This "foretaste" of the Parousia allows them to avoid the snares of chronos time, to "hear" the reproaches John addressed to the seven churches of Asia—above all, his pleas for penitence. He admonished the faithful to avoid succumbing to accommodation, to live in expectation of the coming Christ, hence the Day of Judgment.[146]

Similarly, the "as though not" (*hôs mê*) preached by Paul to the Corinthians indicates the dual path that will allow one to live henceforth in both Chronos time and Kairos time: "Those who have spouses should live as though they had none, and those who mourn as though they were not mourning."[147] None of these responses goes beyond the present. They indicate how to live, day after day, the mystery of Kairos, aware that the Judgment Day is coming but never succumbing to the apocalyptic feverishness nurtured by those whom the authors of the New Testament denounce as so many false prophets, false Messiahs, or anti-Messiahs. The future is swallowed up by the messianic present, and as to what is borne into the future by Chronos time, it lacks importance, no matter what tribulations and persecutions may come. Babylon the great "has fallen!" Read: she—the new Babylon—will fall, just as the ancient Babylon well and truly did.

In his second letter to the Thessalonians, Paul goes further, confronting the question of the gap between Kairos and Krisis, not from the point of view of the daily lives of the faithful but from the larger perspective of a veritable theodicy. Before the advent of the Day of Judgment, it is essential to displace the "person" or "thing" holding back the complete "revelation" of the man of *anomia*, as that entity occupies a position parallel to and the very opposite of that of Jesus the Messiah.[148] This is why he has traditionally been seen as an Antichrist figure. Then, but only then, will the Lord eliminate him permanently. From that episode, the subject of many exegeses and comments, I shall underline in conclusion just this: in his sketch of the end, Paul mobilized both kairos time and chronos time. Because talk of a force that holds or holds back may refer at the same time to a human power (Rome or, at any time, some other) and to a tool devoted to the eschatological divine. The *katechon* is one way to deal with the gap between Kairos and Krisis, providing a representation of it and a meaning. A story is on its way, and here is what it will be until its conclusion. Similarly, the millennial reign of Jesus referred to by John belongs to a kairos time not completely separated from a chronos time. This structural homology between the positions of Paul and John offers a solution to the need to offer a certain substance (a raison d'être) to the inevitable gap between Kairos and Krisis.

The Christian regime of historicity, defined by that gap, fosters not what has often been called a "delayed Parousia" but the willingness to live from now on under two temporalities. Kairos is the first; the second is peculiar to human beings, who became "temporal" when Adam's sin condemned them to death. There is no knowing when the situation will change. Augustine's two cities will illuminate the consequences, his city of God and his city of humans, where two loves are found. This twofold form, fully elaborated, will inform the profound structure of Augustine's universal history.

That is how the first Christians, employing for the first time the Greek concepts of krisis and kairos, waged and won a great battle of encirclement against Chronos; the outcome was the birth, establishment, and spread of the Christian regime of historicity. For the Greeks, the immediately operative pair was chronos and kairos; krisis entered as a third party, marking a before and after the verdict (whether this verdict pertained to a battle or to the course of a disease) but opening no new eschatological perspective. With the apocalyptic prophets, everything changes: Chronos is, as it were, preempted and destituted by Krisis and Kairos. From that time on, the two concepts are linked, though Kairos assumes the task of announcing the approach of the decisive moment, the imminence of the Judgment Day, and the coming onset of a completely different time for those who cross over (the righteous, the chosen).

While they inscribe themselves from the outset in this perspective of imminence, the first Christians will transform it very quickly. Jesus himself says and repeats that time is short. Until here, Jesus has played the part of, if I may put it so, a classical apocalyptist. But from the moment when he presents himself as the Kairos, when the incarnation becomes the Kairos, a gap opens between him and the apocalyptists. The Judgment Day does not vanish—certainly not. It definitely remains on the horizon, but as happens with the horizon, every time one advances, it retreats. The link between Kairos and Krisis is not broken—it cannot be—but Kairos tends to have the upper hand in a world that becomes more and more Christ-centric. The Christly Kairos extends in the direction of the Judgment Day, all the while feigning ignorance (because it is entirely at the discretion of God the Father). Exiting the apocalyptic framework is not possible. In spite of everything, might labeling this final moment the Parousia (namely, the defining presence) of Jesus Christ be the means to "Christianizing" the Judgment Day? The gap between Kairos and Krisis leads, in any case, to the key distinction between the end of times and the time of the end; acting like a wedge, it will be plunged into chronos time. Without this distinction, no history is, from the Christian point of view, possible, and once a history does exist, it must comprise the continual and interwoven advance of the city of man and that of God, until the true, apocalyptic ending.

2

THE CHRISTIAN ORDER OF TIME AND ITS SPREAD

A **CHRISTIAN REGIME** of historicity no doubt exists, as the previous pages have shown. But what is it? A time with a definite beginning and a well-defined end. A time, bookended by the Incarnation and the Parousia, that has no duration. An interval lacking in coherence, as it were, since it exists as the permanent present of the new covenant. We have minutely traced its development, focusing on how it reshaped our relationship to time, on how it recast the very texture of its by-product, chronos time. It was hoped that weaving Kairos and Krisis into a new net for snaring Chronos would make it possible to regulate Chronos permanently. Still, as much as Kairos and Krisis are yoked together, they remain quite distinct.

Let us now zoom out, so that we can take in the margins of the Roman world as a new temporal regime impinges on the rhythms already at work. Adopting a different angle, how did the shockwave of the advent of Jesus affect the division of the world's history into epochs? How did this regime manage in a few short centuries to upend the relations of distant communities to time and the world? Far away from the birthplace of a small apocalyptic sect, the Incarnation became a pivotal date for the world. In the beginning was a reorganization of time, which led to the emergence and then the affirmation of a new order of time, with the church claiming the role of guarantor and official exegete.

The Christian defeat of the Roman Empire, along with those power struggles of the fourth and fifth centuries, clears the way for a remarkable, unprecedented reversal. Only once Constantine embraces the new faith and defeats in 312 his rival Maxentius near the Milvian bridge can Christianity throw off its denomination as a "sect" and command respect.[1] When the Edict of Milan, issued in 313, authorizes the practice of all religions, Christianity is accorded a privileged position. "We have granted to the said Christians free and unrestricted ability to attend to their own worship. When you see that this has been gifted to them by us without restriction, Your Devotedness will also understand that permission has been granted to those who plan to attend to their own observation and worship. . . . We have done this, so that we not be mistaken to be taking away anything from any honor or worship."[2]

That edict of toleration is replaced some eighty years later, in 392, by an intolerant edict in which Theodosius bans all sacrifices and all pagan religions.[3] Many pagan sanctuaries were demolished in the interim, often by zealous bishops intent on driving out demons. One of Constantine's reforms institutes a weekly day of rest, managing "to slip at least a few aspects of the Christian religious calendar into the course of the civil year, doing so without encroaching upon the freedom of individuals."[4] Blending the seventh day of the week—the day of the sun (Sunday)—with the day of the Lord (*dies Domini*) is discreet yet for our concerns enormous; Paul Veyne calls it "a less painful but cunning blow."[5] Justinian is determined to finish the job. He does so in 529 by outlawing religious liberty and closing the Athenian school of Neoplatonism. Shape-shifting Christianity is now the state religion.

With an understanding of the general situation and the key moments leading up to that victory, we will consider in greater detail the vicissitudes of apocalyptic presentism in the first centuries of the Christian era. How will the Christians infiltrate, colonize, and finally master chronos time? This involved the ordinary time regulating daily life and the philosophical time of universal history with its eras and broad intervals. Adding up the founding and the spread of this wholly new order of time, one can speak of an advance spread over ten centuries. The history is long and complex, rich in conflicts and quarrels, and experiences vary considerably in Jerusalem, Alexandria, Antioch, and Rome. To cite but one example, the notable controversy surrounding the date of Easter lasted to the eighth century, when the Venerable Bede made his decisive intervention. We will return to this later in the chapter.

The trio adopted here, Chronos-Kairos-Krisis, came to rule heads and hearts—but only after it ruled calendars. Tracing that trajectory, ever faithful to our unifying thread, we shall investigate how Chronos fell under the sway of Kairos and Krisis. And Augustine will remind us, for it is he who serves as the great regulator of time (*ordo temporum*) during this era, that with the Incarnation the world entered its final age, senescence. Yet though this is without question the time of the end, it is far from the end of times, over which only God will rule. There you have the principal leitmotiv of this book.

ORDINARY TIME: CALENDARS AND ERAS

We have already touched on calendars, those common records of time, in our discussion of the jubilees, and a brief addition will suffice.[6] Calendrical time, Paul Ricoeur wrote, was a "third form of time" that "cosmologizes lived time and humanizes cosmic time."[7] By contrast, Émile Benveniste believed, "the calendar is exterior to time"; he called the calendar "intemporal," a form of "socialized time," adding that it "does not flow on with time. It registers [a] series of constant units, called days, which are grouped into larger units (months, years)."[8] Such comments are no doubt true, but they trivialize a time (assuredly "socialized" and "intemporal") informed, installed, and shaped by the believer. Calendrical time divides the year into positive and negative days, directly linking God to days. In other words, chronos intersects with kairos.

For the Greeks, kairos was discrete, reliable, and catalogued. At the end of *The Works and Days*, Hesiod offered a precise calendar of the "days of Zeus," noting the days of the month best and worst suited to this or that enterprise: "The middle sixth of midmonth is very unfavorable for plants, but good for the birth of males; not favorable for girl-children, either to be born in the first place or to go to their marriage."[9]

Those who wish to live "innocent toward the immortals" will therefore wish to know the precise nature of each day, the goal that shaped Hesiod's advice to his brother Perses.[10] Such a calendar sets us at eye level with the days, and observing the noted routines calls for deep knowledge. One's world becomes a cycle of days and of the routines associated with each, and no wider vista opens, month after month, season after season. How might one best and most propitiously disseminate the proper use of days? Such is the brief set for the calendar that has come to dominate the faithful. How is one to recognize and seize the kairos?

It is evident that this is something utterly different from the ambitious role assumed by the jubilees, which present themselves as the official version of "the divisions of the seasons," a transcription of the "laws of time," as well as a calendar of memories and a liturgical calendar to be followed to the dot. Let us consider what this meant for the law of Easter, a major holiday. "Now you remember this day throughout all your lifetime, once a year on its day in accord with all of its law. Then you will not pass over a day from the day or from month to month. For it is an eternal statute and it is engraved on the heavenly tablets regarding the Israelites that they are to celebrate it each and every year on its day, once a year, throughout their entire history. There is no temporal limit because it is ordained forever."[11]

Inscribed on the heavenly tables, this day, on which the first Passover meal was celebrated in Egypt, must be commemorated on its day forever. In due course fixing the date of Easter will be a bone of contention between Jews and Christians, a nettlesome issue for the latter, who are intent on selecting a date different from the Jewish Passover to be observed in every Christian community, all the more delicate as this occurs even as Rome sets out to claim primacy over Antioch and Alexandria. As it happens, efforts to set a date for Easter and frame a perpetual calendar fuel the adoption of the new *Anno Domini* dating system. Yet it is a curious fact that this is not the first issue to be addressed in the dating controversies.

Apocalyptic writers regularly invoke broad intervals, extending beyond days and months, in which the figures ten or twelve appear. In the so-called Apocalypse of Weeks, for instance, the entire history of mankind is divided into ten weeks.[12] What Baruch calls a time of "tribulations," on the other hand, is an end time in twelve parts.[13] Such broad intervals are not visible to the ordinary eye, but the visions of the apocalyptists give them access to the heavenly tables, which enable them to calculate just how far we are from the end.

THE CHRISTIAN CALENDARS

Above all, and this will surprise no one, the Christian calendar is a liturgical calendar. Over several centuries, from the second to the ninth, debates and conflicts divided the main Christian groupings as they issued, by fits and starts, a variety of liturgies and calendars, culminating in the triumph of the Roman outlook.[14] Chronos time had been laid out through conventional calendars, and our sole enterprise here is tracing how the concepts of Kairos and Krisis infiltrated it, reorienting and recasting the calendars, that is, colonizing and subverting them. As to the liturgy, one may think of it as "a manifestation of the time of God within the time of men," which is the conversion of divine time into chronos time, as the former is "at once a remembrance of the resurrection of Christ, an expectation of his return, and communion with him."[15] The liturgical calendar must offer a place for the past, the present, and the future, adding a linear dimension to the typically cyclical time of the calendar. To effect this, cyclical time and sagittal time must be combined, the latter inscribed in the former without assigning it an inferior role.

Two principles must be obeyed. The first is from Tertullian: "We must pray at all times and 'in all places.'"[16] The second derives from a third-century treatise: "Every day is the Lord's."[17] So true is this generalization that, in contrast to pagan calendars, here time is (or should be) saturated, erasing the distinction between *fasti* and *nefasti* days. Monks take over liturgical time, pushing to its logical extreme the notion of perpetual prayer. The two principles are fully embodied in monastic rules, beginning with those Saint Benedict draws up circa 530; these ensure that every action of the twenty-four-hour cycle of day and night becomes a form of "prayer." The books of hours are fashioned from this liturgy. Jean-Claude Schmitt describes the monastic day: "To conduct services, reciting a different postion of the psalter each time, the monks rise nightly from their beds for matins (roughly two o'clock by our measure), assembling again before sunrise for lauds, then at dawn (about six o'clock) for prime, later for terce (about nine), sext at noon, nones at three o'clock, vespers at sunset, and compline in the dark of night."[18] Connecting astronomical time to canonical time, the psalter serves as a veritable monastic clock closely attuned to kairos. One might speak of monastic time as a perpetual kairos-keeper.

The lives of the faithful see, through calendars, a gradual intrusion of a new sort of time into chronos time, as different cycles are layered atop a linear time defined at either end by Creation and the End of Times, with the Incarnation at the center. The non-Christian origins of the week and the month do not hinder their new functions, as they cycle in new settings. While the week evokes the Bible and the seven days of Creation, Sunday—the Lord's day, *dies domini*—takes its place at the beginning of the week, seizing the position held by the first Latin day (*feria prima*) and assuming the role held by the Sabbath. As Ignatius of Antioch says, Sunday is the day when "our life also arose through Him [Jesus] and his death." The months of this calendar are those Julius Caesar inaugurated, but the liturgical year begins not on January 1, when the consuls' terms of office begin, but on the first Sunday of Advent, four Sundays before Christmas. Only at the end of the fourth century does the Feast of the Nativity come to be celebrated on December 25. It replaces Saturnalia, a celebration of the god Saturn associated with the winter solstice. As fixed and movable festivals populate the calendar, the division of the year's time in accordance with months and seasons undergoes another segmentation: it obeys the sequence of holy days that energize calendrical time by replacing cycles with a time centered on a single point.

Easter dominates the movable holidays. Once it is established in the second century, dependent holidays follow in its wake—Holy Week, Lent, Ascension Day, Pentecost, and so on. Christmas dominates the fixed holidays, and it too has an entourage of subsidiary holidays—Annunciation, Advent, Epiphany, and so on. Both cycles track the main events in the life of Jesus, and each in its own fashion lends it a calendrical beat, supplementing each phase with a time (think of kairos), their attributes shifting in line with the shifting cycles. The faithful live variously, the weeks of Advent distinct from Lent, their experience of the span from Easter to Pentecost different too, until they approach once again the beginning of the cycle, Advent. Each phase dresses in different priestly colors its readings and celebrations. Liturgical time enjoys a variety of moods and colors.[19]

What had been labeled by the Middle Ages "the temporal," namely, that great founding cycle and its gradual arrangement, received a supplement, "the sanctoral." This was the calendar of the feasts of the saints. The cult of saints had first focused on the martyrs, only to grow into an expansive, codified phenomenon. As the date of a saint's death was typically more reliably recorded than the birth date, this day became "an act of memory. It was a commemoration." Jacques Le Goff pointed out that the death of the saint became, over the Middle Ages, less the subject of commemoration than the life, which gave rise to a proper festival (*festivitas*). Turned into "new markers of time, the earliest saints were the first workers of Christian times."[20] These exemplary figures opened the way toward salvation. The sanctoral cycle was celebrated on November 1 as All Saints' Day; the festival of the dead, All Souls' Day, has been celebrated on November 2 since the eleventh century.

When we zoom out further, the broader intervals enveloping the cycles come into view, juxtaposing liturgical time, the time of the Old Testament, and the seasons. The *Rationale divinorum officiorum* (Manual of divine offices) is a work in eight books written by the celebrated thirteenth-century Dominican jurist Guillaume Durand. The sixth book, a study of the liturgical year, proposes a division of time into four eras. First is the "time of deviation," initiated with Adam's fall and the consequent deviation of humankind from righteousness; its liturgical analogue is the period from Advent to the Nativity, while its seasonal analogue is winter. Next is the "time of renewal" (or of "revocation," repeal), which for the liturgy proceeds from the Septuagesima to Easter, a period of sixty-six days, while for biblical history it corresponds to the period from Moses to the Nativity. This is springtime. Summer is the "time of reconciliation," from the Nativity to the Ascension of Jesus, or the first Sunday following Easter to the first Sunday following Pentecost. The fourth era, fall, a "time of pilgrimage," opens with the first Sunday following Pentecost and continues to Advent; this is the "present day" leading from the Ascension to the Final Judgment.[21] Here we have the year in decline and the world sinking into old age. All history since Adam is accounted for in the liturgical calendar, a potent engine whose elaborate gear trains regulate all times. Nothing is left out; everything makes sense. This calendar reminds us, over and over, that every day is far more than a twenty-four-hour span.

In 1300 Pope Boniface VIII proclaims a Catholic jubilee to parse, reenergize, and modernize the time of the fourth era, that of pilgrimage or peregrination. Rather than review the details of the initial proposal and its vicissitudes over several pontificates, let us only point out that linking the remission of sin (via indulgences) and a sort of revival of time opened a series of gaps in the church's chronos time.[22] Originally conceived as a centenary event, the interval shrinks to fifty years, then, recently, to a jubilee every twenty-five years, a tool that the papacy wields to manage stretches of time beyond the scale of the liturgical year.

ENTER THE CHRONOLOGERS

Now that we have traced the spread of the economy of Kairos from the Book of Daniel and its role in calendrical cycles, we shall consider how it transformed—or better, subverted—the domain of universal history.

When the debate broke out in first-century synagogues, the stakes were the acknowledgment of Jesus as *Christos*, Messiah, a role his disciples and apostles asserted as they testified to his teaching, his death, his resurrection and ascension. Beyond the evidence of their eyes and ears, they offered the testimony of scripture. Typological readings meant that all the Old Testament could be reckoned prophetic of the New. What more evidence was needed to show that here and now the time of Kairos had begun? If one preferred a longer view, the periodization offered in Paul's three stages and in the four successive kingdoms sufficed to segment all past history and all time to come. But change was afoot, Christian groupings were cropping up outside of Palestine, and the role of Judaism in universal history had begun to look different from that of its offshoot, Christianity. It would remain for Paul to quit Athens, shaking the dust from his sandals, having vainly tried to explain to the Athenians that the "Unknown God" to whom they had erected an altar was the very same as the one he had come to tell them of: "From one single principle he not only created the whole human race over the whole face of the earth, but he determined the times and limits of their habitation." He related this universal history, then added a few ill-advised words regarding "resurrection from the dead." This proved too much for the Athenians: "Some of them burst out laughing; others said, 'We will hear about this from you another time.'"[23] Those who wish to be heard soon need to step outside of the Bible's self-referencing universe.

Those who accepted that challenge, the first Christian writers, set down a universal history between the second and the fourth centuries. With an apologetic impulse and a chronicler's temper, they faced a number of challenges.[24] As they could no longer dwell in a purely scriptural realm, it seemed essential to link the Bible story to the chronicles Greeks had been elaborating since the sixth century BC.[25] Tempting as the rise and fall of empires appeared, it proved if anything too eschatological: How could the wide variety of vanished and surviving kingdoms be mapped onto just four movements?[26] Above all their task meant drawing a line from Adam to Jesus, marking parallels along the way between the biblical and the pagan chronologies. Chronologers had long ranked synchronism first among their devices, and now the Christians ran with it. But "unlike pagan chronology, Christian chronology was also a philosophy of history," or, more precisely, a theology of history.[27]

A second enterprise flowed directly from the first: synchronisms had to be identified, but the point was to prove that Moses had anticipated the earliest pagan legislators. Beginning with Plato, possibly with Herodotus (he mentions with a smirk how proudly Hecataeus of Miletus presented to the Egyptian priests a genealogy tracing her line back sixteen generations before arriving at a god), the reputation of the Greeks as a young people was firmly established.[28] During the Hellenistic era, as Flavius Josephus happily reported in *Against Apion*, historians from Egypt, Babylon, and Phoenicia had loudly laid claim to ancient roots.[29] These peoples had carefully preserved, said he, annals since ancient times, and the entries regarding the Jews in all these records supported the declaration he had made in *Jewish Antiquities*: the Jews were a people of "extreme antiquity."[30] The Christians embraced this aspect of the book. It was much in their interest to lay claim to the great age asserted by the Jews, yet they scoffed at the extravagant figures cited by the Babylonians and Egyptians in dating their ancient kingdoms, sheer madness when juxtaposed with the biblical chronology. No, such numbers had to be instantly rejected. This contradiction resurfaces periodically up to modern times, undermining Christian time.[31]

The age of the world is the third issue addressed. A consensus gave six millennia as the lifespan of the world, so if Jesus had been born in 5500, as Hippolytus of Rome, Julius Africanus, and other third-century authors believed, the end was advancing swiftly. What to do? Rejoice? Agonize? Revisit the math? An erudite named Eusebius took up the challenge. The bishop of Caesarea was not the first to do so, but the book that he wrote, *The Chronicon*, instantly became the standard work because it pursued the question far further than had any previous treatise. After Jerome had translated it into Latin, it had a remarkable influence over the West until the seventeenth century.[32] And at the end of the sixteenth century Joseph Scaliger deployed historical criticism to reconstruct Eusebius's lost Greek text—an immense project.[33] Written in 1681, Bossuet's *Discourse on Universal History* retains, for the most part, the chronological frame employed by Eusebius.

JULIUS AFRICANUS

Before Eusebius, Julius Africanus (ca. 170–240) wrote *Chronographies*, a work in five books that covers 5,732 years, beginning with Adam in the year 221. A Christian citizen of the Roman Empire, Julius

Africanus was probably born in Ælia Capitolina, in other words, Jerusalem.[34] This accomplished polyglot traveled in the East and spent time in Rome, where he belonged to the circle of Emperor Severus Alexander. He exchanged letters with Origen. Evidently the tools he needed in order to take on this project were at his disposal, and he was aware of its importance, if not its urgency. Yet so little survives of the work, such paltry fragments, that even hazarding a reconstruction is sadly unthinkable. This has not prevented editors of Julius Africanus from crowning him the first true Christian chronologer, from characterizing Eusebius as an epigone—top-notch, yes, but working from a pattern.[35] Eusebius specialists view the subject of their research as an innovator who went well beyond listing dynasties, Olympiads, archonships, consuls, and other phenomena, beyond providing glosses, commentaries, and narrative dilations; they insist that he invented a new genre, a map of time. The irresistible advance of kairos time into chronos time, that flood of the rising tide, drew Eusebius to trace a line from Abraham to Jesus and beyond.

As much as he seeks synchronism, Julius Africanus relies on the unifying thread of the Bible story, which he views as axial. Whenever he can, he inserts links to Persian and Greek chronologies. For instance, the Old Testament dates the return from exile to the first year of Cyrus's reign, which corresponds to the Greeks' first year of the fifty-fifth Olympiad (560/559 BC). With this benchmark synchrony set, links are opened among the three histories, and gradually others can be opened. As nothing related by the Greeks before the advent of Olympiad dating had proven reliable, Africanus does not examine Greek history "in detail." The Hebrews are a different story: he is not concerned about equal treatment. While the importance of comparing the history of the Hebrews to other notable groups cannot be denied, more important still is showing that the Hebrews were first, starting with Moses, who preceded all of Greece's philosophers.[36]

This issue leads straight to the duration of the world. Six thousand years, a reflection of the six days of Creation, is the span allotted to the world in the mind of Africanus, as of Tatian before him. The seventh millennium will welcome the Kingdom of Heaven. Within this framework, which the Christians took up and embraced, room must be found for the prime interval of the Incarnation. To this Daniel held the key, as his famous seventy weeks of years could be recast to prophesy the coming of Jesus. (The pivotal role of Daniel has previously been noted.) Now the birth of Jesus occurs in year 5500 after Creation, halfway through the sixth and final millennium.[37] As in his compilation Julius Africanus traced the elapsed time to 5732, very little time remained. Nonetheless this was not the era of apocalyptic hysterias.

When Africanus adds Daniel to his company, he highlights the links between chronography and an apocalyptic eschatology that serves as the horizon and remains at the horizon. To lend history a meaning, the chronologer arranges a series of dates, calculating the date of the end. Unlike the apocalyptist feverishly stalking omens, he links one date to another, thereby illuminating the future, the coming of the final Kairos. An essential linkage will be the intersection of the birth of Jesus and the chronologies of Rome, Greece, and the Bible; even as chronos time beats along, year after year, whatever date is assigned within the regulation six thousand years will, until the time of the Venerable Bede in the eighth century, shift the Parousia a bit nearer or a bit farther. The date of the birth of Jesus, rocked back and forth, bestows on us a world now younger, now older. The irruption of a Christly Kairos was never about to reverse the sentence of six thousand years; instead it entrenched it, rendering it an article of faith even as it radically transformed it.

Handy as the Egyptian, Babylonian, and Phoenician historians are when the prattling Greeks need to be humbled, they soon become an embarrassment if they make claims for histories leading back 9,000 years for the Egyptians, 30,000 for the Phoenicians, and 480,000 for the Chaldeans. So long as the rule of six thousand years prevails, such figures can only appear extravagant to Africanus. Eusebius, following him, will devote considerable energy to rebutting these pagan claims, and Augustine will do the same. The issue will resurface in the seventeenth century, as new contenders enter the lists, contenders who prove far more resilient, beginning with the Chinese.[38] For the moment, though, Eusebius has recourse to two arguments that others will revive. What were called years, runs the first argument, are not real years. What the Egyptians call a year is in fact, due to their reliance on a lunar calendar, a single lunar month—thirty days. This contraction, drastic yet simple, makes honoring the six-thousand-year limit possible, more or less. While it is not *our* chronos time, this is certainly *a* chronos time. Egypt's king lists include numerous dynasties said to have reigned successively, while in truth they existed as contemporaries governing distinct regions within the country—such is the second argument, deployed when needed.

EUSEBIUS OF CAESAREA

While Eusebius certainly remains faithful to Africanus's general approach, he avoids offering any apocalyptic speculations. He distinguishes chronology from predictions—after all, had Jesus not called the latter "pointless investigations"?[39] But when he takes up the Septuagint to review the genealogies of the most prominent men since Adam and Eve, the date he calculates for the birth of Christ is about 5200, not 5500. At first glance it is a more precise reckoning, but with consequences: the world becomes younger, and the end of time is postponed by three centuries. This is three centuries of chronos time, an additional measure of present but with a set duration. A century after Julius Africanus, a new horizon had been defined without a word uttered about the millennium—a happy outcome. When apocalyptic impulses are eliminated from the present, millenarian speculation is staved off, and that impermeable horizon is acknowledged. Richard Landes showed that the horizon marks a permanent boundary, though it has shifted a bit nearer at times—circa 200 and again a century later.[40] Very roughly speaking, a chart of apocalyptic trends extending to the modern era, to today even, may be sketched in line with a backdrop of major crises. Chronos time stretches out, but standing at the end of that road is always the Kairos of Judgment Day, or of some form of that day. There is no alternative.

Eusebius's *Chronicon* comprises two books.[41] The first, *Chronography*, consists of all the material available on pagan and biblical chronologies, mapping the synchronisms of the two as far as possible. But that compilation amounts to a mere sketch for the second book, the *Canons; or, Chronological Tables*, which constitute a true universal chronicle. Here is a work of unprecedented breadth: Eusebius manages to compare as many as nineteen different kingdoms. As synchronism is gradually expanded, the very ground of history expands. Chronos time is growing: this is due in part to all those kingdoms, but they are all at once linked to biblical time, the bearer of kairos. The aura of kairos time was filtering into the various pagan chronos times.

Eusebius's radical innovation lay, above all, in his *Tables*. He chose to use parallel columns, one per kingdom. Connecting them and determining their positions are the synchronisms, so many passageways between the columns. As the number of synchronies increases, the connections among the various columns ramify; should a dynasty dissolve, the column abruptly ends. History is read doubly: the first reading is vertical and diachronic, as one proceeds from the top of the column to the bottom, and traces the history of a kingdom year by year; the second is a horizontal reading based on synchronies, which open up communication among the columns.

What was the source for this extraordinary layout? No doubt Eusebius borrowed and reworked the model he knew so well, Origen's design for his great edition of the Bible.[42] He had in fact been employed in Origen's library in Caesarea, where he had handled the book in question; after Origen's death he had worked on the reference text, a compilation of all the versions of the Bible Origen had collected, arranged in columns. The six juxtaposed versions gave the edition its name: the *Hexapla*. Readers could opt simply to read a single edition (the Hebrew Bible, the Septuagint, Symmachus's translation, Theodotion's translation, and so on), but more significantly they might shift from one to another, picking out the variant readings of the same passage. Here were the vertical and the horizontal readings. Origen's monument to philological and editorial excellence made possible a range of new editions and commentaries. One such was Eusebius's *Chronicon*, on which he labored—revising it and enlarging it—to 325, the tenth year of the reign of Constantine. If Origen's was the Bible of Bibles, Eusebius's *Tables* was the book of times: it anatomized the penetration (and exploitation) of Chronos by Kairos.

Eusebius provided, in addition to his synchronized columns, a ladder of times beginning with the birth of Abraham and worked out in accordance with a unit, the decades of that patriarch. A canny choice, Abraham is a foundational figure for both Jews and Christians. And inasmuch as he takes to heart the promise made him by God, Augustine considers him a prophet—of the coming of Jesus Christ.[43] His decades, considered as a chronological technique, mark time like the Greek Olympiads, themselves an element in Eusebius's design. But as they begin far earlier, the Abrahamic decades possess a great advantage, and then they bear a sense of history, as one moves from Abraham to Jesus. Numbering the decades identifies at a glance the contemporaries among the Jews, the Greeks, and the barbarians, and the system is quite "independent of the histories of the different nations," Eusebius notes.

One may truly speak of Abraham as a historical personage, as one may his coevals Ninus, first king of Assyria; Europs, king of the Greek city-state Sicyon; and the Theban rulers of Egypt. These first synchronisms constitute the real beginning of the *Chronicon*. As to the preceding period, the three thousand years and more (by Eusebius's calculation) that bore witness to Adam and the Flood, Eusebius felt their presence keenly, yet he also knew that dating from that period "no completely Greek, or barbarian or, to speak in general terms, gentile history is found."[44] Ergo no synchronism whatsoever. Spotlighting the past from the time of Abraham and Ninus thrusts to the rear considerations of when the very beginning occurred and when the end will come. How can we dwell on the subtraction of the age of the world when Abraham is launching a temporal arc destined to reach its terminus in Christ?

After Abraham, Moses serves as the next essential landmark. Identifying his contemporaries enables us to tote up the years between him and the pagan philosophers. The precedence is acquired, and Eusebius "proves" that Moses lived at the same that the mythical Cecrops allegedly ruled Attica, some three hundred years before the Trojan War. This places Moses well in advance of Homer, Hesiod, and all the others. Moses was revived by the Christians, with Augustine referring to him as "our true theologian." The third landmark is effectively the first: the birth of Christ. That took place in the forty-second year of the reign of Augustus, and it was in the fifteenth year of the reign of Tiberius that he began to preach. Working backward, those dates make it possible to link the chronologies of the Bible, of Greece, and of Persia. A gap of 148 years separates Tiberius from Darius; the first Olympiad, in 776 BC, occurred during the time of Isaiah.[45] By applying this regressive method, moving from one synchronism to another, Eusebius reached Moses and, finally, Abraham. The chronological advance relies on running time backward.

Having erected lists measured out by synchronisms and a landmark ladder runged with the decades of Abraham, Eusebius's final addition, in the blanks between lists of dates (what Scaliger was to call *spatia historica*), was a series of notes composing a compact political, religious, and cultural history. These notes were often consulted up to the sixteenth century, and in fact the full title of his work was *Chronological Tables with a Precis of the Universal History of the Greeks and the Barbarians*, proof that he meant to make something that went beyond a simple chronography, even one such as Julius Africanus's.

Such was the appearance of this new order of times leading from Abraham to Jesus and beyond. And we have seen how the very development of that order placed Christ at the center, as he was the starting point for all calculations. Columnar design highlighted the decline in the number of kingdoms to the moment when only one remained, the Roman column. That of the Jews terminated in the year 70, when Titus took Jerusalem and destroyed the temple, and Eusebius informs us that this was on the anniversary of the savior's Crucifixion. Jesus had prophesied the destruction of the temple, and it had come to pass. The story is endowed with a strong sense of history, as humanity travels from dispersion, wars, and a multiplicity of gods toward kingly rule (that of Augustus), peace, and a single god.[46] To the twofold chronological reading, which has a vertical and a horizontal orientation, is added an eschatological reading, which is also political. Here theology and politics are combined in a political theology. Elevation to the bishopric of Caesarea assured Eusebius of having Constantine's ear, and he won imperial honors. His biography of the emperor was left unfinished.

Through the Christian chronologers, Christly Kairos seeped into the temporal fabric, a single thread of weft woven into the warp of pagan times. These early chronologers, fond of extensive, pointed synchronisms, conveyed a history one may call universal. Practically all the known peoples set out on an adventure, and whether they knew it or not, wished it or not, biblical history stood over them all. It was their adventure, yet it passed them by. Eusebius pointed out the launch of each, the achievements of each within its own chronos time—yet a unique time flowed over all these, a time inaugurated by the God who became a man and instantly recast all earlier time as a long, unsuspected preparation. Paul and the evangelists recognized that as a time spent awaiting the plenitude.

Other works like the *Chronicon* fall in line, borrowing the Christian order of times. Jerome goes first, composing the *Book of Times* (*Liber temporum*) by translating, completing, and extending Eusebius's *Tables*. Taking the story up to 378, the year Emperor Valens died, he acts as both "translator" (*interpres*) and "author" (*scriptor*), or perhaps historian, so he tells us. At the book's conclusion he writes, "From the founding of Rome to the last year of this work there were 1,131 years."[47] He had just pointed out that he was writing for Romans, for whom the supreme date was that of the city's founding. After that, universal chronicles ranging from Adam to the date of writing become the norm. I shall note a few: that of Cassiodorus ending in 519, that of Count Marcellinus ending in 534, that of Isidore of Seville ending in 615; that of Bede ending in 725.

OROSIUS'S *HISTORIES AGAINST THE PAGANS* AND AUGUSTINE'S *THE CITY OF GOD*

A pathway marked by chronicles can always be lengthened by redefining a starting point and a terminus, and once we step just beyond the genre we are struck by two outstanding efforts that combine the chronological approach of Eusebius and Jerome with the figure of successive empires, a notion the chroniclers never addressed. (In that they followed the Greek chronologers, who never engaged with eschatology.) Yet from the time of Daniel the rise and fall of empires had offered an apocalyptic horizon; the empires marked time with a plunging beat up to the last one, the one that had no end. Early in the fifth century a priest named Orosius published *Histories Against the Pagans* (417) and Augustine published *The City of God*. The first three books of the latter—"the task is long and arduous"—appeared in 413, a response to the massive shock felt throughout the empire when Rome was sacked by the Visigoths, with Alaric at their head. If it could perish, if it was to perish, then Rome was not the eternal city! "If Rome can perish," wrote Jerome to a correspondent, "what can be safe?"[48] Jerome's year 410 might have been (setting aside the apocalyptic horizon) Paul Valéry's year 1914, five years before he wrote, "We modern civilizations have learned to recognize that we are mortal like the others."[49] Augustine felt the need to distance himself from the event, and the result, sustained, powerful, and enduring, is *The City of God*.

HISTORIES AGAINST THE PAGANS

Orosius's book owes its existence to a request from Augustine. The abominations of history were to be itemized in a compact volume. This would constitute a rebuttal to those who blamed Christians for the sack of Rome in 410, attributed to attacks on the former religion, to the rejection of traditional piety and the former order of times, all of which had driven the gods from the city. Anyone ignorant or vicious enough to make such claims needed to be reminded that the world had, before the birth of Christ, seen a parade of evils both unending and multifarious—Rome's pillage was only the most recent. The synchronism of the reign of Augustus and the birth of Christ gave rise to the coincidence of the peace of Augustus (which triggered the closure of the temple of Janus) and the Christian peace, known as *pax augusta, pax christiana*.

What had been envisioned as a brief monograph offering nothing but facts swells into a *History* in seven books celebrating the good works of the *tempora christiana*, which had succored the true religion. This could hardly have pleased Augustine, as he was in the midst of unfolding a grand vision of the advance of two mingled but radically different cities, that of God and that of human beings. Instead of the examples he needs, Orosius offers a sketch of political theology in which the empire plays a providential role. There is no comparing the significance of Augustine, the church father, to that of Orosius in Christian history, yet the latter proved a great benefactor to the clerics of the Middle Ages, who treated his book as a guide to universal history. Witness the large number of manuscripts (at least 275) that have survived from the period, largely in monastic libraries.

At the beginning of book 2, Orosius returns to Daniel's framework of the four kingdoms, which he boldly modifies. Only Babylon and Rome truly matter; the other two, Macedonia and Carthage, did not last long and never rose to true prominence. The latter never inherited the mantle; they acted as "tutor and regent," and their part in the succession was temporary. The relation between Babylon and Rome, by contrast, was that of "an old father and his young son."[50]

"I noted the many points of similarity between the Assyrian city of Babylon, which was the leading nation at the time, and Rome, which dominates the nations in a similar way today. I showed that the former had the first, while the latter has the last, empire; that the former slowly declined, while the latter gradually grew."[51]

Even as he shifted the framework westward, Orosius never discarded the number four. Daniel had spoken, in his description of the four beasts emerging from the sea, of "the four winds of heaven stirring up the Great Sea."[52] In Orosius, the four winds become the four points of the compass, with one of the four empires at each point (*mundi cardines*): Babylon to the east, Carthage to the south, Macedonia to the north, and Rome to the west. By borrowing Daniel's notion of the succession of the four kingdoms, Orosius both preserved and reenergized the apocalyptic horizon (with Rome as the last empire) and the six-thousand-year span. Chronology, through Orosius, is explicitly reinscribed in eschatology and apocalypse.

It comes as no surprise that a number of synchronisms reinforce his view. "The former [Babylon] lost her last king," he writes, "at the same time the latter [Rome] gained her first; . . . while, when Cyrus invaded, Babylon fell as if dead, Rome was confidently rising and, after expelling her kings, began to be governed by the counsels of freemen."[53] Furthermore, Rome and Babylon were fated to endure for the same period: 1,400 years after its founding, Babylon saw its might obliterated by the Persians. The Medes had inflicted damage earlier, 1,164 years after the founding. If we consider Rome, we find that precisely the same period had elapsed when Rome was taken by Alaric. Alaric was to Rome what the Medes were to Babylon. Chronology becomes typology: the history of Babylon foreshadows that of Rome, which duly repeats the example.

What is to be made of the remaining time, the difference between 1,400 and 1,164? Orosius's silence on this head does not keep us from doing the math. But a problem arises. How are we to reconcile Orosius's depiction of Christian *felicitas* with his underlining of the final troubles, not least the arrival of the Antichrist then the return of Christ and the Final Judgment? Are we to see in the barbarian invasions a sign of his coming? No. There was, yes, a certain amount of pillaging and destruction (though Orosius tells us that they never went too far), but here is a group that can be converted—the coming of the barbarians meant "that the Churches of Christ throughout the east and west alike should be filled."[54] As they bear the Gospel to distant lands, they hasten the coming of the end. These barbarians were, in sum, less the heralds of an imminent apocalypse than tools facilitating the extension and the triumph of "Christian times" (*tempora christiana*) and the advent, precisely scheduled, of the Final Judgment.[55]

THE CITY OF GOD

While rejecting Orosius's approach as well as his conclusions, Augustine does adopt in *The City of God* the chronology of Eusebius and Jerome, the basic idea of the rise and fall of successive empires, and the scriptural six thousand years. These are certain, hard-won truths, and Augustine turns them to account in his work, whose scope far exceeds all of the chronological tables and all of the chronicles drafted before him—his subject is the heavenly city and the earthly city, from the beginning to the end of times. He declares in his preface that he will examine "the glorious City of God" in terms of its dual temporality, for if it dwells among the "ungodly," in the flow of chronos time, living by faith, it also experiences "the security of its everlasting seat," the eternity of God, all the while fully aware that it will experience that fullness only after the Final Judgment.[56] The city of God exists, then, both within and without chronos time, within the chronos time of human affairs and within a kairos time, or concerning Kairos.

Up to this point, the earthly city per se has not appeared, except as the ungodly among whom passes the city of God. It might as well be

the world or even the age. But Augustine will summon and unfold the history of humanity from the days of Cain and Abel, turning to Eusebius and his synchronism in order to link biblical history and the pagan histories, and for that he will need a true city. So venerable a concept lends form to an otherwise atomized universal history, structure to a city of God none can see.

How did this able rhetorician usher the second, earthly city into his preface? He turned to a pair of citations. Quoting from scripture, he noted first that God, founder of the divine city, "resists the proud, but he gives grace to the humble."[57] Then he turned to a well-known passage from the *Aeneid* in which Virgil declares, on the subject of Rome's power, that the city boasted of having to "spare those you conquer, crush those who overbear."[58] As we shift from one formulation to the other, we are expertly shuttled between the two cities. For the latter passage bespeaks a spirit marked by "swelling pride" and the urge to dominate (*libido dominandi*), that perpetual drive of the earthly city. Later Augustine concludes that "the two cities were created by two kinds of love: the earthly city was created by self-love reaching the point of contempt for God, the Heavenly City by the love of God carried as far as contempt of self."[59]

Usually divided against itself, the earthly city was built on fratricide: the city's founder is Cain, while the stranger already making his way toward the city on high is Abel. Fated to occupy the leading position in the earthly city, Rome reenacted this "archetypal" moment when Romulus murdered Remus. Still, there is a difference, as both Romulus and Remus were "citizens of the earthly city," both seeking "glory."[60]

While Augustine's narrative can but alternate between the progress of one city and then the other, starting from the first man, the author reminds us more than once to bear in mind that the cities' progress is "simultaneous." While the earthly city has both feet firmly planted in chronos time, the other city has only one. For now, meaning until the last day of the "century," that other city is called on, by the one who, in Paul, had come to have faith, to exist in chronos time as though it did not.

* * *

From the time of Abraham—"father Abraham," as Augustine calls him—to that of our Savior, one might imagine that only the city of God managed to "proceed on its course," but that is not so.[61] The first of Eusebius's synchronisms, matching Abraham and Ninus, makes it a simple matter for Augustine to switch over to the earthly city. This opens the way to the Assyrian Empire, and Augustine sets out over a landscape already well mapped by Greek chronologers.[62] But ever since Daniel, the Assyrians have been closely associated with the succession of the four kingdoms, mentioned earlier, which Eusebius rejected. Chapter 7 of the Book of Daniel details the vision of the four beasts emerging from the sea, each beast standing for one of the four kingdoms; the chapter is quoted at length by Augustine, who evidently knows the book well. But he wastes no time discussing the details. "Some commentators have interpreted those four kingdoms as the Assyrians, the Persians, the Macedonians, and the Romans. Those who would like to know how appropriate this interpretation is should read the commentary on Daniel by the presbyter Jerome, a most learned and detailed study."[63] While he cites Jerome, it is noteworthy that he makes no mention of Orosius's quadrilateral (the Carthaginians held no interest for Augustine). Only the two kingdoms whose "glory eclipsed the others" mattered to him—Assyria and Rome. Here Augustine turns to synchronisms, notably those drawn up by Orosius, though he does not name him. As we have seen, Rome begins at the very moment that Babylon ends. Rome is a second Babylon, or Babylon a first Rome.

"Rome," Augustine summarizes, "was founded to be a kind of second Babylon, the daughter, as it were, of the former Babylon."[64] The other kingdoms are no more than "appendages" of the two great powers whose drive to dominate renders them the very incarnation of at once the grandeurs and the miseries of the history of the earthly city.[65] The first of the kingdoms is Babylon, and Rome the fourth and last, but Augustine carefully avoids any computations related to the six thousand years; indeed, he forbids them. And yet, like Julius Africanus, Eusebius, and Orosius, Augustine nonetheless wields this axiom to sweep away the foolish claims to antiquity made by the Egyptians. So far from the truth are they that argument is futile: claimants should be "laughed out of court" rather than "refuted."[66]

The City of God concludes with a vast chronological tableau where Augustine, the master clockmaker to all times, synchronizes days, ages, generations, and eras like so many eschatological gear trains. Chronos is wholly regimented, locked up tight. The whole assumes a coherence; it adjusts; it reflects itself. In this mode all time is reviewed, from the first day to the perpetual Sabbath. One finds the six days of Creation and the time of rest on the seventh day, the six ages of mankind from infancy to old age (a sequence through which the human race passes just as an individual does), the six ages of the world. The first age, "the first 'day,'" spans the period from Adam to the flood; the second continues to Abraham; then come the three ages from Abraham to David, David to the Babylonian exile, the exile to the birth of Christ in the flesh. The sixth age, representing the old age of the world, "cannot be measured by the number of generations, because it is said, 'It is not for you to know the dates: the Father has decided those by his own authority.'" And then it will be the seventh age, "our Sabbath, whose end will not be an evening." The Sabbath becomes Sunday, "the Lord's Day, an eighth day, as it were, which is to last forever."[67]

Through a combination of typology, allegory, and chronology, Augustine sets for some time to come the temporal framework and horizon of the city of God, and of the earthly city as well. Rome, the home of the Christians, is truly the final kingdom. While the framework confirms that the end is drawing near, whatever time remains loses all apocalyptic character, for this is not a time for agitations, speculations, or apocalyptic calculations. At the same time, the apocalypse itself has not been derailed—not at all. It is instead postponed, to a date none too distant yet unrevealed. On the horizon, it remains and must remain the horizon of all Christians. As to the sack of Rome in 410, it is but a reversal of fortune, a disaster, possibly the last the earthly city will undergo—but it does not signal the imminent conclusion of the fourth and final empire. Think of this more as a sign of age. Over the years Augustine said it in sermons time and again: "The world is passing away, the world is losing its grip, the world is short of breath. Do not fear, Thy youth shall be renewed as an eagle."[68] For the Christian, conversion amounted to gaining entry to kairos time, offering renewal and rejuvenation. Even as the Christian participates in the old age of the world, in chronos time, he escapes chronos: the Christian can and must live as being in the world and not belonging to it.

Has Augustine, by drawing up this powerful ordering of times, strangled all apocalyptic speculation, ridding the church for good of that font of recurring unrest, anxiety—and hope? Absolutely not, as the work of Richard Landes, mentioned earlier, convincingly demonstrates. And while Augustine does not offer an opinion on the duration of each age, noting that the sixth "cannot be measured by the number of generations," he links the days to the ages.[69] And the much revived formula that, for God, one day might as well be one thousand years and one thousand years one day implies an equivalence among the sixth day, the sixth age, and six thousand years, a rate of conversion never far from hand.[70] At the beginning of the seventh century, Isidore of Seville overtly applied the formula in his universal history, all the time reciting the prohibition on reckoning the date of the end.

On that final day, the end time of the present will annihilate itself against the end of time, the subject to which Augustine devoted the last books of *The City of God*. Such an ending had been inevitable since that first day when the city of God began its advance, determined to flee the misery of chronos time, shifting from the tension of Kairos to unchanging eternity via the eighth day, which will never end. Inevitable, yes, but when Augustine dwells on how the moment (Krisis) effects a permanent division that can never be reversed, he is repeating the claim that the end is coming—and severely restricting how key texts can be understood. Thus his focus in book 20 on the Final Judgment, then on punishing the evil and rewarding the just. He takes up and reinterprets, effectively, the three chief writings on these topics: the Book of Daniel, Paul's second letter to the Thessalonians, and chapter 20 of John's Revelation. He acknowledges the obscurities of these canonical works, but never for a moment does he doubt their depiction of the end.

"Christ," Augustine resumes, "is to come from heaven to judge both the living and the dead, and that is what we call the Last Day [*ultimus dies*], the day of divine judgement—that is, the last period of time [*novissimum tempus*]."[71] How then does one read Revelation? One must admit right away that "there are, to be sure, many obscure statements, designed to exercise the mind of the reader; and there are few statements there whose clarity enables us to track down the meaning of the rest, at the price of some effort." Here we find advice to exegetes of the past, present, and future. "This is principally because our author repeats the same thing in many ways, so that he appears to be speaking of different matters, though in fact he is found on examination to be treating of the same subjects in different terms."[72] Once he has issued his cautionary note and handed the reader the key, Augustine cannot resist holding forth on the mysterious kingdom of one thousand years. But will he offer a literal or an allegorical reading? He opts of course for the second. The thousand years without any doubt "stand for the whole period of this world's history, signifying the entirety of time by a perfect number."[73] That worldly time, the span that opens with the Incarnation and corresponds to the early church, surely belongs to the sixth age and the sixth millennium, but it slips free from the dangerous boundary of the six thousand years.

Furthermore, Augustine cannot "pass over" the comments made by Paul in his second letter to the Thessalonians. As "obscure" as these are, Augustine has no doubt whatsoever that when Paul spoke of the "man of *anomia*"—in the Latin translation "the rebel"—he meant the Antichrist.[74] Yet when Augustine turns to the thing or person who restrained "the rebel," he admits that "the meaning of this completely escapes me." Still, he is willing to relate "some guesses" he has heard or read. Some reckon that this is a reference to the Roman Empire, more precisely, to Nero, who may come back to life or perhaps never died at all, and who could reappear as the Antichrist at just the right moment. Or perhaps, as others claim, the apostle's comment about the *katechon* and the "secret power of wickedness" refers to "the evil people and the pretended Christians who are in the Church"; on departing from it, they will constitute the people of the Antichrist. In every example, the coming of the Antichrist must precede that of Christ.[75]

It is Daniel, Augustine points out, who links the Final Judgment and the series of empires culminating in the eternal kingdom. He has a "prophetic vision of the four beasts, symbolizing four kingdoms, and the fourth of these is overcome by a king who is recognized as Antichrist. This is followed by the eternal reign of the Son of

Man, who is understood to be Christ." Without lingering to name the four kingdoms (which is prudent), Augustine underlines that final, vicious confrontation between the church and the reign of the Antichrist, lasting "only a brief space of time."[76]

In the end, Augustine discards none of the elements of the Christian regime of historicity, which amounts to an apocalyptic presentism, while precluding the possibility of millenarian ferment. He recasts Paul's duality, and his earthly and divine cities offer us a universal history rather than the individual's perspective. Now Paul's "as though not" is applied to the city of God in its entirety. Of the world "as though not," the city of God has a mission in chronos time even while it is hooked up, as it were, to kairos time—it has two natures. Augustine's innovation ensures that the notion of two cities will leave a profound impression on the theology of history. Just as one can be of the world even as one is not, so can one be of a time while existing in another time—this is the temporal application of the idea of Paul's "as though not," Augustine's infusion of "the contemporaneity of the noncontemporaneous" into Christian time will carry over into the time of history.[77] So the city of God swings between chronos time and kairos time, torn between them and, as often as not, torn asunder.

THE PASCHAL TABLES, THE YEARS OF THE INCARNATION, END OF TIMES

From the most ordinary times to the most complex, we have traced the Christian economy of the Kairos, as it spread and consolidated its control. As we take on the date of Easter and its consequences, we address the last of the questions essential to Kairos, reaching the very heart of its mystery. This is a subject we glanced at earlier, in surveying the development of the Christian year: the celebration of Easter is the linchpin that regulates the yearly cycle of the faithful. But it is a far bigger issue still, transcending strictly liturgical considerations. The fraught, challenging task of crafting a Paschal table acceptable to all Christians takes us to the birth of the Christian era, the adoption of

Jesus Christ as the starting point for numbering the years. Only in the seventeenth century is a gradual revolution completed, upsetting conventional guidelines and settling a new order of time that has survived to today. The triumph of Christly Kairos means not only counting by years after Jesus Christ but also in years before Jesus Christ.

Very gradually, dating practices shift from *Anno Mundi*, the Year of Creation, to *Anno Domini*, Year of the Lord. The innovation is the work of Dionysius Exiguus, technically, but virtually no one noticed it when it appeared in 525, including Dionysius himself. Few controversies are as rich, few have stretched on as long as the dispute over the date of Easter. From the second century to the eighth century, disciplines from mathematics to astronomy, exegetics, and theology were enlisted to address the question, which was fought out against the backdrop of a rivalry between Alexandria and Rome, not to mention Byzantium; each round drove Christians further from the Jewish position. The final result was a date, more accurately a series of dates making up a perpetual Paschal table, whose contents imply nothing beyond a set of simple calculations. So even if we dodge the more technical issues, an intimate understanding of the Christian regime of historicity demands that we take the time to unfold the principal issues.[78] Let us drill into the core of the reactor that powers the Christian regime.

How did Kairos become chronos? Chronos not in the sense of the large intervals of which Paul spoke (*ante legem, sub legem, sub gratia*), not in the sense of the inception of the sixth age, but in the precise sense of calculating the day and year of the Crucifixion. Beginning with Eusebius, chronologers labored to turn it into an event of world significance by inserting the Crucifixion into existing calendars and chronologies. Prior to that, there was no interest at all. Indeed, to say that the evangelists were unconcerned about chronology is putting it very mildly. Matthew and Luke offer some vague indications of the date of Christ's birth, while the only precise year that appears in the New Testament is Luke's for a prediction offered by John the Baptist—the fifteenth year of the reign of Tiberius, or AD 28/29—also the moment when Jesus began to preach. With that in hand, and the knowledge that the Passion occurred on Passover, calculating its date should be easy. But the evangelists disagree on the length of Jesus's ministry: the synoptic Gospels say one year, while for John it was at least three.

THE PASCHAL TABLES

The earliest Christians situated the Crucifixion on Passover, the fourteenth day of the first month of the Jewish lunar year, Nisan. This was essential, since Jesus was the Paschal Lamb. Difficulties arise the moment this date, fixed in the lunar year, needs to be inscribed in the Julian calendar, which is solar. How different from the Nativity, which occurs every year on the twenty-fifth of December! Yet assigning Easter to a fixed date is unthinkable, just as it is inconceivable that the Easter holiday simply be erased—it is the cardinal date, on which a linked series of liturgical dates depends. The solution: a set of Paschal tables reducing to a known quantity all Easter's future dates, subduing its mobility. This makes it possible to determine the date of the first Easter, inscribing it in chronos time. He who longs to free himself from the synagogue must turn astronomer.

How can the lunar and solar cycles be reconciled? How long does it take for the moon to exhaust its phases? Centuries of observation would be needed before one could determine that a complete lunar cycle lasts 19 years, a solar cycle 28 years, and the conjoined lunisolar cycle 532 years—19 multiplied by 28. It follows that the Paschal table drawn up by the Venerable Bede covers the years from 532 to 1063. But we have gotten ahead of ourselves, as a number of other constraints and consequences must be considered. A calendrical concern that surfaced early was the difference between the Crucifixion—which must fall on a Friday—and the Resurrection, which could only be on a Sunday (the Lord's day). And in the third century, as the divide widened between Jews and Christians, offsetting by no less than a day the death of Jesus from Passover became imperative.

There is more. Between Nisan marking the arrival of spring and the embrace by early Christians of March 25 (the vernal equinox in the Julian calendar) as the date of the death of Christ, which became the traditional date of the Crucifixion in the West—in the East March 25 was the Resurrection. Now, at last, the calculations could begin. Which year (and one must not forget the lunar constraints) saw March 25 fall on a Friday (or a Sunday)? And then one learns that the vernal equinox occurred not on March 25 but on March 21, setting off a new flurry of calculations. But already the date March 25 had acquired a symbolic resonance, and in fifth-century Alexandria a monk determined that the first day of Creation and the Incarnation had occurred on that date. Here was a truly cosmic, universal date, loosing a radiant Christly Kairos from day one. Its mark is felt on the periodicity of the celestial bodies and the seasons. The regular rhythm of chronos time plays out, finally, in the assignment of the Nativity to December 25, the winter solstice, as chronos is taken up and transformed in the great Christian narrative.

The Council of Nicaea decrees in 325 that every Christian is to celebrate Easter on the same Sunday. Furthermore, Easter must not fall on the same day as Passover—even if 14 Nisan happens to fall on a Sunday, which is bound to happen routinely. The church proposes a solution: Easter will be celebrated on the Sunday following the first full moon of spring. However, this leaves room for variations in the cycles calculated by Alexandria and Rome, never mind that Egypt's mathematicians are known to be better than the West's. One Roman constraint bears mentioning. Up to the middle of the sixth century, the Roman Church refused to contemplate celebrating Easter after April 21. Why? The rationale had no basis in mathematics or astronomy; it was simply that Rome was founded on April 21, and one could not mix pagan and holy festivities. Endless hybridizations and compromises attended the process of assigning a date to Easter. Somehow it was done: chronos time was reconciled with kairos time by acknowledging the quantitative basis of the first without sacrificing the sublimity of the second.

By any standard, Easter had woven momentous phenomena together, from determining the profile of the liturgical calendar to updating universal chronologies and bridging the gap between East and West. Positioned at the intersection of different times, it laid claim to the role of prime synchronism. But there was more, two shocks one could nearly envision as outgrowths of the controversy: at the same moment, the world had been rejuvenated and the age of

Christianity had appeared. Employing his familiar method of serial synchronisms, Eusebius concluded that Jesus was born in the forty-second year of the reign of Augustus and began to preach in the fifteenth year of the reign of Emperor Tiberius. "That year, 548 years had elapsed since the rebuilding of the temple, which took place in the second year of the reign of Darius, king of the Persians; 1,060 years since Solomon and the building of the first temple; 1,539 years since Moses and the people of Israel fled Egypt; 2,044 years since Abraham and the reign of Ninos and Semiramis; between the flood and Abraham 942 years had passed; between Adam and the flood, 2,242 years."[79]

Eusebius places the year given by Luke for the inception of the ministry of Jesus in the Roman, Jewish, and Persian chronologies, then begins to work his way back, stepwise, to Adam. Adding all his figures, we find that he recorded 5,199 years between Jesus and his typological double. Typology now has a temporal form, and Kairos assumes a fully temporal aspect. This silently shaves three centuries off the age of the world, when compared with the widespread belief that Jesus had been born in World Year 5500, in the middle of the sixth age, of the sixth and final millennium—in the eleventh hour. So five hundred years remain, a bit less by the time Julius Africanus righted his *Chronographies* around 5500. Sliding the apocalyptic horizon back must have begun to seem pressing by the beginning of the fourth century; it became, as we have seen, one of Eusebius's explicit goals. The Venerable Bede took up the cause in a short work entitled *On Times* (*De temporibus*), written four centuries after Eusebius, in the 5900s. Appealing to the "Hebrew Truth," namely, Jerome's translation of the Hebrew Bible (the Vulgate), he boldly chopped thirteen centuries from the world's age.[80] Revisiting the genealogies of the patriarchs from Jesus back to Adam, he arrived at *Anno Mundi* 3952 for the year of Jesus's birth. His reasoning is sound, the breathing space is generous, and he manages to postpone for a time those last, turbulent moments.

If this sounds like idle hair-splitting, consider that Bede's treatise so incensed a fellow monk that he accused the writer of heresy, alleging that he had excluded Christ's advent from the sixth age. Not at all, replied Bede in a letter dated 708 and directed to his accuser, whom he invited to read the letter to the bishop. As to the notion that the world will last six thousand years—utter nonsense! How many times had he been accosted by "rustics" plaguing him with inquiries about the time that remained? Bede deprecated this outlook, noting, "The course of the world is not defined for us in any fixed number of years, and is known only to the Judge himself."[81] No matter how fed up with ignoramuses Bede was, a formal complaint of heresy lodged in the bishop's court constituted a proper clerical dispute, and though nothing is known of his accuser, he cannot have been as *rusticus* as Bede made out. The disparaging language belongs to a strategy, rejecting the charge as millenarian superstition.

The *rustici* come in for further abuse in 725, when Bede expands in *On the Reckoning of Time* (*De temporum ratione*) the argument presented already in *On Times*. Once again the Paschal table occupies the center, yet this does not keep Bede from assailing those who would, baselessly, synchronize ages and millennia. An expanded universal chronicle sweeps past the end point of *On Times* (it wound up with nothing beyond "the rest of the sixth age is known to God alone") to follow Augustine into "Future Time and the End of Time."[82] The end of the sixth age, the persecutions of the Antichrist and the Final Judgment, guide us forever beyond the oceanic waves of chronos time to the calm equilibrium of eternity.

The apocalypse, fended off by meditations on the dawn of the Christian era, does not vanish; short of Christianity itself ending, the apocalypse will always be with us. With us in those parts of the Old Testament read by Christians; with us throughout the New Testament; with us in the background of the chronologers, who have made the world younger—always there, as feared as it is hoped for. Orosius closes his upbeat history of Christianity with that final spectacle of unleashed persecutions and savagery, the Antichrist opening the way to the Final Judgment. Augustine leads his two cities on a journey that ends with the apocalypse. And Bede accomplishes much the same in the final chapters of his universal history.

―――――

DIONYSIUS EXIGUUS AND THE CHRISTIAN ERA

Beginning in the third century, efforts to assign dates to the Passion, the Resurrection, and the Incarnation mingled with the growing conviction that a veritable Christian era had begun. Some even adopted a dual dating system, combining the traditional Years of the World with the new Years of the Passion. As the latter waxed, the former waned. That is the context for the work of Dionysius Exiguus, whose epithet, meaning "Little," has led some to minimize his achievement. But his exiguity was neither of stature nor of achievement—he was just a modest, retiring sort. In 525 this able scholar of Latin and Greek, a learned theologian, master of canon law, and chronologer, issues *Book on Easter* (*Liber de paschate*), a sequel to the Paschal table of Cyril of Alexandria, due to expire in 531. Bishops needed, as we might say today, great visibility, and Dionysius responds to that need. Having elucidated the method used to calculate the date of Easter in Alexandria, he adds the following: "Holy Cyril began his first cycle from the 153rd year of Diocletian, and ended his last in the 247th [Note that this was the standard dating system used in Egypt]; we, rather than beginning from the 248th year of that tyrant, have refused to tie to our cycles the memory of that impious persecutor; but we have chosen instead to designate the period of the years *from the Incarnation of our Lord Jesus Christ*: in so far as the beginning of our hope would be more obvious to us, and the cause of human salvation, that is, the passion of our redeemer, might shine more clearly."[83]

Gone is the impious persecutor! That is why Jesus comes to replace Diocletian in the first column of Dionysius's table, and the Christian era makes its inaugural appearance in a Paschal reckoning. Justice is done, and a useful tool supplied. Dionysius does not linger over his accomplishment; he continues to rely on conventional dates for his own writings, giving the consular year and the indiction. Indeed, commentators have pointed out that Dionysius had only an "incidental interest" in chronology; he was devoted above all to promoting Alexandria's Paschal calculations.[84] For him, writes Georges Declercq, "the incarnation era . . . was nothing more than a consecutive numbering of years in a liturgical document," and it is apparent that he "did not have the intention to create a new era for everyday use."[85] A good thing, as it will only be after the lapse of five hundred years, in the eleventh century, that dating from Christ's birth becomes widespread.

On Time, the textbook Bede composes for his students, really launches the movement that culminates with the West adopting Dionysius's calculations and the era of the Incarnation. His goal is a correct date for Easter, and to get there he scrutinizes the various temporal increments, from the shortest (*momentum*) to the longest (the age), all before addressing the lunisolar cycles. At the center of this catalogue that ranges from the instant to the sixth age of the world is a Paschal table, which Bede describes, providing a brief history of its development. Then he turns to the table drafted by Dionysius, and he explains that the numbers in the first column indicate the time elapsed since the Incarnation, increasing each year by one. To read this as a boundless future would be too bold, but determining that a Paschal cycle lasted 532 years was well within human abilities, meaning tables that continued up to the year 1063, with no end in sight. Such a table enables anyone, notes Bede, to "with unerring gaze, not only look forward to the present and future," but also "back at each and every date of Easter in the past; and in order to clarify an ancient text, he can clearly identify all the years, since it sometimes is doubtful when and of what sort they were."[86] The date of Easter orients us toward the future no less than the past, illuminating both. Christly Kairos floods Chronos with light, penetrating its very texture.

The dating system used in the *Ecclesiastical History of the English People* is the years from the Incarnation, an apt choice for a work set in the last age of the world, addressing the Christian era, on the theme of "the particular providence of God with regard to the English."[87] Never before had a work of history employed this system. A timeline at the end of the book provides the year from the Incarnation for each of the events mentioned. The inclusion of Caesar's expedition to Britain, dated 60 before Jesus Christ, confirms the priority assigned to the Incarnation. Bede's books were widely dispersed, his ideas well known, in Britain and on the continent (disseminated by Anglo-Saxon missionaries), as we know from the 250 manuscript copies of *On the Reckoning of Time* and the 170 copies of the *Ecclesiastical History* that survive. By 742 the first Frankish document—a capitulary—bearing a year from the Incarnation had appeared. Increasingly, annotations detailing concurrent historical events filled the margins of Paschal tables, and these annals in due course detached themselves from the tables, instanced by the *Royal Frankish Annals*, written at the end of the eighth century. Lives of the saints, biographies, histories of abbeys, universal chronicles—every historical genre gradually succumbed to the Christian era. Entitled the *Book of Time Since the Incarnation of Our Lord*, the first universal chronicle to adopt as its starting point not Creation but the birth of Christ was written in 908.[88] By the eleventh century, *Anno Domini* dating had become the norm, though the papacy held out until 1431.

This phase of the material conquest of time, a rather long one, ends there. It is nothing less than a new order of time adopted by the medieval church, embodying calendars, universal histories, and the era of the Incarnation. The very raison d'être of the church, it marks the encroachment of Kairos and Krisis on Chronos. That net, cast by the first Christians, envelops all pagan times, which are boxed in, colonized, undone.

3

NEGOTIATING WITH CHRONOS

WHEN THE Incarnation became the axis defining a universal chronology, the labors of the first Christian chronologers had born fruit. This triumph of the Christian regime left a deep mark on space (*Urbi et Orbi*) and time (from Creation to the Final Judgment). Henceforth Christian time extended everywhere, by decree, connecting to everything and every place. The Christly Kairos shines down on the world, penetrating chronos time, determining the Christian order of time.

As the church called the tune, the faithful adopted the rhythms of the liturgical year. The Christian era became widespread, and the use of *Anno Domini* gradually gained supremacy. And Chronos, pinioned in the mesh of Kairos and Krisis, looked utterly defeated. The Italian anthropologist Ernesto de Martino offers the following summary: "The liturgical year wholly absorbs natural, worldly time, as well as the astronomical year. The regular repetition of the liturgical year itself repeats the time of the central event culminating in Easter. At its ideal limit, the image of the liturgical year involves the utter dehistoricization of time—as if in an echoing cavern, where the reverberations vary in pitch, Christ is endlessly repeated."[1]

No matter how sound the theology, such an extreme dehistoricization must in practical terms remain an untenable ideal. There is no making the world one enormous monastery, and after all monasteries do rely on natural, mundane time for their everyday existence. The same is true of all big organizations—kingdoms, empires, the papacy—and of all individuals. To the extent that we live in an apocalyptic present situated between the Incarnation and the Parousia, a time that has been with us, is with us, and will remain with us for some time yet, how might we make sense of it? What are we to make of it without somehow affecting its very character, which is that of in-between? After all, ontologically speaking it is a superfluous time, nothing but the interval between the inception of the time of the end and the end proper. The solution first proposed in the Gospels is the conversion of the world (not omitting the Jews), so that the end can come. That message was repeated at Pentecost and reinforced by Paul in his mission to the Gentiles. Time is short, we are told by the first apostles, and their calls for conversion have remained fundamental over the history of the church.[2] The spiritual conquest of the New World owed everything to this apocalyptic countdown.

To spread the Christly Kairos meant injecting it into the chronos time of others—a strategy adopted early and never revisited. Clerics themselves turned to strategies fashioned for local contexts: while this meant adapting and relaxing the Christian regime, ultimately they reinforced it. Finding space for Chronos without sacrificing anything essential meant adopting a range of temporal instruments functioning in dyads: these strategies were anchored in kairos time and affected chronos time as well. Put to work from the earliest days by the church fathers, their Latin names were *accommodatio* (the accommodation of the divine to human nature), *translatio* (the succession of empires), *renovatio* (renewal), and *reformatio* (reform, in every sense). These learned instruments were used by theologians, in particular the famous abbot Joachim of Fiore, who during the twelfth century increased the part played by chronos in these mechanisms, offering them an articulation among the past, present, and future. The interconnections the four instruments formed in practice encourage us to take the rare step of considering them as a group, a network, a fine and supple mesh that enables them to control Chronos while allowing it a certain play. Equipped with these powerful concepts, the people of the Middle Ages found a space outside of the dehistoricized time of the liturgy where history could act. This was unmistakably a period of triumphal conquest for the Christian regime.³ Yet the same clerics who set out to strengthen the Christian regime of historicity by "modernizing" it opened up deep rents in its fabric. Soon these rents were called heresies, or possible heresies. Those very rents, though they occurred within the Christian frame, unleashed forces that precipitated modern time, defined by a chronos feeling its way free from the meshes of Kairos and Krisis.

ACCOMMODATIO

As God unfolded his divine economy, he relied on *accommodatio* to guide human beings along the path to perfection. This was "accommodation" or "divine condescension," as God descended from on high to speak to humans in their language. The first two instances, outstanding and irrefutable, were the presentation of the Mosaic Law and the Incarnation. An article of faith for church fathers, medieval clerics, and leaders of the Reformation, accommodation remained essential to the modern era, when its crown was stolen by progress, a notion that served as both echo and executioner to accommodation.⁴ At that moment, the leading role passed from God to humankind. For us, the significance of accommodation resides in its close association with time. It played the part of intermediary between the eternity of God and chronos time—or, to be precise, the different times experienced by human beings. (We should note, however, that accommodation occurs wholly on God's initiative.)

When Paul said to the Corinthians, "You are still of the flesh," he became the first to underline the gap between godly perfection and human coarseness. He had seen that his listeners were but infants in Christ, so he had provided for them accordingly: "I fed you with milk."⁵ When the church fathers returned to this image, they used it to convey the weakness of human nature. "Short of the perfect" is how Irenaeus characterized, at the end of the third century, every being in creation; surely little children should not be offered the same food as adults.⁶ After some time the children will grow, mature, advance a bit closer to perfection, growing a bit less fleshly and a bit more spiritual. Tertullian believed that "nothing comes into existence without time."⁷ Because the task of accompanying and guiding the child along that path falls on the church, accommodation must be a pedagogy. The law, for Paul, was "our pedagogue [*paidagogos*] leading us to Christ"—but only to him.[8]

There is a second basis for accommodation, supplementing that applying to human beings in general (i.e., allowances based on their sinfulness, their created nature, their experience of birth, maturation, and death). Also articulated by Paul, this is the notion that Jews and Christians represent different stages of development. The Mosaic Law suited an idolatrous people just departing from Egypt: step by step the Jews needed to be guided to the truer faith. Yet, since they denied the Messiah and rejected the New Testament, Jews remained somewhat backward, wedded to a literal reading of the Old Testament. They had missed the spirit of the text; by failing to read typologically, they had missed the ways it prepared and prophesied the coming of the Savior. To employ an anachronism, they clung to a stage of accommodation that had been superseded. For the Messiah had added a temporal quality to the symbols God had always relied on and in doing so had revealed—retroactively—their true meaning. "All these things," noted Paul, "happened to them [the Hebrews] by way of example, and they were written down to instruct us on whom the ends of the ages have come."[9] Accommodation possesses a history, such that we can speak of accommodation before and after the Incarnation, itself the portal leading to the end of times.

Comments made by Augustine on the nature and impact of accommodation in the Roman West have never been bettered. Marcellinus, to whom *The City of God* was dedicated, had expressed astonishment that "this God, who is proved to be the God also of the Old Testament, is pleased with new sacrifices after having rejected the ancient ones. For they allege that nothing can be corrected but that which is proved to have been previously not rightly done, or that what has once been done rightly ought not to be altered in the very least."[10] Augustine replied in a letter, opening with some general remarks to the effect that "the processes of nature itself and the works of men" change "according to the circumstances of the time," though the reason (*ratio*) for these things does not change. One could say the same of one season leading to the next, the ages of life, and how teachers adopt different methods though the subject matter remains the same. Think too of medicine: a remedy suited to a certain stage of an illness when the patient is a certain age is not suited to another stage and another age. So does "the difference in the times" lead to other sorts of changes."[11]

Then Augustine takes on the question Marcellinus posed regarding sacrifices. "The divine institution of sacrifice was suitable [*aptum fuit*] in the former dispensation but is not suitable now. For the change suitable to the present age has been enjoined by God, who knows infinitely better than man what is fitting for every age [*qui cuique tempori accommodate adhibeatur*], and who is, whether He give or add, abolish or curtail, increase or diminish, the unchangeable Governor as He is the unchangeable Creator of mutable things, ordering all events in His providence until the completed course of time, the component parts of which are the dispensations adapted to each successive age, shall be finished, like the grand melody of some ineffably wise master of song, and those pass into the eternal immediate contemplation of God who here, though it is a time of faith, not of sight, are acceptably worshipping Him."[12] Accommodation advances in step with all human history; it plays the part of baton to the divine conductor-composer.

Augustine's definition, since his day the preeminent account of accommodation, fully accounts for liturgical vicissitudes. That is the subject of a book—arguably the first liturgical history—written in the ninth century by Walafrid Strabo, abbot of the monastery of Reichenau Island.[13] As each practice comes into use, the book shows how "over time [*processu temporis*] it developed." Accommodation makes it possible to account for these developments and changes, while performing the essential task of connecting them to a God who (we are always told) never changes. While accommodation, that temporalizing instrument, functions within chronos time, that time does not impinge on it.

ANSELM OF HAVELBERG

Anselm of Havelberg was a twelfth-century member of the Order of Canons Regular of Prémontré who became bishop of Havelberg. While an ambassador to Constantinople, he had conversations with Greek theologians that formed the basis of his *Dialogues*. He explained, in a history of salvation, that while there could be but one faith, its forms varied considerably, "from Abel to the last of the elect." Accommodation never ceased to be relevant, given the "two extraordinary transmissions [*transpositiones*] called the two Testaments." A third, the Apocalypse, had yet to occur.[14]

"In these two transfers or mutations, divine wisdom has displayed over time [*paulatim*] such variety that after banning idols it authorized sacrifices. Later, when it proscribed sacrifices, it did not prohibit circumcision. Then, proscribing circumcision, it introduced baptism.... So it made Jews of gentiles, Christians of Jews. Bit by bit, by means of elimination, modification, exemption, relying on education [*pedagogice*] and medication [*medicinaliter*], it guided humanity almost furtively [*furtim*] from idolatry to the Law, then from the Law that did not lead to perfection to the perfection of the Gospel."[15]

Anselm offers a nearly verbatim rendering of Augustine's definition of accommodation. Here is a true engine of history, closely engaged with time, which it manipulates in accordance with its plans. But Anselm ventures beyond Augustine, conceiving a force that never pauses. Rather than stop once it has turned the Jews back to the distant past, accommodation continues and will continue to work up to the very end—"bit by bit," "almost furtively," "pedantically," "as medicine works." The movement, he emphasizes, never ceases to advance. The "diversity" and "novelty" animating religious practices "on a nearly annual basis" (one thinks of the Byzantine theologians whom Anselm debated) ought to provoke neither fear nor outrage within the church.[16] This apology for innovation adds something to previous ideas about accommodation. God remains as unchanging as ever, yet novelty can be welcomed, justified, even validated. Every use to which tradition has been put is now comprehended under accommodation, up to what we have taken to calling the "invention of tradition." Anselm saw a church perpetually youthful, renewing (*renovatur*) itself with each new era. For Marie-Dominique Chenu, such "triumphant optimism," shared by Anselm and other twelfth-century theologians, amounted to an optimistic take on history itself.[17]

Christians wielded accommodation as a transformative formula; it enabled them to endow chronos time with a certain heft. Chronos time ceased to be the vacant in-between of the present, the gap separating the Incarnation from the Parousia that one crossed "as though" one did not exist. All the variety and variability and diversity and novelty of yesterday's religion and today's religious practices—all might be clarified and accepted. Clarified and illumined, the present became an object to act on. Looking back on past times, one sees now that waves of divine condescension had announced the coming of the Christly Kairos. Time has ever flowed onward, from Abel to the last of the elect.

Over time, accommodation slowly came to serve as a handmaiden to history, and while it addressed the history of salvation, it also heeded "the memorable changes the passage of time has wrought in the world." Bossuet, the author of that remark, went on to note, in the *Discourse on Universal History*'s dedication to the dauphin, dated 1681, "You will see how empires succeeded one another and how religion, in its different states, maintains its stability from the beginning of the world up to our own time."[18] The book that follows traces the majestic unfolding of accommodation over the centuries.

THE ABBOT OF FIORE: TEMPORALIZED ACCOMMODATION

Tracing the spread and eventual triumph of the Christly Kairos is impossible without touching on the abbot Joachim of Fiore (ca. 1135–1202), though one of his most astute readers, Gian Luca Potestà, accurately characterized Joachim's output as a "wasps' nest." Potestà informs us that Joachim was "an eminent clergyman, active in the Norman and Swabian regions of Italy; he reformed monasticism; he was also a biblical exegete, and had become convinced that in the past lay clues that enable him to unlock the mysteries of the present and the future. Like every true apocalyptist, he believed that the key to the present lay in the words of scripture and in history, correctly interpreted. This belief led to Joachim's insistence that endless links be made from history to the texts, then from the texts to history, all to resolve the enigmas that he confronted."[19]

Three accomplishments assured Joachim a place in the present account—not that I will consider venturing into the "wasps' nest." Every self-respecting exegete since the earliest days of the Christian faith offers a typological reading of the Old and New Testaments, but Joachim pushes the approach to its limits, making of it a device in which he reads the future. Such feats should be possible once a temporal dimension is added to typology. Alongside such a consistently binary logic is Joachim's three-part theory of history, based on the divine Father, Son, and Holy Spirit. So far, so good. But the true novelty of Joachim's approach emerges when he links the trinitarian figures to three "states" (*status*) in chronos time. Most significantly, he places the Holy Spirit in the future. While he is acknowledged during his lifetime as a prophet, Joachim's renown as a seer only increases after his death. In *The Divine Comedy*, Dante presents him as "the Calabrian Abbot Joachim, who had the gift of the prophetic spirit."[20] The Franciscans, in particular, make much of him, and the thirteenth century witnesses a wide circulation of his writings—along with many more ascribed to him—works Henri de Lubac identified as "so-called millenarist utopias."[21] The spiritual legacy of Joachimism stretches to modern times, as Father de Lubac has shown. He comments, "Since the thirteenth century Joachimism has undergone a ceaseless metamorphosis, its impact felt not only within and around churches but in modern secular thought. . . . It has acted as a stimulant ever since."[22]

At the beginning of 1191, when Richard the Lionheart halted at Messina on his way to the Third Crusade, he asked the abbot a simple yet pressing question: Would he capture Jerusalem? The answer Joachim gave—"Not before 1194"—was inspired by an apocalyptic sign: a seven-headed dragon, with Saladin the sixth head (and the Antichrist the seventh). His faith in an exact "concordance" between the Old and New Testaments extended to history, which for him proceeded along two parallel lines. The time of the Old Testament, comprising forty-two generations, matched the forty-two of the New Testament, counting from Jesus Christ to the Parousia, with Joachim himself a member of the fortieth generation. Any rigorous exegete will find history quite predictable: every detail of the Bible prefigures what follows, including events yet to transpire. It is a recursive process, the calculus forever reworked until the last days, since any event, as it occurs, casts light on the true meaning of scripture. What we call a prophet is one who can see the "not yet," which amounts here to being able to read. When Joachim declared himself an "exegete" above all, his reasoning closely resembled that of Pope Gregory I, who had previously said, "We call 'prophet' not just those who predict events to come but those who reveal [scriptural] matters until now hidden."[23]

Such ideas suffice to draw those who sought advice about temporal matters to Joachim. He goes further, though, and his major works outline a true theology of history constructed around the Revelation of John. Adding a three-part historical approach to his "corresponding" dualism, he systematically maps the holy trinity onto the three orders (*ordines*) of Christian society. Lay figures and married couples are associated with the Father and the Old Testament. Clerics are associated with the Son and the New Testament. Monks, endowed with the "spiritual intelligence" of both Testaments, are associated with the Holy Spirit; they act as the avant-garde bringing God's plan to fruition. By virtue of introducing his schema into chronos time, Joachim lends the Trinity a temporal quality, and the three states reveal themselves as overlapping, distinct stages. The Holy Spirit stands ready, and only after some hesitation does Joachim declare that it will begin its era in 1260. Contrast such a dynamic model with the Augustinian tripartite vision of history before the Law, under the Law, and under Grace, all of which ended with the advent of Christ. Joachim adjusted that vision, placing his first state under the Law, the second under Grace, and the third under a "larger" or a "fuller" Grace. The adjustment swells into a real deviation, for while Augustine's seventh era opens with the Parousia, Joachim's is coterminous with the third state and belongs very much to worldly time. Even as one begins to hear echoes of Revelation's chapter 20, with its enigmatic kingdom of one thousand years, Joachim backs away from offering the vaguest estimate of the duration of his "spiritual age" and the faintest hint that the sitting pope is the Antichrist (though, yes, it could be that the Antichrist has been born, and in Rome). Without reviving the old warnings of an imminent apocalypse, he offers a present full of watchful waiting, a third state that, in spite of much exegetical labor, lacks precedent. The time to come, in which Jews, pagans, even Saracens will undergo conversion at the hands of monks, is a time in the making, where those "spiritual men" have an essential role. Where is the future? It starts right here, in chronos time, and no longer is it "only in the distance."[24]

This third stage, in sum, endeavors to preserve Augustine's ambitious vision of an airtight and interwoven history while opening some space between the day of the Son and Judgment Day. Pushing back against the telescoping of that period by Christly Kairos, Joachim of Fiore worked in the same key as those who read the Bible through an accommodationist lens, though in lending that in-between a chronological fullness, he proved a more apocalyptic and more systematic thinker than they. He gracefully advanced the spread of Christly Kairos while carrying on a delicate dance with the chronos time of the past and of—still more—the future.

One wonders, though, whether this professedly rigorous exegete, this theologian devoted to rigor, may have undermined the Christian regime of historicity through his attempts to demonstrate its relevance. Declaring the Trinity subject to time, assigning parts of Revelation's twentieth chapter a temporal moment, intimating that between the time of the end and the end of times one might find space for a history—a history of Salvation, yes, but still a history into which might flow all the aspirations of a new era—these acts can hardly be called inconsequential. Those who followed, acknowledging his impact explicitly or implicitly, will return to these openings, extending them much further than had Abbot Joachim, and, in hastening things along, will bring distortions.

TRANSLATIO

No matter how valuable liturgical calendars, intent on accounting for each day and hour of the year, may be as anchors in securing the conquest of time, they tell us nothing of our progress along time's path and offer no assistance as we wrestle with the meaning of events. Nor does the political complement to the calendar's chronos loop, the swell and tumble of dynasties and empires, convey any special message. A dynasty ends; another begins. Succession is tedious, meaningless—Assyrians, Medes, Persians yielding one to the other had no significance for Greek historians. Those scholars recorded events; they even tried to explain them; they turned them into chronological markers—but they could offer no sense of a meaning that took the events outside of themselves. A way out exists: lodge events in the weave of prophecies or apocalypses, and everything changes.

As I have mentioned, prophets and apocalyptists know full well that all has been inscribed on the heavenly tables, the beginning as well as the ending. The chosen of God decrypt those tables, set them down, in whole or in part, and pass them along in keeping with the Lord's commands. To whom should they confide their visions—to all or only to their trusted intimates? Must they speak promptly or await the chosen moment? It all depends. But for every one of them, the question of the end—or an end—remains central. For the prophets, time advances by fits and starts: after announcing the dawn of an era of punishment and destruction, they offer consolation and rebuilding. After that moment when the covenant is forgotten, the "rest" of Israel will experience a renewed commitment to the covenant. The end, declares every apocalyptist, is both certain and soon—proved by the burst of warning signs. The afflictions of the present offer no alternative: only a radical change can follow. Whichever tendency a prophet inclines toward, the fall of Jerusalem in 587 BC and the ensuing reenactments of that disaster have woven a historical fabric based on a repeated motif.

DANIEL'S UNIQUENESS

An emblematic instance is the Book of Daniel, already mentioned twice. Writing from the point of view of a hostage in sixth-century Babylon who spends his days in the court of Nebuchadnezzar, Daniel receives a vision, startlingly vivid, of the temple in Jerusalem profaned by Antiochus IV. By linking the catastrophe of 587 with that of 168, he offers a universal history as apocalypse, underlining the idea of one empire succeeding another until the last.[25] A royal dream announces the future: the four metals making up the statue described in Daniel's chapter 2 stand for the kingdoms of Babylon, the Medes, the

Persians, and the Greeks, whereas the stone that pulverizes them all stands for a fifth kingdom destined to "last for ever." Daniel becomes the visionary in chapter 7, projecting the four kingdoms onto four enormous beasts that "emerged from the sea." The last beast, the most horrifying, is a stand-in for post-Alexandrian kings. The four beasts will lose their authority, which is claimed by the "son of man," whose rule will be "everlasting."[26]

The head of the fourth beast, seen in close-up, sports ten horns that stand for the Hellenistic kings; the eruption of an eleventh can only be that blaspheming monster, Antiochus IV. Chapter 11, allegedly a prediction to Darius of the sequel to the fall of the Persian kingdom, amounts to a history of the doomed Hellenistic kingdoms. Once the lonely death of Antiochus, struck down by the hand of God, is prophesied, the story lurches to the Parousia and the escape from history's afflictions of "all those whose names are found written in the Book."[27] The sequence repeats itself: the statue is destroyed, the beasts are overwhelmed, Antiochus vanishes, and in each instance the (same) eternal reign begins.

Why do we see the recurrent number four when talk turns to what has long been known as the "succession of empires" (*translatio imperii*)? Was Daniel the first to enumerate four empires, or was he part of a tradition within prophetic writing? The truth is somewhere in between. Was this a Greek invention, as Arnaldo Momigliano thought, or Persian (specifically Zoroastrian), as David Flusser insisted, or something else altogether?[28] Momigliano declared, "The notion of a succession of empires is as old as Herodotus."[29] I am not certain that the issue is so cut-and-dried, but Daniel took it for granted that there were four metals, four winds, four beasts, and four kingdoms. He never wondered *why* power passed from one to the other, noting only that God "controls time and seasons, he makes and unmakes kings."[30] In Ecclesiasticus, dating shortly before Daniel and set down in Hebrew in Alexandria, the transfer of royal dominion from one people to another is linked to injustice: "Sovereignty passes from nation to nation because of injustice, arrogance and money."[31]

The Greeks thought differently about translatio, endowing it with no guiding eschatology. Herodotus and, later, Ctesias knew that the Assyrians had stood supreme, then the Medes, then the Persians.[32]

The Trojan War had marked the true beginning point for the Greeks, and their part in the succession of empires began only once Alexander had conquered Asia and founded the Hellenistic kingdoms, which the Greeks depicted as their inheritance of the Persian Empire. Thucydides made no mention of those kingdoms, skipping from the Trojan War to the Peloponnesian War with only a brief account of the Median wars.

Polybius, conveying Scipio Africanus's reaction to the ruins of Carthage in 146 BC, gives us a weeping figure who cites Homer on the fall of Troy: "There will come a day when sacred Ilion shall perish, / and Priam, and the people of Priam of the strong ash spear."[33]

As he repeats Hector's words on the destruction of Troy, Scipio offers something like a prophecy of Rome's fall.[34] From the old Troy we pass to the new, and that image of a fallen city serves as a warning to the present. But this has nothing to do with the succession of empires, since Polybius sees Rome as unique. He does enumerate, at the beginning of his book, the powers that went before Rome—the Persians, the Lacedaemonians, and the Macedonians—making Rome the fourth. Here we again have four. Still, Polybius has little interest in succession and the number four; Rome, he tells us, outstrips all the great powers of the past.[35] Later, under the rule of Augustus, Dionysius of Halicarnassus makes a similar claim, ranking Rome far above past empires. He lists four—the Assyrians, the Medes, the Persians, and the Macedonians—then adds Rome to the list, much as Daniel did the eternal kingdom.[36] (He knew nothing, mind you, of Daniel's writings.) Romans adapted the succession-of-empires formula, laying claim to special status with the formula "4 + 1." They hoped to counteract the use of that formula in the East, where it was used to stir up opposition to Greece, then Rome, both fated to fall.[37] In that conception, four represents a limit: Rome can be the fourth empire but never the fifth. This entailed rebranding, for instance, the Medes and Persians as a single kingdom. Might the Roman claim to fifth place be a strategy for eluding the "four kingdoms rule"?

Two prophecies, one ancient and the other a more recent patchwork, appear in book 4 of the Sibylline Oracles, dated to the eighth decade AD. The first foretells the four canonical kingdoms, while the second predicts the fall of Rome's savage might and the vengeance of

Asia, followed by the end of times. The redactor sees that the power of Macedonia "shall not always continue," so it forfeits its claim to real dominion.[38] Rome will not in any sense be a fifth kingdom since Macedonia never managed to be a fourth kingdom. Daniel's framework, with its eschatological implications, holds off all challengers, while its apocalyptic horizon serves anti-Hellenic propagandists well, and later those antagonistic to Rome. We have Daniel to thank for the long-term correspondence between the number four and a certain sense of history, a blending of chronos time and kairos time whose simplicity and flexibility have assured its continual reformulation up to the present.

A CHRISTIAN DANIEL

But well before the moderns had their way with Daniel's program, the Christians pioneered harnessing the succession of empires to their program. And by acknowledging his prophetic gifts, they opened a passageway between the Old Testament and the New. When he offered a fresh reading of Jeremiah's vision of the end of the exile in Babylon and his talk of building the temple anew, Daniel really meant the coming of Jesus. He figures out, with help from the angel Gabriel, that each of Jeremiah's 70 years should be understood as a "week of years," totaling 470—more or less the interval between the date of the prophecy and the desecration wrought by Antiochus IV. The cryptic passage had previously lent various formulas the leeway needed to align the prophecy and the chronology. When their turn came, the Christian exegetes soon recognized their own Jesus in the "Anointed One put to death" mentioned in these same verses.[39] A remarkable sequence of mathematical gymnastics is performed by Jerome in his *Commentary on Daniel*, but many had done likewise before him and more will follow. After all, the issue had already been debated by the "most learned" men.[40]

The resolution of that key issue opens the way for reading the entire book as a prophecy. Irenaeus, for instance, understands that when the dream vision shows a statue pulverized, "Christ is the stone which is cut out without hands, who shall destroy temporal kingdoms, and introduce an eternal one."[41] No longer can anyone doubt that the fourth and final empire is Rome. Certainly Jerome, who had read Daniel, has no doubts. And this had been set forth by John, whose narration of the fall of "Babylon the Great"—Rome, it happened—races through the succession of empires, from first to last. Typology ensures that Antiochus becomes a stand-in for the Antichrist, long retaining that role, with its implication of an end hastening nearer. Other Antichrists will punctuate the trajectory of the church, never shedding that apocalyptic quality, and yet at the front of the parade stands Antiochus, distinguished by his appearance (and his unmasking) in the Old Testament. Satan's lieutenant, he also heralded the end.

Invested (in the strictest sense) in the Book of Daniel, the earliest Christians did more than endorse a prophetic interpretation of the Old Testament. Daniel was woven into the catastrophic fabric of the history of Israel. As I have indicated already, Antiochus comes to serve as the agent who turns the disaster of 587 into a cyclically repeating event that will end only with the apocalypse. The moment Christians subscribe to the prophetic message, the loom is back in motion: what ended with Daniel is transformed into the beginning of a new time, through Jesus. His advent and death, seen now as part of Daniel's vision, upend the very meaning of the disaster of 168. It was presented as the final iteration; those who drew up the Book of Daniel experience it as such. It is now read, however, as the exit from an age of catastrophe, set to the tune of Jewish rebelliousness. What was the end of times becomes the overture to the time of the end, changing everything, including the very nature of history. Nonetheless, the apocalyptic structure of history I call *apocalyptic presentism* is not lost: Antiochus has been identified as the Antichrist. In the little time left to them, believers must surrender to Kairos, messianic time. After all, Jesus explained, in words still echoing, that his Kingdom was not of this world, utterances recast by Paul when he insisted that the city of Christians is elsewhere.

The succession of empires is an organizing principle of universal history. Daniel, pioneer of the addition of apocalypse to that framework, never counted beyond a fourth empire, since the fifth could only be the eternal kingdom. The Christians who followed in his footsteps saw things as he had. His system suited them—so long as the Roman Empire took up the number four spot. It was the Romans who embraced the five when they learned about the succession of empires, fairly late, yet before they merited it.[42] Still, no one could claim that they had not succeeded to the Greeks, who were in turn successors to the Persians, the Medes, and the Assyrians. Had they read Daniel? Certainly not. And they had no interest in apocalyptic limits.

At the outset, the succession of empires belongs entirely to *chronos* time—a dynasty begins as another ends. "Succession" (*translatio*) of empires describes it less well than "transfer." And the chronos element does not fade, but Daniel and the Christians attach to it a kronos element, eschatology impinging on universal history. The beneficiaries included peoples whose lands were occupied by foreign powers, as the idea of the succession of empires shone a spotlight on expiration dates. Waiting on the street corner is the apocalypse.

THREE STATES, FOUR OR FIVE KINGDOMS?

Another approach to organizing universal history, drawn up first by Paul then richly elaborated by Augustine, arises from the establishment of the Law, a fundamental event. Since the time of Adam, humankind has known three states—before the Law (*ante legem*), under the Law (*sub lege*), and after the Law the state of grace (*sub gratia*). Paul even knew that the period between the promise to Abraham and the covenant sealed with Moses totaled 430 years. That early promise ensured that the time before the Law was anything but ceaseless ignorance—a light shone, anticipating the fulfillment of the promise by Jesus Messiah. But this tool lacks the breadth of translatio, for as much as it regulates time from the Old to the New Testament, it overlooks the efforts of the Christian chronologers to link the advance of the city of God and the city of human beings, to use an Augustinian image.

Comparisons have been made between the three states and the tripartite division of time offered by Varro, the great Roman antiquarian active in the first century BC. (Varro may have borrowed his model from Eratosthenes, the erudite Alexandrian of the third century BC.) Varro distinguishes three times: "the first from the origin of man to the first Cataclysm, which because of our ignorance is called the 'Uncertain' [*adêlon*]; the second from the first Cataclysm to the first Olympiad [776 BC], which, because many legends are ascribed to it, he calls the 'Mythical' [*muthikon*]; and the third, from the first Olympiad to our time, which he calls the 'Historical' [*historikon*], because the events which occurred in it are contained in factual histories."[43]

The most cursory glance reveals that these two triplets share nothing but the number three. One delimits temporal spaces according to advances in knowledge and truth, while the other proceeds according to the transition from law to faith. When Augustine set to work on the latter, he increased the total number of states to four: before the law, under the law, under grace, and then for the elect *in pace*, in peace.[44] In the twelfth century Abbot Joachim of Fiore's addition of a temporal component thoroughly transforms this schema.

Whereas Herodotus had envisioned only one sovereignty replacing another, succession (*translatio*) served as the key for the Hellenistic kings and later the Romans. The kings fancied themselves the successors of the Persians and the pharaohs. The Romans, conquerors of the East, played the part of Alexander's successors, only to assume the role of masters of the world, a role they anticipated playing forever, as Rome had been promised eternal dominion. (There was to be, for that matter, no further extension of the empire after the reign of Augustus; the task was now one of preservation.) Daniel had already limited the number of empires to four, with the fifth entity God's everlasting kingdom. His book was seized on by the Christians, for reasons previously noted, who turned it into the cornerstone of the regime of Christian historicity. Only a few adjustments were needed: the identity of the fourth and fiercest of the beasts—for the Greeks they substituted the Romans; Antiochus IV took on the role of the Antichrist; and the entire book was now reconceived in terms of Jesus Christ.

Above all, the schema of four kingdoms had to be preserved, the image of succession emphasized. No more than four, the sovereignties yield one to the other; Rome, in last place, is the time of the Incarnation. Cast your mind back to the tables drawn up by Eusebius of Caesarea, where the last column, that marking the end of time, is assigned to Rome. If we picture succession as a motion, it points us toward the endpoint of the advance of history. In all chronos time, the optimal moment for the expansion of Christly Kairos as a plenitude of time was the Pax Romana. Babylon had been the first empire, and Rome, the new Babylon, was now the last—this was true for Orosius and Augustine, and indeed the first and the last eclipsed the others. The notion of a "Christian era" and of a Christian empire had a certain appeal for Eusebius and Orosius, and one can make out the silhouette of a fifth empire there. But Augustine, appalled by the prospect of the theology of history declining into a political theology, firmly drew the line. Yes, he had called on Orosius to take on the task that grew into the *Histories*, but regarding the book he maintained a silence that made his sentiments clear. Had not Jesus said, "My kingdom is not of this world" and "Pay Caesar what belongs to Caesar"?[45] Every universal history must terminate in the apocalypse and the Final Judgment, the defeat of Chronos by Kairos followed by the absorption of the latter into the eternity of God. That thesis, as I have pointed out, occupies the bulk of *The City of God*'s final books.

But we now have a problem. Given the strict rule that the history of the earthly city stops at the number four, and the assumption that Rome is the final empire, what will happen if the Roman Empire manages to tumble, or seems about to? The city's pagans, quite devoted to tradition, were quick to blame the Christians. For them, the eternity promised to Rome was an article of faith, rendering Theodosius's decision to ban the ancestral gods and their cult a sin. As for the Christians, their denials, particularly the rebuttals promptly issued by Orosius and Augustine, depicted a world on its last legs. The fall of Rome to Alaric proved only that that the sixth age had nearly run its course. Any suffering attendant on that should not be mistaken for the onset of the apocalypse—the horrors to come will far outstrip recent troubles. The Lord and the Antichrist had not yet taken up arms. Two scenarios, two temporalities—it was essential to keep them straight.[46]

THE MEDIEVAL TRANSLATIO

Talk of a "renaissance" of the Roman Empire preceded medieval historians' doctrine of a "transfer."[47] Charlemagne himself had *renovatio imperii Romani* added to the imperial seal, and other practices promoted this imagery: coronation in Rome and popular acclamation as "emperor of the Romans." It is important to point out that the term *translatio* was applied to his coronation no earlier than the end of the eleventh century.[48] While every renaissance is by definition punctual—over the preceding centuries a number of rulers had proclaimed them—*translatio* aims higher, demanding continuity and a sense of history. It is one thing to bring Rome back to life; it is quite another to trace the continuity between Augustus and the present. The Germanic kings had a new motto: our empire is a sequel to Rome's. Other mottos: "We are Romans," "Justinian is our predecessor," "Rome (where not one of them lived) is the capital of the empire." Certainly the capital was not Constantinople, least of all in 1054, when it was ruled the city of schismatics.

Mobilizing this legitimating device when their power sank to a low ebb, the German kings, whether in Germany, confronting the pope in Italy, or in Byzantium, claimed for their empire the number four spot, last in line. The strategy adopted, first renovatio, then translatio, cast the Holy Roman Empire as an enduring reenactment of Rome. Daniel, the model for Jerome, Orosius, and Augustine, remained the framework and the horizon for universal history. Translatio effected a double legitimation of the Holy Roman Empire, supporting it politically as an institution, theologically as the fourth empire. For all their protests that the timing of the end was unknowable, these charters of empire dwelt in the time of the end, muttering perpetually about the world's advanced age.

Tertullian believed that the arrival of the end was "held back" by the Roman Empire, an opinion that gained force with the doctrine of translatio. Recently Carl Schmitt and Giorgio Agamben have revived the interpretations of the Pauline *katechon* offered by Tertullian and other theologians.[49] This tradition has made of the Roman Empire a great theologico-political formation, the site proper of the advance of history and the very measure of its limits—Rome as history's unsurpassable horizon. Translatio, in sum, equipped the Christian regime of historicity with a novel, powerful mechanism for ideological, political, and theological enterprises. One might also see it as a form of temporalized accommodation:

without abandoning its commitment to Daniel, it turned to account Roman antiquity (reaching back beyond Constantine to Augustus) and unleashed the writing of history.

OTTO OF FREISING

In *Chronicle or History of the Two Cities*, Otto of Freising (1112–1158) fully applies the theory of translatio. Scion of a distinguished family— King Conrad III was his half-brother—Otto wrote fine works of theology and history upon completing his education in Paris. He served as the bishop of Freising, joined the Second Crusade, and was intimate with Frederick I. While his book's title bespeaks a debt to Augustine, Otto envisioned a difference. Seven of the work's eight sections address the history of the earthly city from Babylon to the middle of the twelfth century; the eighth, appropriately, examines the end, complete with the Antichrist, the resurrection of the dead, and the end of the two cities. But if we consider the vision presented in the book, we find that two distinct cities existed only until Constantine.

"From that time on," he emphasizes, "since not only all the people but also the emperors (except a few) were orthodox Catholics, I seem to myself to have composed a history not of two cities but virtually of one only, which I call the Church. For although the elect and the reprobate are in one household, yet I cannot call the cities two as I did above; I must call them properly but one—composite, however, as the grain is mixed with the chaff."[50]

The vocabulary is Augustine's, yet Otto distances himself from *The City of God*, edging closer to Orosius and Eusebius. Seven centuries had elapsed, and he is leaving behind Augustine's theology of history to create the political theology Augustine rejected. Should this be ascribed to accommodation, or would it be more accurate to call it a betrayal, an utter capitulation? Does it settle the Christian regime of historicity more firmly by bringing it into alignment with the present without giving up the essential division into four empires and an apocalyptic horizon?[51] Devoted as he imagined himself to Augustine, Otto unwittingly broke with him. Can it be that by embedding the Christian regime of historicity more deeply in chronos time, connecting it to the century's affairs, he undermined it?

For reasons already cited, the concept of translatio provides the structure for *Two Cities*. And Otto dwelt on the analogy between the two empires that dominated the quartet, Babylon the pioneer and Rome the last. What will he do to address the first transfer? He explains that while "in fact" (*in re*) power shifted after the fall of Babylon to the Chaldeans, then the Medes, then the Persians, "in name" (*in nomine*) it never left Babylon.[52] Why bother fabricating this distinction between the name and the thing? Orosius and Augustine had crafted a parallel between Babylon and Rome, and with it in hand Otto could apply his distinction to the Roman Empire. Thus Constantine shifts the seat of the empire to Constantinople, the Eastern Roman Empire falls, and power—real power—is transferred to the Greeks, but "under the name of Rome" (*sub Romano nomine*). Dominion is passed on to the Franks in the West, from them to the Lombards, and then to the German Franks.[53] This device enables translatio to retain its theological import without contravening the reality of the facts, making it a historiographic device. While it amounts to a temporal shift, translatio is also a spatial movement traveling from east to west. Here is a transfer in power and in knowledge: they begin in the East and finish in the West, with Spain at the westernmost limit.[54] For is not a march always moving toward the end?

Constantine mediated the folding of the two cities into one while urging the concept of translatio to its full expression. One may speak of the reality of power and the name of the power, yet the name itself possesses power, a fact only partly explained by appealing to the concept of legitimation. Evoked by the grand name "Rome," an entire imaginary of power grows up, and any who lay claim to it reinforce, if not their power, at the least their authority (*auctoritas*). Consider the contests to decide who would name an emperor—the bitterness of these struggles can readily be imagined. The long and conflictual history of the Holy Roman Empire, itself a strange theologico-political enterprise (up to at least 1600), grew out of translatio's binary nature. For that reason, Otto of Freising did all in his power to convey the efficient character of the concept.

The Holy Roman Empire cast itself as the heir to the Roman Empire, and we now have a better understanding of why: so as not to advance beyond that canonical "four." This empire—Roman, German, and holy—was meant to be the last. For Carl Schmitt, this lent further credibility to its role as "delayer" (*katechon*) of the end. The end could also be "hastened." Such was the outcome of Father Vieira's announcement that a Fifth Empire, temporal and spiritual, will commence any day, a discovery this astonishing seventeenth-century Jesuit based on an updating of the Book of Daniel. The first emperor of this final empire, explains Vieira, will be the king of Portugal. Joachim of Fiore had placed the Spirituals, the monks, at the head of the final empire; as he introduced (or reintroduced) an apocalyptic perspective, Vieira seated the Portuguese king on that throne.[55]

✳ ✳ ✳

To extend the Christian regime of historicity, bringing it into the present while enriching its temporal dimension, three innovations are put forward in the twelfth century—Joachim of Fiore's third age, state, or stage; Anselm of Havelberg's version of accommodation; and Otto of Freising's approach to translatio. In their various ways, all set out to show that history had not ended. Joachim showcased prophecy and the apocalypse to direct thinking toward the future. Anselm also faced the time to come, deploying accommodation to account for "novelty" in a church perpetually renewing itself. And Otto, his considerations more institutional and hegemonic, trained his gaze on the Roman Empire, that ultimate horizon, contending that the troubled empire had not run out of time.

Much as all three professed their reverence for Augustine, whom they would never—so they claimed—contradict, each proved in his way unfaithful. Might they have remained faithful to the powerful Doctor of the Church even as they slipped out of the closed, imposing system of *The City of God*? Here is the problem they faced, or a good part of their difficulty, and all along they had, it seems, no interest in breaking with him. Yet in the end they weakened the strong form—the definitive, canonical form—of the Christian regime of historicity by distancing themselves from it. These fissures might become weak points, offering openings to doubts, then dismissals. The moment chronos time becomes part of history, in short, it plays the part of the wolf on the fold, patrolling a growing space, even as kairos time undergoes a reverse transformation, shrinking until it has nearly been expelled from history, or history as the early Christians understood it.

REFORMATIO

Of the main temporal instruments, the one remaining, reformatio, is also of great significance. It has been present for the whole of Christian history, but more than that, it dwells in the very heart of religious life, both of the believer and of the church. Like accommodatio and translatio, it belonged to the clerics' toolkit, but it chanced to become Luther's Reformation, lending its name to a rupture.

Human beings having been created in the likeness of God, a series of terms emerged to designate the path to rediscovering a resemblance that perished with the Fall: *reformatio, renovatio, regeneratio*.[56] For Paul, *re-formatio* referred to conversion, that act in the present that transmuted the believer into that original form. From divergence the soul graduates to that lost resemblance. Baptism leaves behind the old person so as to take on the new person. In times to come, taking monastic orders will accomplish the same. Reformatio offers the sinner mired in chronos time a portal into kairos time and sets him or her on the path to perfection. The imitation of Christ means a return to the truth of the gospel.

During the papacy of Gregory I (590–604), he emphasized personal reform, while under Gregory VII (1073–1085), reform targeted the entire church. Bit by bit the notion that the church ought to experience a perpetual reform took hold, an effort to return to the "primitive church" (that of Constantine, that of Gregory I, the church that the various monastic reforms sought). Though in Paul's day reformatio lacked a temporal component, we are beginning to see how that was reversed as the *re-* of *r*eturn to the past supplanted the *re-* of *r*esemblance. (Still, the latter was hardly dismantled, since the final goal was unchanged.)

During the Middle Ages, the term *reformatio* also had a specific meaning—a parallel meaning—in political contexts. There it was not a question of rediscovering and reviving the primitive church; the model was the Roman Empire. We have just seen how potent translatio could be: the Carolingians knew perfectly well how to pair it with reformatio so that the two instruments were working in tandem to legitimate their empire. Charlemagne, as the successor to the Roman emperors, could legitimately attempt to bring the empire back to life; by announcing the restoration of that empire, he proved himself the legitimate successor to the Roman emperors. Likewise, Emperor Otto III (crowned in 996) proclaimed on his seals "the renaissance of the Roman Empire."[57] Although it possessed a temporal nature from the outset, this political reformatio stood no less in need of the epiphany of a renaissance.

Over the course of the twelfth century, the weaving together of a temporal hub lent reformatio yet another meaning. Remarkably, the re- of reformatio can reveal novelties, things that had never existed. While its attention is trained on the past, reformatio can also look straight ahead. Novelty (novitas), that object of suspicion and cursory rejection in a world where newness might well be heresy, might be smuggled in via reformatio, wrapped in the mantle of reform. A survey of reformatio takes in the revival of religious practices from the near and distant past as well as the advocacy of practices never before seen, justified in light of a newly unveiled phase of God's plan. At that point, reformatio and accommodatio come together. Anselm of Havelberg, for instance, who viewed reformatio in a confident and optimistic light, believed that over time the understanding of the truth increased.[58] Dwarfs on the shoulders of giants, in the formulation attributed to Bernard of Chartres, may be no wiser than their great predecessors, and yet they see farther. The image aptly combines the reverence due to church fathers and a modest opening for the growth of knowledge.

There is more. This optimistic understanding of reform soon meets an older, pessimistic reading built on the Augustinian certainty that a world thrust into old age with the Incarnation is coming to a close. Here too, old age temporalizes itself, as it were. Chronos time, standing between us and the end, amounts to a series of downward lurches. The more drawn out the period, the worse things get. As the end nears, no better means of preparing ourselves exists than reformatio. In a letter to Abelard, Heloise writes, "Almost everyone [is] now rashly running to monastic life."[59] In the midst of all this, the collapse did at least force men to rewrite the old rules or, hoping it might foster some improvement down the line, draft something a bit more suited to the present. Thus even the pessimistic vision of reform contains the seeds of new forms.

That is the moment when reformatio encounters divine accommodatio, though it was up to human beings to adapt accommodation, recasting it as reformatio.[60] Reform must serve the word of God, even as God unfolds his plan for mankind, adjusting it to suit shifting circumstances. That divine plan, woven into concrete history, permeates the interpenetration of reform and accommodation. Rich in promise, fraught with hazard, that encounter could have seen accommodation, which is a holy device, slip into worldly compromise. In a barrage laden with irony, Pascal's *Provincial Letters* took up that very point. This diatribe against the Jesuits, written in the middle of the seventeenth century, faulted them for stunning compromises with the times and scoffed at the reformatio tradition.[61] But that moment, when chronos time held sway, followed long after Anselm of Havelberg, Otto of Freising, and the twelfth-century reformers.

* * *

On October 31, 1517, when an Augustinian monk named Martin Luther posts his ninety-five theses on the door of Wittenberg's castle church, he still approves reformatio in its familiar meaning. Luther targets the sale of indulgences, thought to hasten the transit of souls through purgatory on their way to heaven, but above all he calls on the faithful to set Christ at the heart of their existence. Thesis 94 reads, "Christians should be exhorted to seek earnestly to follow Christ, their Head, through penalties, deaths, and hells."[62] Evidently the stakes extend well beyond indulgences. "When he rose up against the Church in 1517, what did he propose? To reform Germany? To found a Lutheran Church? No. Luther started out to change the foundations of the Christian church . . . to rediscover lost springs that no longer flowed into the church courts and convent cloisters."[63] In a few lines, Lucien Febvre conveys the gist of Luther's movement. As has happened time and again within different monastic orders, Luther calls for a new reformatio. But on this occasion he goes beyond posting theses and inviting a debate on them. On this occasion, he has them printed. That changes everything.

Luther's theses, rapidly reprinted and translated from Latin into German, were widely read and assumed a political character. Theologians lost their grip on them as princes, the newly elected Charles

V, and then the pope took them up, each with his own goals. Through all this, Luther held his ground. The reformatio he had longed for and encouraged ended as a break with Rome, initiating the Reformation and what the Catholic Church was to call "the Pretended Reformed Religion," asserting its monopoly over true reform.[64] The Reformation drew inspiration from the medieval understanding of reformatio, yet it placed great weight on temporal powers as Luther denied the authority of general councils, canon law, and the pope himself—he rejected the entirety of the church's secular tradition in order to recover the untainted starting point.

A radicalized Reformation reenacts the gesture of the humanists, who also set out to overleap the shadowy centuries of the Middle Ages, though in their case the goal is the rediscovery and resuscitation of pagan antiquity. The methods are analogous and equally daring, the goals different. Erasmus alone will set out to reconcile the two—scripture and the ancients. Yet one finds many parallels between the Protestants and the humanists; to start with, they shared an interest in Latin, Greek, and Hebrew. The early Protestants insisted on returning to the sources, to scripture alone (*sola scriptura*). This paralleled the aspirations of the humanists to rediscover, edit, translate, and print the texts of the ancients, so as to begin anew on that basis. Hence we see Luther, that champion of Latin, Greek, and Hebrew curriculum, inveigh against a strictly utilitarian education "for money and for the belly."[65] Yet while the Reformation represented a crucial moment in the temporalization of reformatio, it was anything but the ending. Far from it! Having served the church for centuries, this instrument will become, as we shall see, a useful tool in the hands of a Chronos become modern time.[66]

By taking a series of soundings, we have confirmed the importance of the leading temporal instruments, used by clerics to throw out bridges—sometimes risky—between Kairos and Krisis, and between Kairos and Chronos. These effective tools lent Christian presentism a certain heft, adding room for the old and the new, and taking the future into account. And this was done without casting doubts on the quality and limits of a new time that opened with the Incarnation and was to end with the Final Judgment.

4

DISSONANCES AND FISSURES

THE LEADING temporal instruments used by clergy kept pace with divine accommodation, and though at times they threatened to outstrip and betray it, their commitment to the Christian regime of historicity never slackened. Each of these churchmen was determined to offer the most accurate reading of his part of the Christian regime, and the whole was conducted, as Augustine wrote, by the great musical director Himself. Nonetheless, over time dissonant chords and false notes resonated in increasing profusion. The clergy lost its monopoly. New interpreters took on new orchestrations—their own. Most worrisome of all, fissures opened up in the Christian order of time.

From the appearance of an Old Testament paired with a New Testament, an Old Covenant and a New Covenant, the familiar relations between old and new were upended. From that shock arose a new economy of time, something unprecedented, within which the old bowed to the new—not eliminated but outdistanced. This brings us to the very heart of the Christian regime of historicity. Not the first to express the thought, Augustine nonetheless conveyed it best when he wrote, "What is the 'Old Testament' but a concealed form of the new [*occultatio novi*]? And what is the 'New Testament' but a revelation of the old [*veteris revelatio*]?"[1] Or one might say the "old" is the "shadow" of the "new"—we make out the true nature of the old by the light radiating from the new. David reigned over the earthly Jerusalem, "a shadow of what was to come" (*in umbra futuri*).[2] In such a scenario, the past is no longer a model; it has become a prefiguration. So let us read it typologically, as the prelude to and advance toward the moment of temporal "plenitude" announced by the outpouring of Christly Kairos, the light of the new. To do so, we turn back to Augustine, and his seemingly paradoxical dictum, "The scriptural narrative . . . [is] more concerned—or at least not less concerned—with foretelling the future than with recording the past."[3] It is essentially prophetic. This represents the antithesis, or nearly, of *historia magistra vitae*, whose structural figuration plots the past before (in all senses of the term) the present. It precedes the present and takes precedence over it. The direction is from the past toward the present, not the reverse. Reversing Augustine's figure, the past casts a shadow over the present. The reasoning may be extended to its limit, where nothing is new—and there we find Ecclesiastes. In a time that knows only repetition, nowhere is there anything new.

> What was, will be again,
> what has been done, will be done again,
> and there is nothing new under the sun![4]

Compare that to the Christian regime, which makes allowances for the new—to a remarkable degree—yet none for repetition. Jesus is, to be precise, the one who comes, and the Parousia is, in the strictest sense, the only event yet to come. How is it possible to call "new" that event that has been announced, even trumpeted, and is awaited, yet will still be without precedent?[5] Let every person convert so as to be ready, experiencing a new birth and rebirth (*regeneratio, renovatio, reformatio*). This time that remains, whose duration remains unknown, a matter known only to God, this apocalyptic present enclosed by the Incarnation and the Final Judgment, is the focus of the Christian regime of historicity. It will become the time of the history of salvation.

A region that should be governed in its entirety by Kairos and Krisis has yielded a surveyed portion to Chronos, a progressive operation carried out, as we have just seen, by clerics at work on the leading temporal instruments. Thus we have Otto of Freising deploying all the resources available to translatio to offer an orderly picture of the time that remains, a history stretched over twelve centuries, anchored to the great, enduring name of Rome, and throughout he maintains that apocalyptic horizon. Yet the book looks to the past far more than it does to the future. Apart from holding on, preserving, could the Holy Roman Empire lay claim to any sort of future?

During that same period, other twelfth-century figures turn to "modernity" in their efforts to recast the relation between past and present; for the future, they rely on renovatio. One who wrote at the end of the century, Gautier Map, lauded the preceding one hundred years as "our 'modern times.'"[6] Anselm of Havelberg cleared a space for "novelties" by making accommodation fair game in the present and even the future. After all, novelties are not absolute; they emerge from renovatio. Renewal, for the church, is perpetual, the means of proceeding toward perfection. More than others, Joachim of Fiore saw novelty on the horizon of chronos time even as he anticipated the approaching Third Age of the Spirituals. The unique and unparalleled "novelty" of the Christly Kairos is never in doubt, yet clergy found the means to acclimate novelty to the course of history, as a positive thing.

RENOVATIO DEFLECTED: THE HUMANISTS

The humanists, working the same terrain already surveyed and brought into use by clergy outfitted with effective tools—the modern, renovatio, reformatio—completed an audacious maneuver. How? They carried out a transfer and a deflection, laying the groundwork for a break. In adopting renovatio, they made it their own; they revived antiquity by undergoing a rebirth into the ancient world. This is conversion by another name. When the church first conceived of renovatio, it meant rebirth in Christ, but eventually the church needed renewal and reform for practical reasons, and renovatio became a bit of a routine. As for the humanists, they discovered that returning to the classical past could be a true renaissance, so they made off with the idea, shifting it to a new locus. The timeline in Anselm of

Havelberg's recasting of renovatio was unbroken, whereas that of the humanists broke off when the barbarians took Rome, initiating a long period of darkness that ended only when the humanists' legacy bore fruit.

That intervening time between the two dates will be known (and maligned) as the "in-between time" (*media aetas*), a benighted interval to be sealed off. Beyond glitters ancient Rome. To return: that is the significance of renovatio/renaissance—the return *of* Rome, which will rise again, and a return *to* Rome, a mission that can be accomplished only by mobilizing every erudite procedure connected to restoration (*restitutio*).[7] Pursuing that thought, return was also conceptualized as reformatio, albeit pagan. We cannot but be struck when Machiavelli compares, at the outset of the sixteenth century, the discovery of the New World and the return to antiquity. Indeed, that land of the ancients, where our guide Livy blazes a "path as yet untrodden by anyone," can readily be compared to a new world, so long has it been overlooked and forgotten. The very term "New World" conveyed much of the imaginative power of the new, something Machiavelli hoped might be applied to ancient practices, not for their own sake but as models to be imitated. Models might be found in the realms of medicine and law, but also, Machiavelli emphasized, among those dedicated to the founding and, especially, the preservation of the state.[8] And here we have the very starting point of *Discourses on the First Ten of Titus Levy*. Certainly we return—to the new—in order to revive an aged world, perhaps twice aged. Its age is reinforced by contrast with a world newly discovered ("so new and so infantile," as Montaigne puts it), and by all within it that still belongs to the Middle Ages.[9]

Along the very path marked out for the return to the classical past come the footsteps of a time, traveling in the opposite direction, that draws on the past for guidance, history as "teacher of life." That is the temporal regime rejected by the Christian regime of historicity. For how else is the relation between Old Testament and New possible? It is the same with the recognition of the new, hence renovatio and accommodation as well—in short, the unique attributes of the Christian regime of historicity itself, so able in its response to the "variety in time."

The rejection of a principle, which was a necessary beginning, had not engendered a wholesale rejection or bracketing of classical culture. (That would have eliminated patristics.) The church's tradition of authorities assigned a prominent place to the past—its own past. The first of these, Eusebius's *Ecclesiastical History*, relied on an unbroken chain of witnesses, beginning with eyewitnesses, then witnesses of witnesses, and so on down to his own time. This witnessing lineage formed the backbone of church authority, validating its role as servant of Jesus Christ. It inculcated a reverence for the locus of this past, a need to honor and preserve it—the first disciples saw and believed. Their time, which saw the unsurpassed novelty of the life of Jesus Christ, sparked the rebirth of a *historia magistra* unique to the church. At the heart of the idea of history as teacher lies imitation, and the church ceaselessly preached the imitation of Jesus.

The humanists did not break any new ground as they adopted the approach of *historia magistra*, yet taking on the ways of antiquity permitted them to shake off the shackles of scholasticism. This meant running the risk of mistreating those generations of monks who had labored in scriptoria, copying and recopying ancient manuscripts, as it was they whose work the humanists edited and distributed. In correcting these texts, practicing "good letters," mastering Ciceronian Latin, they act on the belief that the republic will return, will be reborn in Rome. Appealing to antiquity has political implications, and in this case they run counter to France. Advocating a return amounts to an attack on *translatio studii*, the theory of transferal—of empires and scholarship—so warmly embraced, as we have seen, by clergy. When the humanists laid their hands on the texts and monuments of Rome, they short-circuited the notion of a migration of power and even more so of scholarship. With, by, and through those texts and monuments, Rome is reborn here and now. If the humanists were to launch their audacious assault, they had no alternative to treating the medieval past unjustly. They needed "a model, and it had to be . . . all the reality, known from written records, of an ancient world covered in glory, self-sufficient before the birth of Christianity."[10]

While one can offer Christian readings of some pagan authors and a typological reading of Plato—Augustine did it himself—by bracketing the era labeled "intermediate" one introduces a very grave snag into the continuum of the Christian present. Could one sideline the centuries between the Incarnation and the Parousia simply because a few partisans of pagan antiquity denounced them as benighted? As to the suggestion that their "hopeful fervor" regarding the past grew out of an alienation from their world—quite the reverse was true. That fervor amounted to a plan of action for their own times, a "vision of a new world rebuilt on an ancient declaration."[11] Elevating their present to the heights of the glorious Roman past was their ambition. Augustine's portrait of an aging world ran contrary to the humanists' optimistic valorization of the present, a sense of "plenitude" that endowed their renovatio with a nearly Christly force. Here is a body of apostles and missionaries dedicated to a new time, a new Kairos that is somehow worldly and grounded in chronos time, all inspired by the return to Rome. In the end, recycling the form of the resurrection, that quintessential Christian event, for a renovatio of a wholly other sort constitutes a second grave snag threatening the Christian regime of historicity. These snags or fissures demand attention all the more insistently as the trouble they caused was unintentional. Breaking with the Middle Ages, with the "dark centuries" first decried by Petrarch, the humanists meant no direct harm to Christian time or the history of salvation; they longed for only a full experience of their own age, and a spectacular showdown was not part of the plan. Still, that aspiration to plenitude induced a sort of presentism (a recourse to *imitatio*) that raised probing questions, even doubts, about the apocalyptic presentism of Christianity.

Should anyone retrace the path taken by the humanists, who seized and adopted such instruments as renovatio, the resulting trajectory assuredly diverges from the Christian regime of historicity, beyond heresy. The troubled times are evidenced by the changing fortunes of Lucretia, her depiction of humanity's sorrowful origins, and the revival of a cyclical vision of time.[12] Can Lucretia and Genesis be reconciled? To ask the question is to answer it. One might say that the humanists employ the very words they risk losing to narrate their enterprise. In addition, a grand drama overshadowed this entire period, as Luther drove the shift from reformatio/return to rupture.[13] The Protestants never wage open battle with the Catholic Church over the Christian regime, but the church loses its grip when its foes accuse it of corruption.

A series of shocks had just reopened the Chronos case, throwing into question its subordination to Kairos and Krisis, when thinking was again shaken, now by the appearance of peoples unknown to and unforeseen by both the Bible and the ancients. And yet the Indians of the Americas undoubtedly existed. They provoked in their conquerors a disorienting sense of the contemporaneity of the noncontemporaneous. We partake in the same moment, that of the encounter, making us contemporaries, yet everything about them shows that they are not. Yes, they are savages, barbarians, but more than that, children-peoples—all these labels evoke distance, including temporal distance.[14] And the only good way to address the distance is to hasten them into Christian time via baptism. They too come to live under the regime of Kairos and Krisis, which had been off-limits to them. This has been an essential element of the church's mission since its earliest days, effectively universalizing the Christian regime while contributing to preparations for the end of times, which can occur only after the whole world, including the Jews, has been converted. The horizon event, for the New World as well, can only be the Apocalypse. Christopher Columbus wrote in 1500, "Of the new heaven and the new earth, which Our Lord made, as St. John writes in the Apocalypse, after he had spoken of it by the mouth of Isaiah, He made me the messenger and He showed me where to go."[15]

TRANSLATIO RECUSED AND TRANSFORMED

Translatio, that potent instrument with its hand in matters theological, apocalyptic, historical, and political, finds its foundation and starting point in the Book of Daniel. It provides, at the largest scale, the structure for the Christian regime of historicity and measures out the history of empires, treating them as an eschatology. The Holy Roman Empire, in particular, was constructed and justified in terms of translatio. And Bossuet, naturally, chose it as the organizing principle of his *Discourse on Universal History*. And yet it has not escaped criticism. In a chapter of *Method for the Easy Comprehension of History* (1566), Jean Bodin unleashed a devastating assault on this "long established, but mistaken, idea about four empires." As the idea had the support of Daniel and had "won over countless interpreters," among them Luther, Melanchthon, and Sleidan, Bodin had been slow to adopt the "formula of the courts, 'it doth not appear [*non liquet*].' "[16]

Once the providential perspective is abandoned, the entire edifice crumbles. Why, after all, is it four empires? Why those four, when no definition of *empire* or *monarchy* is offered? Here we have the jurist speaking. Next Bodin attacks the Germans, who "claim" they rule the (last) Roman Empire. Their claim to the Roman mantle is "a bit much," particularly since they occupy only "the hundredth part of the world," while the kings of Spain and Portugal possess far vaster territories. Truth be told, the only ruler possessing true "majesty of empire" is the "sultan of the Turks," not to mention the prince of Ethiopia or the "emperor of the Tartars, who rules tribes barbarous in their savagery, countless in number." Set beside those, Germany looks like "a fly facing an elephant." And anyone who takes a good look at the world as it is today will "interpret the prophecy of Daniel as applied to the sultan of the Turks."[17]

Having provoked his readers with a strikingly heretical proposition (the Ottoman sultan often doubled as the Antichrist in exegetical writings), Bodin arrived at his conclusion. What is one to make of Daniel today? His words must be preserved, naturally, even as one reduces the scope of his prophecy to involve only Babylon, bearing in mind that it "fell to the might of Medes, Persians, Greeks, and Parthians, in succession." The long-established but mistaken idea may be attributed to the belief that "each man should interpret the prophecies of Daniel according to his own judgment, not according to accurate history."[18] Thus was Daniel drawn back within the limits of history and the limits of a completed chronos time.

After he has pulverized the statue dreamt by Nebuchadnezzar, Bodin moves on to another error of the same sort, the translation of the metals making up the statue—gold, silver, bronze, iron, and a mixture of iron and clay—into the four ages of humanity. From the age of gold, gone forever, one moves toward the age of iron, that is, mud. To the suggestion that the species has only "degenerated" since its earliest days, Bodin replies with a defense of the advances mankind has made since its savage beginnings.[19] What a golden age! Nowadays "our men . . . lead colonies into a new world." The result has been not only "an abundant and profitable commerce (which formerly was insignificant or not well known) but also all men surprisingly work together in a world state, as if in one and the same city."[20] And so he sweeps away the Augustinian vision of the order of time that casts the world as aged, approaching the end. Yet this is not to impose an image of perpetual progress; progress there is, but it is neither open-ended nor definitive. Far from it. "By some eternal law of nature," after all, "the path of change seems to go in a circle."[21] It merits noting that in order effectively to rebut what we now call "declinism," a different model must be adopted, the ancient figure of cyclical time, which is quite antithetical to the Christian order of time. Augustine disproved that model in *The City of God*. Bodin never pushes his critique to that point, nor does he envision the consequences of such a shift in the temporal paradigm. At the outset, when he distinguishes three types of history—human, natural, and sacred—he declares that the first will be his focus.

Bodin opposed Protestant commentators "from Germany," and he dynamited Daniel and translatio as a polemical reaction to those who presented the Holy Roman Empire as the successor to Rome, as the final empire. His "objective" interpretation was in reality connected to his present.[22] Others had cast doubts on Daniel's model, but Bodin enlisted history and geography to drive his critique further than had any predecessor: a comparison between the vast world of today and the far narrower world of Daniel implies the need to see his prophecy, already dated, in relative terms.

The Jesuit priest António Vieira reacts quite differently to the expansion of the Earth, since he finds that Daniel and the other prophets painted a precise picture of the New World, grounds for elevating them further. The work of Bossuet, likewise, continues to evoke the succession of empires, taking it for granted, never pausing to defend it. A century after Bodin, as these two examples show, translatio is still being used to regulate universal history. As the fourth empire, that of Rome, reaches its limit, Vieira sets out to break the links between the Holy Roman Empire and translatio, opening it to the future so that a fifth empire can rise. But just as Daniel's translatio bore an apocalyptic potential, even before he became a "Christian" author, so it was with the revived translatio, as we will see. This draws the attention of the Inquisition, which existed to stem the confusion of times (particularly the confusion of the time of the end and the end of times) and put an end to any millenarian impulses.

TRANSLATIO AS CHRONOLOGY

António Vieira (1608–1697), a Portuguese Jesuit renowned for his sermons, served as a missionary in Brazil. His career also included routine visits to the Portuguese royal court, diplomatic missions, and a stay at the papal court in Rome.[23] Yet, as established and well known as he was, Vieira tangled with the Inquisition on more than one occasion, for reasons far from trivial. Any inquisitor, even the most unflappable, would have blanched at his talk of Portugal becoming the "Fifth Empire" due to the resurrection of King John IV.[24] His trial was long, much ink was spilled for his defense, and in the end he escaped a guilty verdict only by a papal amnesty—proving that there were doubts regarding his thinking. His exegetical writings owe much to his early conviction that Portugal had been chosen by God, which is best understood through a reading of Sebastianism.[25]

Vieira extended—or revived—the historico-apocalyptic approach of Joachim of Fiore, echoing his faith in the predictive powers of the Bible. Christian presentism admits of some futurity. The key, for Vieira, is less the church fathers' allegorical reading of the Old Testament, effectively a search for Jesus, than a close reading of the text. In addition, he labored over a book, never completed, that he brashly titled *History of the Future*. Whereas historians as a rule wrote "histories of the past for people of the future, we are writing the history of the future for people of the present," an unprecedented project. Carried away, Vieira added that his history "starts at the very moment of its writing, continues along the entire duration of the world, and ends when it ends."[26] The end is surely near. For Vieira, translatio possesses more than that temporal quality—it possesses both a chronological and an apocalyptic quality. It makes a measurable future possible.

The doctors of the church reckoned Moses a prophet because he wrote the history of how things began, making him a prophet of the past. "So why should there be no historian of the future?" Note that

Vieira does not fancy himself a prophet of the future, but a historian. (Not so Joachim.) When Richard the Lionheart sought him out, it was the prophet he consulted. By the mid-seventeenth century, Vieira felt he could use the terms *history* and *future* in his title without "injuring" either: the key was following "all the laws of the [historical] story religiously and precisely." The future told in his *History* lay close at hand, a time of "imminent, happy hopes offered by me to Portugal," which "those who are alive today will get to see, though they may live only a few years more." Like John the Baptist, who both announced the imminent coming of the Christ and saw him with his own eyes, Vieira (it is he who drew the comparison) announces the kingdom of Portugal today and will, as John did with the Christ, point to it with his own finger.[27]

All issues from Daniel, so Vieira naturally summons him after Moses and John the Baptist, then goes on to scrutinize the prophecies of Isaiah. His goal: showing that all of them spoke about and for the world they inhabited, and about the future as well. That world was shaken between the time of the abbot of Fiore and Otto of Freising, and the time of Father Vieira. If Christianity manages to remain coterminous with "the surface of the earth, in spite of the area under Islamic occupation," the discovery of a new world never imagined by the ancients changes everything.[28] Plus, the landmarks set up in the Bible help not at all with the Far East, though it was an area previously known. Vieira contends, nonetheless, that when the fruits of experience and the accumulation of knowledge are taken into account, the prophecies apply to the new lands as well. Consider the antipodes, rejected by Augustine on the basis of the knowledge of his day. Well, the Portuguese "managed to reach by means of the sword that place that Saint Augustine could not reach by means of his understanding."[29]

The Portuguese discoveries, it seems, shed a light on certain texts. Vieira walks us through passages from Isaiah, explaining word by word their relevance to Brazil, even to the state of Maranhão, where he had carried out his ministry. And it works. On the one side, Isaiah describes Maranhão, while on the other, aspects of the local culture illuminate misunderstood or obscure passages from the prophet. Reproaching the ancients for missing the point would be senseless:

How could one "suspect that the prophets were talking about Americans if one had no idea that America existed"? That insight regarding the Brazilian Indians applies to the people of Japan and China as well. This was God's plan: "The provisions of his providence ensured that all these things will be unknown and concealed until the time it determined, a time when it was decreed these things will be known and revealed."[30] Matters visible only to the prophets through revelation become in time visible to common mortals.

Vieira's mechanism is a temporalized form of accommodation. From the beginning the prophecies had been true, yet their fullest meaning revealed itself only over time. In the words of Bernard of Chartres, "Truth is the daughter of time."[31] Vieira simply relies on Christianity's core hermeneutic principle: the past is illuminated by the present. Just as Jesus Christ is the truth of the Old Testament, so does the world of the seventeenth century illuminate the prophecies of Isaiah and Zechariah. All our Jesuit does is consider the prophesies as realized, concluding that all the new lands belong to the universe of the Bible—the prophets had spoken of them, they are clearly mission territories, and the Christian regime of historicity reigns over them.

And Vieira goes further still. Just as he traces the outcome of Isaiah's prophecies, so he does with Daniel, the cornerstone of all thinking on the succession of empires, and with John, considering chapter 20 of Revelation. To found his fifth empire, at once Portuguese, terrestrial, and Christly, he combines Daniel and Revelation. The successive empires were Assyrian, Persian, Greek, and Roman—the last deemed by Vieira, who outlines its vicissitudes down to his day, "much degraded." When he offers his own reading of Nebuchadnezzar's dream, the statue's legs and feet naturally stand for the eastern Roman Empire and the western. The statue's ten fingers, "small and large," signify the ten kingdoms that the empire "will break into when it goes into decline." Next was the clay that accounted for parts of the statue's feet, interpreted as "the provinces and nations that had belonged to the Roman Empire and are now breaking away," in the process "weakening it." One can see there France, England, Sweden, and Spain. Only a single task remains, providing a name for Daniel's fifth empire, that rock that fell away and smashed the statue. That falling stone inaugurated God's eternal kingdom, with its own fifth empire prophesied by the cobbler Gonsallanes Bandarra, and premised on the resurrection of John IV. Chapter 20 of Revelation serves this need admirably, as the authority promised to the chosen people of Portugal stretches over an "earthly" empire "both spiritual and temporal."[32]

At a certain moment, in speaking of this new Portuguese kingdom, Vieira speaks of a "third state [*status*]," an unmistakable link—particularly in this apocalyptic context—to Joachim of Fiore's third state, that of the Spirituals, which will begin soon. Perhaps Vieira imagines his fifth Portuguese Christly kingdom just where the abbot set his monks, but without uttering a word about the duration of that kingdom. And he steps right over Otto of Freising and his apology for the Holy Roman Empire, dreaming instead of a Portugal returned to glory. To ensure the hegemony of the Christian regime of historicity over a world far more extensive than that of the twelfth century, and to restore that hegemony over the Old World, our obsessive exegete turned to the House of Bragança. Even presenting his views as a history of the future rather than a prophecy, however, could not rescue the situation. His rescue from the Inquisition, as I pointed out, came through the pope. As an exegete he counted for little, while his prominence as an orator carried the day; evidently no one at the Vatican took his prophecies seriously. His heretical *translatio*, to which he had added temporal and spatial dimensions, provoked few misgivings.

***

A comparison of Vieira's prophecies and Bossuet's *Discourse on Universal History* (1681) points up striking contrasts between the two contemporaneous works. The bishop of Meaux never considered straying beyond the limits set by Augustine, nor did he offer speculations on a fifth kingdom, earthly or not. He taught the Dauphin that when the Roman Empire fell "Rome . . . preserved its ancient majesty through religion," that Rome had "given rise to the greatest kingdoms of our world," and that Charlemagne's new empire displayed "the conclusive end of the ancient Roman Empire."[33] For the sake of his royal pupil, Bossuet moves briskly ahead, slowing neither to ruminate on whether it was one or two cities after Constantine nor to weigh the impact of translatio on the Holy Roman Empire.

Above all else, Bossuet believed in dwelling on the "secrets of divine Providence" and how it functioned. God "creates kingdoms in order to give them to whom he pleases," yet he also "knows how to make them serve . . . the plans he has for his people." This begins to look like the cunning of God, which Bossuet calls the "plans of Providence." "With the exception of certain great reversals," he explains, "by which God wished to demonstrate the power of his hand, no change has occurred without causes originating in preceding centuries." The task of the historian is to scrutinize those particular causes; he "uncovering for each age the hidden tendencies which have prepared the way for great changes and the important combinations of circumstances which have brought them about." On the one hand, we have the register of particular causes, each differently suitable or efficient, which the future ruler must learn to recognize, while on the other, we have the divine register, where "from the highest heavens God holds the reins of every kingdom." None but prophets can behold God's revelation of what he "had resolved to accomplish" then shift from one register to the other, from one temporality to another. Consider Daniel, whose "admirable visions" enable us to see "the successive fall of these famous empires."[34] History serves as an aid to those who have not received that gift, including princes, as it unveils the divine design after the fact, adjuring them to both humility and prudence in their own deeds. History offers retrospective prophecies, lessons for those who know how to decode them: history is indeed of history.

ACCOMMODATIO PERVERTED

Bossuet presents his *Discourse on Universal History* as the unfolding of accommodation over the course of the centuries, a temporalized accommodatio become a historical instrument, functioning in a history that could only be that of salvation. Accommodatio monitors "the memorable changes the passage of time has wrought in the world." Writing to the Dauphin, he explained, "You will see how empires succeeded one another and how religion, in its different states, maintains its stability from the beginning of the world to our own time."[35] Precisely Augustine's advance of the two cities! God very correctly "sees change everywhere without changing himself," and "all change is wrought by his unchanging decree." He "watches over things at all times." Human beings, by contrast, never do what they set out to do, since "all rulers feel that they are subject to a higher power." Here we have accommodation acting invisibly, and when he makes it the law of all human action, emphasizing an unknowable outcome, Bossuet performs a pair of inimical feats, advancing as far as can be done within the earthly city, while reaffirming the omnipotence of Providence: "God alone can subject everything to his will."[36]

Bossuet reaffirms and reinforces accommodation, but he also transforms and adapts it. For him, the secrets of Providence are linked to the secrets of power, those *arcana imperii* we associate with Machiavelli and Tacitus. Thus the age of absolutism, when many undermined accommodation through calls for compromise, found common ground with Bossuet's defense.

Just a few years before Bossuet wrote his *Discourse*, one of Molière's characters was singing a different tune. Addressing Elmire, the wife of Orgon and the object of his secret desires, the devout hypocrite Tartuffe speaks not of accommodation but, in his treacly tones, of compromise: "Some joys, it's true, are wrong in Heaven's eyes; / Yet Heaven is not averse to compromise."[37] The moment talk turns to compromise, the status quo is reversed. No longer is it a matter of God taking human weakness into account or acting secretly; now human beings feel qualified to recast the divine commandments as they like. Such a volte-face opens another fissure in the Christian regime, posing a deep threat to the economy of accommodation. The fissure can only deepen as human beings conceive of themselves as extending their agency, increasing the position and role of chronos time.

Others kept Tartuffe company. Even clerics played leading parts in this perilous deviation, as Pascal attested in his *Provincial Letters*. Medieval clerics had been trailblazers, too, but they had sought to strengthen and extend the Christian regime, while Pascal viewed the casuistic Jesuits as the gravediggers of Catholic tradition. What displeased him? First and foremost, they had perverted divine accommodatio via human (all too human) compromise. They had reversed accommodation through "'obliging and accommodating' conduct," signing up a mass of casuists he deemed "lax" to serve those who "want laxism."[38] The fictitious provincial father to whom Pascal's letters are addressed, a target of the author's biting ironies, does not see the casuists as excessively prone to compromise; for him they are simply "new" and, much like the Church Fathers, faithful to the morality of their day.[39] Chronos was here.

So corrupt are human beings today "that since we cannot make them come to us, we must go to them. Otherwise they would forsake us; they would do worse, they would give way to utter abandon." Under such circumstances, "the basic policy which our Society has adopted for the good of religion is not to rebuff anyone lest people fall into despair." The morality of casuistry conveyed by such statements amounts to utter desperation, out of which has sprung a compelling need for an infinity of rules governing every sort of person and situation. Thus, since we cannot prevent actions, at least we can "purify" the motives and "correct the viciousness of the means by the purity of the end." And then Pascal brings the good father around to the topic of confession, and the latter explains the need to "smooth" it "out" in order to render it easier, which would be meaningless without softening penitence as well. At that point, the author breaks off, so exasperated by the endless "artifices of devotion" and "aberrations" of the new casuists that he abandons the provincial to his blindness.[40]

The Provincial Letters marked a tipping point, Pascal's polemical exaggerations notwithstanding. With this book, he loosed a wail born of deep misgivings, inspired by a century he saw casting off tradition, a custom this devoted, assiduous reader of Augustine meant to champion. Chronos gulped down accommodation as it had been endorsed, transmitted, interpreted by fathers, councils, and popes, and then vomited it forth as compromise, itself subject to countless revisions. This went beyond the inversion of accommodatio as compromise—quite unavoidable, according to the provincial father—since such concessions twisted and perverted reformatio too. From that idealization of the monastic existence, that appeal to recast one's life in keeping with the gospel, we arrive at the very opposite.

Jesuit casuistry rejects the aspiration to lofty perfection, orienting itself instead toward the faithful, who seem less and less so. Kept at arm's length, then, are two of the temporal instruments that the Christian regime relied on to maintain its hegemony over chronos time, and those driving them away are the very people who claim to be their sworn protectors. Pascal and Molière called them hypocrites.

In addition to his fierce opposition to compromise and his commitment to tradition, Pascal stands out as a firm protector of Christian presentism. "We wander in the times which are not ours, and do not think of the only one that belongs to us. . . . We scarcely ever think of the present . . . the present is never our end. . . . We never live, but we hope to live."[41] These reflections on our distorted connection to time are drawn from the famed fragment on amusement. Incapable of dwelling in the Kairos of the present, we surrender ourselves to the amusements of chronos time, turning to the doctrine of compromise and its hollow facility.

UPDATING THE CHRONOLOGY OF THE BIBLE

We saw in chapter 2 that from Julius Africanus to the Venerable Bede, the calculations of Christian chronologers constituted a discrete but crucial strategy for confronting Chronos. A world younger than had been thought, they showed, implied a later finish date, rebutting those who spoke of an imminent end. The gospel was right: the day and the hour of his coming were known to the Lord alone. The chronologers supported eschatology while delivering blows to the millenarians. Still, no quarrels broke out over the precise date of Creation. Where disagreements arose was in the calculation of the age of the world, which really meant the elapsed time from Creation to the Incarnation; it came down to whether one relied on the Septuagint or the Hebrew Bible.

The sixteenth and seventeenth centuries introduced peoples into the debates over the span of chronos time whose very inclusion in the biblical framework posed challenges, for instead of the ancient Egyptians and the Mesopotamians, peoples still present occupied rapidly expanding spatial and temporal horizons—the peoples of Mexico and, preeminently, the Chinese. Controversies over origins sharpened. Joseph Scaliger emerged as the peerless master of the science of chronology. Many within the church confronted an intractable question, how to account for a time more ancient than that of the Bible's chronology, a time, as it were, before time. The solution proposed by Isaac La Peyrère has long been forgotten, but its relevance makes it required reading. Working from canonical texts, he advocated the existence of human beings prior to Adam. Heresy! He barely had time to publish the results of some reflections that had created a buzz when accusations struck him down.

ISAAC LA PEYRÈRE (1596–1676)

We have nearly forgotten him, but in his day La Peyrère won infamy as a great heretic, worse even than Spinoza—who was among his readers. The Catholic Church thoroughly succeeded in silencing him by rebutting his claims, attacking him, imprisoning him, and forcing him to recant. In a book anonymously published in Holland in 1655, he had made his most grievous claim, contending that Adam was not the first man, that there had been pre-Adamites. From the moment it appeared, the book was subjected to prolonged attacks. Yet La Peyrère was far from a nobody. Secretary to the prince of Condé, he had hobnobbed with the great minds of the time and traveled to northern Europe, where he even had the opportunity to read extracts from his manuscript to the young Queen Christina of Sweden. Yet here was a millenarian who awaited the coming of the Jewish messiah—far from a Vieira. In a new age reigned over by a messiah (in partnership with the king of France) from a rebuilt Jerusalem, he explained, all will be saved—Jews, Christians, pre-Adamites, and post-Adamites.[42]

We shall dwell only on La Peyrère's theory of pre-Adamites, while noting that it nestled within his convictions regarding the Apocalypse. His thinking comprised a fully developed theology that ranged from Creation to the end of times and remained utterly faithful to the Christian regime of historicity. Once he proved the existence of human beings before Adam, overleaping the barrier of six millennia without breaching it became possible—a remarkable feat. All the claims of the ancients and the moderns could now be acknowledged, the one for the great age of the Egyptians and the Chaldeans, the other for the inhabitants of China and Mexico. How to accomplish this without contradicting or challenging biblical conventions, without abandoning tradition?

La Peyrère believed he had a solution. The Bible, he reckoned, is a Jewish history. It mentions only Jews. Adam and Eve are only the first Jews, and the Flood is just a regional event that happened in Palestine and took the lives of sinful Jews. After all, many other peoples have recounted stories of floods. An objection may be raised at this point: as Genesis never gives a hint of any human beings in advance of Adam, how can he be certain of their existence? His reply: the proof is that Moses recounted only the history of the Jews.[43] Arguments from silence can seem specious, so La Peyrère needed positive proof, which he found in Paul. This impeccable authority, in three verses from the letter to the church in Rome, clarified the precedence of Adam over Moses as bearer of the Law. Before Adam, then, sin existed, but it took the Law (and Adam) to assign it a moral quality. After all, if there was no Law before Moses, how could sin have begun with Adam?[44] Before the Law, before Adam, a Lawless world of pagans existed, the outcome of a first creation. In due course, God decided on a second creation, the one recounted in the Bible, for the sake of the people he had chosen and whom he finally abandoned. Still, he did not abandon them permanently; soon "the recall of the Jews" will happen and their messiah will appear.[45] From the existence of human beings before Adam, it follows that between that first creation and the appearance of Adam a long, indefinite time elapsed, possibly that the world has existed for all eternity. The divine plan marked only the history of the Jews, a beginning and an ending.

La Peyrère believed his interpretation (some might call it crude sleight of hand) would serve religion, not hinder it. No one else saw it that way—neither rabbis, ministers, nor priests. The Catholic authorities decided to take him in hand, to stop his heresies from spreading: he would be obliged to recant. Ultimately, in 1657 he was given to understand that if he went to Rome, made an act of penitence before the pope, and converted from Calvinism to Catholicism, no more would be said of the matter. Reports that have come down to us make of the occasion a gay affair. Both the pope and the superior general of the Jesuits had laughed uproariously over La Peyrère's treatise on the pre-Adamites, so when the author entered, they said, "Let us embrace this man who is before Adam."[46]

In spite of the charges brought against him, La Peyrère had no intention of dislodging the Christian regime of historicity, though a Jewish millenarianism—or was it a Marrano theology?—might well sidetrack the Parousia by lining up a redeemer from the chosen people. And yet he had cleared virtually unlimited space for chronos time by removing the insuperable barrier of the day of Creation. Every chronology in the world, the well-known and the newly discovered, could readily be accommodated. No longer would one make light of the calculations of this group or that, denying that their years were actual years. The strict limit of six thousand years underwent a change from within the Christian tradition; because it applied only to the community described in the Bible, it could be relativized. Such heresy led to severe punishment. Yet a bit like his contemporary António Vieira, excused from the Inquisition by the pope in spite of his millenarian belief in Portugal's imperial future, La Peyrère never struck anyone as a real danger, if we can rely on the tale of his papal audience. But of the two men, it was La Peyrère who left a deeper mark, a result of his ideas about biblical criticism and human polygenism. He was praised in an article that appeared in the second volume of the *Anthropological Review* (1864) above the byline Philatheles ("lover of truth"). "Peyrère was two centuries before his time" and naturally suffered persecution. For daring "to step out of the magic exegetical circle which theology had drawn around all the sciences," he was promptly punished.[47] The tracers of that magic circle were Kairos and Krisis.

JOSEPH SCALIGER (1540–1609): EUSEBIUS UPDATED

Joseph Scaliger, working fifty years earlier than La Peyrère, devoted his life to pinpointing the time of the beginning. Here was a real scholar pursuing a quite different path: he took his lead from the tables of Eusebius of Caesara. Central to his achievement—elevating chronology to its most elevated, most advanced form—was the breadth of Scaliger's knowledge of calendars and his mastery of the methods of both philology and astronomy. Rather than applying chronology to reading the Bible and the historians of antiquity or to correcting the errors of other chronologers, he set out to create a fully distinct discipline. This science of times, a result of bringing together every available source, will comprise all times and all places. This will be a universal tool for parsing the world of both the past and the future.

The erudite, outstanding reconstruction of Scaliger's project by Anthony Grafton spares us the need to trace that massive effort, but I shall touch on an innovation relevant to biblical times.[48] Scaliger is not satisfied with having examined every calendar he can find; he needs a temporal yardstick along which he can set each past, present, and future date, something like Eusebius's decades of Abraham. But he departs from that initial approach to biblical time by discarding an existing chronology and creating a universal chronology (*chronicon absolutissimum*). The new cycle is called the "Julian period," its debt to Julius Caesar's "Julian year" quite explicit. To construct the period, Scaliger multiplies the twenty-eight-year solar cycle by the nineteen-year lunar cycle, giving the 532 years of Dionysius Exiguus's Paschal cycle, which he in turn multiplies by the fifteen-year cycle of indiction.[49] The Julian period therefore equals 7,980 years. Each year is assigned a precise location, a "character" defined by its unique position within each of the three cycles. This makes the Julian period a powerful tool for ordering the various extant chronologies. Scaliger, a religious man who has no interest in casting doubts on biblical chronology, produces a system utterly independent of that chronology. He has something else in mind. Countless hours went into an attempt to reconstruct the Eusebian tables, and then he outstrips Eusebius. By plotting every date, including those that have not yet occurred, it becomes possible to connect any given date to any other, and to compare them. This double opening constitutes, naturally, the crucial innovation.

Once he knows the "character" of the year of Christ's birth, he looks for the year in the Julian period endowed with that same character; it turns out to be year 4713. This implies that the Julian period must have begun in 4713 BC. Now we can picture a vast temporal envelope enclosing Christ—more than three millennia of that margin remained. Every event that has transpired in any location—as well as all future events—should fit within that envelope. (In the early seventeenth century, 1,700 years of that cycle remained unspent.) Yet no matter how scientifically this hypothetical time, declared absolute, was fashioned, it took the Nativity as its starting point. In the quest for a universal chronology, the Julian period marked an original and erudite accomplishment, and it convinced at least one person, an Anglican priest named James Ussher. Scaliger's work enabled Ussher to name the year, the day, even the hour of Creation: "In the beginning God created Heaven and earth which happened at the beginning of time (according to our chronology) in the first part of the night which preceded the 23rd of October in the year of the Julian Period 710."[50]

God is in the details! Still, even the Julian period cannot solve every chronological problem, and Scaliger runs headlong into the Egyptian priest Manetho and his list of dynasties. We have seen that the antiquity of the Egyptians presented problems for the first Christian chronologers, but as a serious philologist, Scaliger cannot adopt the course they had. Indeed, he had confidence in his grounds for accepting the testimony of Manetho (active in the third century before Christ). But Manetho's dynasties stretched far further back in time than Creation (3949 BC), surpassing even the early limit of the Julian period (4713 BC). Scaliger the believer could not believe in the existence of anything before Creation; Scaliger the chronologist had reasons to accept Manetho's testimony. To set out Manetho's list in his new book, *Thesaurus temporum* (1606), he needs to resolve the contradiction; the solution is an additional period as long in duration as the original one. He gives the first Julian period, which occurred before and anticipated the second, the name "proleptic." All the space the Egyptian dynasties need they now possess, thanks to a mathematical invention, and there is room for others, should the need arise. Still, though this may satisfy chronological standards, it falls short by historical measures. What "history" can be found in a time before Creation? It does no good to loose the term "mythical." Scaliger himself notes that to speak of events from before time means treading in the land of what the Greeks call the oxymoron. He knows full well that his proleptic period presents more problems than it resolves, not least due to its inevitable clash with the Bible. Grafton explains that he never attacked the Bible head on, yet he also never ruled out such an attack.[51] While several champions of the Bible's version of chronology took up cudgels against Scaliger, he had unleashed a whole series of problems. There was Manetho and the age of the Egyptians; there was the duration of chronos time before Moses and Abraham—the lapse of time before Creation assumed real importance.

DENIS PÉTAU (1583-1652)

Chateaubriand bestowed on Father Denis Pétau, an erudite Jesuit, the title "oracle of chronology."[52] Yes, another Jesuit, but as different from apocalyptic Vieira as from Pascal's provincial priest, so ready to defend compromises as a function of the times. A devoted critic of Scaliger, Pétau shared his commitment to making chronology an orderly discipline distinct from history. The evocative titles of his two studies, *Opus de doctrina temporum* and *Rationarium temporum*, convey their briefs: there is a "doctrine" of times and a rational, practical approach to chronology.[53] Thus the work of the chronologer obeys three principles, assigning dates in line with authority, demonstration, and hypothesis, that is, the analysis of sources, irrefutable proofs drawn from astronomy, and conventional dates serving as reference points for the others.[54]

Like Scaliger, Pétau could not do without an absolute time, yet he chose to rely on the date of the birth of Christ, as the Julian period, rife with impasses and connivances, struck him as unthinkable. This was far from a trailblazing choice, though he did isolate the date of the event, treating it as a moment determined by "convention" that offered a basis for connecting all the other dates. The Greeks began their count with the first olympiad, while others worked from the creation of the world; like them, Christians had a starting point, the Incarnation. To the extent that Christians adopted one time and other groups chose something different, we seem to be stuck in a relative time. To bypass that problem, Pétau made the birth of Jesus an absolute date.

The system would succeed only if one could count *just as readily* forward (into the years after Christ) as backward (into the years before Christ). Pétau stressed that such an arrangement made the year of the Nativity a "pivot" (*cardo*) of times, the "center point of history and chronology" from which "the years of varying numbers" set out, like—and here his image is telling—"lines propagating into limitless space, as much toward the past as toward the future," only to "return toward the unique center point, where they meet."[55] For his absolute time, Scaliger still needed a starting point that could stand in for the date of Creation. Not so Pétau, a Catholic theologian and man of science, because he treats the Christly Kairos as a "hypothesis," a convention, which somehow both absolutizes and chronologizes it. From that moment, the Incarnation becomes an object. This is no common object, but an object it undeniably is, one firmly associated with chronology. One day, as a result, a weighty date may turn into a quite normal date, the basis for what will be referred to, modestly, as the Common Era.

In a world less inclined to heed the six-thousand-year boundary, the appearance of this twofold opening to past and future offered, at least for a time, a potentially limitless chronological tool, despite the church's steadfast stance. Christ as temporal "pivot," facing both directions, stood at the end of a long enterprise initiated by those early Christian chronologers who rejuvenated the world by advancing the date of his birth. The question of when the world had been created slipped out of the spotlight as the time to Apocalypse stretched out. Chronos time may have been utterly Christ-centric, due to Pétau, but it also gained—or regained—some space. Such is the paradox. Opening out the temporal possibilities, as much to the past as to the future, loosened the grip of biblical chronology, though the grip remained. From this time onward to the end of times, an inscription will appear on the tablets of time, declaring that the Christly Kairos shines down on time's every moment.

TWO SENTINELS: BOSSUET AND NEWTON

Rifts have opened, weakening and undermining the Christian regime of historicity in a multitude of ways. At such a time, in the final moments of this chapter, let us consider two great partisans of Christian time—Bossuet and Newton. The former is a prelate in the Catholic Church, the latter a confirmed antipapist. The comparison seems nearly blasphemous, so why pursue it? After all, they could hardly be more different: one the greatest scientist of his time, if not among the greatest of all time, the other a priest, admittedly celebrated, singularly eloquent, who never slackens in his defense of Catholicism and France, a habit that draws him into more than a few controversies against Protestants. Protestant Newton (for whom the pope is the Antichrist) versus Bossuet the prelate: they have nothing in common save a history of championing the Christian regime of historicity. Their willingness to stand sentinel as the first assaults begin may make sense for the priest, but in the case of the scientist they come as a shock. It is easy enough to imagine that Newton's main temporal interest was that of universal gravitation, where time lacked both a beginning and an end, while in fact he researched ancient chronologies over the course of his entire life and even defended the chronology found in the Bible in a work entitled *Observations Upon the Prophecies of Daniel, and the Apocalypse of St. John*.

Bossuet revived divine accommodation by allowing history some acreage—with Providence, shrouded in mystery, beetling over all.[56] He, too, was drawn to the "divine mysteries" found in Revelation, offering an elucidation of that which was and remains indispensable. Quite naturally, he adopted a historical approach. "Who will deny that one may find a perfect match between a straightforward reading of Revelation and the fall of Rome to Alaric" yet "still be able to keep one's mind open to other meanings that may come to fruition at the end of the centuries?" Placing Revelation in a historical context appealed to Bossuet because John's "Babylon," which is to say Rome, had nothing to do with the pope. "He always had in mind the Roman Empire," a place "profane through and through," rendering null and void the Protestant readings of Revelation that cast papal Rome as the throne of the Antichrist. In the Revelation to John, one finds "no trace whatsoever of a corrupt Church."[57]

When one shifts to reflect on Isaac Newton (1642–1727) and time, classical mechanics comes to mind. The definition of time in *Principia* (1687) calls for a smoothly flowing, universal, absolute time. "Absolute, true, and mathematical time, in and of itself and of its own nature, without reference to anything external, flows uniformly and by another name is called duration. Relative, apparent, and common time is any sensible and external measure (precise or imprecise) of duration."[58] Condorcet believed that "Newton perhaps did more for the progress of the human mind than discover this general law of nature; he taught men to admit in physics only precise and mathematical theories, which account not merely for the existence of a certain phenomenon but also for its quantity and extension."[59] As Étienne Klein has written, "The movement of bodies in space is described by giving their positions at successive moments. When calculating trajectories, the parameter of time is treated as something external to the dynamic, while Newton postulated that it flowed from the past toward the future, never varying. . . . For Newton, time is scrupulously neutral: it creates nothing and destroys nothing. It does nothing but keep the beat and trace trajectories. It flows always the same, without a ripple. It reigns outside of history. Indifferent, lacking any character, devoid of incident, this time makes each instant the equivalent of every other."[60] This time is absolute.

As a physicist, Newton does not comment on beginnings, limiting himself to the laws governing the movements of heavenly bodies. Still and all, one might well wonder how such a time might connect to Christian time and the Christian regime. In fact, they do not connect, but for Newton they readily coexist. Does that mean that Newton devoted his labors exclusively to ordering celestial phenomena, addressing time only to the extent that it "kept the beat"? The notion that he had nothing to say about history, with its tiresome time, could hardly be less accurate.

Frank Manuel offered the following portrait in *Isaac Newton, Historian*: "A devout Protestant Englishman writing world history about 1700 could combine an unquestioning acceptance of every fact in the Bible, a euhemerist historicization of pagan myth, and a literal reading of the later Greek and Roman historians into one grand concordance. If he had the requisite training he might attempt to amalgamate even a fourth element, the new physico-astronomical science."[61] That captures Newton, of course, precisely. *The Chronology of Ancient Kingdoms Amended* appeared one year after his death, the summation of thousands of pages he had devoted to the question in his lifelong, determined pursuit of chronology. Why this pursuit? Because Newton reckoned that while great chronologers such as Scaliger and Pétau had done much, their countless errors had yet to be corrected—much improvement remained to be made. To that end, he believed that astronomy, a field in which none could gainsay his achievements, might prove essential. After all, astronomy's predictive powers offered insight into the future, while it also assayed the past by verifying past events. But far more than accurate dating was at stake. First of all, the truth of biblical revelation had to be proven, beginning with the historical precedence of the Hebrews. This places Newton, chronologer, in line with all the Christian chronologers from Eusebius to Scaliger, not to mention Augustine's powerful image of the two cities. If the time of physics is pure chronos time, that of chronology, as practiced by Newton, is a blend of chronos and kairos, the former subordinated to the latter.

While he relies on the same sources as other chronologers—the Bible, classical authors, and astronomical observations, three guarantors of truth—Newton fancies himself a more scrupulous reader, and in any case he knows more than they about astronomy. The precession of the equinoxes, in particular, serves him well. A phenomenon long known, it allows him to prove that the voyage of the Argonauts, that first significant Greek adventure, took place nearly a half-century after the reign of Solomon.[62] He was certain that the voyage, a subject that preoccupied Newton for thirty or forty years, had really happened, but only after that earliest of civilizations, Solomon's kingdom, had left its mark. He went further: having divined the date of the voyage of the Argonauts, he applied it to framing a scientific chronology that included the Trojan War and hence the founding of Rome. A fragment found among his manuscripts revealed his assessment that he had "given an idea of dark ages more consistent with the course of nature & more consonant with Scriptures which are by far the oldest records now extant."[63] To arrive at his chronology, Newton combined the Old Testament, Eusebius and a few others, and the precession of the equinoxes. He considered even Genesis accurate—bearing in mind that Moses, who knew a thing or two about Copernican astronomy, had to make himself understood by ordinary people. The language was figurative, but no less scientifically accurate for that. Buffon was to say roughly the same thing.

But Newton viewed things differently from Eusebius: he had no fear of the apocalyptic horizon (quite the contrary) and did not hesitate to make the world younger. In several fragments he evokes "the coming of the kingdom for which we pray daily."[64] His attitude toward the apocalypse is one of expectant waiting. In his posthumous *Observations Upon the Prophecies*, he insists on the historical accuracy of the Book of Daniel and the Revelation to John, an argument like Bossuet's yet different, since Rome is, after all, the city of the Antichrist. Newton feels that John's predictions have all come true, and he means to prove this in a work that never does get written. Inevitably he needs to wrestle with Nebuchadnezzar's dream of the statue and the four creatures that emerge from the sea. And now the horns of the fourth point not toward Hellenistic kingdoms but the Visigoths, the Huns, the Franks, and so on. And as to the eleventh, the last and the worst, what used to be Antiochus IV is now the church of Rome. (Normally, since Luther, it will be the Antichrist.) There is no mistaking this for anything but the Christian regime of historicity, but now it is in the hands of a rather zealous Puritan.

In his study of prophecies, Newton defended a quite traditional viewpoint. "As the prophesies of the Old Testament remained in obscurity till Christs [sic] first coming & then were interpreted by Christ & the interpretations became the religion of the Christians: so the prophecies of both Testaments relating to Christs second coming may remain in obscurity till that coming," when they are cleared up and "become the religion of God's people" until Christ "shall deliver up the kingdom to the father."[65] Manuel rightly concludes that as a joint pendent to the history of the physical world, *The Chronology of Ancient Kingdoms Amended* and its complement, *Observations Upon the Prophecies*, offer "a fairly complete universal history of mankind, both sacred and profane, since the Creation." Once history's events have been placed in order, one can see that they belong to an organizational scheme, much as a system underlies planetary motions. The same Creator made both worlds, and it had fallen to Newton to improve our understanding of them.[66] Newton may not have considered himself a Daniel, but his astronomy foretold the movements of the spheres after the fashion of Daniel's accurate prophecy of the kingdoms to come, so perhaps he was close.

* * *

The Christian regime of historicity codified by Augustine never ceased to preserve and extend its control over time, adapting and enduring, adapting to endure. Augustine explained the continuous involvement of God with history through accommodation, clearly articulating its machinery. Accommodation permitted us to recognize a variability within time and provided a firm ground for the new. It meant as well that chronos time could matter without depriving kairos time of its dominance. From this emerged the universal history of Bossuet, a tour-de-force that embodied the final blossoming of translatio and accommodatio. As I have pointed out, the bishop divided the agents of change into two categories, history's "discrete causes" and the "secrets of Providence," which belong to God alone. He never meddles directly, practicing accommodation instead through "the cunning of God." Even when rulers think they are acting in their own interest, quite often they are advancing the divine plan—and thwarting themselves. In spite of his explicit plan to write a sequel, Bossuet proved shrewd enough to end his story with Charlemagne, the endpoint of ancient history.

As faithfully as *Discourse on Universal History* followed the chronology of Eusebius of Caesarea and the interweaving spirit of Augustine, it managed to attract many critics. Voltaire opened the scrap in *Essay on Universal History, the Manners, and Spirit of Nations* (1756), craftily labeling Bossuet an "eloquent writer," then laying out the opposing position. Above all, this history is far from "universal." Focusing on the destiny of the Hebrews, "he wholly omits the ancient peoples of the East, such as the Indians and the Chinese, nations more ancient yet just as prominent as any."[67] Once he had made his point about priority, Voltaire has precious little to say about times, time, the Christian regime—the history that mattered to him had unrolled over his own century. He wrote in his *Philosophical Dictionary* (1764), "Bossuet and Newton both commented on the Apocalypse; yet, considering everything, the eloquent declamations of the one and the sublime discoveries of the other have done them greater honor than their commentaries."[68] Voltaire was not impressed.

The sixteenth and seventeenth centuries swept by, and the Christian regime of historicity remained the obligatory frame of reference, the horizon of the worldly city. Nonetheless, fissures were appearing, ruptures were throwing things into question. While they remained central, Kairos and Krisis yielded more room to Chronos—it was either that or lose everything. How then to preserve the Christian regime of historicity? The duty of reinforcing and reshaping it fell to the clergy equipped with temporal instruments—then others besides the clergy. They overdid it, extended Chronos too much, rendering the regime too flexible, until it was truly fragile. Fragile, mismanaged, losing its grip, its bodyguards overwhelmed, the Christian regime was swept away.

5

IN THE THRALL OF CHRONOS

TO GRASP the rise of the Christian regime of historicity—its formation, expansion, and triumph, narrated in chapters 1 through 3—one must grasp how Kairos and Krisis circumscribed Chronos. Dissonances and fissures cropped up in chapter 4, some of them threatening the very existence of the regime. The whole thing begins to tip. Granting space to Chronos becomes more challenging at the very moment when a victory over time seems imminent; the cause is a dating system centered on the appearance of Jesus Christ. That event is the pivot of chronos time and kairos time—or perhaps one should say it had always been, will always be the pivot. Those who cast doubts on the biblical framework and the Christian temporal horizon confronted two sentinels, a papist and a ferocious antipapist. The former, Bossuet, historicized the Revelation of John without abrogating the range of its prophetic potential, while the latter, Newton, maintained the literal truth of the Book of Daniel.

They were overwhelmed. Chronos, though it existed at a lower scale than Kairos, broke free from its grip and emerged the victor. Such is the topic of this chapter: the triumph of Chronos between the late eighteenth and mid-twentieth centuries. The city of man, after considerable struggle, passes under the yoke of Chronos. The fullest, most powerful expression of the Christian regime appears in *The City of*

God, a twin portrait of the titular city and the earthly city, separate yet mixed, obliged to proceed in lockstep to the final day. Since Constantine, Christians had believed in only a single city, the Christian city represented by the church. That was the central argument pursued by Otto of Freising in his great book. The single-city thesis, in spite of the long-lived fable that presented the Holy Roman Empire as the heir to Rome, lost its credibility. In its stead, the two cities reappear, but the rearguard action fought by the church involved surrendering all control over chronos time and renewing its commitment to kairos time, its true domain.

That retreat from the temporal sphere culminated with the dissolution of the Papal States in 1870 and, in France, the separation of church and state in 1905. But in the meantime Kairos had discovered a new vessel for the church. In 1846 the Virgin Mary appeared to two young cowherds near the village of La Salette, and she had them take down a letter that spoke of famine and punishments to come. Pope Pius IX promulgated in 1854, as an element of his campaign against the modern world, the dogma of the Immaculate Conception. Bernadette Soubirous, fourteen years old, experienced in 1858 eighteen visitations from the Virgin, all in the cave of Massabielle, near Lourdes. She was told, "I am the Immaculate Conception."[1] Kairos had manifested these apparitions, like bolts of lightning, to innocent children, loosing a burst of excitement and controversy. The mother of Jesus had opened new avenues for the church to be present in the world, including pilgrimages to Lourdes and to Our Lady of La Salette.

Temporally speaking, the dismembering of the Christian regime of historicity made possible the massive transformation that has given us modern time. The Christian regime did not vanish—far from it. But efforts to grasp it by means of such rubrics as the secularization of society or the secularization of politics cannot succeed, for even though these concepts are convenient and have been widely used, they lack the precision and multivalence needed to pinpoint the transfer from one regime to another. The change took time and entailed a convergence of political, social, economic, and cultural factors, but once the incremental change was complete, the apocalyptic presentism of the previous era had yielded to the futurism of the modern regime of historicity.[2] Let us follow, as the theme of our inquiry suggests, the tracks of Kairos and Krisis, along with the leading instruments of temporalization—translatio, renovatio, accommodatio, and reformatio. Unveiled by the church fathers, the instruments were put to work, with adjustments made up to the end of the seventeenth century. And now, is there a place for them, a task? What might it look like, in the new economy of time? Does it turn out that these instruments are, effectively, recyclable? As unwieldy as the issue may be, we cannot understand how modern time took shape (and took over) without grasping it.

KICKING IN THE BIBLICAL DOOR

The chronology of the Bible was always in play. The church's determination to establish and preserve it, defend and—explicitly or tacitly—adapt it, involved chronologers, theologians, and exegetes, acting as the advance guard, with millenarians and apocalyptists from several denominations also playing a part. All along, the subject attracted considerable attention. And yet it became, as I have emphasized, a straitjacket. Different modes of escape were attempted, all the while insisting that biblical chronology had to be upheld, even reinforced.[3]

Then, during the eighteenth century, the straitjacket loosened. It would be pointless to describe that era in terms of fissures and fault lines in the Christian regime of historicity; the whole thing was being demolished. At the center of the controversy lay the age of the Earth, since sacred chronology's six thousand years looked less and less plausible. Consider Count Buffon and the Marquis of Condorcet, two scholars who lived during the latter half of the eighteenth century. Their works exemplify the de facto abandonment of the Christian temporal horizon; all temporal boundaries, whether in the past or the future, had fallen away. As the Flood sank into irrelevance and Genesis came to seem nothing but a naive fable, the landmarks were collapsing—Christian presentism felt the world going topsy-turvy. Voltaire crowed.

"THE DARK ABYSM OF TIME"

But it was the Count of Buffon's *Epochs of Nature*, far more than Voltaire's opprobrium, that undid the Christian regime. According to Buffon, he revered the biblical truths, yet his determination to shine a light onto "the dark abysm of time" drove him to reject the chronological framework, dismembering the Christian regime.[4] When chronos time found itself alone onstage, it assumed an active role sufficient unto itself. In his telling, time alone governs the Earth as it slowly cools from its molten state, inaugurating a history of nature whose different eras Buffon describes. "The great laborer of nature is time," he wrote in volume 6 of *Natural History*, published in 1756. In 1778 he traced the connections between the history of living nature and the history of the Earth in *The Natural History of the Epochs of Nature*. Consider the words of the title. As a natural phenomenon propelled onward by time, this history dispenses with God. We call the regular divisions of nature's distinctive history *epochs*, a word that brings to mind the epochs of Bossuet. But the word enjoyed a certain currency during the eighteenth century, as Jacques Roger, Buffon's modern editor, points out, and others had previously used it to indicate the principal events marking the history of the Earth.[5] Later the meaning of the term changed. It had meant a fixed point from which one might survey the past and the future, but now it referred to a period, the duration of which was to be calculated. That fixed point, that perspective, is what Bossuet had in mind when he used the word, and his usage was in keeping with the Greek etymology.

"As in civil history," wrote Buffon, "one consults documents, studies old coins, and deciphers antique inscriptions to determine the epochs of human revolutions and to establish the dates of moral events, so likewise, in natural history, one must rummage through the world's archives, draw ancient monuments from the entrails of the Earth, collect their remains, and assemble in a body of evidence all the clues to the physical changes that can send us back to Nature's different ages. This is the only way to ground some points in the immensity of space and set some milestones along the eternal road of time."[6]

Complementing "the immensity of space" is "the eternal road of time." Words matter. To his opening declaration, a majestic, calmly sanguine preamble setting out the approach and ambition of this new history, Buffon adds, "Natural history embraces equally all of space, all of time, and has no limits other than those of the universe." Civil history, by contrast, functions only within a narrowly delimited space and time. Consider the limits imposed by "the six or eight thousand years of religious traditions."[7] They cannot align with the time needed for the Earth to return to inhabitable temperatures, as Buffon discovered when he developed chronologies based on experiments with white-hot balls of iron left to cool. Compared to others he preserved among his papers, the timeline he finally elected to have printed is brief: 75,000 years had elapsed between the formation of the planets and the eighteenth century after Christ. Further cooling will kill off all the Earth's flora and fauna in 168,000 years.[8] Such spans far exceed those found in the Bible; they exceed even, as Buffon notes, "the limited power of our intelligence." Had he communicated his longer chronology, which estimated that by the eighteenth century three million years had elapsed, with the end coming at the seven million mark, the Sorbonne could hardly have been more outraged, and in any case none of his contemporaries would have taken it seriously. It would have meant swapping one tall tale for another. To quote Jacques Roger, "The minds least beholden to dogmatic thinking had not freed themselves from intellectual habits of very long standing. They could not imagine a 'dark abysm' so very distant in time, an abyss where human beings were nothing, an abyss harder to imagine than the endless spaces pervaded by the eternal silence so terrifying to Pascal. The features of all Creation were changing."[9] Perhaps Buffon was addressing posterity when he concluded, "Instead of pushing the limits of duration too far back, I have drawn them as near as I could."[10] As far as was possible, so as not to go too far beyond the believable.

Since Buffon is determined to "reconcile forever the science of nature and that of theology," his strategy for coping with the first few verses of Genesis involves lending the narrative a temporal framework: he injects time, a great deal of time. The familiar translation of the first verse, "In the beginning God created heaven and earth," should read, "In the beginning God drew out of nothingness the matter for heaven and earth." It will only be later that these take on the forms with which we are familiar, for it is written that "the earth was a formless void" and "there was darkness over the deep."[11] As to the six days, they must not be units of twenty-four hours; it stands to reason that they are "six spans of time" capable of accommodating the "physical truths." Was he aware that he was reviving a version of accommodation? In any case, his contention that Moses's story had to resonate with "the common man" rather than "demonstrate the world's true system" was in no sense original.[12] He does go further in that direction, declaring, "The truths of Nature will appear only with time." After all, God "uses man to reveal and display the marvels with which he has filled the bosom of nature." We have here, once again, "truth, the daughter of time." The implication is that as science advances, taking accurate measurements of time, it does not contradict what Bossuet called the designs of Providence. He concludes his ad hoc exegesis with a recantation. Those who were "too insistent on a literal reading" might find his ideas unacceptable, but they ought to bear in mind that "as my system is entirely speculative, it do no harm to revealed truths, which are immutable axioms never affected by hypotheses, and to which all of my ideas are subordinated."[13] As the axiom trumps the hypothesis, all is well and orderly, even though the hypothesis appears to dispense with the axiom entirely.

Buffon anticipates, early in his work, describing six epochs of nature. The symbolic power of the number six, what with the six days of Creation and Augustine's six ages of the world, is considerable. In his *First Discourse* (1773), he still discusses six epochs. But he did end up adding a seventh centered on man rather than nature.[14] Would this day, the seventh, complete and crown nature's handiwork? One may certainly think of the seventh epoch as a sort of human Parousia, yet it unfolded slowly and gradually from utterly pathetic beginnings that more closely resemble the picture conveyed by Lucretius than that in the Bible. Time remains the crucial issue, and the sovereignty of mankind does not derive from God: human beings are the fruits of toil, far from finished. "Nature had need of six hundred centuries to build its great works.... How many will human beings need before they can arrive at the same point and put an end to worries, disturbances, and destroying each other?" Human beings are not born masters of nature—they become masters. That achievement depends on them, but it cannot be done without assisting and improving the power of nature. "Is there anything he cannot do for himself, by which I mean his own species," asks Buffon, "if his will were forever guided by the intelligence? Who can say how far the perfecting of human nature—moral or physical—might go?"[15] From the extended time of nature, we shift to the time of human beings, whose principal strength is their perfectibility, a quality increasingly evident in recent times. As it has gained in temporality, the seventh epoch has come to resemble a utopia.

"INDEFINITE PROGRESS"

Once humanity has arrived at that seventh epoch, with all those happy perspectives opening ahead, Condorcet readily takes the baton, offering a vision of the "indefinite progress of the human mind."[16] No longer need there be any pretense of coordinating the advance of reason and theology. The French Revolution had come and gone, freeing Condorcet to censure the deadweight of superstition. No more condemnations will issue from the Sorbonne, a change from Buffon's time. In another change, Condorcet set aside the time of nature, addressing only the seventh epoch, that of man. No great admirer of Buffon, Voltaire had explicitly declared in his article on history drawn up for the *Encyclopedia* that natural history was "inappropriately termed *history*" as it was "an essential part of Physics."[17] For him, the most philosophically rewarding history was that of "the human mind," an idea he applied to the century of Louis XIV. What he wrote was not "the annals of his reign; it is rather the history of the human mind, examined in the century that sheds the most glory."[18] Condorcet could have seized on the moment when that history neared its climax, but instead he began with the very "first state of civilization."[19] Sent off toward physics, nature will not put in an appearance in the painting; the subject is the time of human beings.

What did he hope to show in writing *A Historical Picture of the Progress of the Human Spirit?* "That nature has set no term to the perfection of human faculties; that the perfectibility of man is truly indefinite; and that the progressions of this perfectibility, from now onward independent of any power that may wish to halt it, has no other limit than the duration of the globe upon which nature has cast us."[20] Before his proscription drove Condorcet into hiding, he had time only to draw up a sketch of *Picture*. When Madame de Condorcet published the sketch in 1795, the Convention bought and distributed three thousand copies. Rehabilitated through that act, Condorcet was recognized as the official intellectual of the new regime. Since their earliest days, human beings have never ceased to advance toward perfection—history shows this. The theory of sensations—the foundation of the idea of perfectibility—suffices to explain this, from that first mental faculty consisting of receiving sensations, initially simple and more elaborate with time. Clearly there is no longer any need for the overseer, the patron of the divine perfection toward which human beings, fallen and redeemed, have tended. Instead of accommodation we have sensations; rather than reformatio there is progress. Obstacles have hindered the march forward—prejudice and superstition still do; yet the march never comes to a halt. "Everything tells us that we are now close upon one of the great revolutions of the human race."[21] For a wanted man with a price on his head, these were optimistic words indeed.

Condorcet's *Picture* is conceived as "the hypothetical history of a single people." The progressions of that history are divided into nine "stages," with a tenth devoted to "the future destiny of the human race," acknowledging the possibility of advances in those "natural faculties" themselves.[22] Peeking out of this passage is a Condorcet whom we would nowadays call a transhumanist. Or, more accurately, today's transhumanists and posthumanists are continuing Condorcet's legacy. Life expectancy, Condorcet foresaw, will only increase with improvements to medicine, housing, nutrition, and lifestyles. And he went further, wondering whether it was "absurd then to suppose that this perfection of the human species might be capable of indefinite progress; that the day will come when death will be due only to extraordinary accidents or to the decay of the vital forces, and that ultimately the average span between birth and decay will have no assignable value?" That final epoch will unroll as he describes, and none will see that it is without end, this time of a humanity "emancipated from its shackles" and "advancing with a firm and sure step along the path of truth, virtue, and happiness."[23]

We have left behind Augustine's six ages and Buffon's seven epochs to arrive at Condorcet's *Sketch* and his ten epochs. One senses the influence of the metric system with its all-conquering rationalism: even epochs obey almighty decimals. Kairos time is nowhere to be found, and chronos time carries on by itself. Yet such concepts mean nothing to the revolution. Condorcet wants to know what, in the wake of the American Revolution, "precipitated" the revolution in France. His answer: the "maladroitness of her government," bearing in mind that "philosophers guided [the] principles" of the revolutionaries, and that "the power of her people destroyed the obstacles which might have stood in its way." Even "chance" can be pinpointed using statistical methods, as "only by the study of this calculus" is its true meaning revealed. Much as calculus enormously improved the precision of the sciences, the social mathematics of statistics opens a vast new field that "can determine the probability of unusual facts" and "the different degrees of certainty that we can hope to attain."[24] Even the future becomes susceptible to rational inspection and calculation. No longer will time be elusive and inscrutable.

In sum, the expansions of all sorts that Condorcet foresees result not from wild leaps in the atemporal utopias of old but rather from lucid extrapolations, even when he addresses the extension of the human lifespan. If he refers to them as indefinite, he means that we know only that they must not end, that they have no previously set boundary. Chronos time and its mastery, including the mastery of future time, is the topic, even when that future time is very distant. The study of statistics makes predictions possible, and it shrinks further and further the role of kairos. Christly Kairos expanded its power over chronos time by spreading, while statistics reverses the course. As Chronos marches forward, Kairos retreats; it is pinpointed, pressed, dissected, and led (or should I say forced) to account for itself. And then, it is driven out.

TEMPORALIZED CREATION

Time, after Buffon and Condorcet, no longer respected any limits, whether in the past or the future. But it was Darwin who delivered the coup de grâce to the Christian regime of historicity. For a long time naturalists had believed that species were "immutable productions, and had been separately created." Darwin proved the opposite, that the transformations of living species were themselves the result of time.[25]

In the long preface that Clémence Royer wrote for the French edition of *The Origin of Species*, published in 1862, the translator dwelt deliberately on the ideas of revelation and progress. Linking that oxymoronic pair, this positivistic philosopher meant to provoke theologians of every stripe and jolt Catholics in particular. Royer wonders what Darwin's thought might boil down to, and she replies, "The rational revelation of progress." That revelation is, then, brought about by scientific progress, most recently the law of natural selection discovered and proven by Darwin. Natural selection is a matter of time—time over an extended, continuous period. Nature never leaps. The full title of this edition could not be clearer: *On the Origin of Species by Means of Natural Selection; or, On the Laws of Progress in Higher Beings*. "I believe in progress" are the preface's final words. Evidently Royer was determined to insert Darwin's theory into human history's sequence of "revelatory epochs" (note the echo of Condorcet).

With *The Origin of Species* (1859), the notion of species as immutable productions that had been separately created was devastated. "All the chief laws of palæontology plainly proclaim, as it seems to me," writes Darwin, "that species have been produced by ordinary generation: old forms having been supplanted by new and improved forms of life, the products of Variation and the Survival of the Fittest." What was needed, quite simply, was time, vast amounts of time. But just as "the mind cannot possibly grasp the full meaning of the term of even a million years," he notes, "it cannot add up and perceive the full effects of many variations, accumulated during an almost infinite number of generations."[26]

The Creator appears briefly at the end of the book, very much in passing: "It accords better with what we know of the laws impressed on matter by the Creator, that the production and extinction of the past and present inhabitants of the world should have been due to secondary causes, like those determining the birth and death of the individual."[27] For Darwin, speaking of secondary causes conveys a loftier sense of the divine than does a picture of a creator ceaselessly involved in acts of creation. Such a view governs his declaration, a result less of conviction than of prudence, that he sees "no good reason why the views given in this volume should shock the religious feelings of any one."[28] He had offered a token acknowledgment of religion, yet "every negative criticism of Darwin from a naturalist [was] inspired by motives that were, at their essence, theological."[29] In particular, Adam Sedgwick, a friend of Darwin's who had been his geology instructor at Cambridge, considered his book "mischievous" since it had thrown the "natural order" into question and cast doubts on the place of human beings at the center of nature.[30]

In the period leading up to his formulation of transformism, Darwin immersed himself in James Hutton's *Theory of the Earth* (1788) and, especially, *Principles of Geology* (1830–33) by Charles Lyell, the leading geologist of the day. Hutton embraced a cyclical theory of time and had concluded that searching for either the Earth's origin or signs of its end was vain; he declared, "We find no vestige of a beginning,—no prospect of an end."[31] In a comment on this aphorism, Stephen Jay Gould explains that while the Earth certainly had a beginning, incessant metamorphoses ensured that no geological traces remained. If no insight into an end is available, it is because "time's cycle governs the earth only while it operates under the regime of natural laws now in force." The end, or some change of state, will occur when the "higher powers" terminate the reign of the "current regime of natural laws."[32] A professed Newtonian, Hutton was no more willing than his idol to comment on beginnings or endings. While chronos time is sufficient unto itself, it does not preclude the existence of a kronos time, which in any case belongs to another sphere, that of "higher powers."

During his voyage on the *Beagle*, Darwin read the three volumes of Lyell's study. The two men later became close friends, and Lyell stoutly championed Darwin. He viewed geologic change as the outcome of natural causes no different today from yesterday, yielding the same effects, quite different from the view that assigned change to catastrophes occurring with some regularity. That theory of "revolutions of the globe," which Georges Cuvier defended, and the ideas of the Christian catastrophists contradicted Lyell's uniformitarianism. "The mind," he wrote, "was slowly and insensibly withdrawn from imaginary pictures of catastrophes and chaotic confusion, such as haunted the imagination of the early cosmogonists. Numerous proofs were discovered of the tranquil deposition of sedimentary matter and the slow development of organic life."[33] Even Lyell's selection of modifiers appears to be calculated to convert his reader to the view that change has always been gradual, progressive, and continuous. No disaster, ergo no flood either. Chronos is enough; there is no need for a Kairos—or even a kairos.

Cuvier's theory, on the other hand, suits religion nicely: was not the biblical flood the world's most recent catastrophe? This sort of thinking comes in for Flaubert's withering satire in *Bouvard and Pécuchet*. The parish priest happens to be passing by when the two idiots, in the throes of their geological phase, are digging flints from the middle of the road. He sings out "with an ingratiating voice, 'You gentlemen have taken up geology? How wonderful.' For he approved of this science. It confirmed the authority of the Scriptures by proving the Flood."[34] One need hardly add a word. As it turns out, Bouvard and Pécuchet had just finished reading with relish Cuvier's *Discourse* on the revolutions of the globe. When they call on the priest and pester him with questions about the opening verses of Genesis, he sheds that earlier friendliness. Cuvier and Lyell occupy positions, notes Gould, that speak to two antithetical notions of time. Theirs was a struggle that "pitted a directional view of history as a vector leading toward cooler climates and more complex life, and fueled by occasional catastrophes, against Lyell's vision of a world in constant motion, but always the same in substance and state, changing bit by bit in a stately dance toward nowhere."[35] Time seen as cyclical confronts time like an arrow. The former comprises a much extended chronos time that seems never to advance, while the latter, a sequence of ruptures, seems to extend Christian time by combining Chronos and Kairos. The priest of Chavignolles (still) feels quite at home there.

PROGRESS

When the work of these three scholars is assembled, the dominance of Chronos becomes clear. Each of them brashly acknowledged this, pursuing the implications at remarkable length. Chronos is enough, sufficient unto itself. Yet what is Chronos if not a large amount of time, time to be reckoned in millions of years? Buffon rightly noted—and Darwin chimed in—that it was effectively impossible to conceive of such vast timespans, beyond the capacity of the human mind. Here is a slow, ever-flowing time that exists long before the appearance of human beings, with no use (or next to no use) for the compass needle of a kairos. With reason to direct it, humanity's march forward advances on a wide-open future. The great age of the world cannot be doubted, but the Augustinian ages of the world, with Earth proceeding along its final age, makes no sense. If anything, human history is simply the most recent date on the calendar. Each of the sciences laid out in 1863 by Ernest Renan is assigned "a moment of the duration." This makes each discipline equally historical, with "history itself, the youngest of the sciences," shedding light "on that final period."[36]

With Buffon, the impulse to assign a date to the Earth's beginning—and its exhaustion—has not vanished. Things change with Condorcet, who evades that task with the word "indefinite," applied to all future advances. Now limits fall away, both canonical and conventional, and the very idea that present time lies between the Incarnation and the Parousia, between the onset of the time of the end and the end of time itself, ceases to matter. As I have pointed out, the Christian regime depends on maintaining a clear distinction between the time of the end and the end of times. We are told that that distinction will one day melt away—precisely when, no one knows—but, nonetheless, between those two poles a pure, presentist present gained in temporality over time, resolving into a historic time, all the while preserving that gap between the already and the not yet, between experience and suspension. Those first Christians had only an ahistoric apocalyptic presentism, which after a hasty negotiation came to dominate Chronos, only to press it into the service of the city of God, itself grounded in Christly Kairos. The part played in that sequence of events by the leading temporal instruments was decisive; we have seen how some of them were used and recycled.

Now that the network they formed has nearly dissolved, let us summon to mind one last time their dream, which was to guide fallen and redeemed human beings toward divine perfection. God was able to employ accommodatio to meet human beings halfway, as they remained children in many regards. Their response involved renovatio and reformatio, two means of making sense of chronos time, and then there was translatio, offering a meaning for the entirety of universal history. A system so balanced was rent by fissures, due in part to efforts made by clerics to preserve—and to strengthen—the hold that Kairos has over Chronos. The efforts of Joachim of Fiore and, more naively, more nakedly, António Vieira sometimes ran the risk of lapsing into heresy.

Most grievous were the efforts of the humanists because of a tendency to repurpose elements of the Christian system, stepping out of the standard framework to invest those elements with novel content. Fond as they were of renovatio, they put it to wholly new ends: they did not hope for a rebirth in Jesus but to rediscover and foster the rebirth of antiquity, in spite of their awareness of an unbridgeable chronos interval between themselves and the distant past. And in addition, if renovatio was to succeed, bearing in mind that it belonged largely to Kairos, it will be obliged to seek out the erudite techniques of restitutio so dependent on a chronos timeline, laboring to measure its effects and minimize its harm. Renovatio saw that Chronos was pushing it aside. When Jean Bodin aggravated this trend by rejecting the providential claims of translatio, he dealt the Christian regime of historicity a fatal blow. To break free of convention, he turned to an alternative temporality, the cyclic model familiar from the classical past.[37]

PERFECTION, PERFECTIBILITY, PROGRESS

One hundred years elapsed, and then the issue of perfection sank like a wedge into the Christian order of time. Perfection has nothing to do with chronos time; it belongs to God and his eternity. A temporal instrument is indeed a tool that conveys human beings along the path of a perfection unattainable in this world. During the quarrel of the ancients and the moderns in the seventeenth century, perfection, which descends from heaven, was somehow secularized and temporalized. What was the perfection ascribed to the ancients? Which should be crowned in the contest of perfection, the ancients or the moderns? Charles Perrault marshaled two forms of perfection in *The Parallel of the Ancients and the Moderns* (1688). First was the "point of perfection," and second was the "degrees of perfection."[38] The idea behind the former was a curve that rose upward. The idea behind the latter was a steplike ascent to the pinnacle. Never explicitly posed, the question implied by the two images is: What comes after the highest point? As soon as one goes beyond the point of perfection, does one tumble? This returns us to cyclical time, known as the time of "vicissitudes." Or is there a deceleration, a braking or progress that happens when one nears the "highest degree" of perfection? A bit like Perrault himself, we shall set aside these knotty questions to focus only on the temporal effects of these spatial renderings of perfection. Whether we address the perfection of the point or of the degree, their progressions depend on time—a purely chronos time, with no connection to kairos. As soon as perfection entered human time, its temporalization was preordained.

This displacement advances a step further as we shift from perfection to perfectibility. Viewed from this perspective, the drive to perfection is understood in terms of the perfectibility of the actor, humanity's ability to perfect itself—over time and on its own. Rousseau, who identified this attribute as the key difference between the human species and animals, served as its leading disseminator. In *Discourse on the Origin of Inequality* (1755), he writes of the

> very specific quality that distinguishes them and about which there can be no argument: the faculty of self-perfection, a faculty that, with the aid of circumstances, successively develops all the others, and resides among us as much in the species as in the individual. On the other hand, an animal, at the end of a few months, is what it will be all its life; and its species, at the end of a thousand years, is what it was in the first of those thousand years. Why is man alone subject to becoming an imbecile? It is not that he thereby returns

to his primitive state, and that, while the animal which has acquired nothing and which also has nothing to lose, always retains its instinct, man, in losing through old age or other accidents all that his *perfectibility* has enabled him to acquire, thus falls even lower than the animal itself?[39]

Perfectibility is as characteristic of the human species as of any individual, and it is inseparable from chronos time. The skill human beings display in exploiting chronos time sets them apart from animals. Time belongs to humans alone, very much along the negative lines set out by Augustine, who blamed Adam's sin for the fall in time.

Condorcet outdoes Rousseau. He traces human perfectibility to the cardinal ability to receive sensations, declaring "truly indefinite" a "progress" that has "no other limit than the duration of the globe upon which nature has cast us." Passing from perfection to perfectibility may seem like a simple transition, but when we realize that everything can now be traced to human nature, we see that a true rupture has occurred. At that very instant, the Christian system loses control, as do its increasingly temporalized instruments, renovatio and reformatio, devised in response to God's accommodatio to draw people toward their original state of perfection. When Pascal attacked the casuistry of the Jesuits, decrying their leading part in making compromises, he was an early critic of this noxious capitulation.[40] Perfection and accommodatio had long formed a pair; they had been succeeded by perfectibility and progress.

While Condorcet wrote of "progressions," soon enough the singular collective "progress" prevailed, the nineteenth century's god of progress, emblematic of modern time. Writers clung to the image of the city of humans marching forward, but the destination of that march was changing. Hadn't Condorcet, for instance, seen the city striding "with a firm and sure step along the path of truth, virtue, and happiness"?[41] And in *The Legend of the Ages*, Victor Hugo conveys human experience as "a single, immense ascending movement toward the light." For him, the twentieth century was to be "Liberty in the light."

> Where is this ship going? It is going, all dressed in day,
> To God's pure future, to virtue,
> To the science we see gleaming,

To the death of the scourges, to generous oblivion,
 . . . it rises to the stars!⁴²

At a time of countless declarations, proclamations, and manifestos, all lauding progress, the universal expositions offered a glimpse of the future.⁴³ One cannot readily imagine a better way to celebrate, promote, and popularize progress as "the general religion of modern time," to borrow language from the Universal Exposition of 1900. By drawing the maximum numbers of visitors into this new world, which was theirs to see and touch, the expositions hope to convert them to the new religion.

A number of the most emblematic displays spoke eloquently. The first in this series is the famous Crystal Palace, the great metal and glass greenhouse erected for the Universal Exposition held in London in 1851. Next, in 1889, is the Eiffel Tower at the Universal Exposition in Paris. Another Parisian exposition, this time in 1900, saw the American historian Henry Adams spending long hours at the Palace of Electricity. "As he grew accustomed to the great gallery of Machines, he began to feel the forty-foot dynamos as a moral force, much as the early Christians felt the Cross. . . . Before the end, one began to pray to it."⁴⁴ This comparison made by Adams is very suggestive—even though it is unlikely that every visitor shared his thinking. Because there are grounds for an analogy between the mystery of the cross and that of electricity; generating electricity amounts, according to Adams, to a form of kairos, but one that has been produced and controlled by technology. Again in 1900 a moving walkway is installed between the Champ de Mars and the Invalides; it is called the "Road of the Future." With equal parts optimism and foolishness, the last in this series, 1939's New York Universal Exposition, announces the "World of Tomorrow." That world, we are told, has arrived; we need only reach out our hand to touch the future. But what future? Tomorrow will lead, in a few years, to Auschwitz and Hiroshima.

MODERN TIME AND THE MODERN REGIME OF HISTORICITY

Evoked time and again, progress is presented through the image of a figure striding forward, but it will be time itself that strides, with a quickening tempo. Those who wish to be modern, to become modern, even to remain modern will be obliged to keep up. Time now sets the pace. No longer is chronos only, to cite Aristotle one last time, the number of motion with respect to the before and the after; we now perceive it as an independent agent. As Reinhart Koselleck showed in his extended analysis, that which occurs "in time" now also occurs "by time": through it.[45] This marks the advent, between the end of the eighteenth century and the middle of the nineteenth century, of what I have called the modern regime of historicity.

The new regime is characterized by a new insistence on the future and, to borrow categories from Koselleck, a widening gap between the field of experience and the horizon of expectations.[46] The future becomes the goal in this new temporality, and the light cast on the past comes from that future. From its former taxonomic identity, time becomes the instrument of history as process, another name for (the real name for) progress. None other than Alexis de Tocqueville offered the most lucid description of the new regime of historicity: "When the past no longer lights up the future," he wrote at the end of *Democracy in America* (1840), "the spirit walks in darkness."[47] These valedictory remarks on the old regime of historicity, whose passing left the world in darkness, might also serve as the motto of the modern regime, decoding the post-1789 world. In that realm, the future bears the onus of lighting up the past and indicating the path forward. The spirit, then, does not advance in darkness, not any more. The past dominated the old regime of historicity, but its time is done, and likewise does the modern regime break with the Christian regime—which it has undone.

As the doors behind which biblical chronology lay safe are kicked in, Chronos breaks free from its dependence on kairos time. Without any temporal limits, whether toward the past or the future, Christian presentism loses its rudder. Having long performed ably, the leading temporal instruments are rendered useless, since they manifestly rely on limits, namely, the time of the end inaugurated by the Incarnation and the end of times that will accompany the Parousia. What began as a simple, vaporous present had become, once limits are imposed, a fully chronological space. Forging a chronology involves growing a space for chronos time while ensuring that it remains subordinate to kairos time—this makes history possible. What history? Ecclesiastical history of course, Church history, a universal history of Providence that Bossuet, the eloquent official guardian of the Christian regime of historicity, hopes to set down as a lasting and glorious guide for the future king. Bossuet's history, however, did not extend beyond Charlemagne.

ACCELERATION

Contemporaries perceive modern time, a process, as time speeding up. When Koselleck identifies acceleration as the central experience of modern time, he points to the French Revolution. We can see the disruption most markedly in the rapid succession of different regimes between 1789 and 1815. But there are other examples. Robespierre marks the Constitutional Festival of 1793 by declaring, "Our duty is to accelerate this great revolution made possible by advances in reason." This statement presupposes that the course of history can be accelerated by a decisive action. Time is already speeding up, but the task, the duty of the revolutionary, is to make history, a matter of accelerating time even more.[48] This was conveyed by that hero of Goethe's, who said, "One can no longer learn anything once and for all. Our ancestors observed their whole life long the instruction they received in their youth; but we have to learn anew every five years if we do not to fall completely out of fashion."[49] We have entered a new time, one that "is always surpassing itself," and always forcing those under its sway to do likewise.[50]

In a discussion of what he called the "apocalyptic premises of the modern axioms of acceleration," Koselleck sharply distinguished between two phenomena: compressing time and accelerating time. Compression belongs to that Christian attitude of waiting, with an attendant apocalyptic quality of variable intensity.[51] "May the Lord bring the end soon!" (One thinks of Newton's daily prayer for the coming of the heavenly kingdom.) The alternative appeal, amounting to much the same thing, is: "How much longer?" How much longer must we wait for the return of Christ? Bear in mind that for God one day is as one thousand years, and one thousand years is as one day. Anything is possible when an unchanging, eternal God is sole master of time. No matter how righteous the believer's hope that the end comes soon, God alone has the power to cut short chronos time. Luther himself, the great reformer, hoped for a short wait, and in his *Table Talk* he reveals a decidedly apocalyptic streak. The sixteenth century also witnessed the advent of a different relation to time fostered by scientific breakthroughs and technological advances. This is exemplified by Francis Bacon (1561–1626), who pointed out the wide array of ever more impressive improvements realized over briefer and briefer timespans: *per minora intervalla* was his phrase.

Time itself has yet to accelerate, but things are heading that way. From noting inventors' quickening pace to endowing time itself with agency is a short step. And all the while the only device used to measure that quickening tempo is the clock made by human beings. Where once heaven and earth had stood in opposition, and the time of God had opposed the time of human beings, now there is the past versus the future in a time strictly human, and the gap between the two increases exponentially. To express the gap between the Incarnation and the Parousia, the Christian regime employed the temporalized *already* and *not yet*, which become part of chronos time itself, taking the form of experience and expectation. Koselleck makes of them his metahistoric categories: the space of experience and the horizon of expectation.[52] Under the cover of this new application of familiar categories, a profound transformation is taking place, something that amounts to a rupture. The *already/not yet* structure has survived, but its contents are completely different. The very temporal limits imposed by the Christian regime's *already* and *not yet* are cast off in the modern regime. Freed of limits, *already* and *not yet*, which can be thought of as experience and waiting, become properties of *processus* time itself, a way of thinking about its effectiveness and of the possible forms of experience it offers. For every hermeneutics of time, from Koselleck to Ricoeur and beyond, modern time or historical time actually emerges out of the gap between the field of experience and the horizon of waiting. When we think of the Christian regime of historicity, there is nothing of historical time in the essential gap between *already* and *not yet*, because it was first lived as a simple apocalyptic present. Only gradually did it take on a temporal quality, thanks in large part to the actions of the leading instruments; but again it failed to establish autonomy. So long as limits constituted an insuperable horizon, alternatives were inconceivable.

REFORM

At the instant that the limits vanish, however, those instruments became useless—with a single exception. From our perspective, it is fascinating that reformatio, now known as "reform," remained in uniform, though it defected to modern time. Inasmuch as reformatio functioned since the twelfth century like a veritable temporal confluence, the switch was easy enough; do not forget that reformatio always had, simultaneously, its eyes to the front and to the rear.[53] Once reform adjusted its gaze, looking only to the future, it could serve as an active instrument of modern time. Yes, the Lutheran Reformation did initially keep an eye to the past, but its role as pioneer of a new Christian era certainly facilitated the movement of reformatio into modern time, and the very idea of reform came to include severing connections to a past that had been surpassed—a past that would otherwise hinder and slow things—facilitating the emergence of all that was new and superior.

Thus "reform" became a political slogan in France circa 1840, and during the July monarchy a republican journal with that title was founded. Those who wished to proceed shrewdly, and to remain resistant to censure, embraced reform as a means of laying claim to the revolution. For revolution was essential, but it had to be gained one step at a time: first of all is universal suffrage, foreseen in the Constitution of 1793 but never adopted. Reformist republicans believe that their approach allows all the improvements the revolution failed to bring about to unfold in chronos time, more slowly, hence more effectively. In the final years of the July regime, reform reignited the march toward progress, a confrontation with all those who labored to block it. The call for universal suffrage did not imply a return to 1793, but rather an unleashing by the new era of progressive forces long held in check. So reform comes to be a political concept of motion, characterized by order and gradualism, bearing within itself and itself borne within modern time. It had functioned as an instrument in the name of the Christian regime, but so flexible was it that it came to serve as a leading instrument of the modern regime of historicity.

HISTORY AND THE REVIVALS OF KAIROS AND KRISIS

The new regime coincides with the consecration of history. Between the end of the eighteenth century and the middle of the nineteenth century, the collective singular "history" (much like the singular "progress") announces itself as the dominant force in the modern world. Among the notes left behind by Novalis (1772–1801) are two aphorisms: "Time is the surest historian" and "History engenders itself."[54] Seventy years later, in his dictionary entry for the word "history," Pierre Larousse goes further: "Recently history has become, as it were, a universal religion. In every soul it has come to fill the place vacated by unsettled and expired beliefs. . . . History will become for modern civilization what theology was for the Middle Ages and the ancient world, namely the spirit prevailing over and regulating consciousness."[55] Larousse, a secular republican, both recognized and demanded this transformation of the sacred—which was anything but unusual. Just as there is a religion of progress, there is a new universal religion of history; both in fact amount to the same thing, a belief based in a world regulated by a *processus* time that explores the most distant of pasts, surveys an open-ended future, and experiences acceleration as the new normal.[56] When Charles Peguy confronts the "plight of history in modern times," twenty-five years after Larousse, he bemoans the harm that had been done. In particular, he attacks Ernest Renan, whom he sees as the forerunner of the modern world. For Peguy, humanity has "become God," and the historian too has made himself God, "half unconsciously, half compliantly."[57] Larousse may have praised the change while Peguy deplored it, but both had in mind the same phenomenon: the replacement of the Christian regime of historicity by the regime of history. Soon enough Marxism was to erect a secular religion that set history the task of saving and perfecting humanity.

Is that it? Has Chronos taken over the world? Has it rid itself of Kairos and Krisis, the fripperies of days gone by? Will Chronos be able to take on every historical situation, accounting for and making sense of everything? For the Greeks, the role of kairos was to animate chronos. From Buffon to Darwin, from the geologists to the naturalists, Chronos did a good job of explaining the Earth's transformations and the evolution of species, so long as one thought of it as dealing in millions of years. One no longer needed the theories of the catastrophists, which turned out to be another way to smuggle kairos back in, dressed in Christian colors or not. But will this do for the time associated with modern societies, such as we have witnessed? It is a *processus* time, a futuristic time of accelerating progress, the motor of a history made—we are told—by human beings, though, to echo Marx, the circumstances are not of their choosing. Clearly the uniform time of nature (now speaking like Buffon) is inadequate; to hope to grasp the complex tempos of societies, we need not one time but several. Bear in mind that Voltaire's natural time belonged to physics while Condorcet spoke of the indefinite progressions of a single humanity.

I shall, for now, address only the means by which Kairos and Krisis were absorbed and extended by Chronos, becoming traits and properties of their host. Well before that, Kairos and Krisis were put to task by the Christian regime of historicity as part of its ambitious—and successful—effort to control and transform Chronos, a reworking of concepts borrowed from the Greeks. That was the subject of my first two chapters. But even once Chronos was liberated, it did not dispense with Kairos and Krisis, which had demonstrated their utility over a long span. He took them into his service, if I may put it that way, under his authority, if not his control. But a change has come: so long as Krisis remains active and on the horizon, the Judgment is with us, but God no longer judges. Instead it is history that bears that responsibility; the image of the tribunal of history becomes a cliché. "The world's history," Schiller famously declared, "is the world's tribunal," and soon Hegel and many more took up the chant.[58] When the socialist Karl Liebknecht addressed the topic of privileges at the Reichstag in 1910, he declared, "As you know, gentlemen, there is much truth in the dictum 'The world's history is the world's tribunal,' and the trumpets of the Last Judgment—the trumpets of the Last Judgment, the trumpets of the peoples' judgment, gentlemen, will sound awesomely in your ears, the day of vengeance and of retribution will come. *Dies irae, dies illa*!"[59] One apocalypse yields to another, and from heaven we pass to Earth. Looking at it in reverse, Schiller's aphorism could serve to justify the supremacy of the strong. That is how Oswald Spengler read it. "*World-history*," he wrote, "*is the world court*, and it has ever decided in favour of the stronger, fuller, and more self-assured life. . . . Always it has sacrificed truth and justice to might and race, and passed doom of death upon men and peoples in whom truth was more than deeds, and justice than power."[60] For Hegel, though, the world tribunal was "the world-spirit," the advance toward liberty, something quite different from how the cynics and "realists" interpreted it. Still, the time of history remains a space where all is in play.[61]

KAIROS AND REVOLUTION

Between the advent of the Christly Kairos and the Judgment Day stretched out an intermediate time; between *already* and *not yet*, all is accomplished and all is not yet accomplished. Krisis manages to find work as the judge acting in and through history, while Kairos ensures the French Revolution is seen as a disruption, as the starting point of a new time, much like the situation after the Incarnation—or, from a radically different perspective, like the situation to come after the Apocalypse. Everything is different. No one could call this a planet predictably returning to a fixed location; time has split open, and the revolution has erupted into history. Consider the adoption, in 1793, of the revolutionary calendar. This brutal symptom of the eruption was meant as an alternative to the time of the church, in fact a substitute. When the Republic was proclaimed, on September 22, 1792, the Convention issued a decree stipulating that henceforth every official document was to be dated from "Year 1 of the Republic." On crowning himself emperor in 1806, Napoléon rescinded the act creating the calendar; its brief existence had been marred by vehement intransigence. A new era had begun, but it took place in the flow of traditional time and set a limit on the unprecedented experience of a revolutionary time.

Gilbert Romme, the architect of the new calendar, believed that "time is opening a new book to history, and as it advances, its step as new, majestic, and simple as equality, it must take up a new chisel to engrave the annals of a France reborn."[62] Time the actor has opened the new book; its step is measured by the laws of reason. It fancies itself the tool by which the city will be regenerated. The moment had come to replace the mixture of chronos time and kairos time that constituted the Christian calendar, as well as the time of kings, with pure, neutral chronos time. According to Romme, this process would honor two principles, "matching the republican year to celestial motions" and "measuring time by more precise and more symmetric measurements," namely, the decimal system. While it may be neutral, this new time is far from empty.[63] Once it is properly weighted with symbols and imagery, it can serve as a proper means of educating the public. Soon republican festivals will set it humming.

The experience of time will not readily accede to the novel forms a calendar prescribes, no matter how blazingly new it may be. As we have seen, it took the church centuries to fully implant Kairos and Krisis in Chronos. And we must ask whether the revolutionaries had really renounced kairos time once and for all. They had not, as their rapid and frequent application of "regeneration" shows. According to Lamourette, later the constitutional bishop of Lyon, "Lycurgus' regeneration . . . proceeded from laws to mores," while "the regeneration of Jesus Christ," the true rebirth, the sort the revolution hoped for, "first changed hearts." Mona Ozouf writes, "Even people who never dreamed, in the manner of Lamourette, of making the Revolution consubstantial with Christianity could accept the idea of the Revolution as a form of conversion—a sign of the religious dimension and singular nature of the enterprise."[64] The notion of regeneration in turn gave rise to the ideology of the new man and the Republic's revolutionary messianism. Regeneration also features in a different context, that of the counterrevolutionaries whose eschatology presents rebirth as a punishment. Only through persecution and expiation can a new age come into being, meaning that the final realization has yet to occur. Just as it had during the high tide of biblical prophets and apocalyptic seers, Providence keeps watch over all.

Such is the credo of Joseph de Maistre (1753–1821) and of all those who, calling for restoration of the old order, openly endorsed a reactionary posture, or touted tradition while musing over compromises. Two examples mark the extremes: Maistre and Chateaubriand. Both are members of the nobility who fared poorly during the revolution, both are Christian apologists, but ultimately they have little in common. Maistre took up a position directly in front of modern time and rejected it completely; Chateaubriand ferried back and forth between the old and the new regimes of historicity. In the spirit of Edmund Burke, Maistre angled for the title of theoretician of the Counter-Revolution. What was his approach? He believed that simply censuring the "satanic character" of the revolution, like Burke and the Abbé Barruel, would not do; more important was to identify the role played by Providence. Here we see the return of Bossuet, his take on the ways of Providence enlisted by Maistre to make sense of a century so impious, so monstrous, so incomprehensible that it could not be faced.

"'I do not understand it at all' was the fashionable phrase," recalls Maistre. But as soon as they realized that this was an "ordained revolution" that could not be hindered or blocked, everything was clear. It swept all before it, including "the very rascals who appear to lead the Revolution yet are involved only as simple instruments; as soon as they aspire to dominate it they fall ignobly."[65] He noted, "*It goes all alone*. . . . If the vilest instruments are employed, punishment is for the sake of regeneration." The great word is dropped: regeneration is well and truly remobilized. This is the dark side of regeneration, and crimes are now "the instruments of Providence." One should think here not of a rebirth but of a purification. After all, Providence is judging and chastising the French: the darker the crime, the more grievous the punishment. Providence goes beyond that, and when the armies of the Republic prevented France's dismemberment, they unwittingly supported "France and the future king." Punishing the French, it protects France. "If Providence *erases*, it is no doubt in order to *write*."[66] Such were Maistre's thoughts on the secrets of Providence and the ways of regeneration.

Far from Maistre's theocracy, Chateaubriand seeks a compromise between the ideals of progress to which he subscribes and the Christian faith in which he believes. He tries to mark out a path that might be called modernist even though he is aware that "the old society is giving way beneath itself." While he has no illusions about the prospects for the Bourbons, Chateaubriand is a devoted Legitimist, and he hopes to persuade his readers—and possibly himself—that "the Christian idea is the future of the world." Maistre rejects chronos time and focuses only on a theocracy where kairos time is restored, whereas

Chateaubriand believes in allocating chronos time an important role albeit wrapped in the church's kairos time. "Christianity is stable in its dogma and mobile in its enlightenment."[67] Another way of expressing that fluidity is to say that Christianity knows how to negotiate with chronos time. Writing in 1831, Chateaubriand declares, "Man inclines to an indefinite perfection. . . . He climbs, never pausing, the precipitous incline of this unknown Sinai, at the peak of which he will once again behold God. As society advances it effects a number of general transformations, and the human species has now reached just such a great change."[68] To reconcile the old Christian notion of perfection, that of *imitatio* and *reformatio*, with Condorcet's ideas of indefinite progressions and perfectibility, he offers the expression "indefinite perfection." For the author of *The Genius of Christianity*, who was also a champion of the free press, this twofold profession of faith added a measure of coherence, at least, to a life suspended between two times.

THE HISTORIES OF FRANCE

To grasp the revolution, histories of France drawn up over the nineteenth century adopted, to varying degrees, a form of Kairos. They drew an analogy between the revolution and the Incarnation, nothing that both represented key moments that revealed not just the entirety of the past but what lay ahead for France. It had happened; it could not happen again—we find ourselves in the *already*. Still, it had been interrupted, missed, derailed (by the Terror), and so it remained incomplete—all was not yet realized. Partisans of the Revolutions of 1830 and 1848, and of the Commune all came to believe that the promise of their movement will come to fruition in a transitional, committed time—and that history itself will end with a sort of Parousia. This is that time.

In 1869, when he comes to write the preface to his *History of France*, Jules Michelet looks back over the book: "The work of forty years or so was conceived out of a single moment, the lightning of July. In those memorable days, a great light suffused things, and I saw France."[69] Surely he is telling us that the task to which he has devoted forty years of his life was inspired by a mystical experience! That "lightning" of the July Revolution revealed France to him, much as Christ revealed himself to John in the first lines of Revelation. Writing becomes a way of bearing witness to what he had seen. Yes, 1830 is only a sequel to 1789, yet it succeeds, and the creation of a constitutional monarchy, with minimal resistance, remedies the broken promises of 1789. The success is such that in the ensuing years the victors, principally the historians of liberal stripe, come to believe that history has ended. That conviction means that the events of 1848 leave some—Guizot, Augustin Thierry—glassy-eyed. But surely, they think, the Parousia had occurred in 1830! This has been recorded in the one and only time, chronos. Roland Barthes pushes this insight to its extreme. For Michelet, he thinks, the French Revolution "fulfills time," meaning that anything after that could be experienced as "reprieved from History." So it is experienced in that deferral. Michelet is, according to Barthes, "a Republican only in History," yet he manages to "make the nineteenth century enter into that trial of time only as an Apocalypse."[70]

✳ ✳ ✳

While Krisis and Kairos enjoyed important renewals—the former because history was cast as alpha and omega, the latter because the revolution resembled Christly Kairos—one should also speak of their minor renewals, which were often nearly invisible. Briefly, these rendered it more flexible, better suited to grasping how human beings functioned; they enriched chronos time by "humanizing" it. Bossuet was at pains to distinguish between two levels of human action: the "particular causes" that engendered intentions and the "secret decrees of Divine Providence" that determined the real outcome of action. As a result, "every event is unexpected if we perceive only its specific causes; and yet the world goes forward in a foreordained sequence."[71] At the tiller is kairos time, as it must be, but clandestinely; such is the fee Bossuet must forfeit to preserve—active, presiding—the Christian order of time. Hegel, writing less than two hundred years later, offers a different answer to the same question. "The cunning of Reason" is his name for the gap between the universal and the particular, the actualization of the Idea and the individual action, but in the end everything takes place in accordance with the plan shaped by History, conceived as the true doctrine of Salvation.[72]

The great man, object of much scrutiny and celebration in the nineteenth century, could also serve as the vector of kairos time. So it was with Napoléon, he claimed, born of himself and always living in advance of himself. When Hegel caught sight of him crossing Jena on horseback in 1806, he recognized "the world-soul," a moment when the Spirit was unfolded. Usually seen as ahead of his time, the great man changes the course of ordinary time. He may sometimes labor to fit into that time, and indeed his historic mission is to transform it, generally by accelerating it.[73] By acting as the leading wedge of chronos time, he served as the bearer of a certain kairos.

FROM KRISIS TO CRISIS

Krisis was going through even more important changes. The old connection with medicine was revived: krisis as crisis, a simple crisis, one might almost say. As employed in Hippocratic texts, *crisis* refers to a change, which takes us back to the beginning of this study. One spoke of a crisis when an illness worsened, weakened, underwent a change to a different illness, or ended for good or ill.[74] The Hippocratic crisis belongs to a larger cycle in chronos time, which differs from that Krisis linked to the Final Judgment, the exit from time. Three definitions of the word are found in the *Grand Larousse du XIXe siècle*: a medical meaning, a metaphorical meaning conveying an "uncertain situation," and a new meaning. That third definition, referring to a commercial crisis, cited *On Commercial Crises and Their Periodic Occurrence in France, England, and the United States* (1862), a work in which Clément Juglar offers the first analysis of cyclical crises: "Crises, like illnesses, appear to occur in every society dominated by commerce and industry. We may foresee them, we may mitigate them, we may build limited defenses against them and facilitate a recovery from them, but up to the present no one has been able, in spite of the most varied connivances, to stop them. We find ourselves incapable of offering a solution where others have had so little success, and after all, the natural evolution of a crisis restores balance and lays a solid foundation for fearless enterprises to come."[75]

Crisis, according to this optimistic, liberal view, is neither unusual nor deadly. One could even call it normal, with a regular, observable pattern. Once it has been relieved of its apocalyptic associations, it recurs as a basic element of chronos time. That element is one of four—prosperity then crisis, depression then recovery—that make up the ten-year cycle to which Juglar gave his name. As the new time of economics equips itself with its own key dates and periods, crisis becomes part of that. Yet as devoted to cyclical time as he could be, Juglar never forsook linear time; he felt that the time of economics functioned cumulatively, perpetually offering a sunnier prospect. His was a chronos time with a direction.

As the decades swept by, economists and then historians who studied both economic and social questions developed and articulated this approach, adding long cycles—very long cycles—alongside Juglar's shorter cycles. The study of crisis, which belonged fully to chronos time, remains a way to grasp and manage events. Both illnesses and crises follow standard patterns, and just as a doctor can use symptoms to frame a diagnosis and a prognosis, so an economist can use initial conditions to predict how a crisis will develop. I must point out that as a science of crisis grows up, progressing from the visible to the invisible, the briefest to the longest (which ends up almost motionless), room for any sort of intervention in the "critical" event on the part of kairos time diminishes. This is truest of *longue durée* history, serial history, and structural history, all of which downplay chance events and highlight repetition. The historian Ernest Labrousse was to conclude that the structure of an economy determines its crises.[76]

As reflections on crisis acquired true profundity, their textbook example, throughout the nineteenth century and much of the twentieth, was the French Revolution. As we have just conveyed, the revolution could be interpreted in radically different ways, at times as a modern embodiment of the Christly Kairos, and at other times as a forerunner of the Judgment Day. The champions of History, guardians of chronos time and no other, took a very different tack: they set out to prove that the revolution had been swept in and swept along by ordinary time, as clouds bring storms, without the need of any other time. The stakes were high, as this will determine whether History can justly lay claim to being a science, can in fact state with authority what was and was not true. Since the concept of crisis had been considerably refined, particularly since the crisis of 1929, it might answer the need. We return here to Labrousse, because of the program he embarked on to grasp the French Revolution through an ambitious analysis of crises that theorized the ancien régime–type crisis or the "old-fashioned" crisis. He thought of the revolution as the intersection of several crises—an old-fashioned crisis (the shortage of grain that occurred in 1789) paired with an "abnormal" or "intercyclic" recession that overlapped with the reign of Louis XVI, all of which took place during the century's "long wave" of increased wealth among rentiers and merchants.[77] He concluded that it was "the economic situation that caused the revolutionary situation."[78] This revolution is no apocalypse, we should note; instead, its roots are sought at a deeper and more explanatory level, where everything is a matter of rhythms, which vary in character as their depths are plumbed and sometimes end up at variance with one another.

In the end, crisis comes in many forms, each with a distinctive rhythm and temporality, in spite of interferences and overlaps. The result is a truly geologic representation of crisis, since there is no more a single crisis than there is a single time. Doctors, historians, and economists all seek clarity, and just as the first makes calculations and imposes order, the latter two are obliged to divide up crisis, taming it by parceling it into a range of times, each of them a chronos time. As the study of crisis becomes fully ramified, kairos time is shrunk almost to zero; this is true even of revolutions, no matter how emblematic and puzzling such seminal events may be. The ancient alliance of Kairos and Krisis has so devolved that, in an astounding and nearly paradoxical turn of events, every species of kairos time is under siege by krisis, itself a crisis fully internalized by chronos time. After a long partnership, one might say, Krisis turned on Kairos, so as to return to the Greek fold.

Modern historiography, fancying itself ever more scientific, will reduce kairos time to insignificance. It turns human events into statistics, generates series, calculates indices, charts curves—no longer studying great men but crowds, its subjects quite nameless. In his role as mathematician, Condorcet anticipated a gradual transformation of what was blindly referred to as chance into a set of probabilities. Presumably future chronos time will undergo an analogous disciplining. As tools developed to assist with decision making, forecasts and projections served to systematize this trend, coming together for quite some time under the banner of futurology. Companions of the modern regime of historicity in its march toward the future, such systems and specialties strengthened the absolute grip of chronos time, a time without rivals, a time complete in itself, the sole time of the past, present, and future.

THE CASE OF ERNEST RENAN

As chronos time expands, it assumes an active role, becoming the unique actor. Ernest Renan (1823–1892) not only witnessed this change, he hastened it.[79] The former seminarian often alludes to "the incalculable series of centuries" and "the infinity of duration." Within the modern regime of historicity, he adopted a strong position, declaring becoming the great law. There will be no further talk of the age of the Earth or the time of the end, whereas the end of time will occur, but millions, billions of years in the future. "Time," he writes, "seems to me more and more the universal factor, the great coefficient of the eternal becoming." Understood in terms of becoming and refined by progress, Chronos is the mainspring that explains the universe, "driving everything into life, a life ever more complex."[80] So committed is Renan to this new gospel that he reformulates all of the natural sciences and the humanities along its lines. But as unremitting and eloquent as is his advocacy of chronos time, he does not entirely renounce kairos—the author of *The Future of Science* is also the author of *The Life of Jesus*.[81] While the blazon of chronos hangs over the religion of science, pure kairos saturates the religion of Jesus. Renan's twofold profession of faith casts him as a liminal figure. The same may be said of Chateaubriand, despite differences.

APOTHEOSIZED HUMANITY

What does progress mean to Renan? At the most general level, everything on Earth "inclines toward progress"; this is "an advance . . . where everything links together, where the basic cause of every moment is the preceding moment." Such a "regular development," much like the growth of an embryo, encouraged "the slow fabrication of humanity," amounting to the advance toward consciousness.[82] Progress also occurs on another level, one more strictly historical, as its Hegelian reading makes it the moment when humanity "began to understand and reflect upon itself" for the first time. The French Revolution marked "the first attempt of humanity to take the reins in its own hands and to drive itself." To speak as Michelet did in his translation of Vico, many agreed that humanity was acting as its own Prometheus: human beings fashioned both the world and historical time. Renan declares, "Right is the progress of humanity; there is no right in opposition to this progress, and, *vice versâ*, progress is sufficient to legitimize everything. Whatever serves to advance the work of God is permissible." With the future comes understanding of all of the development that has come before. The Incarnation, to a Christian, is the vantage point from which all is revealed; revelation, to Renan, lies in the future, in that moment when humanity achieves a full awareness of itself: "The aim of humanity is . . . that perfection should be made flesh."[83] Such will be the Parousia. No wonder the church condemned Renan as a dangerous heretic, something like the Antichrist.

Humanity will one day give up an existence *in fieri* (in becoming), will once and for all be rather than become, and on that day, as Renan drives home in his "Letter to Marcellin Berthelot" (1863), humanity will be a perfect God. Ever since Paul, Christians had conceived of a "plenitude" investing time from the moment of the Incarnation. Now that will come only in the future; it will in fact be the Future. Here is the telos, a destination offering the universe its reason for existing. Thus Renan reprises and alters (or derails) the principal paradigm of Christianity. And here he breaks decisively with Christianity. By prioritizing the extension and the forward motion of chronos time, nothing but chronos, one ensures that kairos plays a part only at the end, when humanity achieves fullest realization and, experiencing a sort of chronological apocalypse devoid of all drama, becomes God. Waiting for Godhood, one might say, the God in question is (already) something like "ideal," and he will (some time) be something like "reality." Whether one is inserting God-Humanity into chronos time or reducing God to chronos time, there is something of Joachim of Fiore here, seven hundred years later. For Joachim temporalized the Trinity by distinguishing the gospel of the Father from those of the Son and the Holy Spirit—he believed that the last would begin in the near future and would serve as the eternal gospel.[84] Similarly, Renan's future-oriented religion could be called an eternal gospel *in fieri*—and its completion will be millions of years in the making. The beginning, according to Joachim, will come in 1260.

Advances do not always happen peacefully; they are marked by halts, tumbles, and retreats, all the wars, defeats, and revolutions that beset the future, which appears to grow more distant. Such is the experience of Renan in 1870 and 1871. Though he tosses between despair and exaltation, his faith in the future sustains him, at times to a fault. In his *Philosophical Dialogues* he offers a self-portrait, painting himself as a divine fool named Theoctistes, "founder of God." Compared to the fantasmagorias confabulated by this fellow, the transhumanists of Silicon Valley come off as a bunch of pleasant, somewhat fearful interns. In a series of fragments jotted down in May 1871, he sketches something beyond humanity as it is, since that entity seems unlikely to muster a reign of reason. "Science will create an omniscient, omnipotent being. A learned body, master of the world, armed with potent weapons." Also: "Era when science eliminates humans and animals and replaces them, much as fats in nature are replaced by something better."[85] The future has retreated, possibly by millions of years, but it will come. The transhumanists of our day, who see things differently, want the future in the present. The time of the transformed, improved human being is now. Renan, by contrast, could not imagine an acquaintance with the future, even for a moment. It lay far further away than tomorrow. While the transhumanists draw the future into the present, Renan works from a distant future to shine a relativizing light onto the present (and its maladies). The former set the future within a presentist context, while the latter stretches the modern regime of historicity as far as it will go.[86] The catalyst for both, however, was a time of crisis regarding the future, meaning the present.

THE JESUS KAIROS

Renan's image of an apotheosized Chronos disconnected from the Christian regime did not begin to exhaust his thinking about religion and time. Never in his life does he offer a single, unequivocal thought, inclining always to duality and ambiguity. Devout though he is in his commitment to Chronos, he cannot renounce kairos completely. He announces in *The Future of Science* a plan to blow up the "barrage" of moribund Christianity, but in *The Life of Jesus* he sets out to show that now more than ever Jesus has a future. This will mean, first of all, a break with theology, scholasticism, the papacy—everything that had long smothered the original spark. We have already examined the central part played by reformatio, an instrument taken up by many earlier Christians intent on reclaiming that originary truth.

If he is to offer an exegesis and bring about a reform, Renan will do it through modern science, meaning philology and a certain historical psychology—miracles and revelations will be excluded from the outset. Finding the historical Jesus, what Renan calls the "fact" of Jesus, can be done by relying largely on the Gospels to get at the figure who predated the Gospels. Finding the "spontaneity" of Jesus that had not yet been distorted by the "legend," including the betrayals of disciples who misunderstood him, will mean setting aside the font of dogma to which he was quickly reduced.[87] To get at the true spirit, one had to bring the most exacting scrutiny to the text, though even better was working at a remove from the text, while drawing on it. The outcome is a Jesus both incomparable and unsurpassable.[88] The creator of a "heaven of pure souls," he founded "a universal and eternal religion." And Renan explains, "Men did not become his disciples by believing this thing or that thing, but in being attached to his person and loving him." Rather than frame a dogma or fashion a symbol, Jesus brought a new spirit into the world. "The least Christian men were, on the one hand, the doctors of the Greek Church . . . and, on the other, the scholastics of the Latin Middle Ages. . . . To follow Jesus in expectation of the kingdom of God, was all that at first was implied by being Christian. . . . Jesus gave religion to humanity, as Socrates gave it philosophy, and Aristotle science."[89]

For Renan the time occupied by Jesus is his own, yet even as he dwells in it he surpasses it. (We managed to rid ourselves of him, yet he is infinitely more present today than he ever was during his lifetime.) So much so that ultimately he both belongs to chronos time (like Socrates and Aristotle) and eludes it, much as he eludes the limits of Christian Kairos. Suddenly and inexplicably present, he is that kernel ever ready to spring back to life, always available—there is no question of having "surpassed" him. It was in his inaugural lecture at the Collège de France that Renan defined Jesus as a man (definitely) who was both "incomparable" and "unsurpassable," words that cost him his professorship and won him considerable renown.

The Life of Jesus evinces a dual necessity: rupture (or departure) and faithfulness. The only way Renan can be truly, deeply faithful to his vocation, he sees, is to break things off. "The idea that in abandoning the Church I should remain faithful to Jesus got hold upon me, and if I could have brought myself to believe in apparitions I should certainly have seen Jesus saying to me: 'Abandon Me to become My disciple.'"[90] The result is the religion of Jesus on one side, a sort of pure love inscribed in kairos time (that cannot be measured), and on the other the religion of humanity, which applies science and the (slow) passage of chronos time to achieve the fullest awareness of self. The latter echoes Condorcet's paradigm, but with the difference that the progressions of reason are set in a temporal horizon. Such a procedure is unthinkable for the former, the religion of (Renan's) Jesus, as it resists situation in a place or time. Jesus may beckon anyone to follow him, at any moment. "His worship will constantly renew its youth; the tale of his life will cause ceaseless tears."[91]

Always between two extremes but never occupying the happy medium, Renan serves as our compass as we trace the crisscrossing paths of chronos time and kairos time. Chronos time had won him over, in spite of his deep attachment to an unchanging present free of all time. That kairos time affects only private life off limits to the state, whereas public life is wholly regulated by chronos time. "Religion must become wholly free, something about which the State has nothing to say."[92] Such sentiments—his advocacy of the separation of church and state and his defense of secularism—won him laurels from the Third Republic. An example might be the dedication in 1903 of a statue erected in Renan's honor in Tréguier, his birthplace; officiating at this event was the new president of the Conseil d'État, Émile Combes. Two years later, the law guaranteeing the separation of church and state was enacted.

A SHAKEN, DISPUTED CHRONOS

Viewed in 1900, the empire of Chronos comprised, on one side, a world time that proceeded a varying speeds and, on the other, the absolute time Newton defined as "sensorium Dei." When the Christian regime falls apart, absolute time faces a new challenge from within physics, in a test case involving simultaneity. In its practical form, the puzzle is known as the synchronization of clocks, and a great deal rides on the outcome. This is because it is situated at the intersection of power and various intellectual specializations. At play are physics, technologies, trade, and colonial and imperialist rivalries.

SYNCHRONIZING THE CLOCKS

In 1889, at Paris's Pavillon de Breteuil, the burial of a standard meter and kilogram makes them official. Just as science is the measure of all things, the metric system is its prophet. Next on the list is time. As a first attempt to synchronize clocks, a telegraph cable is run from the mother clock in Paris's observatory. The idea is to extend the network from one clock to the next until the entire nation is covered, then the world. It does not quite work out. As synchronization gains ground, railroads play the leading role, particularly in the wide open spaces of the United States and Canada. In a statement to the American Metrological Society, William Allen says, "Railroad trains are the great educators and monitors of the people in teaching and maintaining exact time."[93] Next comes the laying of the great transoceanic cables linking and synchronizing the continents, making possible precise longitudinal calculations and improved maps. When European time, in its electrical form, arrives near Bahia, Emperor Don Pedro II of Brazil goes to salute it. The nexus lies in Paris's Bureau of Longitudes, with director Henri Poincaré playing the leading role in the creation of a network that embraces the nation, France's global empire, and finally the world. Because American and British networks also expand during this period, pressure mounts to select a prime meridian. Which? Since the location is purely conventional, any longitude would do. When the International Meridian Conference is convened in Washington in 1884, France's representatives make a strong case for the meridian of Paris, but they lack support and must give way to the partisans of Greenwich as prime meridian. France loses and Britain wins the battle over the world reference time, becoming master of world time. Germany proves quite willing to accept Greenwich, and in a speech given to the Reichstag in 1891, former field marshal Helmuth Graf von Moltke lauds the benefits synchronization provides for trains, notably for the rapid mobilization of troops.

Because it formalizes the descent of kairos time into chronos time as the "pivot" of universal time, the victory of the Christian regime is now legible in the tablets of time in the form of the *Anno Domini* dating system. The "pivot" of world time (Universal Time) now appears at Greenwich, selected as the prime meridian in 1884. The world has been synchronized—no one can now speak of coordinating clocks as an innocent pastime. Indeed, one of the consequences of this innovation is far from trivial: Albert Einstein's theory of relativity, first announced in 1905. When he conceived of a system for synchronizing clocks, it "reduced time to procedural synchronicity, tying clocks together by electromagnetic signals."[94] The theory of relativity extinguished all reference time, every central clock. Newton's absolute time was dead.[95] Likewise, Henri Poincaré (1845–1912) views simultaneity as a "convention." Peter Galison has written, "Poincaré's was a hopeful modernism of relations graspable by us, without God, without Platonic forms, and . . . without Kantian things-in-themselves."[96] Thinking about simultaneity led Poincaré, like Einstein, to the idea that time is not an absolute truth, but a convention. Time had been altered, jolting physics, philosophy, technology, even history. Simultaneity had belonged to God's eternity; replaced by "a convention given through machines," it is tumbled from its "metaphysical pedestal."[97]

As we have seen, one alteration triggered the transition from the Christian regime to the modern regime, even as it sundered all relations between the two. Here Chronos takes unique control, casting off the scissoring blades of the time of the end and the end of times even as it reclaims and recycles Krisis and Kairos, two great concepts, not to mention reformatio/reformation. And progress fuels the process in which it serves as the grand finale. All this and History too, the vessel into which the various factors flow, even as it assumes a new meaning that permits it to unite these different elements, offering a unique rubric and making sense of things. In our modern regime, the odyssey is undertaken not by the city of men but by time and History; human beings are told to follow, to outstrip the leaders if they can. In a familiar metaphor, History is the train on which we all have reservations, destined to hurl us into the future. For the entirety of the twentieth century, the watchwords will be *catch up*, *surpass*, *reform*, *modernize*, and *develop*. In 1929, a "watershed" year, Stalin writes, "We are marching at top speed toward industrialization and socialism, leaving behind our 'Russian,' secular backwardness."[98] Backwardness gets left behind. Mao Zedong will echo him thirty years later, when he launches the Great Leap Forward—and the "collateral damage" will be the same. India will gain independence, and under Nehru it will set out to modernize, more than once.

DOUBTS REGARDING THE MODERN REGIME OF HISTORICITY

In addition to those who stood up to modern times and those who hoped to revive a hopelessly shattered Christian regime, we find, at the very heart of the modern regime, malcontents. An event that flushed some out was what Lucien Febvre called the "great drama of relativity." Yet we have noted that synchronization can also strengthen the grip of Chronos on world time. In spite of everything, these are no longer simple queries regarding Chronos; these questions throw the whole enterprise into doubt.

There had been difficulties, and already the new relationship among Chronos, kairos, and krisis had suffered. Krisis, driven by Chronos, had found itself at the heart of chronic crises endemic to societal processes, much like the health crises that afflict individuals. When such crises are protracted, Chronos can be contaminated, leading to stoppages, breakdowns—Chronos becomes a time of unremitting crisis. This was the outcome of the crisis of 1929, a chronic state of crisis that ended only when a novel type of crisis was unleashed. The war to which I refer also reactivated apocalyptic scenarios and gave new life to that old instance of Krisis, the Final Judgment.

As for Kairos, it learns little from modern time and its future-oriented process; it assumes the form of contingency, which in its purest form, a series of random events, eradicates all sense of history.[99] It is only, to cite Macbeth's famous words on life, "a tale told by an idiot, full of sound and fury, signifying nothing." In *Ulysses* (1922) James Joyce recasts the thought, stating, "History . . . is a nightmare from which I am trying to awake." As for the discipline of history, there are those who feel that what they call a "history of battles"—or a history of events—sacrifices all hope of understanding, opting instead for the fun of surprises, distractions. Such a history was subjected to a critique by the first generation of *Annales* historians.

More serious problems arose as real-world assessments of progress put the modern regime of historicity, which had adopted progress as its motor and destination, to the test. At that moment what had been a religion of progress was reduced to a myth.[100] The ancient image of regeneration (*regeneratio*) was brought out of storage after the Franco-Prussian War of 1870, though the form had been emptied of all content. Various groups spoke up to glorify war, presenting it as the means to a rebirth, a bloody baptism that will wash away the apathy of modern society and succor the spirit of sacrifice. Nationalists and militarists everywhere joined voices to acknowledge a necessary evil, as regeneration came to look much like a mystical vision of progress. After a brief exposure to the War of 1870, Frederic Nietzsche declared during the 1880s, "Learned and therefore weak, the Europeans of today are in need not only of wars, but bigger, more terrible wars."[101] An occasional barbarous interlude is needed if civilization is to survive. That old saw.

Nietzsche stood apart. One might easily assign him a distinguished place among the most radical critics of the modern regime of historicity, but here I shall limit myself to pointing out what set him apart from the critics we might call traditionalists or simply reactionaries.

This herald of the coming of a superman combines fierce opposition to Christianity (God is dead) with a rejection of modernity. One might say that Nietzsche rejects modernity twice, inasmuch as the world, despite its pretensions to modernity, remains deeply steeped in Christian values. Does it really not know, or is it merely pretending not to know, that God is dead? Yet while Nietzsche deeply despised "imperialistic and industrial Europe, mass society, faith in progress, liberalism, democracy, humanitarianism and egalitarianism in all their ancient and modern forms, from Christianity to socialism," he refused to accept decadence and nihilism, placing his faith instead in regeneration—just like his prophet Zarathustra.[102] He is intent on a tragic encounter with "The Crucified One," and for that he equips himself with the entire Christian apocalyptic toolkit. If, as he believes, the modern world has not shaken off the Middle Ages, then he has no choice but to enter the lists armed with Christianity's foundational documents, suitably refashioned; he will present a countergospel. If he is, though, to bring about a true "transmutation" of values, if he is to slice history in two, he will need to start from the beginning. The only tactic suitable to the attack appears to be that of doubling the foe.

"THE CORPSE OF THE GOD OF PROGRESS"

What doubts had arisen about progress after 1870 were amplified and radicalized by the enormous bloodshed and technological breakthroughs of World War I. Any thought of regeneration was sidelined as the outbreak of hostilities shifted all thinking to a special version of apocalypse: stunted and wholly negative, it had shed its final rebirth. This is apocalypse as cataclysm ending in the extinction of humanity.[103] A sole figure, Léon Bloy, held out against this revision. He knew the Bible, knew that rather than an apocalypse the war amounted to a prelude. He entitled the journal in which he recounted the years 1914 and 1915 *On the Threshold of the Apocalypse*. His final entry for 1915 reads, "I await the Cossacks and the Holy Spirit." Expiation will come, but it has only just begun.

The 1920s and 1930s saw the application, more or less pointed, of apocalyptic tropes to current and recent events, while a plethora of questions was raised about the modern regime. What became of chronos once it was deprived of the motor of progress? Paul Valéry's prosopopeia, published in 1919, soon won fame: "We modern civilizations have learned to recognize that we are mortal like the others.... *Elam, Niniveh, Babylon* were vague and splendid names.... *Lusitania* is a lovely name. And now we see that the abyss of history is deep enough to bury all the world."[104] The suicidal clash of the great powers offered a view of global shipwreck, an end of history. Buffon had encountered a different sort of abyss, that of the time of Nature; here is the abyss of History, of the time of History, where beautiful vague names lie scattered about. Condorcet's great hopes for reason no longer hold. By 1937 Lucien Febvre was bluntly speaking of the "corpse of the god of progress" that had enriched dictatorships, adding, "The sudden collapse of a power as revered as this—no other drama in our lives compares."[105] *Power, revered, drama*: strong words. Those a bit younger than Febvre, such as Henri-Irénée Marrou, had been "born to self-awareness and the life of the spirit immediately after the butchery of the First World War." That conflict "had forever dispelled an illusion—a comfortable and ingenuous belief in a linear, continuous progress which vindicated Western civilization as the last stage of evolution reached by humanity."[106]

When De Martino assembled a compilation of apocalyptic traits as part of his great unfinished study of cultural apocalypses, he seems to have included only negative materials, on the "crisis" of the West, the "crisis" of progress, the "death" of the West. Every one of these apocalypses lacks an *eschaton*.[107] Borne on chronos time, they lack any connection—at least in principle—to kairos. De Martino traces the roots of the crisis notable for amassing "a distinctive weight during the period surrounding the period stretching from the 1920s to the 1950s" to the second half of the nineteenth century. He links the two postwar periods, noting,

> The "nausea" of Sartre, the "absurd" of Camus, the "sickness of objects" of Moravia, and the dramas of Beckett are more than a reflection of the apocalyptic atmosphere of our era, since the "success" of these literary works shows that they resonate with people's hearts, that the sensibility they reflect is widely shared. On a different cultural level, Euro-American science fiction, which regularly offers

obscure prophecies regarding society and predicts the degeneration and extinction of humanity and its world . . . in turn proves that the theme of an *eschaton*-free apocalypse now pervades our world, relying on all of the power of mass communication at our disposal.[108]

Here is an illuminating approach to highlighting an apocalyptic backdrop as well as the ways apocalypse has been worked into many cultural productions. The approach allows us to gauge the persistence of these themes; they come readily to hand when modern time triggers discomfort, doubt, and anxiety.

Roquentin, the protagonist of Jean-Paul Sartre's *Nausea* (1938), a story without any sort of apocalypse, abruptly realizes that only the present exists—there is neither past nor future, absolutely none. Beyond "I exist," there is nothing. And likewise, from the first sentence of *The Stranger* (1942), Albert Camus gives the reader a man who is a "stranger" to ordinary time—he knows only the present. "Maman died today. Or yesterday maybe, I don't know. I got a telegram from the home: 'Mother deceased. Funeral tomorrow. Faithfully yours.' That doesn't mean anything. Maybe it was yesterday."[109] An inability to orient himself in time—he does not even know his mother's age—will play a part in his final condemnation. There is no doubt that he murdered an Arab for no reason, but above all he is an asocial being: a complete stranger. For him, as for Roquentin, it is not so much that time is "off the rails" as it is frozen, halted.

A SINGULAR KAIROS

The theses Walter Benjamin sets out in "On the Concept of History" (1940) belong to this apocalyptic aura, and yet he occupies a quite singular position, that of a Marxist critic of progress. For him the modern regime, with its linear, "homogeneous, empty time" (this is the absolute time of Newtonian physics), leads straight to disaster, hence his fierce attack on it. But he embraces neither a hypothetical superman nor the perspective of a negative apocalypse nor a vague nor viscous present of the sort Roquentin experiences in *Nausea*. Quite the contrary: he searches for a way to open the future and hasten emancipation by reintroducing kairos to chronos time.[110] But which kairos? He offers an alternative to the revolutions Marx compared to locomotives pulling the train of history, the very opposite: "Perhaps revolutions are an attempt by the passengers on this train—namely, the human race—to activate the emergency brake."[111] Revolutions become the things that halt the race to the abyss. Instead of the moment of the tabula rasa and of acceleration, Benjamin seeks that stunning conjunction of a present moment and a past moment. The combination fosters a dynamic connection between the present and the past and a living history at odds with the positivists who would make history a science of the (dead) past.

Such an arrangement permits the (transfigured) future to remain—or to truly become—the guiding category, while emphasizing the contemporaneity of the noncontemporaneous. It is then, as a certain present moment encounters a certain past moment and a recollection comes into being, that revolutionaries discover their potential and their power for making history. This is a messianic time not because a messiah is expected but because "splinters of messianic time" pierce the time. In sum, the coming revolution involves neither Kairos nor Krisis (note the capital letters) but a constellation of *kairoi* both induced and snatched on the fly: "Every second was the small gateway in time through which the Messiah might enter."[112] Open to these *kairoi*, a revived Chronos is not empty, homogeneous, or linear; it comprises messianic bursts or flashes (*Jetztzeit*) and is essentially discontinuous.[113]

Benjamin's hastily drawn up theses, completed shortly before he killed himself, appeared in print only after the war and left nary a ripple until the 1960s, the very moment when the modern regime of historicity was subject to radical reevaluation. In the interim, the regime was routinely praised (due to rapid technological advances and the triumph of Marxism), challenged, torn down; since the conclusion of World War II it had been impossible to believe in human progress. The "firm and sure" step that Condorcet announced—or planned to announce, on the brink of his demise—had ended, for Europe at least. Chronos lay in pieces, and two names came to mark that moment: Auschwitz and Hiroshima.

6

CHRONOS DESTITUTED, CHRONOS RESTORED

WHAT BECAME of Chronos in the latter half of the twentieth century and the beginning of the twenty-first? What new economy of time commenced with Auschwitz and Hiroshima, those names heavy with symbolism? And what of two concepts we have traced, kairos and krisis (with and without capital letters), from their unprecedented, potent mobilization by the early Christians, those zealous readers of the Bible? How have they fared? After dominating Chronos for as long as the Christian regime of historicity existed, how did they end up as the subordinates of that same Chronos, now triumphant? How have they managed to linger like phantoms on the margins—and not just the margins—of the Western world's temporal horizon, agents of a truncated apocalypse? Have their roles changed over the course of this new period, nearly eighty years old now? Have they been assigned an active role? Are they somehow once again weaving the present?

The previous chapter ended with the challenges faced by Chronos, which ranged from the modern regime of historicity and its critique of progress, of the illusions or the myth of progress, to what De Martino called "an apocalyptic atmosphere," which for him involved only negative apocalypses. The "firm and sure step" of humanity that Condorcet anticipated had already been shaken before World War II, but by the end of the conflict it has lost any connection to reality. What doubts had existed regarding progress are now radicalized, and Chronos is split between a halted time that cannot advance and a time of pure acceleration, moving ever faster until it is outlawed. This time never ceases to contract, much like the ass's skin in Balzac's novel, until it has nearly vanished.

A NEW SPLIT WITHIN CHRONOS

Since the Greeks first fashioned the nets that separated time and eternity, on the one hand, and chronos and kairos, on the other, that split has characterized the Western tradition—including elusive Chronos. This was the principle of the first mesh designed to trap Chronos, before the Christian regime set about weaving the two aspects of time together, well before Chronos broke free and forged its empire. In the next installment, the newer net I call the modern regime of historicity gradually lost its hold, until it had no hold at all. The rents left in the netting after World War II made any repairs challenging. At that time, a new split appeared, its consequences lingering over several decades. How time is experienced changes gradually, as we have found over and over, and there is nothing universal about those changes. Only after a time can an adjustment or a challenge to such changes arise, and that only once we appreciate what has occurred.

After the Nuremberg trials (1945–1946), the modern regime of historicity was given new life. The trials, and the punishment of an array of leading Nazi criminals, set chronos time marching again into the future—or at least that was the hope. As the first significant instance of transitional justice, it had accomplished something. Germany "year zero" could now give birth to a new nation—two, in fact, one democratic and the other socialist. Digging out of the ruins, Western Europe rebuilt and modernized quickly; the Marshall Plan was meant to keep it in the free-world camp, while the Cold War enlisted the two blocs in a protracted contest over who would control the future. With Chronos and progress once again marching in lockstep, a freshly mounted modern regime of historicity would soon be gaily galloping. Working alchemists' magic were Western-style modernization and the development of postcolonial states. Setting the tempo and handing out loans was the United States of America.

Few then noted a time issuing from Auschwitz. We might call it halted, a past that went nowhere, a prolonged present. This is the time that escapes all statutes of limitations. During the Nuremberg trials, the crime of extermination becomes the crime of genocide and a crime against humanity.[1] The existence of crimes against humanity creates a temporality until then unheard of, a time that does not advance—this is explicit, as there is no statute of limitations for the crime committed. Judicial time, which typically limits the period within which litigants may lodge a suit, does not advance. In its suspended state, it must not advance so long as the accused shall live. This intrinsic temporal discord has confronted cases of crimes against humanity (and complicity in crimes against humanity) from the trial of Adolf Eichmann, held in 1961 in Jerusalem, to that of Maurice Papon, held in 1997 and 1998 in France. There was no choice but to get used to that discord.[2]

THE ATOMIC BOMB

What was the impact on Chronos of the atomic bombs dropped on Hiroshima and Nagasaki on August 6 and 9, 1945, ending World War II? A headline in *Le Monde* read, "A Technological Breakthrough." Paul Langevin, a famous physician who played a part in the interwar peace movement, viewed the event as the opening of a new era: "It is impossible to overstate the significance, for mankind's future, of the appearance of the atomic bomb. This is actually something quite different from the invention of a new weapon that, awful in its efficacy, has hastened the end of a conflict burning up the planet for the last six years. The truth is that we are witnessing the beginning of a new era, an especially dramatic form of controlled transmutations."[3] In an editorial for the newspaper *Combat*, Albert Camus admitted to anxieties regarding the potential applications of scientific progress, yet he did not reject such applications in general: "Technological civilization has just reached its final degree of savagery. We will have to choose, in a relatively near future, between collective suicide and the intelligent use of scientific conquests."[4] He was prepared to bet on intelligent use.

Writing in the first issue of *Les temps modernes* (October 1, 1945), Jean-Paul Sartre pondered "the end of the war," which left "man naked and without illusions," having "at last understood that he has only himself to rely on." After all, "humanity had, one day, to come into possession of its death. . . . Here we are, back at the millennium. Each morning, we shall be on the eve of the end of time. . . . After the death of God, the death of man is now announced. . . . The community that has appointed itself guardian of the atom bomb stands above the realm of nature, being responsible now for its life and death." Two possible conclusions follow: "there is no longer any *human species*" or our "freedom is purer," since "if the whole of humanity continues to live, it will do so . . . because it will have decided to prolong its life."[5] The bomb drives us, definitively, out of nature. It finishes the process of dividing the time of Nature from that of human beings. We hear an echo of this in the editorial that appeared in the same issue of *Les temps modernes*: we write for today, for our contemporaries, burdened with this duty which is also liberty. "We refuse to view the world with future eyes."[6]

Emmanuel Mounier, founder of the magazine *Esprit*, directed fresh light on the situation in a series of lectures given between 1946 and 1948. These texts, brought together and published as *Studies in Personalist Sociology* (the original French title could be rendered as "The Minor Fright of the Twentieth Century"), look more original than they are. A well-informed Christian, Mounier agrees with Léon Bloy on the importance of distinguishing apocalypse from catastrophe, without being led to endorse Bloy's conclusions. Linking the bomb and the apocalypse strikes him as a nihilism of hopelessness: "The Apocalypse is now available to distract us from whatever measures of public health may be necessary to deal with the malady of Europe. . . . The guilty conscience of Europe is about to give itself the Apocalypse." Far better is to see in the instant of that explosion the end of "the immaturity of man. He became, indeed, within the limits of his range, the master of creation."[7] The trajectory begun with the Enlightenment had arrived at its terminus, for Mounier as for Sartre. This was *"mankind's exit from its self-incurred immaturity,"* to quote the phrase

Mounier alludes to, the famous opening of Kant's "What Is Enlightenment?"[8] With this new mastery went a duty, also without precedent. The future to which humanity had long been condemned was now its slave.

Speaking in 1956, the philosopher Karl Jaspers joins the discussion of the atomic bomb and mankind's future. He believes that when facing a grave threat to mankind, "this is no time to sleep," that "unless it undergoes a conversion, the life of mankind is over." In spite of a fondness for religious terminology, Jaspers never considers an apocalyptic outcome. The reasons are two: the current situation had its origins in technology, and "reason warns us against issuing fearful statements on inexorable catastrophes." He too is averse to "bringing on the apocalypse."[9]

That same year, another philosopher, Günther Anders, publishes a book in Munich entitled *The Obsolescence of Human Beings*. And while he does discuss the apocalypse, it is certainly not, pace Mounier, for lack of courage. Once the apocalypse is summoned, one is able to reflect on how it transforms the experience of time. By obliging us to dwell on the end of times, apocalypse turns humans into "the dead-in-waiting." Mounier spoke of humans as "masters of all creation" who were leaving behind their "immaturity," whereas Anders evokes "lords of the Apocalypse" who possess the power to "destroy one another." We are the first "to be mortal as a group, not merely as individuals"—a point made by Sartre. To think of this in temporal terms, we must give up the old adage, "What was, will be again" (Ecc. 1:9), or simply "What has been, has been" (there is no undoing what has occurred), in favor of "Nothing has been." After all, nothing will be left after a nuclear war.[10]

For Anders, the "lords" are "blind." He cites two complementary reasons: the faith in progress is first and more general, while the second, more specific, is the growing gap between "human beings and the world they have made." Faith in progress erases the idea of an end (in particular, our end), thereby blocking our view of the apocalypse: "Our lot must be the duty of suffering." Among the erasures that Anders cites is death, an event found nowhere in the United States, where the latest euphemism is suffering a *"change of residence."* As to being outpaced by our own handiwork, losing hope of "catching up with those devices that inched out ahead of us," progress moves too quickly (that acceleration again), and "the human body" falls back. Anders refers to the perpetually growing desynchronization as the "Promethean gap."[11]

One last consequence of faith in progress is a shift in the relations between humanity and its future. As Anders points out, citing the planned economies of the East, progress has become a "project." As for the West, was it not General De Gaulle who spoke of such planning as "an ardent duty"? We now picture the future as a "sort of space" within which the objectives of our plans are realized (or not, but that is another question). The future no longer "comes" to us; "it's we who make it." This has caused the future to shrink: "The day after tomorrow no longer belongs to the future." This implies the possibility of a break, a time without future. That break could happen tomorrow, the day after, or in the "seventh generation," all "the result of what we are doing today." Anders emphasizes, "The *persistence* we see in those consequences of what we do today means that today we have already arrived at the future, which pragmatically speaking means it is already *present*."[12]

Here was an insight that few shared, yet Anders drew from it a practical lesson. He called for a change in the relation between humanity and time, for adopting a "broader temporal horizon." To do that, we must "take hold of the most distant future events so as to synchronize them—since they are in fact occurring now—with our unique point of insertion into time, namely, this very instant. As they are the result of our present, they are very much happening now. And we are involved with them to the extent that they are happening now, since it is now that we are preparing them through our actions."[13] If we are to begin to shrink it, we must be aware of that unprecedented gap.

From that he draws the following conclusion: "From now on the future must not stand *before us*; we must capture it; it must be *with us*; it must become our present." And he adds: "This is no minor adjustment. We can only hope that the time remaining to us is sufficient to take on this task and bring it to a happy conclusion." A new net is needed, as we learn to master—Anders says "capture"—the coming chronos. We need only replace "atomic bomb" with "global warming" to appreciate the path that is opened, or that might have been opened, by Anders's broader temporal horizon, offering us the means of grasping our present moment, our time of no return. The adjustment to the atomic bomb happened more easily, in all likelihood, as there could be no doubt that the bomb was entirely of our own doing. The bomb belonged to the world's time, humanity's time, meaning the chronos time of the war, then of the Cold War, and of rapid technological advances. At the time we thought little of the long-term effects of radiation, even less of nuclear waste, two issues of real gravity today. The energy of tomorrow: such was the hope for abundant and inexpensive nuclear power, which was going to "improve humanity's standard of living," to adopt a phrase from Langevin. The De Gaulle era would see France make the most of its nuclear program (both military and civilian), vaunting its rapid advance toward the future.

CHANGES IN THE SEVENTIES

Then, in the 1970s, things change. Auschwitz time outstrips Nuremberg time; protests and other challenges to nuclear power appear. The philosopher Michel Serres explicitly links Hiroshima and the death camps. "The death camps were echoed by Nagasaki and Hiroshima, which were just as destructive of history and consciousness—in both cases in a radical way, by attacking the very roots of what makes us human—tearing apart not just historic time but the time frame of human evolution."[14] These words expand the temporal horizon, going beyond history's "torn" time to include the time of hominization, which is shaken to its core. Taking Anders and his "lords of the Apocalypse" as a starting point, Serres focuses on the science and what he sees as "scientific optimism." He writes, "We now know what is signified by mastering nature: it means making machines equivalent to it, creating parity between the natural and the artificial." We now make things on a planetary scale: he calls them "world-objects." So much so that "time no longer defines itself according to the successive rounds of the game, on the promises and risks involved in starting over, but according to the bleak wait for the only blow that is now possible. Time has no path, no definition: it has only an ending and a limit. Our history is a suspended inchoate."[15]

So, drawing on "Hiroshima's way," one becomes aware of a time that has halted, more or less, and of a history that has not ended but remains in suspension.

In 1982 Paul Crutzen and John Birks offered a forecast of nuclear winter, joining a growing number of scientists alarmed by the impact a massive nuclear war would have on Earth's atmosphere.[16] The modern era, brief as it was, and humanity's unique chronos time fall away under the impact of such reports, as once again the time of Nature—better, of planet Earth—takes hold. A new configuration appears, in which the future evades capture by the ever progressing time of history. The future is now "quantifiable, thanks to models and diagrams that convey the exponential increase of physico-chemical agents, such as temperature, carbon dioxide, nitrogen, etc."[17] While they stem from a range of backgrounds, the reflections noted here (I shall limit myself to three examples) share a sense of what is occurring, an anxiety, and a conviction that modern chronos time has failed; to repeat what Serres writes, there is no path, no definition. Anders calls for an enlightened adjustment to a broader temporal horizon, but how? It would involve nothing less than developing a new concept of Chronos structured by a new set of splits, even though such an innovation is neither needed nor wanted by the roaring technologies or the states locked in Cold War rivalries. As a result the modern regime of historicity, futurism and all, retains the title, wedded to acceleration, its main catalyst. Still, suspended time will be the rule, particularly in Europe, during the closing decades of the twentieth century—an apparent paradox. Here is a Chronos that might be called degraded, destituted, in which nearly all time is present time. The moment of presentism.

A DEGRADED, DESTITUTED CHRONOS: PRESENTISM

One text, more than any other, plunges us into the destitution of modern time. Samuel Beckett's *Waiting for Godot*, first performed in 1953, excelled *Nausea* and *The Stranger* in its extremity, attesting to the impoverishment of a time without past or future, a time that exists only as an unredeemable present. When the play's two "heroes," Vladimir and Estragon, discover that time is not advancing—"Time has stopped"—they anxiously set about finding out how to set it going again, by inventing pastimes. But exactly where have they come from? What are they doing in this lamentable state? We never find out. Their days pass by and never pass at all: Is that night coming on or the dawn breaking? Lost in time, lost in space, they do not know up from down. Are they where they were last night, was that yesterday anyway, has evening really come?

The only clue that act 2 differs from act 1 is Beckett's precise stage direction: "Next day. Same time. Same place." Yet the tree is described as leafless in act 1 and leafed in act 2, which is another absurdity. One at a time wants to leave, but neither moves. They barely remain upright, as if they have just disembarked after a long crossing. Forever scolding one another for their forgetfulness, there is only one thing they must not forget: they are waiting for Godot. And then he sends a boy to tell them that he will be coming tomorrow. Is it all a dream or a nightmare? Are there but two survivors of some late disaster? They need something to do, maybe, and it occurs to them a few times to hang themselves. But they decide not to—for the time being.

> VLADIMIR: We'll hang ourselves tomorrow. [*Pause.*] Unless Godot comes.
> ESTRAGON: And if he comes?
> VLADIMIR: We'll be saved.[18]

At a certain point, in the middle of their talk, there is this:

> All the dead voices.
> They make a noise like wings.
> Like leaves.
> Like ashes.
> Like leaves. . . .
> They murmur.[19]

Also:

> VLADIMIR: Where are all these corpses from?
> ESTRAGON: These skeletons. . . .
> VLADIMIR: A charnel-house! A charnel-house!
> ESTRAGON: You don't have to look.[20]

Yes, who is murmuring? Where do the dead voices, the ashes, the corpses come from? We cannot help hearing the voices of those so recently murdered, incinerated, exterminated.

A NEW PRESENTISM

In the aftermath of Auschwitz and Hiroshima, a reconsideration of the modern regime took place, and Chronos was subjected to what could be called an ethical destitution or degradation—a freezing of time, like a freeze frame. In the social sciences and the humanities, this retreat took the form of a rejection of evolutionism and a critique of leading functionalist theories, which are basically futuristic. Fernand Braudel, who had spent five years in a prisoner-of-war camp, devoted himself increasingly to long time spans and structural history—as he noted, events never meant much to him. In due course, the situation came to resemble an oxymoron: motionless history. The 1960s witnessed the triumph of structural anthropology when Claude Lévi-Strauss returned to France after sheltering in the United States. Synchrony dominates diachrony. Scholars turn their attention to language, the unconscious, systems, and in the meantime the subject fades from view. Soon enough Michel Foucault is announcing the death of mankind. If he acknowledges a connection to the structuralist label, something people in a wide range of disciplines have in common, it is that "one point in common" of trying to "oppose" a philosophy founded on the "affirmation of the 'primacy of the subject.'"[21] He will soon claim that the duty of the philosopher is "to diagnose the present."[22]

The most striking phenomenon is the rise of the present. Such a novel presentism differs markedly from the one that launched the present inquiry and has guided it since, as we investigate Chronos and its modulations between Kairos and Krisis. What, then, is this novelty, and what is its texture? We might begin by defining it in negative terms: the rise of the present takes the stage, rising an octave just as the future slips from the leading role assigned it by modern time. A retreat, and the present is first by default. A coming time rich in promise—"the American dream," "the Socialist paradise," "the

German miracle," "the thirty glorious years"—was our goal in that future-oriented and progress-borne time, which invited—and usually forced—us onward, the pace ever quickening, present and past bathed in its light. Its catchwords were accelerate, modernize, develop, overtake, catch up. For all its concessions, contestations, tumbles, futurism reigned supreme. Roughly speaking, it dominated between 1850 and 1960, by hook or by crook, including the political realm.

But the most glittering promises turned into nightmares, and after two world wars and a number of revolutions the image of scientific advances, technological progress, and the improvement of humanity advancing with linked arms was no longer conceivable. Beginning in 1970 or a bit later, a crisis of the future set in, soon identified as such: as the prospect seemed to close, the present expanded, as though Chronos abhorred a vacuum. Early on, this change was a Western phenomenon, as an independent India, a Maoist China, newly formed African states, and a portion of the Arab world believed—wanted to believe—in the futurism preached by the modern regime of historicity and the benefits it brought to economic development. They labored to increase, rapidly, the distance between their field of experience and the horizon of expectation. During these decades efforts were made to advance swiftly along the pathway of development.

"When the past no longer lights up the future," Tocqueville had written, "the spirit walks in darkness."[23] With those diagnostic words, he hoped to render the present legible, if not deducible. With a single declaration he marked the closure of the old regime of historicity and enunciated the motto of the modern regime, namely, when the future lights up the past (and the present), the spirit no longer walks in darkness. We have here the fast, vibrant, violent path of modern time. Still, should faith in Progress collapse or vanish, should the future cease to light up the past (and the present), the spirit will once again walk in darkness. The modern regime loses its grip, and Chronos experiences a crisis. The future closes, and the past goes black. In 1973 the first oil crisis shook up the economies of the West, provoking anxious recalibrations. A number of petroleum-producing nations managed to threaten the Western way of life. An issue with global repercussions had, for the first time, eluded Western control. The great god of growth wobbled, threatening GDP.

As the years passed, the present came into fashion then into demand—being of one's time did not suffice, as one also had to live and work in the present. Even the word "present" was prized. Additional catchwords were never rest, be flexible, mobile, respond to demand, always innovate. This is presentism's crowning moment. Very soon, the instantaneity and simultaneity known as "real time" has been conveyed, spread, and realized in manifold ways by new information technologies. Overlapping with these changes was an acceleration of globalization, giving rise to new markets and new players in those markets. The short term is prized, not least because global trade is increasingly driven by finance capitalism demanding rapid returns on investment.

"The history of capitalism after the 1970s," explains the economic sociologist Wolfgang Streeck, "is a history of capital's escape from the system of social regulation imposed on it against its will after 1945."[24] Anything that imposed limits on markets and competition was to be eliminated, while the role of finance in the economy increased. Fernand Braudel declared that the continuity capitalism had exhibited between thirteenth-century Italy and present-day West was an "unlimited flxibility."[25] Wherever the greatest profits could be made, capitalism was always there. But the finance capitalism of today demands maximal profits (more or less) instantly. Since the 1970s, writes Streeck, capitalism has traced the following trajectory: "to defuse potentially destabilizing social conflicts," it boils down to using money "*to buy time*." This deferred or "extended" crisis, first through "inflation" and sovereign debt, then through the development of "private loan markets," and finally, today, through "central bank purchases of public debt and bank liabilities."[26] This strategy for buying chronos time amounts to stretching the present, in the hope that it will last as long as possible. Just hope it lasts!

The present, considered as an instant, contracts almost to nothingness, yet paradoxically it never ceases to expand, both into the past and into the future, becoming a sort of perpetual present. Life expectancy increased, and Western populations aged, contributing their portion as the present enlarged its domain. All were expected to remain youthful, and a dynamic market sprang up to support the various methods. What the present—the omnipresent—needs, it manufactures, appropriating the orders of an available past and future so as to produce its own—first on a daily basis, then each instant, then continuously. From television news broadcast twenty hours daily to news networks that never go dark to Facebook and Twitter. The future, we are told in ubiquitous advertisements, begins tomorrow, better still right now. Was it not François Hollande who announced, in his campaign for the French presidency in 2012, that "change" was coming "now"? Here was a campaign slogan as presentist as hell, which was turned back on him as soon as he was in office.

A SHORT GLOSSARY OF PRESENTISM

Acceleration/Urgency

Just how deeply chronos time—champion of the now, dismisser of duration—has taken control of our daily lives may be gleaned from a study of the terminology of presentism. Modern time possesses an acceleratory nature, as Koselleck showed, yet this attribute has escalated in what the sociologist Hartmut Rosa labels "late modernity," becoming the era's defining quality. The critical theory of acceleration that has emerged from his study of how societies have reacted to this change in velocity states that once acceleration exceeds a given threshold it attacks itself: "The acceleration that is a constitutive part of modernity crosses a critical threshold in 'late modernity' beyond which the demand for societal synchronization and social integration can no longer be met."[27] What are the principal traits of late modernity? Cycles of consumption have attenuated, everything is quickly obsolete, returns on investment happen overnight—the instant and the simultaneous are prized. Within nanoseconds, computers render verdicts, testing the limits of time's compressibility. Presentist acceleration is in charge, providing an essential validation quite different from that of the modern regime of historicity (a.k.a. futurism): at a certain moment, it serves as its own justification. Ruled by its iron law, we have become the hamster in its wheel, racing ever faster, advancing not an inch. That earlier acceleration promised emancipation; all we can now see on the horizon is alienation, possibly self-alienation. The expectation that each of us will match the pace of acceleration provokes a fear of falling short.

Acceleration and innovation are inseparable—the latter one of today's catchwords. We must innovate, always innovate, even innovating to innovate. Racing to be the first to dream up an item or a service, we will worry later about creating demand. After a longer period of invention, innovation has taken the lead. Fostering innovation has become an "urgent obligation" for government, much as planning once was. Mirroring innovation is obsolescence, typically planned obsolescence, without which the machinery of innovation might come to a grinding halt. Instead of basic research—too slow, ungainly, and unpredictable—research and development is prized, short-term studies of projects and public tenders. The new focus on the present integrates all these practices.

Urgency escalates even as acceleration accelerates. Yet another of the catchwords of presentism, urgency amounts to a focusing of chronos time. It permeates the present, rendering any other explanation or justification superfluous: "It's an emergency!" Every facet of society has been affected; urgency is a "total social fact."[28] But the word "urgent" no longer suffices, and intensifiers are widely used: "very urgent," "extremely urgent," and so on. There are never enough contingency plans, and any delay in unrolling a new one is met with outrage. Most urgent of all are medical emergencies, a topic that has drawn much heated comment. France's urgent medical aid service, known as SAMU (Service d'aide médicale urgente), was founded in 1972. The very name the service chose—SAMU is commonly referred to as "the Urgents" (les Urgences)—proved a liability: a surge of patients of all kinds has ensured that wait times have increased. Can they function in two distinct capacities, as clinics ("We went to the urgents") and as specialist services ("We were taken to the urgents")? All our emphasis on urgency has produced the very opposite: a depression that deprives its sufferers of everything but a "lethargic present without past or future" and, more and more, utter exhaustion and burnout.[29]

As urgency contracts our time frame, catastrophe appears. This term occurs often in the presentist context. Historians working in the second half of the twentieth century wanted to maintain a distance from events, only to have the presentists focus so much on events that nothing else seemed to exist. The event is all, and everywhere we find the eventful. No institution, business, or organization can fail to mount events, more events, ever more and ever more quickly. This is where we encounter catastrophe: it occurs, it happens, it is an unexpected event. Yes, it is negative, but how it is discussed and confronted belongs to the eventful. And as with events, it is one catastrophe after another.

"The opposite of an eschatology" is how the historian Alphonse Dufront defined emergency. Think of immediacy standing in for the *eschaton*, or the instant being the only aperture for viewing things. Emergency starts to look like the contemporary regime of presentism's unique variant of kairos. So tight and compressed is the time of the emergency that no decision or action can be accomplished in time—they are almost already too late. There is, in any case, no time to spare. The Greek form of kairos, in which stalking the right moment gives time a break, is no more helpful than the Christly kairos, where conversion provides an opening into the present. These will not help because each emergency is followed by another, then another, and on each occasion there is a chance of arriving too late, coming up short, being left behind. We have seen the rise of the tyranny of emergency, and on the horizon is the (predicted) catastrophe.

A Politics of Presentism

Within the presentist regime, all politics are reduced to presentist politics, always treated as an emergency and governed by shifting emotions. In its modernist form, politics had a loose association with the modern regime of historicity, sometimes marching alongside it, sometimes opposing it, depending on where it stood along the spectrum from progressive to reactionary. Reactionary politics hoped for an about-face—let us refer to this as *pastism*. Progressive politics embraced the future, believed in democratic advances, emancipation, and human progress. Along with countless other texts, the articles on schools written by Jean Jaurès are emblematic of that position. The political man, by definition and by virtue of his position, had a vision of the future toward which he drove matters with great haste, and while that future may not have been radiant, it marked an improvement. Nowadays we reproach politicians with having no vision, though such a thing is entirely beyond them. Yet from the moment that they lose the light of the future, they might as well be blindfolded and have soon made a mess of things. In this they are only following the lead of their fellow citizens, who are no better off. Tocqueville's "theory" has been proven.

Political leaders have roles in governing, communicating, and reacting. They are immediately judged according to the speed with which they react to events, notably their ability to show up at the scene of a disaster. Their reaction time weighs more heavily than their reaction proper. Normal political time comprises a number of strata, each with a distinctive rhythm and duration. One thinks of the imperious time of elections; "saving time" (by postponing a decision), which has existed since the shadowy depths of history; and the most recent, not the least demanding, the time of political communication. Fully engaged with and in tune with the current moment, political communication unites presentism and politics, a risky affair that might end with presentism swallowing politics whole.

As these overlapping, interlocking tyrannies—the instant, the future nearly set in stone (i.e., global warming), and, as often happens, a traumatic or criminal past—defy the awkward efforts of our aging representative democracies to adjust their decision making without compromising the very things that transformed them, bit by bit, into democracies. Can democracy function instantaneously, in real time? How can it address the immediacy of email and, most recently, social networks? What are we to do when politics is reduced to a stream of tweets that constantly appear, are repeated, contradict themselves, then vanish? At the moment we are in the midst of a shift from a politics of the regime of presentism to an utterly (and abjectly) presentist politics defined by an incessant recourse to internet surveys, a reliance on big data and algorithms, both dictating the content disseminated via communication tools and policy briefings, as well as the intended audience, with messaging pursued day after day, strategies readjusted every hour. Of late, the social networks that instantly spread images, catchwords, insults, and artfully orchestrated fake news have reinforced the power of presentism, inasmuch as emotions and egotism now drive our instantaneous information, which lacks any mediation and declares with ever-increasing volume its perfect transparency.

Now

Three weighty words have had a profound impact on modern history: *revolution, emancipation*, and *reform.* Yet these terms have no connection to presentism. How does it address them? Revolution, as we have seen, played the Christly Kairos in chronos time. It was a central element of the modern regime of historicity and of attendant political strife. Either it was initiated by time itself (the transformation of the forces of production was supposed to do it), or it had to be urged forward, in line with Robespierre's hopes and Lenin's efforts. But at the moment the future is called into question, the revolution's guiding beacon flickers. In the West we can date that moment to May 1968, which belonged to both futurism and presentism. Those in the streets still declared that the revolution was oriented to the future, yet they backed away from sacrificing their present for a hypothetical prospect. We need only hear once more those half-joking half-serious slogans: "Everything, right now!" or "Under the paving stones, the beach!"

At least one group from the so-called ultra-left, the radical left, has come out against the present, but only the present. This is the Invisible Committee, a group of unnamed authors whose recent book is entitled, significantly, *Now*. Their approach is quite the opposite of the revolutionary and progressive movements that endorse futurism, as they contend that "a mind that thinks in terms of the future is incapable of acting in the present." Hope itself, they continue, must be banned, since "that very slight but constant *impetus toward tomorrow* that is communicated to us day by day, is the best agent of the maintenance of order." No reform, in their view, could produce the slightest hope. This confirms, negatively, the narrow link between reform and the modern regime of historicity. In that case, might the past serve as a resource? Not really: "Even if the past can act upon the now, this is because it has itself never been anything but a now." Clearly the very notion of learning from history makes no sense. This produced a logical conclusion: "There isn't, there's never been, and there will never be anything but now."[30] All we ever do is leap from one now to another.

Next comes a series of statements defining this now and its implications. First and foremost, it is the locus of "decision." But it is also "the locus of presence" for oneself and to others, because its most evident, most "incandescent" form is riot. As the authors write, "One never comes out of one's first riot unchanged." A riot is "desirable as a moment of truth"; through it "the real is finally legible."[31] Endowed with a certain lyricism, these epigrams go beyond simple elegies to riot: they grant it a specific aura. Riot opens a unique time resembling a kairos time. Riot, for the Invisible Committee's authors and those who followed them, is truly a form of kairos, but it is aleatory, punctual, hopeless. One might call it a detemporalized utopia, set on repeat in the here and now. Under the circumstances, the will to "found" is a trap—only "destitution" matters, and one must see to it that, among others, the president of the Republic is destituted.

As a concept, emancipation conveys motion. One state, slavery, is left behind so that liberty can be approached. In the context of modern politics, it is bound up with the modern regime of historicity, so what happens when emancipation ceases to be borne by a progressive time? Instead of vanishing, it retains a place among the values of the left or, more vaguely, for those who identify with humanism. Much as they mean to promote it, to fight for it, they have lost sight of the pathway. Is a horizon of emancipation compatible with the erasure of a time defined by procedures and progress? If words are to mean anything, one much choose between a belief that progress and time are linked (or that this connection can be revived) or side (as with the revolution) with this detemporalized utopia, rendering emancipation something like a moral imperative.

Yet another institution that is thrown into question is schools, which are by their very nature open to the future and have strongly supported the ideal of emancipation. They have safeguarded the authority of the professor, promising in return benefits no less real for being postponed. Schools nowadays tend to be viewed as a service evaluated by calculating short-term interest. As Philippe Meirieu and

Marcel Gauchet have pointed out, "The focus is strictly on the immediate value of practical knowledge acquired at the lowest cost."[32] The obsession with "skills" (the category comprises a wide range of things) smacks of educational productivity and tends to reduce education to a transaction. More generally, while students want to know, they do not want to learn. Technological advances convince us that instant knowledge is possible without learning. All we need do is click: all that time spent learning has been saved. The click is a "chronophage," devouring chronos time.

* * *

And last is reform, our constant companion throughout this study. Its flexibility ensured that it served as a leading instrument of temporalization, from the reformatio of the first centuries after Christ through the medieval period and the Lutheran Reformation to what are referred to in the modern era as reforms.[33] In the nineteenth century, it was one of the principal slogans of the progressives, a term more palatable than *revolution* that offered the signal advantage of offering a gradual change, heading toward emancipation or leading toward further emancipation.

In a presentist age, reform is always with us, all the more so since it has become a synonym for adjusting, adapting (after too long a wait) to a situation. Reform pushes obstacles aside, aiming to streamline processes, improve the efficiency of systems, and so on. Unlike the reformatio of old, it looks neither forward nor backward in time. All is urgency and acceleration; one reform leads to another—at times before a preceding reform has been fully implemented. Mustn't wait, we are warned, until it is too late. This is urgent. Under such circumstances, it can be no surprise that those affected instantly conclude that this is "regressive," a threat to previous "gains." Two examples should suffice. In France, state education is a hotbed of incessant reform due to temporal conflicts both perennial and intractable. How can one prioritize effectively when faced with the urgent demands of the most recent incident, the need to update programs, preparation for today's world (really tomorrow's, which defies prediction), and the long timespans needed to educate students? A second textbook case is that of pensions, one of the achievements of the welfare state. Since the resources available for pension reform and adjustment have nearly been exhausted, how can the various stakeholders be convinced, above all those toying with the idea of enrolling, that decisions can be made at least thirty years in advance, when, with the exception of the known demographic data, no one can say what the labor market will then look like, not to mention life expectancy, and the whole matter of international relations? To these must be added the uncertainties unleashed by global warming.

The remark of Alphonse Dupront remains broadly accurate: "With each passing day we choke a bit more virtue out of the word 'reform,' in which such great hopes were placed during the long century of the Middle Ages."[34] As we have seen, those hopes extended back far beyond the Middle Ages. Today hope has been replaced by mistrust and anxiety, feelings that have been fomented and amplified.

Protection, Precautions, Prevention

Since the 1970s the three words *protection*, *precautions*, and *prevention* have come to occupy a more prominent place both in the public sphere and in our daily lives. Their shifting trajectories convey a clear change in our relation to the future. Protection arrived via environmentalism. In 1972 the first United Nations Conference on the Human Environment takes place in Stockholm, declaring environmental protection a "duty." That same year, the General Assembly of UNESCO adopts the Convention Concerning the Protection of the World Cultural and Natural Heritage.[35] The same sort of change has been evident in the rapid development of the precautionary principle, to the extent of being added to the French Constitution in 2005.[36] This triggered a series of debates on its application. If we overuse it, do we not risk turning it into nothing but a veto power that simply preserves the status quo? Prevention is not new (it is central to insurance), but lately it has expanded to address security and safety, the subject of bitter debates in elections around the world.

The section of the French criminal code addressing secure detention (February 25, 2008) "permits the convict to be detained, upon completion of sentence, for the period of one year, with the possibility of unlimited renewal, solely on the basis of posing a threat."[37] On the basis of statistical probabilities, the "threat posed" by an individual is assessed, and a decision is made, for instance, to keep that person locked up (even after a sentence has been fully served), thereby denying him or her the possibility of a future. Only one point is being made: because it is viewed as a threat, the future is prevented, or at least postponed, in the name of urgency and for the sake of protecting the present.[38] More broadly, to quote the jurist Mireille Delmas-Marty, some global dangers "can have consequences that never end. Depending on whether these are connected to interhuman violence (global terrorism) or the overwhelming power human beings have over nature (ecological or biotechnological dangers) . . . different sorts of security measures can be imagined. In some cases, a state of emergency becomes permanent, prolonging the present, while in other cases the future is embedded in positive law through strategies ranging from prevention to precautions, from the current generations to future generations."[39] All these decisions, provisions, ways of being reinforce the omnipresent nature of the present, that impenetrable horizon of now. *Preservation, conservation, precaution, prevention*—all these words (and politics) drawing us toward, perpetuating a presentism characterized by retreat and closure, a world of increasing fears where none benefit, save the swelling ranks of those who profit from fears.

Memory

A dimension must be added to our oscillating present that swings between the *nearly all* and the *just-about nothing*—memory. The trial of Adolf Eichmann in 1961 marks the first big public, international acknowledgment of what I have called the time of Auschwitz, a halted time, a past that goes nowhere. For the first time, survivors are summoned to testify, to say what they had endured, although quite clearly they never met the accused in person. This is the dawn of what Annette Wieviorka called "the era of the witness" (her book is *L'ère du témoin*), which we might just as easily call "the era of the victim." Make no mistake: it is in their capacity as victims that these witnesses have come to prominence.[40] As one of them said to Daniel Mendelsohn, "You want to forget, but you shouldn't forget, you cannot forget."[41] So began an era that Pierre Nora would soon name "the memory years." The book he thought up and oversaw, *Les lieux de mémoire* (the places of memory), turned to memory in order to rewrite history, while Claude Lanzmann's film *Shoah* attested—with shattering force—to the impossibility of forgetting. The former appeared between 1982 and 1992, the latter in 1985.[42] During this period public spaces (media, the courts, the cultural arena) in Europe and much of the rest of the world were increasingly dominated by the "demands" of memory, the "duty" of memory, and the "right" to memory.

Memory and its alter ego, cultural patrimony, assumed essential roles in political speech and agendas. Commemorations were ubiquitous and the occasion for great gatherings that could be national, patriotic, chauvinistic, and so on, sometimes taking the form of protests. The politics of memorials arose, sometimes producing laws regarding memorials.[43] While presentism has given up on history, it depends on memory, which is effectively an extension of the present into the past, as moments of the past (most of them painful, hidden, forgotten) are evoked and collected in the present. There is, though, no opening to the future, except through the declaration "Never Again!," which itself implies a review of the past already declared closed. In fact, the moral gleaned from touring the many museums of memory that have appeared around the world is "Do not forget, so as not to experience that again." Such memorials, including examples in South Africa and Chile, often take an architectural form, figures in a landscape marking the conclusion of the process known as "transitional justice." Victims were given the opportunity to speak about what they had endured, a process directed toward jumpstarting time, enabling it to proceed forward once more. Such was the role allotted to various truth and justice commissions, whose moral and political objective consisted of escaping from a frozen time without resorting to forgetting or amnesties. But what time can be restarted once the modern regime's futurism has vanished? How can one escape from frozen time, a present that belongs to the victims, when around us, seeking and enlarging its terrain, is presentism, comprising the perpetual present of the victims and victorious presentism (or presentism's first victorious moment)?

The study of history, which had been deified in the nineteenth century, was a teleological discipline (its heroes the Nation, the People, the Proletariat) that opened onto the future.[44] These attributes tended to place it on the side of the victors or possibly those who, defeated today, would emerge victorious tomorrow. Memory, by contrast, has come to serve as a tool or weapon of those who have been unable to speak or whom we have not heard, the forgotten (of history), minorities, victims. Memory and presentism therefore complement each other while remaining quite distinct. One thing memory can do is offer an escape route from the present, where all landmarks are swiftly erased, without utterly abandoning it. When we confront the past that, as has been mentioned, goes nowhere, that time of genocides and crimes against humanity, we have found a way to confront the present. After all, this past is not only still present; it is of the present. The lack of a statute of limitations on crimes against humanity renders criminals coevals of their crimes for life. This means that time does not "advance" for them, should not, and the same is true for us. Beyond the Nazi criminals, the legal basis for reparations is situated in this juridical temporality of imprescriptibility, specifically reparations for slavery, sustained as soon as it was formally identified as a crime against humanity.

The Presentist Turn of the Faithful

Christianity certainly is a form of presentism. That was established early in the present study. So the encounter of late twentieth-century presentism and Christianity should not go awry. The problem is that contemporary presentism is anything but a revival of Christian presentism. In general the former is neither apocalyptic nor squeezed between Kairos and Krisis, the time of the end and the end of time—it dwells within the instant and sees no horizon beyond itself. It does not see itself as an intermediate time. Furthermore, the institution of the church committed itself to control a place as long as possible, within chronos time and hence within history. We have traced the many compromises, repeated endlessly, that were made between the apocalyptic present and worldly time.

The church, the oldest institution in the Western world, has its own time quite different from the modern time it has long rejected and condemned. Its horizon has long been the presentism of origins, an article of faith, although it has yielded in some areas, negotiated with Chronos, and accepted aspects of the last century. Only when Pope John XXIII launched Vatican II (1962–1965) and *aggiornamento* did the church seek to embrace modern time. While the church was determined (in spite of some resistance from within) to move forward at its own pace, soon enough the rise of the new presentism had thrown it off kilter. It had to adjust to the speed of the media, all the more so as the popes had decided to assume the role of prominent voices on the world stage. Some have become superstars: one thinks of John Paul II, whose very rapid canonization proves that acceleration has lodged in the very heart of Vatican theology. Ever since, the papacy has been subject to the same demands for responsiveness and transparency as any other institution, whether large or small.

That is not all. The church has been obliged to address the competition it faces from the evangelical groups whose global expansion has been exponential. What they offer, above all, is the possibility of a direct, immediate relationship with God.[45] Emotions dominate and presentism reigns among congregations of believers, new believers, and born agains. In addition, evangelicals often adopt apocalyptic outlooks. The entanglements of the Catholic Church in an institution developed over two thousand years that has made compromises with chronos time set it apart from the evangelical groups that can, without interruption, make a transition from the immediacy of contemporary presentism to that of apocalyptic presentism, the movement functioning as a sort of permanent revival meeting.

One can say the same of Islamic State, whose fundamentalism combines apocalyptic presentism with current, technological presentism, atop a basic rejection of modern Western time, that of the "infidels" (who are also former colonizers). Anything before the Prophet is but a past that must be erased (ruins to be dynamited), and between the Prophet and them is nothing but a present opening on apocalypse. Their use of images is in keeping with the most deliberate presentism. Islamic State films killings through the immediacy of digital technology. "Filming, recording, showing, disseminating, uploading to the internet have become," writes Jean-Louis Comolli, "*a single action.*" He adds, "Choosing a cinema of *visual shock* is typical of our time, extending far beyond the clips made by Islamic State."[46]

The early Christians had only the present, yet it would be wrong to depict that present as its own horizon. "Forgetting all that lies behind me, and straining forward to what lies ahead": with these words, Paul described his relation to the present, his way of living as a Christian.[47] I have already emphasized the importance of this passage. Nothing similar exists in contemporary presentism, even though, as we have seen, some shards of a kairos time have lodged there—riots, but also musical events, sports matches, funerals, large demonstrations, all of which suggest "communions." In addition, our current presentism first achieved prominence with the collapse of the modern regime of historicity. That regime guided the advance of time and defined modernity, until a different presentism appeared, borne by the digital revolution and spread by globalization. Back in the nineteenth century, in the time of the great temporal utopias, the modern regime ruled out the marker of the end or (what amounts to the same thing) rejected it in a future so far off that it had no meaning, eluding the mortgage imposed by the apocalypse. Still, once the category of the future lost its guiding function, a space opened wherein apocalyptic scenarios could be activated or reactivated. This was readily accomplished by the evangelicals, who slipped from one presentism to another. One can say the same of Islamic State and its "martyrs." As to the more secular evocations of the apocalypse, they too may turn to the apocalypse, but inevitably negative apocalypses, notable since World War I, including a major strike by France's nationalized railway workers.

LEAVING PRESENTISM

One may speak of a society's temporal norms, which Rosa has inventoried, as a " 'silent language' of time" that each person absorbs, and yet, as this quick glossary of presentism shows, there are also words of time—a language of the epochs of time.[48] Now that we have witnessed four or five decades of presentism, we have enough distance to evaluate its effects. An evaluation of the relative acceleration and desynchronization among places, social groupings, generations, and classes discloses one overarching effect: the formation of a "mosaic of temporal ghettos."[49] There is, in addition, no single presentism that is the same for all; there are types of presentism. Just as chronos shrank like the ass's skin, so is this present riddled with divisions. At one extreme is the chosen presentism that belongs to "the winners of globalization"—they are connected, mobile, agile—while at the other is the endured presentism that belongs to all those "barred from projects," those unable to "pro-ject" (literally) themselves toward the future, instead living—surviving really—from one day to the next. Their entire universe is "precarity," truly "great" or "very great precarity." The most destitute of these today is the "migrant" (neither an emigrant nor an immigrant, but a "migrant"). Locked in an endless present, migrants have a single horizon, the endless present of migration, their destiny.

Between the chosen and the endured presentisms lie all the intermediate possibilities. But all the divergences among temporalities that vary among social groupings, groups defined by age and class, introduce dangers, as we have gradually come to understand. Temporal discord does not produce frictions, and yet it adds fuel to conflicts among different groups. People may share the same present while existing within different sorts of time, and when a discrepancy grows, it may engender a reaction—a rejection, a refusal, bursts of anger and hatred. The distances separating the center from the periphery are matched by the temporal gaps. In Europe this has been driven home on a nearly daily basis over the past few years, evidenced in the political transformations that we have seen, are seeing, and may well see in the future.[50]

After the brief triumph of a dominant presentism came complaints and campaigns to reform it or flee it. The insistence on acceleration provoked attempts to decelerate. Founded in Italy in 1999, the Slow Food movement took on fast food, only to succumb to a rash of problems. The movement has largely devolved to a marketing effort, making a selling point of the Slow this and that.[51] At least there are those for whom slowing down has a market value. Since 1996 the Long Now Foundation has been promoted by well-known counterculture and high-tech personalities. An enormous clock, intended to last ten thousand years, is the signature project—it remains a work in progress. In due course the large hand of the clock will advance by one click annually, the little hand by one click every hundred years, and a cuckoo will serenade the millennia. The plan calls for installing it in Texas on the property of Jeff Bezos, boss of Amazon and a contributor to the project. Pilgrimages will be made to the site, where each visitor will be invited to meditate on longer scales.[52] When the principal peddlers and beneficiaries of technological presentism launch such an initiative, it tells us a great deal. Having done much to destitute Chronos, might they come to regret their actions and seek to reinstate themselves by dedicating a sanctuary to the divinity, whether to revive the cult or make sure he is dead once and for all?

Some of those who become aware of presentism and its excesses take steps to escape it. Breaking with the presentist way of life can mean leaving big cities behind and embracing other life paces, other approaches to consumption. Silently, these small withdrawals are happening, and the number is growing. Tempting as it is to ascribe this to the nostalgic belief that "things were better then," the overriding concern is the future. Many of these are children of presentism who have never known anything else, and the reaction is no revival of the 1960s' "getting back to the land" movement. More and more, from all directions, the call to end "short-termism," to reopen the future and, with it, history, reassures those turning their backs on presentism.[53] Even politicians have begun to move—some more adroitly than others—in this direction, increasing their use of the word "future" in public statements and during campaigns. Nonetheless the mythologized past remains for some the shortest route to the future, notably in the winning slogan of 2016: Make America Great Again.

Criticism of presentism by insiders has been both reinforced and profoundly transformed by the recent emergence of a threatening and unprecedented chronos time: the Anthropocene. Concerns about the future have given way to fears regarding our prospects. Throughout its existence, presentism has seen time shrink continually to the point of near oblivion, and suddenly now it has to face a chronos time, nothing but chronos, that amounts to millions and billions of years. Did this new Chronos arrive expressly to burst the presentist bubble, snatching the attention of so many away from their toes and their returns on investment? The future has well and truly arrived, a future that manages, all at once, to be not quite within our grasp, no longer within our grasp, and lingering a bit in our grasp. The big swings that began in the 2010s have not subsided, with all the anxiety and hysteria that sometimes entails.[54]

Presentism relies heavily on catastrophe (one of our key terms of presentism), treating it as the opposite of an event; the Anthropocene does much the same.[55] For the latter, the term indicates both an ongoing catastrophe (global warming, its advance monitored by reports from the Intergovernmental Panel on Climate Change) and the final catastrophe (the sixth mass extinction). "Collapse" is on the lips of all, as is, of course, "apocalypse" (in its purely negative sense). Many commentators on and around the Anthropocene have the word *apocalypse* at their fingertips.[56] In short, catastrophe glides readily from the context of presentism to that of the Anthropocene, with the signal addition of a notion of finality, unknown to presentist catastrophe.

While indications of presentism abound, we are hearing from the transhumanists and posthumanists, the strident and impatient futurists determined to expand the potential of time to come. What they promise is an improved human being, a "Humanity+," finally a posthumanity.[57] Twenty-five years ago the geneticist Daniel Cohen wrote, "I believe in the possibility of a new stage in human biological evolution that will be conscious and planned, as I do not see *Homo sapiens*, this harried, jealous person, waiting patiently and quietly for the anachronistic path of natural selection to deliver a new species of human."[58] We may wish to accelerate that change, given how slowly natural selection functions—and so the future falls under the spell of acceleration. And while it is quite impossible to evaluate the scientific promise of such schemes, that does not keep them from tapping significant financial resources or from influencing investment strategies—one thinks in particular of corporations like Google.[59] Still, the most interesting thing for us is the light shed by such ideas on the present: What sort of future does this present aspire to? Many feel that we must make haste to leave our present behind, or that those who have the means should blaze a new trail, somewhere else, beyond Earth, beyond humanity. But in the meantime the present, such as it now is, must last a bit longer. Nothing can happen without cryogenics and air conditioning.

Among the prophets of the coming disruption, the most famous is a Google engineer named Ray Kurzweil. This media star of futurism speaks of the coming of the "Singularity" and has founded a Singularity University. Kurzweil has stated, "I have set the date 2045 for the 'Singularity' which is when we will multiply our effective intelligence a billion fold by merging with the intelligence we have created."[60] Inasmuch as transhumanists anticipate using technology to eliminate death, the future in which Kurzweil lodges his predictions is in fact a near future. The exponential growth of artificial intelligence narrows the gap separating us from futures foretold on a daily basis. If we conjure a generalized regime of acceleration, the future itself will be subject to that law of perpetually increasing speed. In other words, this future will incorporate presentist decelerations. Compare that to the futures of Condorcet and Renan, which had so much time ahead of them—the difference is vast. For both men, the coming of a new humanity inhabited a very distant horizon. Before that moment, Condorcet envisioned only "indefinite" progressions (and never gambled by predicting a date), while Renan readily hazarded that only millions of years in the future would humanity achieve full self-realization.[61]

The transhumanists are keenly aware of the threats troubling Earth, including the risk of human extinction—another reason for their great hurry. Finding a way out has acquired a new urgency. Their solution comprises nothing but scientific and technological advances, an outlook taken so far in the case of Kurzweil that he has invented a purely technological apocalypse: the Singularity. Of the apocalyptic thinkers we encountered earlier, he most closely resembles Joachim of Fiore. Much like the abbot in 1260 reckoning the date of the Third Age (that of monks and the eternal gospel), Ray Kurzweil is predicting 2045 as the year of the Singularity. He should be included among the abbot's distant descendants, reminiscent of the title of a book by Henri de Lubac: *The Spiritual Posterity of Joachim of Fiore*.[62]

CHRONOS RESTORED: THE NEW EMPIRE OF CHRONOS

Just yesterday presentism fancied itself its own horizon. But that perspective has been challenged, and a new "dark abysm of time" has opened up. With Buffon, the Christian regime of historicity met the long durations of geology and natural history. A different scenario is shaping up today. Rather than confront the Christian regime of historicity or, for that matter, the modern regime, presentism now confronts presentism. Challenged in any number of areas, presentism has not retreated, particularly as the digital revolution, presentism's leading instrument, continues its advance. If we can speak of a chronos time informing that advance and the concomitant rapid transformations at the levels of both social groupings and the individual, it must be recognized as a very brief *chronos* time adapted to a universe of nanoseconds. Even as individuals and institutions are drawn to—forced to—adjust to instantaneity, directly under their feet another chronos, this one very long, is opening up. This time, quite incommensurable with the digital chronos, rises up before us, taller than that "wall of ages" that Hugo envisioned rising before him as he set out to compose *The Legend of the Ages*.[63]

A restored Chronos follows the destituted time of presentism, and it will have to be faced. In the near future we will assume a new condition, as we try to give the "digital condition" a human face. Seen from another perspective, the near future seems to be swallowed up in a perennially elusive *chronos* time. Maybe we have here a reiteration of the mythical god devouring his children, a truly chronophagous Chronos.[64] What shall we use to net him? But first: what net shall we make, with what mesh? For the first time in recorded history, Chronos is split between a time vanishingly brief and a time so long that it defies representation. Likewise, the new digital condition is torn apart between two radically incommensurable temporalities. Can such a condition, we want to know, give rise to a new historical condition? Between the Anthropocene and the age of the microprocessor, what sort of historical time (or new historical time) is possible?

THE TEMPORALITY OF THE ANTHROPOCENE

What does the Anthropocene look like? What time period does it cover? What is its texture? Since the chemist Paul Crutzen coined the term in 2000, it has been adopted at a dizzying pace, as shown by the appearance of specialist journals, research groups, an organized community, debates, and a list of publications that grows by the day.[65] The word *Anthropocene* has become part of everyday speech, and it is discussed in popular media outlets with increasing frequency.[66] Crutzen received the Nobel Prize for his work on the stratospheric reduction of the ozone layer, then went on to show that the concentration of carbon dioxide in the atmosphere had rapidly increased, concluding that a new era in Earth's history had begun. This marked the end of the Holocene, which accounted for all human history to that point, just short of the twelve-thousand-year mark, and the inception of a new epoch in which the human race had become a geological power affecting, as such, the Earth system, the equilibriums of its various systems.[67] This accounts for the proposed name "Anthropocene."[68]

Whether to endorse the name was now up to the geologists—more precisely, up to the International Commission on Stratigraphy, a unit of the International Union of Geological Sciences. The union serves as the protector of the geologic time scale; it alone has the authority to bring about any change to that scale. Now, Crutzen's suggestion was based on observations recorded in the atmosphere, and the ozone layer has no effect on stratigraphy, so the geologists needed to determine whether there was a properly geologic basis, such as a stratum, for declaring a new geologic epoch. There is plenty of evidence supporting claims for a boundary setting off a stratum. Most conspicuous was concrete, the quintessential manufactured new stone; billions of tons of concrete have been poured. And then there is plastic, that symbol of the modern world, of which hundreds of millions of tons have been produced annually since the 1950s. Plastic waste is quite visible on land and sea, and recently researchers have been tracing microplastics too, and even nanoplastics, which are ubiquitous yet invisible to the naked eye. Since such materials are now found in geologic layers—and will be for millennia—it is apparent that the Anthropocene is no flash in the pan. As the geologist Jan Zalasiewicz has said, it is a "fundamental boundary," which is why it can "be assigned an epoch status." When we think at the scale of geological time, a temporal limit is understood to be "an interface in time, of no duration whatsoever—it is less than an instant—between one interval of time (which may be millions of years long) and another."[69] The Anthropocene is an epoch in two different senses: it is, in accordance with Crutzen's criterion, a stopping point; it is also a long duration, as the geologists showed in the process of arriving at their verdict.

What sort of boundary should we imagine for the Anthropocene? Zalasiewicz very usefully writes, "In terms of the definition of a 'stratigraphical Anthropocene,' we are dealing with change to the Earth system rather than a change in the extent to which we are recognizing human influence." Although it includes the word *Anthropocene*, his definition foregrounds the planet, rendering human actions secondary. "It is important," he adds, "that the planetary system is *recognizably* changing, and it just happens to be the activities of the human species that are currently the main perturbing force. The Anthropocene would remain just as important geologically, because of the scale of the planetary (and hence stratal) effects, if it had some other cause." The mid-twentieth century may strike him as the most likely candidate for the boundary, but that does not mean that the entirety of "'humanity' per se" should be blamed for all the changes.[70] Not every tumbling asteroid and erupting volcano has had the same impact; not every human society has left the same geological traces. So when we think about the Anthropocene, it need not be in anthropocentric terms; in studying it, we may adopt comparative approaches that take variety into account; in acting on it, a range of tactics can be employed.

※ ※ ※

Time in Buffon's natural history could hardly be more different from time as today's geologists conceive it. Buffon wanted, above all, to record and measure Earth's past, while Zalasiewicz tells us that geology has become a fully developed science as focused on the future as on the past. Keeping track of "*everything* that is present or happening on, within and above the Earth, now and over the past four and a half billion years" no longer suffices; now geology must address "the Earth's future," namely, "something like another five billion years," not to mention the evolutions of the other heavenly bodies.[71] From Buffon's limited abyss we have shifted to a general abyss that lies behind us, before us, beyond us. Is there a way to cope with it? After all, we assumed a responsibility when we became a geological force. Not for us is Lucretius's *suave mari magno*, since now, "when the storm-winds roil/A mighty ocean's waters," there is no terra firma where we can stand to watch "another's bitter toil."[72] We cannot spectate. We have embarked, and should a ship go down, it will have been ours. But how is it possible, under such circumstances, to see ourselves as a geological force? In other words, how do we come to understand ourselves as a species? Here we must unravel the sensitive issue of how a point of view is constructed, more challenging still because it is doubled—we belong to both the world and the Earth.

The notion of the epoch calls out for a few additional comments here. Recall that Buffon enumerated seven. Still, the sovereignty of humans over nature was in his day far from settled, so that epoch, his seventh, has to be sorted as "to come" rather than "done." Only once the power of nature had been aided and shrewdly improved on could that epoch be realized, which would take a lot of time. Buffon did not view human beings as innately masters and owners of nature; at best they might earn that after much labor and a great deal of time. If the seventh epoch was to become something other than a fantasy, the Earth's time and human time (the time of the world) would need to come together. Condorcet's outlook could only differ from Buffon's, as he addressed nothing but human time. The final triumph of humanity occupied his tenth epoch and was intended to belong entirely to chronos time, yet he carefully avoided offering any sort of precise chronological prediction. Both examples rely heavily on the powerful notion of perfectibility to imbue mature perfection with a temporality.

Prospects dim with the arrival of a new epoch: the Anthropocene. Having imagined itself free from the time of nature, humanity was now whipped back into line. Geology does not measure perfection; to triumph, for *Homo sapiens* (now *Homo faber*), is to become the subject of doubts. As for its role in the Earth's order of time, humanity can hardly withdraw since, from the moment it was acknowledged as a geological force, it has been an active player. Should becoming a geological force be viewed as a victory? Yes—a Pyrrhic victory. For there are those who wish to see nothing but victory, and they demand triumphs that transcend this triumph, the fruits of further accelerating science, climatic engineering, transhumanism, and more. And there are others who foresee a defeat that will lead to a rout. Just listen to the raised—and rising—voices of the various catastrophists, collapsologists, survivalists, and apocalyptists, whose words are repeated in escalating echo.

The historian Dipesh Chakrabarty published a seminal article on climate in 2009, opening an extended reflection on the ways climate change has affected history, a topic that eventually broadened to encompass the transformation underway in the human condition itself.[73] A leader in the field of postcolonial studies and global history, Chakrabarty takes great care in identifying and underlining the divide between the "global" of globalization and that of global warming.[74] The former offers a homocentric history; the latter, a "zoecentric" history of the planet, with that which has made and makes life possible at the center. These are two profoundly different registers due to their incommensurability, yet they do come into contact at a certain moment, and frictions erupt. One such point of friction (let us call it an epoch) is the Anthropocene. And in fact an awareness of the divide and its irreducibility reside at the foundation of what he calls a new "epochal consciousness," borrowing the concept from Karl Jaspers.[75] Just as the atomic bomb gave rise to a new epochal consciousness, global warming may be seen as ushering in a new consciousness. The appearance of such a historical consciousness is not sufficient, in itself, to resolve aporias, but it does furnish a space inimical to faulty, simplistic diagnoses. Two temporalities perpetually in tension that never intermix: living with them is living in the Anthropocene.

Those familiar with the time of the modern regime of historicity will find the new situation worrisome—even more so those who have known only today's presentism. But just how novel is it? Consider the Christian regime of historicity: Was that not a matter of living in two utterly incommensurable times at once? Can this analogy—it can be no more than that—be fruitful? Can it help us reflect on our situation? Given the trajectory the present inquiry has followed, it is hardly a surprise that the parallel obtruded itself, but let us investigate it a bit before drawing to a close. Might the very gap between the two analogical figures shed a light, however oblique, on the undeducible present of which Valéry spoke?

THE ANTHROPOCENE AND THE WORLD'S TIMES

At this time there are two temporalities, that of the Anthropocene and that of human beings or of the world, which we can think of as a

Chronos that has certainly been restored—but split as well. We never shed that sense of a split, and it was always there, but while the new dividing line may be the result of our existence or our actions, it is hardly under our control. Here is a situation without precedent in human history.[76] That second form of temporality gave rise in the eighteenth century to modern time and the modern regime of historicity. Later, in the second half of the twentieth century, presentism enjoyed a brief tenure. Should we formulate an Anthropocenic regime of historicity based on the temporality of the Anthropocene? The question may be logical, but does it mean anything? If so, what heuristic benefit can we expect? Bear in mind that the only goal the regime of historicity, as a concept, ever had was to serve as a heuristic device.

Evaluating the impact of the Anthropocene on the past, present, and future—the three categories of the world's time—provides some specificity. Chronos time, limitless and bottomless, has abruptly imposed boundaries on the world's time; this is the greatest of the Anthropocene shocks. Looking back, Chronos had freed itself from the grip of Kairos and Krisis after a long struggle with the interlocking end of time and time of the end, those scissor blades that constitute the Christian regime. We mentioned three who undertook this struggle: Buffon, Condorcet, and Darwin. And now a possible ending has materialized—not the end of the Earth's time, but of that chronos time of the world that took over from the Christian regime of historicity. This jolt is shocking, as much for the modern regime of historicity as for presentism. Christian presentism had been set adrift by the modern form of chronos time and its tendency to erase boundaries; today's presentism is under attack by the Anthropocene, as the reappearance of boundaries threatens to unseat it. First the suppression of limits threw things off balance, and now it's the reappearance of those very limits shaking things up.

The moment a possible or probable ending drops into view, the other blade of the scissors rises up, marking the entry into a time of the end. Unmistakably this new time, which feels different, is a chronos time, but one experienced as a time that remains. It feels different from other chronos time and is often perceived as the present, just as was the Christian time between the Incarnation and the Parousia that was bound up in the aura of Kairos. This new situation was bound to evoke reactions ranging from denial through all the apocalyptic humors, including the future-oriented itinerary involving technological innovations and their promises of a ready posthumanity. They were not explicitly summoned, but the shadowy figures of Kairos and Krisis can be made out prowling in the background, on the margins. The guilt of all humanity seems to be pronounced in this ending, but some of us more than others, men more than women, humans as a species in relation to other living things, and regarding inanimate things as well. When Chronos is restored as the time of the Earth, humanity is destituted, for it has set itself up in modern time as the final epoch, the horizon beyond which nothing can travel. So much for Condorcet's tenth epoch or even Buffon's seventh.

Two approaches to the past need to be reconsidered in light of the Anthropocene. What could be called the epic take on modern times, set to the rhythms of European expansion and the industrial revolutions, needs a drastic revision. Any decisions made in the past could be reevaluated by reopening the archives and, by the light of the present situation, proving that the range of possibilities always outstripped the choices made, whether the context was economic, industrial, or agricultural.[77] At any fork, the outcome might have been different. Such a regressive history reads events against the grain, unrolling the reel in reverse. This rewriting of history was the work of scholars who reject the cover provided to capitalism's past and present depravities by humans, whether or not they amount to a geologic force. They insist that responsibility and blame be meted out in accordance with the who-what-how-when. Since the waters of the Anthropocene are rather murky, perhaps we should speak candidly of the Capitalocene? What of the disagreements on the origins of the Anthropocene? Should it take as its starting point the beginnings of agriculture or, somewhat later, the Neolithic? Or a later moment, the conquest of the New World? Or, later still, the industrial revolution? The consensus view gives the nod to the 1950s, when human impacts on the Earth and the biosphere increased with notable speed.[78]

These revisions, while relevant and illuminating, may run the risk of overlooking our unprecedented circumstances. As Clive Hamilton has written, we will not fully appreciate climate change "if it is cast *only* as a problem of power relations and differences between among humans."[79] The second approach leads us away from the brief time of the world—all the briefer if only modern time is considered—to consider the long time frame of evolution, of "deep history," and the still longer time of the planet.[80] In the letter he wrote to Marcellin Berthelot in 1863, we should recall, Renan adopted the same way of seeing.[81] Chakrabarty, when he wants to describe the intrusion of this new past, turns to the metaphor of falling: "We have fallen into 'deep' history, into deep, geological time."[82] We lack any direct access to these temporalities, yet suddenly we are conscious of their presence.

The Anthropocene extends variously into the future. Much as through a significant extension of the past it reopened it, it forces us to contend with a very distant future. Zalasiewicz has proposed as the horizon of geology the next five billion years, a figure that completely foils all human attempts to grasp it: it is unrepresentable. The space assigned to the future by the presentism of the last decades has been meager—a time of urgency and acceleration, of rushing, of a hunger for technological innovation, tender notices, superfast returns on investments. At the crossroads of the futurism generated by the modern regime of historicity and the more recent futurism of the presentist regime, which I have just mentioned, we find transhumanism, also embraced by the apocalyptic presentism of the Singularitarians. This three-way temporal intersection renders it a symptom of our times. Or four-way, as the new awareness that our time is limited must be considered as well.[83] Catastrophe has resurfaced. A functional element of the presentist regime, it is a tell-tale indication of the Anthropocene, a time of catastrophe.

An event whose occurrence lies far ahead and yet, somehow, has made a certain progress—this is the nature of the Anthropocene future, a reality more unnerving and wrenching than any other provoked by this new epoch. Already we know we have altered the climate for the next 100,000 years.[84] This comes from what our predecessors did, what we are doing, and still more from what we are not doing. The future is well and truly here, one might say too here, but it has ceased to be that blank page of history routinely evoked by the rhetoric of origins. Even if we were to alter our habits radically, this future that has yet to occur would continue to give rise to effects in the present and would affect the future too. Feedback loops stretched over very long intervals are prone to this. As agency in our three standard categories—past, present, future—is destabilized, our paradoxical future poses an unprecedented cognitive challenge, prompting questions as to what course to follow. To quote Bruno Latour, who always has the perfect turn of phrase, "We cannot continue to believe in the old future if we want to have a future at all."[85] Is the point of digitally enhancing such classical figures as Destiny (Greek: *Tuchê*; Latin: *Fatum*) and Providence (more or less blind) that they can shift or humanize the Anthropocene?

Such a transformation of chronos time's three categories is destabilizing. Past and future had been absorbed, after a fashion, by Christian presentism, a process on which I have dwelt at some length. Under the modern regime the future served as the guiding category, which is precisely how the regime wanted it. Contemporary presentism foregrounded the present once again, but without the magnetic mentoring of the Kairos-Krisis pair. Then, with the Anthropocene, the deck is shuffled: temporalities forever at odds can never be separated. No longer will the planet's time serve as a mere prop in our self-scripted productions played on the world's time. No longer can we claim, like Diderot in the *Encyclopedia*, that "man is the sole point from which to begin, and to which all must be brought back. . . . Aside from my existence and the happiness of my peers, what does the rest of nature matter?"[86] The happiness of our peers, in order to maintain its worthy status, must adopt new criteria; human beings can no longer be the exclusive standard. While the Holocene was the time of human beings, the Anthropocene should be, Latour tells us, the time of the Earthbound, meaning everything that is found on the Earth, whether living or other, bearing in mind that humanity is a latecomer.[87] Having agreed on this new situation—or better, this new condition—one issue remains unresolved: How are we to reassemble our refashioned temporal categories? What is life in the Anthropocene, and how should it be lived? Specifically, what becomes of the present? Long certain of being entire of itself, the present realizes that it is in reality a tiny islet soon to be submerged by the rising tide of a very long Chronos.

This is a brutal blow. The feeling of some sort of apocalyptic effervescence, spreading through a number of Western groupings, cannot be a surprise—the new orientation resonates with those who hit out against presentism. Its reasoning strikes them as unimpeachable. No longer is it a matter of discomfort or dis-ease; like the planet Melancholia in Lars von Trier's eponymous film, catastrophe is upon us. Flight from the "system" has become a political statement; withdrawing and retreating are on the rise, as are novel cults; hostilities have heightened. Many dream of scuttling capitalism to save the Earth, a reversal of Fredric Jameson's comment that imagining the end of the world came more easily than imagining the end of capitalism.[88] We find such an outlook in France's recent ZAD, *"zones à défendre"* or "zones to defend."[89] On the wall of Paris's Ministry of the Ecological Transition an inscription recently appeared: "ZAD everywhere." No longer a return to the earth, we now have the return of the Earth. The logo of Extinction Rebellion, a group committed to civil disobedience founded in the United Kingdom in September 2018, is a black hourglass shape set in a circle implying the Earth. The message is clear: as mass extinction draws near, the only possible response is rebellion. While the group professes nonviolence, others feel that overthrowing the system demands violence.

Some of these militants, true converts, radiate zeal and intolerance. They scold those who have not seen the light, have seen only glimmers, or are only shamming, faulting them for apathy and hypocrisy. Among the new gurus, those Cassandras and Sibyls, the young Swede Greta Thunberg has lately taken the older generations to task for selfishly seizing her future. Is her sense of mission so different from that of Bernadette Soubirous and the other babes from whose mouths truths once came?[90] Certainly she is bearing witness, in season and out of season, addressing the mighty of the earth regarding the "revelations" she has received. Do not, she repeats, listen to me, but do listen to the scientists whose words I report. On December 14, 2018, addressing COP24, she declares, "Our biosphere is being sacrificed so that rich people in countries like mine can live in luxury. It is the sufferings of the many which pay for the luxuries of the few. . . . And if solutions within the system are so impossible to find, maybe we should change the system itself."[91] She has a form of autism, a difference she emphasizes: "Without my diagnosis, I would never have started school striking. Because then I would have been like everyone else. Our societies need to change, and we need people who think outside the box and we need to start taking care of each other. And embrace our differences."[92] A reporter from the *New Yorker* adds, "Greta's protest serves a dual purpose. It not only calls attention to climate policy, as she intended, but it also showcases the political potential of neurological difference."[93] The global audience she has won, in which young people preponderate, points up a rising conflict among temporalities. By taking away our future, meaning the future in line with the present we have known until now, you created a break in time: our time can no longer be your time. Your side is that of the Old World and the Old Human Being. Somewhere between you and us, something like a religious conversion took place. If you delay too long, alas for you—not so serious—but alas for us too!

APOCALYPSE ON THE HORIZON

If one tries to capture the mood of the times, or one such mood, by speaking of an apocalyptic effervescence, that is no slur. And it is not a matter of differentiating rational and irrational thoughts, slapping the irrational label onto all calls for change and related events, just to marginalize them. Nonetheless, few heed the calls for reason. This holds true both for the "heuristics of fear" of Hans Jonas and the "enlightened catastrophism" of Jean-Pierre Dupuy. Neither is an apocalyptist. Jonas pleaded, much as Jaspers did at the dawn of atomic warfare, for an "awakening." For the sake of the "ethics for the future" he wanted, one had to "take into account futurology . . . so that we do not face the future blindly, but with our eyes open" (alert to what we can learn from science about the consequences of our actions). Then might come "futurology as *warning* in order to bring our unleashed abilities under our control. This warning, however, can affect only those people who, besides being aware of the scientific laws of causality, also have an *image of man* that entails certain duties they consider entrusted to their care."[94] Dupuy relied on Anders and Jonas precisely to avoid all apocalypticism; it was not the catastrophe that interested him, but what came after. If we could project ourselves into the postcatastrophic moment and imagine that it had happened, we stood a chance of preventing it. The root of the problem lay in not believing that the catastrophe would come in spite of our knowledge that it was coming. We need to shift from knowing to believing. This heuristics is far from a surrender to the irrational; it stakes everything on an increase in rationality.[95]

Yet the ineluctable bond linking Chronos and the multiform apocalypse has been a constant of our transit along the avatars of Chronos, Kairos, and Krisis. So at a moment when Chronos once more slips between our fingers—more slippery than ever—we can scarcely be surprised that the ancient figure of apocalypse, ever poised for action, should be summoned, whether explicitly or not, accurately or not, crudely, or crisply. It all happens within a sort of nebulous apocalyptic aura. At such moments, as I have noted more than once, the date of the ending is calculated over and over, which is just what is happening today.[96] Still, nine times out of ten the apocalypse evoked is strictly negative, or it is the truncated modern version that dwells on the discontents of progress and the harm done by technology. One might easily confuse this version of the apocalypse with catastrophe.[97]

It arose during World War I; alongside De Martino we watched it stalking to and fro throughout the interwar years; it peaked with the atomic bomb, the Cold War, the anxieties surrounding a nuclear winter. From the moment a limit is set, a possible or probable ending to the world's time, all relation to time changes. Now the present is what remains to us of time, and that urgency that informed the vocabulary of presentism increases—urgency is everywhere, and massive. The only official reaction, according to watchdogs and activists, is "talk." As leaders sit idly, "the house is burning," biodiversity is plunging, countless meteorological "episodes" are sweeping past—the idle must be assaulted and denounced in every conceivable way. What was the present yesterday, under presentism, is not today's present, which is in flux, transitioning to the decisive moment. You might say that the Final Judgment had already, in some sense, taken place, yet chronos time is taking on a form of kairos. We are guilty: we the humans, the human race. We have rendered a guilty verdict on ourselves. But there are among us those who yesterday bore a heavier guilt, who today are guiltier by far, than others. The roster grows, perpetually, catastrophe after catastrophe.

* * *

So many speak of the apocalypse, wielding references with varying acuity and authority, but one stands apart, an eminent apocalyptist: Bruno Latour. This major figure, who led the way in the study of the Anthropocene, may possess the greatest international renown. In contrast to those who have "obscured" our understanding of the apocalypse by limiting it to a catastrophe, Latour insists on the original Christian meaning: the moment of transition toward the wholly other. Channeling a primitive Christian, he stated in a recent interview, "The apocalypse is a thrill!" His turns of phrase—*ancien régime, new climatic regime, loyalist* ("ci-devant") *human beings, loyalist Nature*—go beyond mere analogies between the Anthropocene Event and the French Revolution.[98] The French Revolution, as we have previously seen, constituted an unprecedented moment experienced by some as Krisis (Judgment), others as Kairos (the opening onto a new Christly time). The Anthropocene is much the same. Latour chooses Kairos.

In addition, taking an approach that seems initially quite odd, he reproaches the Moderns (those who fancied themselves moderns, though in reality they never were) with imagining that they stood on *"the other side"* of the apocalypse, that it had already taken place, with the coming of modern times.[99] This rendered impossible a fresh apocalypse, and the rising tempo of alarms leaves them unmoved. I am not fully convinced by this surprising statement, but it is congruent with Latour's general thesis, namely, that like the early Christians we "tremble once again with uncertainty."[100] For Anders there is a "duty of anguish;" for Latour the goal is to make us "regain the present" by "taking [it] seriously." How? Only if we can "relearn to live in the in the time of the end."[101] One is reminded of the universe encountered in chapter 1, particularly that of Paul, whose words are quite familiar to Latour, and more recently that of Charles Péguy.[102] As we have indicated several times, for Christians everything has already been accomplished—through the Incarnation—but everything has not yet been completed, since they await the Parousia. Latour tells us, " 'The end time has come,' yes, but it goes on." Yes, "there is indeed the feeling of a radical break, but with the crucial nuance that the break must constantly be *taken up again*. One cannot escape from this fundamental instability." And: "This contradiction must not be overcome."[103] The Christian "already" and "not yet" hover in the background, but

Latour transforms them into "already" "again:" already and again. Because no other world is on the horizon, not an "ultra-world" and not a "lowly world." That enables him to say that Gaia "objects to any flight into the beyond," for it is "opposed to utopia and uchronia." It "can welcome the present, but it mistrusts the Apocalypse and everything that claims to jump to the end of time."[104] Imagining an apocalyptic Gaia (the name Latour gives to his creation is drawn from Isabelle Stengers and James Lovelock) is no easy task.

After his countless assertions and turns of phrase, the final result is, without question, a present cast as kairos time and a plea for a new presentism that may not be Christian but belongs to the Christian type. Latour will win no prizes for orthodoxy. Back in the good old days of the Inquisition, he might even have been summoned for a fireside chat on the subject of his "counter-religion."[105] How certain are we that the apocalypse will happen, in the way the early Christians supposed? Not at all, if "not yet" doubles as "again," an again that must be constantly "reworked."

Still and all, he tells us, we must live as if the apocalypse were to arrive soon, in the time of the end. With that "as if" he salutes the apocalyptists he labels "prophylactic," those who labor to keep the apocalypse at bay. He prefers to prepare for it, eyes wide open, treating it as an extraordinary event to be embraced. To turn it into an authentic kairos, both in the Greek sense, meaning occasion, and in the Christian sense, meaning complete transformation, we must be ready to "welcome the present." If the Humans who "take the Earth" understand that the "Earthbound"—their identity from this moment on—are *"taken by it,"* in a "reverse appropriation of land," the apocalypse-catastrophe (Krisis) may not occur, and the kairos will be seized.[106] Standing apart from Krisis, kairos will have warded off Krisis, but not forever.

CONCLUSION

The Anthropocene and History

APOCALYPSE AND history do not, as a rule, go together. In search of the advancing end, intent on its date, the apocalyptist expects nothing from the past and hopes for—or both hopes for and dreads—an ending of the present, which offers no other outcome. The impasse is complete, and the outcome must come from elsewhere. For Daniel, the sole remedy for the abomination of Antiochus IV was the Coming of the Lord. Every millennial movement has arrived borne on hopes for a new heaven and a new Earth. From chronos time, a time of misery, one can expect nothing good, except an ending. Yet Latour, in my mind a singular apocalyptist, has found a place for history. Our entry into the Anthropocene may, he feels, enable humans to "rediscover the thread of history," "a sense of the history that has been taken away from them by what they had viewed up to now as a mere frame deprived of any capacity to react." They had named this context nature and made it the backdrop of the world, of their world with its own time and its own history. But now the scientists have become the historians of nature. Geology, with its billions of years, both past and future, is a historical science. We should not, writes Latour, see Gaia as "a cybernetic machine controlled by feedback loops but [as] a series of historical events," hence a historicizing force.[1] Buffon reckoned that if natural history was to become an authentic discipline, it would have to borrow the methods of "civil history." Latour tells us that today it is the scientists historicizing nature and the Earth system who are recasting "civil history," meaning history and the world's time. Coming from a sociologist and philosopher of science for whom history has not been a central concern, this signals some sort of change. One may conclude that the Anthropocene, far from being yet another end of history, could lead toward a revival—and a new concept—of history.

Decades have elapsed since the reconstitution of nature as patrimony gave law a say in whether nature belonged in chronos time. When the General Assembly of UNESCO adopted the Convention Concerning the Protection of the World Cultural and Natural Heritage in 1972, humanity assumed responsibility for something that until that moment none could own and none could alter. Then, in 2003, the convention to safeguard intangible cultural heritage was adopted, enabling local inhabitants to nominate sacred spaces for protection. Matters have advanced, and today natural entities and living places are endowed with legal personhood: one example is New Zealand's Whanganui River. We have shifted from the cultural heritage of humanity to "goods shared in common by humanity." The commons have acquired a new meaning that takes into account human and nonhuman groupings.[2]

The historian Dipesh Chakrabarty opened his reflections on this question, as we have seen, by asking how history had been affected by climate change, broadening his inquiry to consider the impact of the Anthropocene on the human condition. The existence of two distinct chronologies—that of capitalism and that of *Homo sapiens*—caused a problem, as he acknowledged from the outset: while they are distinct, we must consider them together, without trying to combine them. This tension, Chakrabarty correctly wrote, "stretches, in quite fundamental ways, the very idea of historical understanding," taking it to its limits.[3] Since then he has never ceased to explore the breadth and consequences of that gap, that differend, as it were.[4] We have both the familiar chronos time of the history of the world and the otherness of the chronos time of the Earth. In 2009 Chakrabarty turned to Walter Benjamin to evoke the emergence of a potentially new universal history flashing up at a moment of danger, that "shared sense of a catastrophe" announced by climate change. Truly universal, this history will also be negative.[5] The Benjaminian flash of lightning might be said to correspond to the moment when one abruptly understands.

More recently, Chakrabarty turned to Karl Jaspers, linking climate change to "epochal consciousness."[6] The first trait of such a consciousness is a cleavage, with, on one side, humanity treated as a political subject (with its various parts) and, on the other, humanity as a species and a geological force. The result was a gap between fundamentally opposed temporalities. The concept of epochal consciousness, a sort of artefact, helps us see this more clearly, Chakrabarty believes, by steering us away from a potential confusion between the records and logics underlying the two. But it does not offer a pat solution to the most important question: How do we live the Anthropocene and, more important, how do we live in the Anthropocene?

We have some experience of the world's time—or, better, of its times—but no direct experience of Anthropocene temporality is possible, though we are well aware that ignoring it is no longer possible. From the three categories that structured the world's chronos time—the past, the present, and the future—it was possible to formulate a metabolized version as a heuristic device—the regime of historicity. From the condition that will be ours henceforth, where we find ourselves in both the time of the world and that of the Anthropocene, which may experience contacts and conflicts but can never truly mix in view of their incommensurably different scales, can we hypothesize an Anthropocene regime of historicity?

Could invoking the notion (encountered at several points in the book) of the simultaneity of the nonsimultaneous help?[7] After all, it has already enabled us to identify some moments when time runs into trouble. When the Spanish encountered Native Americans, they experienced the simultaneity of the nonsimultaneous. These beings, until now unknown, unfamiliar to the Bible and the ancients, were in some respects contemporaries and in others not at all. As a result, that temporal otherness is not suppressed; it is channeled, tamed. Once this gap has been recognized, political means may be employed to reduce and suppress it—conversion and colonization, these means are called. These indigenous peoples had to be inserted into European chronos time, given access to Christian kairos time. The Anthropocene is, obviously, not an Indian, nor does it resemble an Indian. Still, the shock of the encounter with Anthropocene temporalities is in some ways analogous to experiencing the simultaneity of the nonsimultaneous, even though the way of handling it must be different. Conversion and colonizing are not part of the plan today. Or, should conversion prove necessary, it must be entirely our responsibility. Nowadays, it is no longer we who take the Earth, but she who takes us, a reversal described by Latour.

The erasure of the modern regime of historicity and of its future-oriented time has opened up a space for presentism and also a multitude of clashing temporalities, hence a growing number of concurrent disjunctive events. Time is growing increasingly individualized: my time is not yours, and not his either, even if we share the experience of instant electronic messages and smartphones. One of the traits of the connection to contemporary time is, then, a generalized dissonance, which has yielded social fragmentation (including the loosening of family ties). Among the times of the world, the time fostered by the Anthropocene is excessive—unique because quite irreducible. Yet if one illuminates it through the notion of the simultaneity of the nonsimultaneous, one adds a measure of clarity to the experience of the Anthropocene (though no direct experience of Anthropocene temporalities is possible).

The notion of the simultaneity of the nonsimultaneous takes us back, it turns out, toward the Christian regime of historicity. Did not Augustine theorize it (without naming it), even placing it in the heart of universal history? The entire history of the two cities, that of God and that of the Earth, which has been with us since the beginning of this study, recounts their combined yet distinct march forward, ever intersected by the experience of the simultaneity of the nonsimultaneous. The history of the Earth, of human beings, of fights for power, takes place within chronos time, chronos alone. The other, while it (still) exists in chronos time, (already) belongs to kairos time. They are and are not part of the same time: one will terminate when time itself ends; the other will join that divine eternity to which it has aspired from its beginning, as kairos time merges with the eternal changelessness of God. But Augustine only generalized the simultaneity of the nonsimultaneous first formulated, if not conceived, by Paul. Living as a Christian is living two times simultaneously, existing in the present of ordinary time while not existing there (the "as . . . not").[8] Keeping one foot in chronos time while the other already steps into the apocalyptic present of the Christly Kairos. Becoming Christian is learning to live in two incommensurable temporalities—in the eternity of God, which is by definition off-limits, unquestionable, and unrepresentable, and in ordinary chronos time. To forge a connection between them, Christians turned Jesus into the Messiah, that is, the mediator—the Kairos. A second mechanism attached itself to this mediation, one more involved in chronos time, namely, accommodatio, whose historical significance has been traced earlier. God is unchanging, yet he adapts his commandments in light of the time and the season, the better to guide humanity along the road of perfection. As divine accommodatio unfurled, the church responded with reformatio, in practical ways making allowances for the world's time. The church had found its way of being in the world; reform made it possible to come to grips with the world's time without ever belonging fully to it. As for renovatio, which culminated with the Eucharist, it became a strictly liturgical matter, whereas translatio informed universal history.

When Pope Francis conveys the magisterium of today's church in his ecological encyclical letter *Praise Be to You* (*Laudato Si'*), he preaches a reformatio aimed as much at nonbelievers as believers. The goal is in fact "to protect our common home"; it must be protected and also restored. The manifesto naturally avoids any reflections on the time of the end or the end of times. It opens with an "analysis of our present situation," in the form of a brief summary and a catalogue of damage. While the pope limits himself to a factual presentation, in order to break "the spiral of self-destruction which currently engulfs us" he calls for a veritable "ecological conversion."[9] Which ecology does he have in mind? An "integral ecology" that must include an "'ecology of man,' based on the fact that 'man too has a nature that he must respect and that he cannot manipulate at will.' "[10] The topic of ecology permits the pope to recall the church's doctrine on the subject of procreation. The pope also faults those who cite the Bible to justify human domination of the world, characterizing such readings as erroneous, decontextualized. Does not the portion of Genesis that grants human beings "dominion" over the earth also say that we must "till and keep" the world's garden?[11]

If the pope does not speak the word *apocalypse*, even so as to reject it, no more does he mention the word *Anthropocene*. By limiting his reflections to the problematic of ecology, he remains within the only time of the world, our common house that must be protected and repaired. The path he endorses is that of reformatio. Christians may understand full well that Christ is the ultimate source from whom ecology flows and that "the Eucharist is itself an act of cosmic love." The "conversion" the pope calls for nonetheless belongs to the world's chronos time.[12] Never does his inventory of humanity's current plight take on the extremes of Anthropocene temporalities, which may not affect Pope Francis due to his Christian faith but have a destabilizing effect on what we think of as the human condition. No, the magisterium of the Catholic Church has nothing to offer those seeking a way out of the aporia, though Christianity is intimately familiar with a life beset by incommensurable temporalities. This is the very heart of the "mystery" of Christianity.

I am not well suited to the task of hastily fabricating an analogy with the devices Christians have conceived to connect eternity and time, and I have no intention of doing so. That would be ridiculous. But we can at least bear in mind that a solution to this aporia has already been proposed, which did in due course lead—sticking with the question of time here—to the invention and establishment of a new regime of historicity, that Christian regime that has so powerfully and lastingly shaped how the West has dealt with chronos; to be sure of grasping chronos, the concepts of Kairos and Krisis were mobilized. One readily understands why, when seeking to mediate between the Anthropocene and ourselves, between an immense time and our own ephemeral time, some will have recourse to the forms of or substitutes for Kairos time and will revive equivalents of Krisis. This is the practice, specifically, of the prophets of doom attached to various denominations, from the moment that the Augustinian chisel dividing the end of times from the time of the end is revived.

But the main difference from the temporality of the ancient Christians is that chronos time, in greater and lesser volumes, accounts for the temporalities of the Anthropocene and ourselves. The Earth's system is not God, and the Anthropocene "Event" is no analogue (not even negatively) of the Incarnation, despite being unique, without precedent in human history, and the herald of a new time. This unprecedented time belongs, as has been stated, to chronos time. While we are facing gigantic differences in temporal scales, we are not confronting essentially divergent temporalities. Furthermore, if we have entered the time of the end, that does not mean the end of the planet but rather the end of the world, an entity the Moderns cast as the engine of universal history—their own. While the sixth mass extinction may occur within a few centuries, that will not keep the Earth system from carrying on, and the Anthropocene era will last for millennia. And "the silence"—less that of "these infinite spaces" than of these indefinite times—will cease to frighten anyone.

Must we, in order to live in the Anthropocene, fabricate intermediaries or mediations capable of grasping that formidable Chronos? Or might we be able to leave behind our chronological "nonage" and adopt as our new historical experience the incommensurable? Yes, no single measure can be applied to both the time of the Anthropocene and the time of the world, yet we no longer have an alternative to dwelling in both at the same time. Chronos has always been split in two, so that is not new, but this time humans are not guaranteed a say in that division.[13] The Greeks never imagined that they had mastered eternity or the endlessness of heavenly motions, yet Plato drew from that his conception of human time as a moving image of eternity and Aristotle his notion of a time without beginning or ending, a "number of motion." The cleavage has thus been a device for thinking time, a way of grasping the Ungraspable. Do we need a Plato, an Aristotle, or an Augustine to reconsider time from the cleavage between the temporalities of the Anthropocene and the times of the world, our own?

While we may not have direct access to the Anthropocene, while we may not be able to see ourselves as the human species, we are nonetheless able to measure the (negative) effects of this era on the world and the times of the world. A sense of urgency about the climate is ubiquitous, and any failure to respond immediately to that urgency is now condemned as inaction. Evidently the illusions of presentism have yet to fade. This is particularly true given the digital bent of our new historical condition, itself structurally presentist. Our condition is, then, the result of a number of gaps: the gap between the time of the Anthropocene and the times of the world (more and more fragmented), the gap between a digital presentism (at the heart of globalization) and the world's other temporalities, and, last, the radical gap between that presentism and the temporalities of the Anthropocene. This condition is an experiment in dismembering. In a similar configuration, one might employ an Anthropocene regime of historicity to link these different gaps (from the smallest to the largest), though without reducing them. It is no longer, as it was in the good old days, a matter of simply articulating past, present, and future, but of taking into account pasts, presents, and futures, whose impacts may differ, diverge, even contradict each other, but which nonetheless form a nexus or a web of temporalities in which, to one or another degree, we act and are acted upon. The first challenge is to orient oneself in a knot of temporalities that no Alexander will sever. Even making the attempt would be foolish. It is here that the concept of the Anthropocene regime of historicity may help—helping to orient us, unravel things, create order so as to release the order of times defining the new human condition.[14]

At the end of *Memoirs from Beyond the Grave*, Chateaubriand concluded that his era was situated within a double impossibility: that of the past and that of the future ("The present world, the world without consecrated authority, seems placed between two impossibilities, the impossibility of the past and the impossibility of the future"). The past of the ancien régime could not return. Any attempt to restore it was a contradiction, as it contradicted the flow of time: the old regime of historicity had lost its command over the new chronos time. Yet the future appeared to be just as unthinkable, since it succumbed to "the madness of the moment," which was "to achieve the unity of peoples and to make but one man of the whole race."[15]

Today we may feel that we find ourselves, in our turn, caught in a double impossibility of past and future—not the same, but analogous. It is highly unlikely that the modern regime of historicity will simply pick up where it left off. It is no longer possible to dwell immured within the narrow time of the world, in which we took such pride, and certainly not within the narrow closet of presentism. But, given those limits, is the future clear? Certainly not. Paradoxically, the very abundance of the future will give rise to its impossibility, as a mass of futurity is unleashed, like a wave surging across the deck of a storm-tossed ship. This Anthropocene future is remarkably long and, what is even more unnerving, part of it has already been enacted due to the role that we, both as humans and as a species, have already played. The role we have had and will have imposes a responsibility in the past, the present, and the future.

What is that role today, and how should it be performed, bearing in mind that as we take on the role of our lives, we are risking our lives, the lives of other human beings, and the lives of nonhumans, those of the present and of the future? Coming to grips with Chronos, a new and improved chronos, requires posing the question and, if possible, answering it.[16] While this pressing inquiry is the most recent—and often it finds itself nudged by a sense of urgency, that pathology of our time—it is not the only one. More than ever, we must untangle the multiple, conflicting, antagonistic temporalities of the world's times, all affected by this sense of urgency, even as they are increasingly systematized, if not controlled, by digital presentism, which is acting as much and as quickly to transform the human condition.

Confronting Chronos nowadays means confronting a new wind, a powerful wind destined to blow through the Anthropocene, but it also means confronting the brisk and commanding wind of presentism. A world is ending, but the admonition Paul Valéry included at the conclusion of "The Graveyard by the Sea" is still with us: "The wind rises! . . . We must try to live."[17] New winds have risen, and we too must try to live, if we want to wake tomorrow to a livable world, one in which the vital overcomes the lethal.

Yes, Chronos is indeed ungraspable. Yet what has been, what is the task of humanity, if not the effort to lay hold of it? If these pages have added something, all is well, not so as to render the present deducible, but to leave it a bit more legible. On September 2, 1850, Michelet added to his diary an entry that included a wish: "May I be the link between times!"[18] Asserting it—surely not. But dreaming it—there lies the reward for a historian's life.

POSTSCRIPT

Chronos was completed before the COVID-19 epidemic swept out of China, leaving its mark on the entire world. As I write, the West has been most deeply affected. Are the few lines left here really enough to say something? And yet, could I say nothing? Impossible. But at the end of April 2020, no one can say how far the shockwaves will spread. Within a few weeks this invisible thing, barely animate, has succeeded in locking away more than half of the world's population and has brought the global economy to a halt. Yes, even more than Valéry imagined, the present is "undeducible." Do the words Chateaubriand wrote in 1794, in the midst of his *Essay on Revolutions*, apply to today's historians? "Often," he recalled, "I was often obliged to undo at night the picture I had sketched during the day: events moved faster than my pen."[19] But he was writing thirty years after the events!

Does the coronavirus crisis (or revolution) invalidate the picture presented here? To the extent that the study began far off so as to capture the installation of the three concepts Chronos, Kairos, and Krisis, to trace the paths of their avatars over a long period, before arriving—and in order to arrive—at today's interwoven temporalities, the answer is "no." The ongoing crisis unquestionably renders things more complex. Some inclinations have been accelerated and reinforced, while others have been curtailed. Presentism has seen its troubles exacerbated, but the painting has not been ruined.

The arrival of the virus meant that within a few days we experienced three new temporalities. As we knew nothing of the virus's own time, medical time applied old Hippocratic precepts to gauge the rhythm of the illness, determine which were its "critical" days, chance a prognosis—all to control the time of the sickness. The sole tool at our disposal to slow the spread of the virus was lockdowns, which suspended time, an unprecedented event. Days go by; the present remains. All three temporalities fully belong to chronos time, and all are subsumed under the concept of krisis in the Greek sense: an extraordinarily massive health crisis. Conflicts soon erupted between the three temporalities. Medical time could not master the time of the virus. It longed to dictate the length of the lockdown, but the political could not afford to lose control of the social time blended into the lockdown time. No generalization is possible about the time of lockdowns.

As we have come to appreciate, universal lockdown is not the same for all. All were obliged to domesticate, as it were, this singular time, and methods varied. The affected include those obliged to combine isolation and work, whether the latter entails telecommuting or going to a workplace. The latter live with one foot in the previous time and the other in the new time. While presentism has come under fire, we have seen that it is still very much with us. It remains to be seen whether lockdown, certainly much like a sudden deceleration, runs into analogous challenges. For the time being, its all-conquering urgency ensures broad support. Everything is urgent; every delay puts us behind; no one will stand for tardiness. Lockdown is also supported because for millions and billions of people around the world lockdown is plugged in, online. We are submerged in immediacy and simultaneity. Already underway, the evolution of the human condition toward a digital condition has undergone an acceleration. We can be present for everything and can do everything, or just about. All that we lack is true presence. What might a telesociety look like, where everything was handled via teleconferences and contactless credit cards? And we must not forget the ceaseless flow of "viral" videos on social networks.

The scale of the present crisis has already engulfed every aspect of what instantly came to be known as "the world before." Might it surpass the Greek concept of "crisis" and impinge on that of Krisis (with the capital letter), known to us via the apocalyptists and Christianity? This is the Krisis of Revelation and the Final Judgment. Because it lent itself to more than one reading, the French Revolution has served as our textbook case, interpreted via the Christian concept of Krisis or the Greek medical concept of crisis—or a blend of the two. How will the process go with the COVID-19 crisis? Only the shrewdest might guess the answer now. If it does earn the status of a crisis-with-a-capital, it will be a revolution freighted with even more of Valéry's undeducibility. Because even those who had planned for the increasingly likely epidemics or pandemics had only thought as far as health crises. Needless to say, that is the horizon within which all the planning of states and international bodies takes place, and they expect and plan for a repetition, though they dread the days that will follow, which they know will be agonizing.

Others see opportunity: if the coronavirus crisis does not quite look like the final crisis of capitalism, these groups see it as that of neoliberalism, whose demise could be hastened. At the least, the world after should not be a copy of the world before. But COVID-19 is only the means. The bat and the pangolin are our doing, this ever-less-biodiverse world we have made, we the guilty (even though some are far guiltier than others). A kairos that must not slip away, the pandemic can help us, once the health crisis proper is behind us, advance toward another world, possibly utterly other. We must use it like an accelerator, either to hasten the end (that is the extremists) or to slow it (or prevent it), thinking in terms of a radical conversion of how we live and act. It is one thing to recognize the kairos, another to put it to use. What sorts of uses? Will there be violence? One last Greek concept, stasis, which long ago powerfully captured urban conflicts, has slipped in between kairos and krisis. How are we, then, to influence crisis, to advance toward Crisis? By translating or transforming the kairos opportunity into *stasis*, whether that means confrontation, class struggle, or civil war. The path is known, as are the risks.

NOTES

TO READERS OF THE ENGLISH EDITION

1. Dipesh Chakrabarty, *The Climate of History in a Planetary Age* (Chicago: University of Chicago Press, 2021).
2. Vanessa Ogle, *The Global Transformation of Time, 1870–1950* (Cambridge, Mass.: Harvard University Press, 2015), 186.
3. Ogle, 197–98.
4. Denis Lacorne, *Religion in America: A Political History*, trans. George Holoch (New York: Columbia University Press, 2011), 127.
5. Pierre Boussel, "Géostratégie du temps au Proche-Orient," Ph.D. dissertation, University of Tours, 2020.

PREFACE

1. Paul Valéry, *Cahiers*, ed. Judith Robinson-Valéry, Bibliothèque de la Pléiade (Paris: Gallimard, 1974), 1490.
2. François Hartog, *Regimes of Historicity: Presentism and Experience of Time*, trans. Saskia Brown (New York: Columbia University Press, 2015), esp. chap. 2 (41–63) on the tears of Odysseus.
3. Krzysztof Pomian, *L'ordre du temps* (Paris: Gallimard, 1984).
4. Saint Augustine of Hippo, *The Confessions* 11.14.17, ed. David Vincent Meconi, trans. Maria Boulding (San Francisco: Ignatius, 2012), 343.
5. Peter Galison, *Einstein's Clocks, Poincaré's Maps: Empires of Time* (New York: Norton, 2003), 322.

6. Pomian, *L'ordre du temps*, 334, 354. This places Pomian in line with Fernand Braudel's propositions on the times of different layers, from the *longue* or the *très longue durée* to the brief time of the event.
7. In *L'ordre du temps*, Pomian addressed the tendency to reflect on time: "We cannot help but try to reconcile intelligibility and time, though we know perfectly well that before we are able to make sense of it time will have made a mockery of our efforts" (347).
8. Carlo Rovelli, *The Order of Time*, trans. Erica Segre and Simon Carnell (New York: Riverhead, 2018), 4–5. For a general view of time based on the history of science, see Étienne Klein, *Chronos: How Time Shapes Our Universe*, trans. Glenn Burney (New York: Thunder's Mouth, 2005).
9. I shall bracket theories about the unreality of time, of which the leading exponent is the British philosopher John McTaggart. See his "The Unreality of Time," *Mind* 17 (1908). See also the study of McTaggart by Sacha Bourgeois-Gironde, *McTaggart: Temps, éternité, immortalité* (Nimes: Éditions de l'Éclat, 2000).
10. Galison, *Einstein's Clocks*, 12n1; Donald J. Wilcox, *The Measure of Times Past: Pre-Newtonian Chronologies and the Rhetoric of Relative Time* (Chicago: University of Chicago Press, 1987); Gerhard Dohrn-van Rossum, *History of the Hour: Clocks and Modern Temporal Orders*, trans. Thomas Dunlap (Chicago: University of Chicago Press, 1996); Daniel Rosenberg and Anthony Grafton, *Cartographies of Time: A History of the Timeline* (New York: Princeton Architectural Press, 2010).
11. Michel de Certeau, *The Writing of History*, trans. Tom Conley (New York: Columbia University Press, 1988), 135.
12. Since the founding documents of the early church no longer belonged to a shared culture, we shall dwell on them all the longer. The time spent reading them will be better spent if one avoids simply rereading them.

INTRODUCTION

1. Saint Augustine of Hippo, *The Confessions* 11.14.17, ed. David Vincent Meconi, trans. Maria Boulding (San Francisco: Ignatius, 2012), 343.
2. Aristotle, "Physics" 4.11.219.22, in *The Complete Works of Aristotle: The Revised Oxford Translation*, ed. Jonathan Barnes, trans. R. P. Hardie and R. K. Gaye, Bollingen Series 72.2 (Princeton, N.J.: Princeton University Press, 1984), 371.
3. Erwin Panofsky, "Father Time," in *Studies in Iconology: Humanistic Themes in the Art of the Renaissance* (New York: Harper and Row, 1962), 69–93.
4. Jean-Pierre Vernant, *Myth and Thought Among the Greeks* (London: Routledge and Kegan Paul, 1983), 88–89.
5. Anaximander D6. From Simplicius, *Commentary on Aristotle's Physics*, in *Early Greek Philosophy*, vol. 2: *Beginnings and Early Ionian Thinkers*, part 1, ed. André

Laks and Glenn W. Most, Loeb Classical Library 525 (Cambridge, Mass.: Harvard University Press, 2016), 283, 285.
6. Plato, *Timaeus* 37d–38c, in *Timaeus and Critias*, trans. Desmond Lee, rev. T. K. Johansen (London: Penguin, 2008), 27–28.
7. Saint Augustine of Hippo 11.13.16 (342–43).
8. Saint Augustine of Hippo 11.29.39 (362).
9. Paul Ricoeur, *Time and Narrative*, trans. Kathleen Blamey and David Pellauer (Chicago: University of Chicago Press, 1988), 3:261.
10. Ricoeur, 3:272.
11. Ricoeur, 3:274.
12. In his *Dictionnaire étymologique de la langue grecque* (Paris: Klincksieck, 1968), Pierre Chantraine noted the dubious etymology of *Kairos* while offering some support for the suggestion that it was related to *keirô*, to cut. Chantraine declared the etymology of *Chronos* a mystery, though *chronos* had also been connected to *keirô*, to cut. Such uncertain or untraceable etymologies suggest how that ungraspable quality of time is manifest from the outset. Links to the verb *to cut* seem promising, not least because of the hypothesized connection between *tempus*, the Latin for time, and the Greek term *temnô*, which also means to cut. Monique Trédé has written, "*Kairos* refers to the initiation of a discontinuity within a continuum, to an opening of time within space, of timely time in spatial time"; see Trédé, *Kairos: L'à-propos et l'occasion* (Paris: Klingsieck, 1992), 54. See also Barbara Cassin et al., *Vocabulaire européen des philosophies* (Paris: Seuil and Robert, 2004), q.v., "Moment," 815. The Alexandrian grammarian Ammonius said that *kairos* referred to the quality of time, while *chronos* was the quantity.
13. Dietrich Boschung, *Kairos as a Figuration of Time: A Case Study* (Munich: Wilhelm Fink, 2013), 34.
14. Aeschylus, *Seven Against Thebes* 1–3, 65, 652, in *The Complete Greek Tragedies*, vol. 2: *Aeschylus II*, trans. David Grene (New York: Modern Library, 1956), 105, 107, 128.
15. Aeschylus 719 (131).
16. This is what befell Creon, who in *Antigone* (1260–62) is led astray by "an unreasoning reason" and succumbs to "obstinate errors, sowing death." Too late, he grasps what has come to pass.
17. Thucydides, *The History of the Peloponnesian War* 1.23.1, trans. Richard Crawley (London: Dent, 1963), 11.
18. The Peloponnesian War, by contrast, was not a "crisis": it was a long time coming, and it lasted thirty years. Thucydides spoke of this as a shock (*kinêsis*).
19. Hippocrates, *Affections* 8. See also Jacques Jouanna, *Hippocrates*, trans. M. B. DeBevoise (Baltimore: Johns Hopkins University Press, 1999), 337–40.
20. As Jouanna points out, Hippocratic physicians were so keen on numerology that they believed hard-and-fast laws governing the progression of a disease could be drawn from its periodicity. See Jouanna, *Hippocrates*, 337–38.

1. THE CHRISTIAN REGIME OF HISTORICITY

1. On the Septuagint, one should consult the research directed and carried out by Marguerite Harl and her team. Under the general title *La Bible d'Alexandrie* (Editions du Cerf), the Greek text of the Septuagint and a translation have been published. The volume published under the direction of Cécile Dogniez and Marguerite Harl, *Le Pentateuque: La Bible d'Alexandrie* (Paris: Gallimard, 2001), is excellent. It comprises, in addition to the translation of the first five books, a series of studies of the Septuagint, of the translation into Greek, of its circulation, and of its use.
2. *The Letter of Aristeas*, trans. H. St. J. Thackeray (New York: Macmillan, 1917), 31. Here I note only that the translation exists, without entering the controversy regarding the letter of Aristeas. Joseph Scaliger first proved it a forgery. The ostensible author, Aristeas, presents himself as a Greek clerk. Modern commentators agree that he was a Jew.
3. Gilles Dorival, "La traduction de la Torah en grec," in Dogniez and Harl, *Pentateuque*, 580.
4. Alain Le Boulluec, "Le Pentateuque dans la littérature chrétienne de langue grecque," in Dogniez and Harl, *Pentateuque*, 682.
5. James Barr, *Biblical Words for Time*, 2nd ed. (Naperville, Ill.: Alec R. Allenson, 1969), 122–34. On time in Judaism, see Sylvie Anne Goldberg, *Clepsydra: Essay on the Plurality of Time in Judaism*, trans. Benjamin Ivry (Stanford: Stanford University Press, 2016), esp. 77–78.
6. Ezek. 7:3. All scriptural quotations are taken from the *Revised New Jerusalem Bible*. See also Ezek. 21:14–15, "Son of man, prophesy. Say, 'The Lord says this. Say: "The sword, the sword has been sharpened and polished, sharpened for slaughter, polished to flash like lightning."'"
7. Jacques-Bénigne Bossuet, *Sermon sur la Providence*, in *Oraisons funèbres; Panégyriques*, ed. Abbé Bernard Velat, Bibliothèque de la Pléiade (Paris: Flammarion, 1936), 1046.
8. Ezek. 7:12.
9. 2 Baruch 14:1, 20:1. See *The Apocrypha and Pseudepigrapha of the Old Testament in English*, trans. R. H. Charles (Oxford: Oxford University Press, 1913), 2:481–524, ed. and adapted by George Lyons for the Wesley Center for Applied Theology at Northwest Nazarene University, 2000, http://www.pseudepigrapha.com/pseudepigrapha/2Baruch.html.
10. Ernest Renan, *History of the People of Israel* (Boston: Roberts, 1895), 5:142, 160.
11. James Barr (*Biblical Words for Time*, 127) declares that in many cases the terms *chronos* and *kairos* are "interchangeable, apart from the stylistic preference for [*kairos*]." I disagree: chronos and kairos offer two different perspectives on time, representing forms of temporality that are qualitatively dissimilar. The person unwilling to see or hear experiences as chronos what the believer experiences

1. THE CHRISTIAN REGIME OF HISTORICITY   243

as kairos. Latin does not distinguish between the two; both are expressed by *tempus*. In translating the Bible, Jerome therefore rendered *kairos* and *chronos* as *tempus*—or, rarely, *momentum*.

12. See Daniel Marguerat et al., *Introduction au Nouveau Testament: Son histoire, son écriture, sa théologie*, 4th ed. (Geneva: Labor et Fides, 2008).
13. Luke 12:51.
14. Luke 2:34.
15. Helpful in untangling the debates on the Bible and history are two books by the Protestant theologian Oscar Cullmann: *Christ and Time: The Primitive Christian Conception of Time and History*, trans. Floyd V. Filson, rev. ed. (Philadephia: Westminster, 1964), and *Salvation in History*, trans. Sidney G. Sowers (London: SCM, 1967).
16. Hans Blumenberg, *The Legitimacy of the Modern Age*, trans. Robert M. Wallace (Cambridge, Mass.: MIT Press, 1983), 43.
17. For these early texts, rendering *Iesous christos* as "Jesus Christ," as though it were his name, will not do. *Christos*, or "anointed," is the Greek translation of the Hebrew word *mashiah*, the messiah. Surely it would be more precise to render it as "Jesus Messiah" or, in some cases, "Jesus the Messiah."
18. Mark 1:15 [*Translator's note* (henceforth *TN*): RNJ translation slightly modified].
19. Jeremiah was the first to announce the coming of a new covenant: "Within them I shall plant my Law, writing it on their hearts. Then I shall be their God and they will be my people. . . . I shall forgive their guilt and never more call their sin to mind" (31:33–34).
20. Luke 22:20.
21. Heb. 8:13. Once it was appended to Paul's letters, the anonymous Letter to the Hebrews (ca. AD 70) was accepted as a canonical element of the New Testament.
22. Heb. 9:15–17.
23. 2 Cor. 3:6.
24. Luke 24:44. See also John 5:39, 46.
25. The first deportation had taken place a decade earlier, in 597. And in 701 BC, when Judea rose up against the rule of Sennacherib, the Assyrian ruler, he had crushed the revolt. The Assyrian annals speak of destruction, booty taken, and populations driven out. The year 722 was marked by the destruction of the Northern Kingdom.
26. "In fact," notes Arnaud Sérandour, "Cyrus followed the convention adopted by newly enththroned Assyro-Babylonian rulers of announcing a general amnesty for all those, human or divine, who had been imprisoned by royal predecessors. Archaeological evidence, be it noted, does not indicate that a significant part of the population returned [to Judea] during the Persian period." See Arnaud Sérandour, "Histoire du judaïsme aux époques perse, héllénestique et romaine. De Cyrus à Bar Kokhba," in *Introduction à l'Ancien Testament*, ed. Thomas Römer, Jean-Daniel Macchi, and Christophe Nihan (Geneva: Labor et Fides, 2009), 84.

244   1. THE CHRISTIAN REGIME OF HISTORICITY

27. To our list we can also add the occupation of Jerusalem by Pompey in 63 BC, as well as the final destruction of the city in AD 135 following the crushing of the revolt against the Romans led by Bar Kokhba.
28. Luke 17:26–30.
29. John 5:39.
30. Marcion was excommunicated by Rome in 144. The church he founded spread across the Mediterranean and into Mesopotamia, surviving until 400. Marcion embraced the loving God of Jesus and rejected the Old Testament God, whom he took to be an evil demiurge. Here the break with Judaism was complete.
31. Gal. 3:14–18.
32. Matt. 6:33–34.
33. Luke 9:60.
34. Phil. 3:13.
35. Arnaldo Momigliano, "Preliminary Indications on the Apocalypse and Exodus in the Hebrew Tradition," in *Essays on Ancient and Modern Judaism*, ed. Silvia Berti, trans. Maura Masella-Gayley (Chicago: University of Chicago Press, 1994), 88–100.
36. André Lacocque, *The Book of Daniel*, trans. David Pellauer (Atlanta: John Knox, 1979); John J. Collins, *Daniel: A Commentary on the Book of Daniel*, with an essay "The Influence of Daniel on the New Testament" by Adela Yarbro Collins, ed. Frank Moore Cross (Minneapolis: Fortress, 1993).
37. Dan. 2:21. "[God] controls time and seasons, he makes and unmakes kings."
38. Dan. 2:29–45. This destruction echoes that found in chapter 7, which befell the four beasts that emerged from the sea. The fourth, taken to be Antiochus IV, was the cruelest of the beasts.
39. Dan. 9:6–13.
40. The original text was probably in Hebrew. Thanks to its inclusion in the Vulgate, it was broadly disseminated.
41. 4 Ezra 3:1. After the Council of Jamnia, Ezra responded to the finalization of the canon of the Hebrew Bible with a defense of the legitimacy of apocalyptic writings.
42. 4 Ezra 4:21.
43. 4 Ezra 11:45.
44. 4 Ezra 4:44–50.
45. 4 Ezra 5:54–55.
46. 4 Ezra 14:11–12.
47. 4 Ezra 9:1–2.
48. 4 Ezra 13:58.
49. For an interdisciplinary and comparative approach, see Emma Aubin-Boltanski and Claudine Gauthier, eds., *Penser la fin du monde* (Paris: CNRS, 2014).
50. *The Book of Enoch*, trans. R. H. Charles (London: Society for Promoting Christian Knowldge, 1917; Mineola, N.Y.: Dover, 2007), XCI.15–17 (134). A great canonical

work of the Essenes set down between the second and first century BC, the Book of Enoch comprises a series of revelations.

51. James C. VanderKam, *Jubilees: The Hermeneia Edition* prologue, 1.4, 1.29 (Minneapolis: Fortress, 2020), 7, 11. Written in Hebrew by a member of a priestly community during the second half of the second century BC, the book is opposed to collaboration with the Greek invaders and favors a strict respect for the Law. See Goldberg, *Clepsydra*, 116–17.
52. VanderKam, *Jubilees* 6.35 (32).
53. See, e.g., *Book of Enoch*, CII.1–3 (145–46).
54. *Book of Enoch*, CVII.1 (152).
55. François Hartog, "Prophète et Historien," *Recherches de science religieuse* 103, no. 1 (2015): 55–68.
56. Isa. 4:2–3. "That day, the Lord's seedling shall be beauty and glory, the fruit of the land shall be the pride and ornament of Israel's survivors. / Those who are left in Zion and remain in Jerusalem will be called holy, / all those in Jerusalem marked out for life."
57. Charles Péguy, *Œuvres complètes*, Bibliothèque de la Pléiade (Paris: Gallimard, 1987), 1:246. See also Paul Ricoeur, "Sentinelle de l'imminence," in *Penser la Bible*, by Paul Ricoeur and André LaCocque (Paris: Seuil, 1998), 229–32.
58. Paul Ricoeur, "Temps biblique," in *Ebraismo, Ellenismo, Cristianismo*, ed. Marco Olivetti, Archivio di Filosofia (Padua: CEDAM, 1985), 30.
59. Ricoeur, "Temps biblique," 31. The entirety of Deutero-Isaiah bears the impress of this thinking.
60. François Hartog, *Partir pour la Grèce*, rev. ed. (Paris: Champs Histoire, Flammarion, 2018), 84–97.
61. Mark 13:1–37; Matt. 24:1–44; Luke 21:5–33.
62. An exception may be made in the case of the Gospel of Mark, dated to roughly AD 70.
63. Matt. 24:15.
64. Mark 13:10; Matt. 24:14.
65. Acts 1:7–8.
66. Matt. 24:34–35.
67. Luke 9:27. See also Matt. 16:28; Mark 9:1.
68. Matt. 3:3, citing Isaiah.
69. Luke 7:19.
70. Matt. 17:11–12.
71. Mark 1:14–15 [*TN*: translation slightly modified].
72. John 21:21–23.
73. Mark 13:4.
74. Matt. 24:36.
75. 1 Thess. 5:2.
76. Mark 13:33.

77. Rom. 1:1. I will not address the issue of the order of the epistles, but there is no question that these are the first truly "Christian" texts.
78. Rev. 1:2.
79. Phil. 3:13.
80. Phil. 3:5–6.
81. Phil. 3:14.
82. Phil. 3:11.
83. Rom. 13:12.
84. 2 Cor. 3:6; Rom. 15:4.
85. 1 Cor. 15:51.
86. 1 Thess. 4:16–17.
87. In Rom. 11:5, Paul refers to that "remnant" of Israel, which the prophets always emphasized and without which the renewal of the covenant would have been impossible. See Marcel Simon, *Verus Israel: Étude sur les relations entre chrétiens et juifs dans l'Empire romain (135–425)* (Paris: Boccard, 1948), 100–107.
88. 1 Thess. 5:1–2.
89. Rom. 13:11–12.
90. Gal. 4:4.
91. Eph. 1:10.
92. Col. 1:19–20.
93. 1 Cor. 15:54.
94. Rom. 5:14 [*TN*: translation slightly modified].
95. Gal. 3:28.
96. Col. 3:10–11.
97. Eph. 6:5–6, 9.
98. 1 Cor. 7:29–31 [*TR*: translation slightly modified].
99. A translation that gives "as if not" for Paul's *hôs mê* misses the point, in my view. Married people are not meant to pretend that they are not married, but to live as though they were at once married and not married. In *The Lives of the Saints* there is a single temporal (kairos) event: death. Life is but a holiday in a foreign land. See Marguerite Harl, "Les modèles d'un temps idéal dans quelques récits de vie des Pères Cappadociens," in *Le Temps chrétien de la fin de l'Antiquité au Moyen Âge, IIIe–XIIIe siècles*, ed. Jean-Marie Leroux (Paris: CNRS, 1984), 226.
100. 2 Thess. 2:2.
101. Rendering *anomia* as "wickedness" or "godlessness" will not do. *Nomos* is the Law; the man of *anomia* is the one who denies the Law, is ignorant of the Law, or suppresses the Law. For Daniel, this was Antiochus IV, followed by the Roman emperors who established the imperial cult. When he spoke to the Corinthians (1 Cor. 9:20–21), Paul stated that he submitted to the Law along with those who were under the Law, but that he had been without Law (*anomos*) along with those who were without Law (*anomoi*).
102. 2 Thess. 2:5–6.

1. THE CHRISTIAN REGIME OF HISTORICITY   247

103. Carl Schmitt, *The* Nomos *of the Earth in the International Law of the* Jus Publicum Europaeum, trans. G. L. Ulmen (New York: Telos, 2006), 59–60. See the remarks in Giorgio Agamben, *The Time That Remains: A Commentary on the Letter to the Romans*, trans. Patricia Dailey (Stanford: Stanford University Press, 2005), 108–11.
104. Until the twelfth century, all that was known was the Antichrist, Christ's very opposite, his negative twin. Then, with the Antechrist, a temporal element is inserted, as he comes before the final return of Christ. The Protestant theologian Oscar Cullman offers a more positive reading of the *katechon* that preserves its apocalyptic import. The idea, previously suggested by several church fathers and taken up later by Calvin, envisioned the *katechon* as the time assigned to Christian missions and the conversion of the world. The *katechon* would hold the end at bay until conversion was complete (Cullmann, *Christ and Time*, 164–66). Why not!
105. 2 Thess. 2:7, 8, 12.
106. Charles Brütsch, *La clarté de l'Apocalypse*, 5th ed. (Geneva: Labor et Fides, 1966); Claude Carozzi, *Apocalypse et salut dans le christianisme ancien et médiéval* (Paris: Aubier, 1999); André Vauchez, ed., *L'attente des temps nouveaux* (Turnhout: Brepols, 2002); Richard Landes, "Lest the Millennium Be Fulfilled: Apocalyptic Expectations and the Pattern of Western Chronography, 100–800 CE," in *The Use and Abuse of Eschatology in the Middle Ages*, ed. Werner Verbeke, Daniel Verhelst, and Andries Welkenhuysen (Leuven: Leuven University Press, 1988), 137–209.
107. Eusebius of Caesarea, *The History of the Church* 7.25.1, trans. Jeremy M. Schott (Oakland: University of California Press, 2019), 368.
108. Eusebius of Caesarea 3.25.1–4 (148–49). On Eusebius, see chapter 2. See also Jean-Daniel Kaestli, "Histoire du canon du Nouveau Testament," in Marguerat, *Introduction au Nouveau Testament*, 496, 498.
109. St. Augustine, *Concerning the City of God and Against the Pagans* 20.17, trans. Henry Bettenson (London: Penguin, 2003), 929.
110. Rev. 20:1–6.
111. Brütsch, *Clarté*, 449.
112. While the author is named John, there is no evidence to support an identification with John, son of Zebedee, disciple of Jesus, or with the author of the fourth Gospel. According to Elian Cuvillier, "He must have been an important figure in the Asian communities of the late first century. The text was written for inhabitants of Asia Minor" (Elian Cuvillier, "L'Apocalypse de Jean," in Marguerat, *Introduction au Nouveau Testament*, 420).
113. Jacob Taubes, *Occidental Eschatology*, trans. David Ratmoko (Stanford: Stanford University Press, 2009), 72. "Two concepts of the Messiah come together in the Apocalypse: the militant Jewish Messiah, who comes to sit in judgment over the power of the world and whose birth is still awaited, and the Messiah in the figure of the Lamb, who has already come" (70).

114. Cuvillier, "L'Apocalypse de Jean," 425.
115. Rev. 22:7, 17.
116. Dan. 9:27, 7:25.
117. Dan. 7:25. One year, two years, and half of a year, or three and a half years, or forty-two months (the number recurs in the Apocalypse of John), say 1,290 days.
118. Rev. 17:5.
119. Rev. 1:3.
120. Rev. 1:2. Pierre Prigent, *Commentary on the Apocalypse of St. John*, trans. Wendy Pradels (Tübingen: Mohr Siebeck, 2001), 79–84.
121. Rev. 19:10.
122. Rev. 22:18–19.
123. Dan. 12:4; Rev. 22:10.
124. Rev. 22:20.
125. Rev. 1:1.
126. Rev. 3:11, 22:7, 20.
127. Rev. 14:7.
128. Rev. 18:2, 9, 11, 17.
129. Rev. 1:8. In Exod. 3:14, God says to Moses, "I am who I am," or "Me, I am the one that is" (*Egô eimi, ho ôn*). John repeats the definition, puts it to use, and transforms it.
130. Rev. 22:12, 17, 20. Prigent points out that "Come!" recalls a very similar formulation to one of primitive Christianity's earliest liturgies. The word *Maranatha*, "transcribed from Aramaic," comprises "two words, of which the first, *Maran* (or *Marana*), means 'our Lord.' The second is a form of the verb 'to come,' either the perfect or the imperative. As a perfect it might be translated, 'our Lord has come,' which might mean 'he has come, he is here.' As an imperative the translation is obvious: 'Come, our Lord!' The patristic witnesses speak more in favor of the first meaning, the book of Revelation in favor of the second, and that at a very early date" (Prigent, *Commentary*, 650). Both the perfect tense and the imperative are possible, yet the Aramaic *Maranatha* conveys the essence of the Christly mystery: he has come and he is coming (soon). This is precisely what drove Jesus's disciples to recast apocalyptic texts and, more broadly, the Old Testament. See also Thomas J. Talley, *The Origins of the Liturgical Year*, 2nd ed. (Collegeville, Minn.: Liturgical, 1986), 79. Talley writes that the term *maranatha* is rendered in Greek as a single word, while "in Aramaic (and Syriac) it is two words, *marana tha*, a form of imperative force oriented toward the future, 'Come, our Lord.' However, that Greek transliteration could as easily present the perfect form expressive of a completed event in the past, *maran atha*, 'our Lord has come.'" In *Christ and Time*, Oscar Cullmann confirms that Revelation contains many allusions to primitive Christianity (104–5).
131. Rev. 2:9, 3:9. [TN: note that while *The Revised New Jerusalem Bible* and most other English-language Bibles translate *metanoêson* as "repent," the term literally means "convert."] John speaks even of those who call themselves Jews but are not so in reality.

132. Rev. 20:1–3.
133. Rev. 20:10.
134. Rev. 21:1–2.
135. Brütsch, *Clarté*, 329.
136. Brütsch, 330–31.
137. Augustine, *City of God* 20.9 (915).
138. Augustine, 20.7 (907).
139. Rev. 18:2, 21.
140. Phil. 3:13.
141. It is imprecise to say that the present will last *until* the Second Coming. This present is permanent, unending, without past or future. Here is yet another way to translate, more or less, kairos into chronos time.
142. Philippe Bobichon, *Justin martyr: Dialogue avec le Tryphon, édition critique* 32.2 (Fribourg: Academic Press Fribourg, 2003).
143. Rev. 18:2.
144. Hans Blumenberg quite rightly wrote, "Christianity laid claim only very late to having initiated a new phase of history. Initially this was totally out of the question for it because of its eschatological opposition to history and the unhistorical quality that was (at least) implied by it." See Blumenberg, *Legitimacy of the Modern Age*, 468.
145. Mark 1:15.
146. "Let anyone who can hear, listen to what the Spirit is saying to the churches" (Rev. 2:7, 11, 17, 29; 3:6, 13, 22). Each of the letters addressed to the seven churches ends with this formula.
147. 1 Cor. 7:29–30.
148. 2 Thess. 2:3, 6–7.

2. THE CHRISTIAN ORDER OF TIME AND ITS SPREAD

1. Paul Veyne, *When Our World Became Christian, 312–394*, trans. Janet Lloyd (Cambridge: Polity, 2010), 2–9; Pierre Chuvin, *A Chronicle of the Last Pagans*, trans. B. A. Archer (Cambridge, Mass.: Harvard University Press, 1990), 23–35.
2. Eusebius, *History of the Church* 10.5.7–8, 480. [TN: Note that due presumably to a proofreading error, no section 8 is indicated in this edition].
3. Guy G. Stroumsa, *The End of Sacrifice: Religious Transformations in Late Antiquity*, trans. Susan Emanuel (Chicago: University of Chicago Press, 2009).
4. Veyne, *When Our World Became Christian*, 91.
5. Veyne, 91.
6. See chapter 1. Also see, among others, Roger T. Beckwith, *Calendar, Chronology and Worship: Studies in Ancient Judaism and Early Christianity* (Leiden: Brill, 2005), 1–4.
7. Paul Ricoeur, *Time and Narrative*, trans. Kathleen Blamey and David Pellauer (Chicago: University of Chicago Press, 1988), 3:105, 109.

8. Emile Benveniste, "Language and Human Experience," trans. Nora McKoen, *Diogenes* 51 (1965): 5–6.
9. Hesiod, *The Works and Days* 782–84, in *Hesiod*, trans. Richmond Lattimore (Ann Arbor: University of Michigan Press, 1959), 111.
10. *Hesiod*, 117.
11. James C. VanderKam, *Jubilees: The Hermeneia Edition* prologue, 49:7–8 (Minneapolis: Fortress, 2020), 160–61.
12. *Book of Enoch* 93.3–9, 91.12–17 (132–34).
13. 2 Baruch 24:3.
14. Aimé Georges Martimort, ed., *The Church at Prayer: An Introduction to the Liturgy*, vol. 1: *Principles of the Liturgy*, trans. Matthew O'Connell, rev. ed. (Collegeville, Minn.: Liturgical, 1985).
15. Jacques Le Goff, *In Search of Sacred Time: Jacobus de Voragine and the* Golden Legend, trans. Lydia G. Cochrane (Princeton, N.J.: Princeton University Press, 2014), 15. The definition of liturgy cited by Le Goff is quoted from Monsignor Albert Houssiau.
16. Tertullian, *Concerning Prayer*, in *Tertullian's Treatises*, trans. Alexander Souter (London: Society for Promoting Christian Knowledge; New York: Macmillan, 1919), 41.
17. Alistair Stewart-Sykes, *The Didascalia apostolorum* 6.18.16 (Turnhout, Belg.: Brepols, 2009), 248. This is a treatise addressed to Syria's Christian communities at the beginning of the century. See also Charles Piétri, "Le temps de la semaine à Rome et dans l'Italie chrétienne, IVe–VIe siècle," 63–97, and Luce Piétri, "Calendrier liturgique et temps vécu: l'exemple de Tours au VIe siècle," 129–41, both in *Le temps chrétien de la fin de l'Antiquité au Moyen Âge, IIIe–XIIIe siècle* (Paris: CNRS, 1984).
18. Jean-Claude Schmitt, *Les rythmes au Moyen Âge* (Paris: Gallimard, 2016), 258. On the books of hours, see 332–37.
19. Schmitt, 304–5. Jacques de Voragine also relies on a fourfold structure, noting in the opening of the preface to *The Golden Legend* that "the whole time-span of this present comprises four distinct periods." See Le Goff, *In Search of Sacred Time*, 18.
20. Le Goff, 25–26.
21. Schmitt, *Rythmes au Moyen Âge*, 300–303.
22. Schmitt, 591–99; Claude Carozzi, *Apocalypse et salut dans le christianisme ancien et médiéval* (Paris: Aubier, 1999), 180–85.
23. Acts 17:23, 26, 32.
24. Richard W. Burgess, "Apologetic and Chronography: The Antecedents of Julius Africanus," in *Julius Africanus und die christliche Weltchronik*, ed. Martin Wallraff (Berlin: Walter de Gruyter, 2006).
25. Alden A. Mosshammer, *The "Chronicle" of Eusebius and Greek Chronographic Tradition* (Lewisburg, Pa.: Bucknell University Press, 1979), 84–112.

2. THE CHRISTIAN ORDER OF TIME AND ITS SPREAD 251

26. See the section "Orosius's *Histories Against the Pagans* and Augustine's *The City of God*" later in this chapter and *"Translatio"* in chapter 3.
27. Arnaldo Momigliano, "Pagan and Christian Historiography in the Fourth Century A.D.," in *Essays in Ancient and Modern Historiography* (Middletown, Conn.: Wesleyan University Press, 1977), 110.
28. Herodotus, *The History* 2.143, trans. David Grene (Chicago: University of Chicago Press, 1987), 194.
29. In *Against Apion*, written between AD 90 and 95, Flavius Josephus replied to a range of insults directed toward the Jews, beginning with the claim that the Jews must be a recent people since they had gone unmentioned by Greek historians. He insisted that the problem in fact resided in the youth and ignorance of the Greeks.
30. Josephus, *Against Apion; or, On the Antiquity of the Jews* 1.1, in *The Life; Against Apion*, trans. H. St. J. Thackeray, Loeb Classical Library 186 (Cambridge, Mass.: Harvard University Press, 1926), 163.
31. See "*The City of God*" section later in this chapter and "Updating the Chronology of the Bible" and "Two Sentinels: Bossuet and Newton" in chapter 4.
32. Mosshammer, *The "Chronicle" of Eusebius*, 29–37; Hervé Inglebert, *Interpretatio Christiana: les mutations des savoirs dans l'Antiquité chrétienne, 30–630 après J.-C.* (Paris: Institut d'Études augustiniennes, 2001), 493–512.
33. See the section "Joseph Scaliger (1560–1609): Eusebius Updated" in chapter 4.
34. When Jerusalem was colonized by Rome, Hadrian renamed it Ælia Capitolina. Subsequent to the revolt led by Simon bar Kokhba (132–35), Jews were barred from Jerusalem.
35. Iulius Africanus, *Chronographiae: The Extant Fragments*, ed. Martin Wallraff, trans. William Adler (Berlin: Walter de Gruyter, 2007). Brian Croke notes that Eusebius's originality was acknowledged in antiquity by Jerome, Augustine, Cassiodorus, and Isidore of Seville, the last describing Eusebius's history as "multiplex"; see Brian Croke, "The Originality of Eusebius' *Chronicle*," *American Journal of Philology* 103, no. 2 (1982): 195–200.
36. Jean Sirinelli, *Les vues historiques d'Eusèbe de Césarée durant la période prénicéenne* (Paris: Université de Paris, 1961), 52–59, 497–515.
37. Writing in the third century, Irenaeus explained, "For in as many days as this world was made, in so many thousand years shall it be concluded. And for this reason the Scripture says: 'Thus the heaven and the earth were finished, and all their adornment. And God brought to a conclusion upon the sixth day the works that he had made; and God rested upon the seventh day from all His works.' This is an account of the things formerly created, as also it is a prophecy of what is to come. For the day of the Lord is as a thousand years; and in six days created things were completed: it is evident, therefore, that they will come to an end at the sixth thousand year." See Irenæus, *Against Heresies* 5.28.3, in *Ante-Nicene Fathers: The Writings of the Fathers Down to A.D. 325*, ed.

Alexander Roberts and James Donaldson, vol. 1: *The Apostolic Fathers, Justin Martyr, Irenoeus*, ed. Alexander Roberts, James Donaldson, and A. Cleveland Coxe, trans. Alexander Roberts and William Rambaut (Christian Literature, 1885; Peabody, Mass.: Hendrickson, 1994), 557, rev. and ed. for New Advent by Kevin Knight, https://www.newadvent.org/fathers/0103528.htm.

38. See the section "Two Sentinels: Bossuet and Newton" in chapter 4. See also Paolo Rossi, *The Dark Abyss of Time: The History of the Earth and the History of Nations from Hooke to Vico*, trans. Lydia G. Cochrane (Chicago: University of Chicago Press, 1984).

39. Eusebius, *Chronicle*, preface, http://attalus.org/translate/eusebius4.html#1, accessed November 12, 2021.

40. Richard Landes, "Lest the Millennium Be Fulfilled: Apocalyptic Expectations and the Pattern of Western Chronography, 100–800 CE," in *The Use and Abuse of Eschatology in the Middle Ages*, ed. Werner Verbeke, Daniel Verhelst, and Andries Welkenhuysen (Leuven: Leuven University Press, 1988), 137–209.

41. Jerome translated only the second book, which he extended to 378, completing the work from the Roman perspective.

42. Anthony Grafton and Megan Williams, *Christianity and the Transformation of the Book* (Cambridge, Mass.: Harvard University Press, 2006), 133–77.

43. Augustine, *City of God* 18.37 (812).

44. Eusebius's *Chronicle*, part 2, translated from Latin by Roger Pearse, "The Translated Preface of Eusebius," *Chronicon*, https://web.archive.org/web/20111204225524/http://rbedrosian.com/jerome_chronicle_01_prefaces.htm, accessed November 7, 2021.

45. Eusebius's *Chronicle*, part 2.

46. Eusebius, *Preparation for the Gospel* 1.4.9d–11d, trans. Edwin Hamilton Gifford, 2 vols. (Oxford: Clarendon, 1903; Grand Rapids, Mich.: Baker Book House, 1981), 1:11–13.

47. Malcolm Drew Donalson, *A Translation of Jerome's "Chronicon" with Historical Commentary* 249d (Lewiston, N.Y.: Mellen University Press, 1996), 57.

48. Jerome, quoted in Peter Brown, *Augustine of Hippo*, new ed. (Berkeley: University of California Press, 2000), 285–96 (quotation on 288).

49. Paul Valéry, "The Intellectual Crisis," in *Variety*, trans. Malcolm Cowley (New York: Harcourt, Brace, 1927), 13, 20. Valéry's letter appeared in 1919 in *La Nouvelle revue française*.

50. Orosius, *Seven Books of History Against the Pagans* 2.1.6, trans. A. T. Fear (Liverpool: Liverpool University Press, 2010), 74.

51. Orosius 7.2.1–2 (320).

52. Dan. 7:2.

53. Orosius, *Histories Against the Pagans* 7:2.2 (320).

54. Orosius 7.41.8 (407).

55. Orosius 7.35.6 (389).

56. Augustine, *City of God* 1.preface (5).

2. THE CHRISTIAN ORDER OF TIME AND ITS SPREAD   253

57. 1 Pet. 5:5 (echoing Prov. 3:34).
58. Seamus Heaney, *Aeneid Book VI* (New York: Farrar, Straus and Giroux, 2016), 89.
59. Augustine, *City of God* 14.28 (593).
60. Augustine 15.5 (600).
61. Augustine 18.1 (761).
62. Augustine 18.2 (764).
63. Augustine 20.23 (945). In fact, in his *Commentary on Daniel*, Jerome identifies the first kingdom as Babylon, the second as the Medes and Persians, the third as Alexander and his successors, and the fourth as Rome.
64. Augustine 18.22 (787).
65. Augustine 18.2 (762).
66. Augustine 18.40 (815).
67. Augustine 22.30 (1091).
68. Augustine, *Sermons* 81.8, quoted in Brown, *Augustine of Hippo*, 296.
69. Augustine, *City of God* 22.30 (1091).
70. 2 Peter 3:8.
71. Augustine, *City of God* 20.1 (895).
72. Augustine 20.17 (929).
73. Augustine 20.7 (908).
74. Augustine 20.19 (931, 933). Note that the Antichrist is not mentioned in the letters of Paul.
75. Augustine 20.19 (933).
76. Augustine 20.23 (944–45).
77. Ernst Bloch, in his study of German society on the brink of Nazism, was the first to offer this formulation. See Ernst Bloch, *Heritage of Our Times*, trans. Neville and Steven Plaice (Berkeley: University of California Press, 1991). Reinhart Koselleck sees this as a fundamental aspect of how history grapples with the world's diversity. Consider the encounter with "savages" that took place in the sixteenth century, a series of meetings between contemporaries and noncontemporaries, that occurred in the same chronological time and in another time entirely. See Reinhart Koselleck, " 'Neuzeit': Remarks on the Semantics of the Modern Concepts of Movement," in *Futures Past: On the Semantics of Historical Time*, trans. Keith Tribe (Cambridge, Mass.: MIT Press, 1985), 242–43 (indigenous peoples), 249 ("the contemporaneity of the noncontemporaneous").
78. Alden A. Mosshammer, *The Easter Computus and the Origins of the Christian Era* (Oxford: Oxford University Press, 2008); Georges Declercq, *Anno Domini: The Origins of the Christian Era* (Turnhout: Brepols, 2000).
79. Eusebius, *Preface*, in Saint Jérôme, *Chronique*, 65.
80. Bede, letter to Plegwin, in *The Reckoning of Time*, trans. Faith Wallis (Liverpool: Liverpool University Press, 1999), 406 ("Hebrew Truth"); Bede, *On the Nature of Things and On Times*, trans. Calvin B. Kendall and Faith Wallis (Liverpool: Liverpool University Press, 2010), 126 (for the math). Some sort of action had

become imperative—or at least useful—as the territory in which Bede was treading could have fueled millenarian upheavals: 5200 + 700 = 5900.
81. Bede, letter to Plegwin, 412–13, 414.
82. Bede, *On Times*, 131; Bede, *Reckoning of Time*, 239.
83. Dionysius Exiguus, "Letter to Petronius 20," quoted in Robert Hannah, *Greek and Roman Calendars: Constructions of Time in the Classical World* (London: Duckworth, 2005), 155. Emphasis is mine. Denys says nothing about how he managed to bring into juxtaposition the 248th year of Diocletian and the year 532.
84. Declercq, *Anno Domini*, 138.
85. Declercq, 150 ("incarnation era"), 139 ("did not have"). See also Mosshammer, *Easter Computus*, 8.
86. Bede, *Reckoning of Time*, 156.
87. Wallis, introduction to Bede, *Reckoning of Time*, lxx.
88. Declercq, *Anno Domini*, 184.

3. NEGOTIATING WITH CHRONOS

1. Ernesto de Martino, *La fin du monde: essai sur les apocalypses culturelles*, ed. Giordana Charuty, Daniel Fabre, and Marcello Massenzio (Paris: École des hautes études en sciences sociales, 2016), 221. For a more general view of the Middle Ages, see Georges Duby, *The Age of the Cathedrals: Art and Society, 980–1420*, trans. Eleanor Levieux and Barbara Thompson (Chicago: University of Chicago Press, 1981).
2. See the section "The New Testament and the Apocalyptic Future" in chapter 1.
3. One enduring negotiation is that which turns on time and money, a topic around which a small scholarly industry has grown. The topic is broached in Luke (6:35): "Lend without any hope of return." Between the twelfth and the fifteenth centuries, the focus turned to usury and credit. The usurer "sells the time that belongs to all creatures." Such unjust appropriation called down theological censure. But then, as Jacqus Le Goff noted in a classic article, "the whole of economic life at the dawn of commercial capitalism is here called into question." Accommodations would be needed. See Jacques Le Goff, "Merchant's Time and Church's Time in the Middle Ages," in *Time, Work, and Culture in the Middle Ages*, trans. Arthur Goldhammer (Chicago: University of Chicago Press, 1980), 29. In addition, see Giacomo Todeschini, *Les marchands et le temple: La société chrétienne et le cercle vertueux de la richesse du Moyen Âge à l'époque moderne*, trans. Ida Giordano and Mathieu Arnoux (Paris: Albin Michel, 2017); Sylvain Piron, *L'occupation du monde* (Brussels: Zones Sensibles, 2018), 170–76 (on Peter of John Olivi's *On Contracts*).
4. Stephen D. Benin, *The Footprints of God: Divine Accommodation in Jewish and Christian Thought* (Albany: State University of New York Press, 1993); Amos

Funkenstein, "Periodization and Self-Understanding in the Middle Ages and Early Modern Times," *Medievalia et Humanistica*, n.s., 5 (1974): 3–23.
5. 1 Cor. 3:1–3.
6. Irenaeus, *Against Heresies* 4.38.1 (521), available at https://www.newadvent.org/fathers/0103438.htm, accessed November 5, 2021.
7. Tertullian, *Le Voile des Vierges 1.6.8, Sources chrétiennes* (Paris: Cerf, 1997), 424.
8. Gal. 3:24 [*TN*: translation slightly modified].
9. 1 Cor. 10:11.
10. Augustine quotes from Marcellinus's letter in his reply. See Augustine to Marcellinus, AD 412, letter 138, in *The Works of Aurelius Augustine, Bishop of Hippo*, trans. Rev. Marcus Dods, vol. 13: *The Letters of Saint Augustine*, vol. 2 (Edinburgh: T. and T. Clark, 1875), 195.
11. Augustine, 196–97.
12. Augustine, 198.
13. *Walahfrid Strabo's libellus de exordiis et incrementis quarundam in observationibus ecclesiasticis rerum*, trans. Alice L. Harting-Correa (Leiden: Brill, 1995), 12.
14. Anselme de Havelberg, *Dialogues: Livre I, "Renouveau dans l'Église,"* trans. Gaston Salet (Paris: Cerf, 1966), prologue, 1141 B (30); book 1, chap. 5, 1147 B (59). [*TN*: Hartog has translated the Latin himself, departing slightly from Salet's reading.]
15. Anselme, book 1, chap. 5, 1147 C–1147 D (59, 61).
16. Anselme, book 1, chap. 1, 1141 D (35).
17. M.-D. Chenu, "Theology and the New Awareness of History," in *Nature, Man and Society in the Twelfth Century: Essays on New Theological Perspectives in the Latin West*, trans. Jerome Taylor and Lester K. Little (Toronto: University of Toronto Press, 1997), 183.
18. Jacques-Bénigne Bossuet, *Discourse on Universal History*, trans. Elborg Forster (Chicago: University of Chicago Press, 1976), 3, 4.
19. Gian Luca Potestà summarizes his biography of Joachim in "Joachim de Flore dans la recherche actuelle," trans. Andrea A. Robilglio, *Oliviana* 2 (2006), http://journals.openedition.org/oliviana/39. The biography is *Il tempo dell'Apocalisse: vita di Gioacchino da Fiore* (Rome: Laterza: 2004). See also Potestà, "Temps et eschatologie au Moyen Âge," in *L'attente des temps nouveaux: eschatologie, millénarismes et visions du futur, du Moyen Âge au xxe siècle*, ed. André Vauchez (Turnhout: Brepols, 2002), 106–21; Henri de Lubac, *Medieval Exegesis: The Four Senses of Scripture*, vol. 3, trans. E. M. Macierowski (Grand Rapids, Mich.: William B. Eerdmans, 2009), 327–419; Brett Edward Whalen, *Dominion of God: Christendom and Apocalpypse in the Middle Ages* (Cambridge, Mass.: Harvard University Press, 2009), 100–124.
20. Dante Alighieri, *Paradiso*, trans. Allen Mandelbaum, canto 12, lines 140–41, Digital Dante website, Columbia University, https://digitaldante.columbia.edu/dante/divine-comedy/paradiso/paradiso-12/, accessed July 26, 2021.
21. Lubac, *Medieval Exegesis*, 3: 352. Lifting the expression from Father Yves Congar, Lubac spoke of "apocalyptic historiosophy."

22. Henri de Lubac, *La postérité spirituelle de Joachim de Flore*, vol. 1: *De Joachim à Schelling* (Paris: Lethielleux, 1979), 14.
23. Pope Gregory I, cited by André Vauchez, "Le prophétisme chrétien de l'Antiquité tardive à la fin du Moyen Âge," in *Prophètes et prophétisme*, ed. André Vauchez (Paris: Seuil, 2012), 68.
24. Henry Mottu, *La manifestation de l'Esprit selon Joachim de Flore: herméneutique et théologie de l'histoire d'après le Traité sur les quatre évangiles* (Neuchâtel: Delachaux et Niestlé, 1977), 272.
25. See "Prophets and Apocalyptists" in chapter 1 and "Histories Against the Pagans" and "The City of God" in chapter 2.
26. Dan. 2:44, 7:3, 13, 14.
27. 2 Maccabees 9:5; Dan. 11:45, 12:1.
28. Arnaldo Momigliano, "Daniel and the Greek Theory of Imperial Succession," in *Essays on Ancient and Modern Judaism*, ed. Silvia Berti, trans. Maura Masella-Gayley (Chicago: University of Chicago Press, 1994), 29–35; David Flusser, "The Four Empires in the Fourth Sibyl and in the Book of Daniel," in *Israel Oriental Studies*, vol. 2 (Tel Aviv: Tel Aviv University, 1972), 148–75.
29. Momigliano, "Daniel and Imperial Succession," 29.
30. Dan. 2:21. See also 4:29.
31. Ecclus. 10:8.
32. Herodotus, *Histories* 1.95 (79); Ctesias, *History of Persia: Tales of the Orient* 32.5, trans. Lloyd Llewellyn-Jones and James Robson (London: Routledge, 2010), 149.
33. *The Iliad of Homer* 6.448–49, trans. Richmond Lattimore (Chicago: University of Chicago Press, 1951), 165.
34. Polybius, *The Histories* 38.22, vol. 6, trans. W. R. Paton, rev. Frank W. Walbank and Christian Habicht, Loeb Classical Library 161 (Cambridge, Mass.: Harvard University Press, 2012), 489, 491.
35. Polybius 1.2.2–7 (5).
36. Dionysius of Halicarnassus, *Roman Antiquities* 1.2, trans. Earnest Cary, Loeb Classical Library 319 (Cambridge, Mass.: Harvard University Press, 1937), 574.
37. Joseph Ward Swain, "The Theory of the Four Monarchies: Opposition History Under the Roman Empire," *Classical Philology* 35, no. 1 (January 1940): 1–21.
38. Michael D. Fortner, *The Sibylline Oracles* (Lawton, Okla.: Great Plains, 2011), 99.
39. Dan. 9:26.
40. *Jerome's Commentary on Daniel* 9.24–27, trans. Gleason L. Archer, Jr. (Grand Rapids, Mich.: Baker Book House, 1958), 95.
41. Irenaeus, *Against Heresies* 5.26.2, trans. Alexander Roberts and William Rambaut, in *Ante-Nicene Fathers*, vol. 1, ed. Alexander Roberts, James Donaldson, and A. Cleveland Coxe (Buffalo, N.Y.: Christian Literature, 1885), 555.
42. Swain cites a fragment from the poet Ennius (d. 172 BC) that indicates that the fall of the Assyrian Empire and the founding of Rome were contemporaneous. Here begins a theme that will enjoy much revival up to and including Augustine. See Swain, "Theory of the Four Monarchies," 3.

3. NEGOTIATING WITH CHRONOS   257

43. This important passage from Varro was reported by the grammarian Censorinus. See Censorinus, *The Birthday Book* 21.1, trans. Holt N. Parker (Chicago: University of Chicago Press, 2007), 48. Augustine lays out Varro's tripartite time in *City of God* 6.5 (234).
44. Saint Augustine, *The Augustine Catechism: The Enchiridion on Faith, Hope, and Love*, ed. John E. Rotelle, trans. Bruce Harbert (Hyde Park, N.Y.: New City, 1999), 118 (131–32).
45. John 18:36; Matt. 22:21.
46. See *"Histories Against the Pagans"* and *"The City of God"* in chapter 2.
47. Robert L. Benson, "Political *Renovatio*: Two Models from Roman Antiquity," in *Renaissance and Renewal in the Twelfth Century*, ed. Robert L. Benson and Giles Constable, with Carol B. Lanham (Oxford: Clarendon, 1982), 359–71.
48. Werner Goez, *Translatio Imperii: ein Beitrag zur Geschichte des Geschichtsdenkens und der politischen Theorien im Mittelalter und in der frühen Neuzeit* (Tubingen[?]: n.p., 1958).
49. See "The Epistles of Paul" in chapter 1.
50. Otto, Bishop of Freising, *The Two Cities: A Chronicle of Universal History to the Year 1146 A.D.*, trans. Charles Christopher Mierow, ed. Austin P. Evans and Charles Knapp (New York: Columbia University Press, 2002), 323–24.
51. To describe the church as the only city, as Otto of Freising does, amounts to reconciling imperial power (*regnum*) and the priesthood (*sacerdotium*). This in spite of the fierce opposition between the two, particularly during the Investiture Controversy.
52. Otto, Bishop of Freising, *Two Cities*, 283.
53. Otto, 94.
54. The westward march is not a theme developed by Otto of Freising alone. Hugh of Saint-Victor believed it a result of divine Providence, reckoning that once the march had reached the world's outermost limits, time itself would end. Cited in Chenu, "Theology and the New Awareness of History," 187. In his prologue, Otto of Freising stated that science was transmitted from Babylon to Egypt, thence to the Greeks, Romans, Gauls, and Spaniards.
55. See "Translatio as Chronology" in chapter 4.
56. *New Catholic Encyclopedia*, 1st ed., s.v. "Reform"; Gerhart B. Ladner, *The Idea of Reform: Its Impact on Christian Thought and Action in the Age of the Fathers* (Cambridge, Mass.: Harvard University Press, 1959); Giles Constable, "Renewal and Reform in Religious Life: Concepts and Realities," in Benson and Constable, *Renaissance and Renewal in the Twelfth Century*, 37–67; Giles Constable, *The Reformation of the Twelfth Century* (Cambridge: Cambridge University Press, 1996).
57. Benson, "Political *Renovatio*," 359–60.
58. See "Anselm of Havelberg" in this chapter.
59. Quoted in Constable, *Reformation of the Twelfth Century*, 163.
60. See *"Accommodatio"* in this chapter.

61. See "Accommodatio Perverted" in chapter 4.
62. Patrick Collinson, *The Reformation: A History* (New York: Penguin, 2004), 58.
63. Lucien Febvre, *Martin Luther: A Destiny*, trans. Roberts Tapley (New York: Dutton, 1929), 303 [TN: translation slightly modified]. See also Marc Lienhard, *Luther: Ses sources, sa pensée, sa place dans l'histoire* (Geneva: Labor et Fides, 2016).
64. Luther seldom used the term *reformatio*. Only one and a half centuries after his death was his accomplishment labeled *reformatio* (and "Lutheranism"). See *New Catholic Encyclopedia*, 1st ed., s.v. "Reform."
65. Jean-Christophe Saladin, *La bataille du grec à la Renaissance* (Paris: Belles Lettres, 2000), 357 (quotation) and, more generally, 355–61.
66. See "Reform" in chapter 5.

4. DISSONANCES AND FISSURES

1. Augustine, *The City of God* 16.26 (687).
2. Augustine 17.14 (744).
3. Augustine 17.1 (712).
4. Ecc. 1:9.
5. See the section "Past/Present, Old/New" in chapter 1.
6. Walter Map's *Of the Trifles of Courtiers* is cited in M.-D. Chenu, "Tradition and Progress," in *Nature, Man and Society in the Twelfth Century: Essays on New Theological Perspectives in the Latin West*, trans. Jerome Taylor and Lester K. Little (Toronto: University of Toronto Press, 1997), 320n24. Based as it is on the adverb *modo*, meaning "recently," the adjective *modernus* means "recent" and has come to mean "now." It distinguishes a qualitatively distinct time from what went before.
7. François Hartog, *Partir pour la Grèce*, rev. ed., Champs Histoire (Paris: Flammarion, 2018), 29–30.
8. Niccolò Machiavelli, *Discourses on Livy* 1.1, trans. Harvey C. Mansfield and Nathan Tarcov (Chicago: University of Chicago Press, 1996), 5.
9. Michel de Montaigne, "Of Coaches," in *Essays*, in *The Complete Works*, trans. Donald M. Frame (New York: Knopf, 2003), 842.
10. Alphonse Dupront, *Genèses des Temps modernes* (Paris: Gallimard, 2001), 49.
11. Francisco Rico, *Le rêve de l'humanisme: de Pétrarque à Erasme*, trans. Jean Tellez and Alain-Philippe Segonds (Paris: Belles Lettres, 2002), 19.
12. Pierre Vesperini, *Lucrèce, Archéologie d'un classique européen* (Paris: Fayard, 2017).
13. See "Reformatio" in chapter 3.
14. François Hartog, "À distance de loge: Découverte du monde et discordance des temps," in *À distance de loge: actes du colloque organisé avec Juan Rigoli en 2010 à Berne et à Genève*, in *Les approches du sens: essais sur la critique*, ed. Michaël Comte and Stéphanie Cudré-Mauroux (Geneva: La Dogana, 2013), 379–94. In my

article, I study a number of instances of the contemporanity of the noncontemporaneous, notably in the pages Montaigne devoted to the Indians of the New World; see "The Paschal *Tables*, the Years of the Incarnation, End of Times" in chapter 2.
15. Cecil Jane, trans. and ed., *The Four Voyages of Columbus: A History in Eight Documents*, 2 vols. in 1 (New York: Dover, 1988), 2:48.
16. Jean Bodin, *Method for the Easy Comprehension of History*, trans. Beatrice Reynolds (New York: Norton, 1969), 291. On the prominent place occupied by Daniel in the sixteenth century, see Claude-Gilbert Dubois, *La conception de l'histoire en France au XVIe siècle (1560–1610)* (Paris: Nizet, 1977), 387–500, 485–95 (on Bodin's chapter).
17. Bodin, *Method for the Easy Comprehension of History*, 291–93 [TN: translation slightly modified].
18. Bodin, 295 [TN: translation slightly modified], 296.
19. Bodin cites the early chapters of Thucydides on mankind's origins.
20. Bodin, 301 [TN: translation slightly modified].
21. Bodin, 302.
22. Bodin, 291.
23. In French, a convenient treatment is R. P. Antoine de Azevedo Vieyra Ravasco, *Histoire du futur*, trans. Bernard Émery (Grenoble: ELLUG-Université Stendhal, 2015).
24. *Espérances du Portugal Quint Empire du Monde, première et seconde vie du roi Jean IV, écrites par Gonsallanes Bandarra et commentées par le père Antoine Vieira . . . et remises à l'évêque du Japon* (1659). A cobbler by trade, Bandarra had prophesied the birth of a great king who would bring back justice and law to the land, unifying the world under a single scepter and a single faith. His prophecies "were enormously popular in Portugal, particularly among newly converted Christians and Jews, who believed that the end of the world was imminent." Lucette Valensi, *Fables de la mémoire: la glorieuse bataille des trois rois* (Paris: Seuil, 1992), 167. See also Hugues Didier, "La fin des temps selon *História do Futuro* et *Clavis Prophetarum* de P. António Vieira," *Eidôlon* 78 (2007): 53–66.
25. After defeat in 1578 at the hands of the troops of Sultan Abd al-Malik in northern Morocco, King Sebastian I vanished. Sebastianism promotes the myth of his glorious return. For Vieira, King John IV of Portugal, whom he served, was in fact the "invisible Sebastian." After the king's death, Vieira announced that he expected him to be resurrected soon. See Valensi, *Fables de la mémoire*, 162–63, 169–70.
26. Vieyra Ravasco, *Histoire du futur*, 87.
27. Vieyra Ravasco, 89, 90, 97, 98.
28. M. D. Chenu, "Theology and the New Awareness of History," in *Nature, Man and Society in the Twelfth* Century, 188 [TN: translation slightly modified].
29. Vieyra Ravasco, *Histoire du futur*, 192.

30. Vieyra Ravasco, 236, 238.
31. Chenu, *Nature, Man, and Society in the Twelfth Century*, 162.
32. Vieyra Ravasco, *Histoire du futur*, 274, 257, 261, 354.
33. Jacques-Bénigne Bossuet, *Discourse on Universal History*, trans. Elborg Forster (Chicago: University of Chicago Press, 1976), 300, 339–40, 5.
34. Bossuet, 299, 302, 303–4, 373, 301, 302.
35. Bossuet, 3, 4.
36. Bossuet, 374–75.
37. Jean Baptiste Pocquelin de Molière, *Tartuffe*, trans. Richard Wilbur (San Diego, Calif.: Harcourt Brace, 1963), 126 (IV, v). The definitive version of the play was performed in 1669. When Molière uses the word "compromises" (*accommodements*), he is referring to laxity, what he terms the "science, lately formulated, Whereby one's conscience may be liberated" (126).
38. Blaise Pascal, *The Provincial Letters*, trans. A. J. Krailsheimer (Harmondsworth: Penguin, 1967), 76.
39. Pascal, 85. [*TN*: Krailsheimer gives "modern" for Pascal's "nouveaux." I have retained the literal translation.]
40. Pascal, 93, 104, 150, 163.
41. Blaise Pascal, *Thoughts*, trans. W. F. Trotter, Harvard Classics, vol. 48 (New York: Collier, 1910), 64–65.
42. Richard H. Popkin, *Isaac La Peyrère (1596–1676): His Life, Work, and Influence* (Brill: Leiden, 1987), 3, 13, 24. La Peyrère's thought is described by Popkin as "Marrano theology" (25). See also Nathan Wachtel, "Théologies marranes: une configuration millénariste," *Annales* 2007, no. 1: 69–100. Noting a series of instances, including both La Peyrère and Vieira, Wachtel charts a "constellation of Marrano theologies." The millenarian impulse was inspired by, among others, Joachim of Fiore.
43. La Peyrère also claimed that close scrutiny contradicted the claim that Moses had written the Pentateuch. Spinoza and Richard Simon would take up this heresy. Simon, a friend of La Peyrère, denied him the title of scholar, rejecting all talk of pre-Adamites and the imminent arrival of a Jewish messiah while endorsing the critical examination of biblical texts. See Popkin, *Isaac La Peyrère*, 87.
44. Rom. 5:12–14. Paul says only that a single man brought sin into the world, that sin brought with it death. "Sin already existed in the world before there was any law, but sin is not reckoned when there is no law. Nonetheless death reigned over all from Adam to Moses, even over those whose sin was not after the model of Adam's transgression, who prefigured the one who was to come."
45. Isaac La Peyrère, *Du rappel des juifs* (1643).
46. Popkin, *Isaac La Peyrère*, 14.
47. Philatheles, "Peyrerius, and Textual Criticism," *Anthropological Review* 2, no. 5 (May 1864): 109, 110.

48. Anthony T. Grafton, "Joseph Scaliger and Historical Chronology: The Rise and Fall of a Discipline," *History and Theory* 14, no. 2 (1975): 156–85; Grafton, *Joseph Scaliger: A Study in the History of Classical Scholarship*, 2 vols. (Oxford: Clarendon, 1983–93).
49. See "Dionysius Exiguus and the Christian Era" in chapter 2.
50. James Ussher, *Annales Veteris Testamenti a prima mundi origine deducti* (London, 1650), cited in Donald J. Wilcox, *The Measure of Times Past: Pre-Newtonian Chronologies and the Rhetoric of Relative Time* (Chicago: University of Chicago Press, 1987), 187.
51. Grafton, "Joseph Scaliger and Historical Chronology," 173.
52. Chateaubriand, preface to *Études ou discours historiques sur la chute de l'empire Romain*, in *Œuvres complètes*, vol. 1 (Paris: Lefevre, 1831), xx.
53. Wilcox, *Measure of Times Past*, 203–8.
54. Wilcox, 207. "That I am writing in 1627 is true not by demonstration but by convention, but it still cannot be disproved. It must be accepted by hypothesis."
55. Adalbert Klempt, *Die Säkularisierung der universalhistorischen Auffassung: zum Wandel des Geschichtsdenkens in 16. und 17. Jahrhundert* (Göttingen: Musterschmidt, 1960), 86.
56. Jean-Robert Armogathe, *L'Antéchrist à l'âge classique: exégèse et politique* (Paris: Mille et une nuits, 2005), 149–50.
57. Jacques-Bénigne Bossuet, *L'Apocalypse avec une explication*, in *Œuvres complètes*, vol. 2 (Besançon: Outhenin-Chalandée, 1840), 12, 9, 10.
58. Isaac Newton, *The Principia: Mathematical Principles of Natural Philosophy*, trans. I. Bernard Cohen and Anne Whitman with Julia Budenz (Oakland: University of California Press, 1999), 54. See also Alexandre Koyré, *From the Closed World to the Infinite Universe* (Baltimore: Johns Hopkins University Press, 1957), 160–62.
59. Antoine-Nicolas de Condorcet, *Sketch for a Historical Picture of the Progress of the Human Mind*, trans. June Barraclough (New York: Noonday, 1955), 150.
60. Étienne Klein, "Le temps de la physique," CIRET website, http://ciret-transdisciplinarity.org/bulletin/b12c5.php, accessed September 8, 2021.
61. Frank E. Manuel, *Isaac Newton, Historian* (Cambridge, Mass.: Harvard University Press, 1963), 37.
62. Manuel, 92.
63. Manuel, 89.
64. Manuel, 165. On Newton and the Protestant apocalyptic tradition, see Rob Iliffe, *Priest of Nature: The Religious Worlds of Isaac Newton* (New York: Oxford University Press, 2017), 222–59.
65. Manuel, *Isaac Newton, Historian*, 160.
66. Manuel, 163.
67. Voltaire, *Essai sur les mœurs et l'esprit des nations, et sur les principaux faits de l'histoire, depuis Charlemagne jusqu'à Louis XIII* (Paris: Ch. Lahure, 1859), 121.
68. Voltaire, *Philosophical Dictionary*, trans. Peter Gay (New York: Harcourt, Brace, and World, 1962), 92.

5. IN THE THRALL OF CHRONOS

1. Ruth Harris, *Lourdes: Body and Spirit in the Secular Age* (New York: Viking, 1999).
2. Hans Blumenberg, *The Legitimacy of the Modern Age*, trans. Robert M. Wallace (Cambridge, Mass.: MIT Press, 1983), 3–120; Jean-Claude Monod, *La querelle de la sécularisation: théologie politique et philosophies de l'histoire de Hegel à Blumenberg* (Paris: Vrin, 2002).
3. See the section "Isaac la Peyrère (1596–1676)" in chapter 4.
4. As early as 1749, Buffon stated during his defense of *The Theory of the Earth* that he had presented "his hypothesis regarding the formation of the planets as no more than a purely philosophical reflection," and he denied "giving any thought to challenging scripture." See Jacques Roger, introduction to *Les époques de la Nature*, by Georges-Louis Leclerc, le comte de Buffon, ed. Jacques Roger (Paris: Éditions du Museum, 1988), c.
5. Roger, introduction, xli.
6. Roger, xli.
7. Buffon, 3, 15.
8. Roger, introduction to *Époques de la Nature*, lxv.
9. Roger, lxvii.
10. Buffon, *Époques de la Nature*, 43.
11. Gen. 1:1–2. Buffon even alleged that the use in these passages of the imperfect verb tense demonstrated the long duration of this period. But the imperfect was found only in the translation he read, not in the Hebrew.
12. In this, he shared the opinion of Newton. See Iliffe, *Priest of Nature*.
13. Buffon, *Époques de la Nature*, 19–24.
14. According to Roger, Nicolas-Antoine Boulanger and the astronomer Jean Sylvain Bailly induced Buffon to make this addition. See Roger, introduction to *Époques de la Nature*, xxxv.
15. Buffon, *Époques de la Nature*, 212, 220.
16. L. Becq de Fouquières, introduction to *Œuvres en prose de André Chénier*, ed. L. Becq de Fouquières, new ed. (Paris: Charpentier, 1872), xvi.
17. Voltaire, "History," The Encyclopedia of Diderot & d'Alembert Collaborative Translation Project, trans. Jeremy Caradonna, Ann Arbor: Michigan Publishing, University of Michigan Library, 2006, http://hdl.handle.net/2027/spo.did2222.0000.088.
18. Voltaire to Abbé Jean Baptiste Dubos, October 30, 1738, trans. Jacques Barzun, in *The Varieties of History: From Voltaire to the Present*, ed. Fritz Stern (New York: Vintage, 1956), 38.
19. Condorcet, *Sketch for a Historical Picture*, 5.
20. Condorcet, 4 [TN: translation slightly modified].
21. Condorcet, 12.
22. Condorcet, 9, 12–13, 199.

23. Condorcet, 200, 201.
24. Condorcet, 146, 160–61.
25. Charles Darwin, *The Origin of Species by Means of Natural Selection; or, The Preservation of Favored Races in the Struggle for Life* (New York: Modern Library, n.d.), 3.
26. Darwin, 277, 368.
27. Darwin, 373.
28. Darwin, 367.
29. Patrick Tort with Solange Willfert, *Darwin et la religion: La conversion matérialiste* (Paris: Ellipses, 2011), 371.
30. For "mischievous," see Adam Sedgwick to Charles Darwin, December 24, 1859, in John Willis Clark and Thomas McKenny Hughes, *The Life and Letters of the Reverend Adam Sedgwick* (Cambridge: At the University Press, 1890), 2:357.
31. James Hutton, *The Theory of the Earth*, in *Philosophical Transactions of the Royal Society of Edinburgh*, vol. 1 (Edinburgh: Royal Society of Edinburgh, 1788), 96.
32. Stephen Jay Gould, *Time's Arrow, Time's Cycle: Myth and Metaphor in the Discovery of Geologic Time* (Cambridge, Mass.: Harvard University Press, 1987), 92.
33. Charles Lyell, *Principles of Geology*, cited in Gould, 122.
34. Gustave Flaubert, *Bouvard and Pecuchet*, trans. Mark Polizzitti (N.p.: Dalkey Archive, 2005), 72.
35. Gould, *Time's Arrow*, 132.
36. Ernest Renan, "Lettre à M. Marcellin Berthelot," in *Œuvres complètes de Ernest Renan*, ed. Henriette Psichari, vol. 1 (Paris: Calmann-Lévy, 1947), 634.
37. See "Translatio Recused and Transformed" in chapter 4.
38. François Hartog, *Anciens, modernes, sauvages* (Paris: Points-Seuil, 2008), 256–59.
39. Jean-Jacques Rousseau, "Discourse on the Origin and Foundations of Inequality Among Men," in *Basic Political Writings*, 2nd ed., ed. and trans. Donald A. Cress (Indianapolis: Hackett, 2011), 53.
40. See "Accommodatio Perverted" in chapter 4.
41. Condorcet, *Sketch for a Historical Picture*, 201.
42. Victor Hugo, *La légende des siècles*, Première série: Histoire—Les petites épopées (Paris: Hachette, 1878), iv, 379, 374–75.
43. Pascal Ory, *Les expositions universelles de Paris* (Paris: Ramsay, 1982). The expositions were a "much-loved real-world laboratory for Saint-Simonianism" (18).
44. Henry Adams, *The Education of Henry Adams* (New York: Modern Library, 1931), 380.
45. Reinhart Koselleck, "'Neuzeit': Remarks on the Semantics of the Modern Concepts of Movement," in *Futures Past: On the Semantics of Historical Time*, trans. Keith Tribe (Cambridge, Mass.: MIT Press, 1985), 246.
46. Reinhart Koselleck, "'Space of Experience' and 'Horizon of Expectation': Two Historical Categories," in *Futures Past*, 271–76.

47. Alexis de Tocqueville, *Democracy in America*, trans. Henry Reeve, Francis Bowen, and Phillips Bradley (New York: Knopf, 1985), 2:399.
48. Reinhart Koselleck, "Modernity and the Planes of History,'" in *Futures Past*, 7.
49. Johann Wolfgang von Goethe, *Elective Affinities*, trans. R. J. Hollingdale (London: Penguin, 1971), 88. Quoted in Reinhart Koselleck, "Does History Accelerate?," in *Sediments of Time: On Possible Histories*, trans. Sean Franzel and Stefan-Ludwig Hoffmann (Stanford, Calif.: Stanford University Press), 90.
50. Koselleck, "Does History Accelerate?" 90.
51. Koselleck, 93–99.
52. Koselleck, "'Space of Experience' and 'Horizon of Expectation,'" 267–88.
53. See "*Reformatio*" in chapter 3.
54. Novalis, *Notes for a Romantic Encyclopædia: Das Allgemeine Brouillon*, ed. and trans. David W. Wood (Albany: State University of New York Press, 2007), 38 ("Time"); Novalis, *Œuvres complêtes*, trans. Armel Guerne, Éditions de la Pléiade (Paris: Gallimard, 1975), 2:395 ("History").
55. Pierre Larousse, *Grand Dictionnaire universel du XIXe siècle*, s.v. "Histoire."
56. François Hartog, *Croire en l'histoire* (Paris: Flammarion, 2016), 9–16.
57. Charles Peguy, *Zangwill*, in *Œuvres en prose complête*, Bibliothèque de la Pléiade (Paris: Gallimard, 1987), 1401, 1416.
58. Christophe Bouton, "L'histoire du monde est le tribunal du monde," in *Hegel penseur du droit*, ed. Jean-François Kervégan and Gilles Marmasse (Paris: CNRS, 2004), 263–77.
59. Bouton, 263–64, citing Hans Ulrich Gumbrecht, "Das neue Millennium als Weltgericht. Über Zusammenspiel von Philosophie, Geschichtsschreibung und politischer Rhetorik," in *Die Weltgeschichte—das Weltgericht*, ed. R. Bubner and W. Mesch (Stuttgart: Stuttgarter Hegel-Kongress 1999, 2001).
60. Oswald Spengler, *The Decline of the West*, vol. 2: *Perspectives of World-History*, trans. Charles Francis Atkinson (New York: Knopf, 1928), 507.
61. There were also the "dustbins of history" to which the enemies of the revolution were condemned, in a vulgar variation on the Final Judgment.
62. Bronislaw Baczko, "Le calendrier républicain," in *Les lieux de mémoire*, ed. Pierre Nora (Paris: Gallimard, 1997), 1:71.
63. Baczko, 76, 87. To match the calendar, the Convention set out to decimalize time. There were to be decades (of ten days) rather than weeks, days composed of ten hours, and right angles measuring 100 degrees rather than 90.
64. Mona Ozouf, "Regeneration," in *A Critical Dictionary of the French Revolution*, ed. François Furet and Mona Ozouf, trans. Arthur Goldhammer (Cambridge, Mass.: Belknap, 1989), 782.
65. Joseph de Maistre, *Considerations on France*, trans. and ed. Richard A. Lebrun (Cambridge: Cambridge University Press, 1994), 4, 5 [*TN*: translation slightly modified].

66. Maistre, 8, 19, 15, 20.
67. *The Memoirs of François René, Vicomte de Chateaubriand, Sometime Ambassador to England*, trans. Alexander Teixeira de Mattos (London: Freemantle, 1902), 6:217, 199, 218.
68. Chateaubriand, preface to *Ètudes ou discours historiques*, cli–clii.
69. Jules Michelet, 1869 preface to *Histoire de France*, in *Œuvres complètes*, ed. Paul Viallaneix, vol. 4 (Paris: Flammarion, 1974), 11.
70. Roland Barthes, *Michelet*, trans. Richard Howard (New York: Hill and Wang, 1987), 63–64. See also Barthes, "Michelet, l'Histoire et la mort," in *Œuvres complètes*, vol. 1, ed. Eric Marty (Paris: Seuil, 1995), 94.
71. Jacques-Bénigne Bossuet, *Discourse on Universal History*, trans. Elborg Forster (Chicago: University of Chicago Press, 1976), 375. See also "*Translatio* as Chronology" in chapter 4.
72. G. W. F. Hegel, *Reason in History: A General Introduction to the Philosophy of History*, trans. Robert S. Hartman (Indianapolis: Bobbs-Merrill, 1953), 43–44. [TN: this book comprises selections from *Lectures on the Philosophy of History*.]
73. Hartog, *Anciens, modernes, sauvages*, 166–71.
74. See "*Krisis*" in the introduction. Also see Reinhart Koselleck, "Some Questions Regarding the Conceptual History of 'Crisis,'" in *The Practice of Conceptual History: Timing History, Spacing Concepts*, trans. Todd Samuel Presner et al. (Stanford, Calif.: Stanford University Press, 2002), 236–47; Paul Ricoeur, "La crise, un phénomène spécifiquement moderne?" in *Écrits et Conférences*, vol. 4: *Politique, Économie et Société* (Paris: Seuil, 2019), 165–96.
75. Clément Juglar, *Des crises commerciales et de leur retour périodique en France, en Angleterre et aux États-Unis* (Paris: Guillaumin, 1862), vii.
76. Krzysztof Pomian, *L'ordre du temps* (Paris: Gallimard, 1984), 59–83.
77. C.-E. Labrousse, *La crise de l'économie française à la fin de l'Ancien Régime et au début de la Révolution*, vol. 1: *Aperçus généraux, sources, méthode, objectifs, la crise de la viticulture* (Paris: Presses universitaires de France, 1944), viii–lii.
78. C.-E. Labrousse, *Esquisse du mouvement des prix et des revenus en France au XVIIIe siècle* (Paris: Dalloz, 1993), 2:640.
79. François Hartog, *La nation, la religion, l'avenir: Sur les traces d'Ernest Renan* (Paris: Gallimard, 2017).
80. Renan, "Lettre à M. Marcellin Berthelot," 640, 634, 644.
81. Renan published *The Life of Jesus* in 1863. While the writing of *The Future of Science* was largely completed by 1849, it was not published until 1892.
82. Renan, "Lettre à M. Marcellin Berthelot," 639, 644, 645.
83. Ernest Renan, *The Future of Science* (Boston: Roberts, 1891), 18, 357–58, 362.
84. See "The Abbot of Fiore: Temporalized Accommodation" in chapter 3.
85. Ernest Renan, *Dialogues philosophiques*, ed. Laudyce Rétat (Paris: CNRS, 1992), fragments 214, 226, 244.
86. See "Leaving Presentism" in chapter 6.

87. Ernest Renan, *The Life of Jesus* (New York: Brentano's, 1863[?]), 32 ("fact"), 150 ("spontaneity"), 300 ("legend").
88. Ernest Renan, "De la part des peuples sémitiques dans l'histoire de la civilisation," in *Œuvres complètes de Ernest Renan*, vol. 2, ed. Henriette Psichari (Paris: Calmann-Lévy, 1948), 329 ("incomparable"); Renan, *Life of Jesus*, 311 ("will not be surpassed").
89. Renan, *Life of Jesus*, 302, 303.
90. Ernest Renan, *Recollections of My Youth*, trans. C. B. Pitman (London: George Routledge, 1929), 273.
91. Renan, *Life of Jesus*, 311.
92. Hartog, *Nation, religion, avenir*, 72, quoting Renan's preface to *New Studies in Religious History*.
93. Peter Galison, *Einstein's Clocks, Poincaré's Maps: Empires of Time* (New York: Norton, 2003), 125.
94. Galison, 292. See also Klein, *Chronos*, 75–80.
95. Galison, 293. See also Stephen Hawking, *A Brief History of Time* (New York: Bantam, 1988), 20–35.
96. Galison, 316.
97. Galison, 319.
98. Stalin, "Discours prononcé à la conférence des marxistes spécialistes de la question agraire" (27 December 1929), quoted in *À l'épreuve des totalitarismes (1914–1974)*, by Marcel Gauchet (Paris: Gallimard, 2017), 315.
99. In *History as Giving Meaning to the Meaningless* (1919), Theodor Lessing sets out to demonstrate that history is a function of belief rather than science.
100. Jacques Bouveresse, *Le mythe moderne du progrès: la critique de Karl Kraus, de Robert Musil, de George Orwell, de Ludwig Wittgenstein et de Georg Henrik von Wright* (Marseille: Agon, 2017). Bouveresse presents thinkers who have offered critiques not of progress but of what the Finnish philosopher Georg Henrik von Wright called, in a collection of that name published in Swedish in 1993, "the myth of progress."
101. Quoted in Emilio Gentile, *L'apocalypse de la modernité: La Grande Guerre et l'homme nouveau*, trans. Stéphanie Lanfranchi (Paris: Aubier, 2011), 195. Gentile is quoting from *Human, All Too Human*.
102. Gentile, 189.
103. Gentile's *Apocalypse de la modernité* considers many instances of regeneration and apocalypse.
104. Valéry, "Intellectual Crisis," 3–4.
105. Lucien Febvre, "Puissance et déclin d'une croyance," *Annales d'histoire économique et sociale* 43 (1937): 89.
106. H. I. Marrou, *Time and Timeliness*, trans. Violet Neville (New York: Sheed and Ward, 1969), 7–8.
107. Ernesto De Martino, *La fin du monde: Essai sur les apocalypses culturelles*, ed. and trans. Giordana Charuty, Daniel Fabre, and Marcello Massenzio (Paris: Éditions de l'École des hautes études en sciences sociales, 2016), 277–319.

108. De Martino, 71.
109. Albert Camus, *The Stranger*, trans. Matthew Ward (New York: Knopf, 1988), 3.
110. Walter Benjamin, "On the Concept of History," in *Selected Writings*, vol. 4: *1938–1940*, ed. Howard Eiland and Michael W. Jennings, trans. Edmund Jephcott and others, 389–400 (Cambridge, Mass.: Harvard University Press, 2003), 395–97 ("homogeneous, empty time"). Benjamin was not alone in seeking a path during these apocalyptic years; one thinks of Ernst Bloch and his *Thomas Münzer as Theologian of the Revolution* (1921). See also Michael Löwy, "Eschatologies et utopies révolutionnnaires modernes," in *Encyclopédie des religions*, ed. Frédéric Lenoir and Ysé Tardan-Masquelier (Paris: Bayard, 1997), 2:2099–2108.
111. Walter Benjamin, "Paralipomena to 'On the Concept of History,'" Eiland and Jennings, *Selected Writings*, vol. 4: *1938–1940*, 402. See also Michael Löwy, *Walter Benjamin: Avertissement d'incendie, une lecture des thèses "Sur l concept d'histoire* (Paris: Presses universitaires de France, 2001), 78.
112. Benjamin, "On the Concept of History," 397. See also Löwy, *Walter Benjamin: Avertissement d'incendie*, 118, 120.
113. The word *Jetztzeit* is Benjamin's term for the lightning that bursts from these temporal short circuits, and it is translated as "the present time" or "now-time." Giorgio Agamben sees it as a reprise of Paul's "kairos of now." See Agamben, *The Time That Remains: A Commentary on the Letter to the Romans*, trans. Patricia Dailey (Stanford, Calif.: Stanford University Press, 2005), 143.

6. CHRONOS DESTITUTED, CHRONOS RESTORED

1. Philippe Sands, *East West Street: On the Origins of "Genocide" and "Crimes Against Humanity"* (New York: Knopf, 2016).
2. Yan Thomas, *Les opérations du droit*, ed. Marie-Angèle Hermitte and Paolo Napoli (Paris: Gallimard, 2011), 255–80; Antoin Garapon, *Des crimes qu'on ne peut ni punir ni pardonner: Pour une justice internationale* (Paris: O. Jacob, 2002).
3. Paul Langevin, *La pensée*, July 5, 1945, 3–16. On this topic more generally, see Bernadette Bensaude-Vincent, "Framing a Nuclear Order of Time," in *Living in a Nuclear World: From Fukushima to Hiroshima*, ed. Bernadette Bensaude-Vincent et al. (Pittsburgh: Pittsburgh University Press, 2022).
4. Albert Camus, *Between Hell and Reason: Essays from the Resistance Newspaper Combat, 1944–1947*, trans. Alexandre de Gramont (Hanover, N.H.: Wesleyan University Press, 1988), 77.
5. Jean-Paul Sartre, "The End of the War," in *The Aftermath of War (Situations III)*, trans. Chris Turner (Oxford: Seagull, 2008), 71–72, 74–75.
6. Jean-Paul Sartre, editorial in *Les temps modernes* 1 (1945): 6.
7. Emmanuel Mounier, *Studies in Personalist Sociology*, in *Be Not Afraid: A Denunciation of Despair*, trans. Cynthia Rowland (New York: Sheed and Ward, n.d.), 26, 23 [*TN*: translation slightly modified].

8. Immanuel Kant, "An Answer to the Question What Is Enlightenment?," trans. James Schmidt, in *What Is Enlightenment? Eighteenth-Century Answers and Twentieth-Century Questions*, ed. James Schmidt (Berkeley: University of California Press, 1996), 58.
9. Karl Jaspers, *La bombe atomique et l'avenir de l'homme*, trans. Ré Soupault (Paris: Plon, 1958), 22, 46, 63. [TN: Karl Jaspers published two works in German with the title *Die Atombombe und die Zukunft des Menschen*. The first is brief and appeared in 1957, subtitled *"ein Radiovortrag."* That is the work translated by Soupault, issued by Plon in 1958.]
10. Günther Anders, *L'obsolescence de l'homme: Sur l'âme à l'époque de la deuxième révolution industrielle*, trans. Christophe David (Paris: Ivrea, 2002), 266, 269, 272.
11. Anders, 309, 31.
12. Anders, 314, 315.
13. Anders, 316.
14. Michel Serres with Bruno Latour, *Conversations on Science, Culture, and Time*, trans. Roxanne Lapidus (Ann Arbor: University of Michigan Press, 1995), 4.
15. Michel Serres, "Trahison: la Thanatocratie," in *Hermés III: la traduction* (Paris: Éditions de Minuit, 1974), 101.
16. Paul J. Crutzen and John W. Birks, "The Atmosphere After a Nuclear War: Twilight at Noon," *Ambio* 11, no. 2/3 (1982): 114–25.
17. Bensaude-Vincent, "Framing a Nuclear Order of Time."
18. Samuel Beckett, *Waiting for Godot* (New York: Grove, 1954), 84.
19. Beckett, 52–53. [TN: the translation has been modified to reflect Beckett's French original.]
20. Beckett, 54–55.
21. Michel Foucault, *Remarks on Marx: Conversations with Duccio Trombadori*, trans. R. James Goldstein and James Cascaito (New York: Semiotext(e), 1991), 85–86.
22. François Hartog, "Michel Foucault guetteur du présent," in *Foucault(s)*, ed. Jean-François Braunstein et al. (Paris: Éditions de la Sorbonne, 2017), 97–104.
23. Alexis de Tocqueville, *Democracy in America*, 2:399.
24. Wolfgang Streeck, *Buying Time: The Delayed Crisis of Democratic Capitalism*, trans. Patrick Camiller and David Fernbach, 2nd ed. (London: Verso, 2017), 19.
25. Fernand Braudel, *Civilization and Capitalism, 15th–18th Century*, vol. 2: *The Wheels of Commerce*, trans. Siân Reynolds (New York: Harper and Row, 1982), 433.
26. Streeck, *Buying Time*, lxii.
27. Harmut Rosa, *Social Acceleration: A New Theory of Modernity*, trans. Jonathan Trejo-Mathys (New York: Columbia University Press, 2013), 20.
28. Christophe Bouton, *Le temps de l'urgence* (Latresne: Bord de l'eau, 2013), 17.
29. Bouton, 132.
30. Invisible Committee, *Now*, trans. Robert Hurley, Intervention Series 23 (South Pasadena, Calif.: Semiotext(e), 2017), 16–17.
31. Invisible Committee, 17, 14.

32. Marcel Gauchet and Philippe Meirieu, remarks made during a debate on the question "Can the University Be Reinvented?" at Rencontres d'Avignon, July 13, 2011.
33. See the sections "*Reformatio*" in chapter 3 and "Reform" in chapter 5.
34. Alphonse Dupront, *L'histoire et l'historien*, Recherches et débats du centre catholique des intellectuels français 47 (Paris: Fayard, 1964), 25.
35. François Hartog, *Regimes of Historicity: Presentism and Experience of Time*, trans. Saskia Brown (New York: Columbia University Press, 2015), 186–91; Isabelle Anatole-Gabriel, *La fabrique du patrimoine de l'humanité: L'Unesco et la protection patrimoniale (1945–1992)* (Paris: Publications de la Sorbonne et Éditions de la Maison des sciences de l'homme, 2016).
36. The definition of the precautionary principle: "Where the occurrence of damage, although uncertain according to the state of scientific knowledge, could seriously and irreversibly affect the environment, public authorities shall, in accordance with the Precautionary Principle and within their fields of competence, ensure that risk assessment procedures are carried out and that provisional and proportionate measures are adopted to prevent the damage from occurring." See *Encyclopedia of the Environment*, s.v. "the precautionary principle," https://www.encyclopedie-environnement.org/en/zoom/the-precautionary-principle/, accessed October 25, 2021.
37. Mireille Delmas-Marty, *Libertés et sûreté dans un monde dangereux* (Paris: Seuil, 2010), 7.
38. Antoine Garapon, "La lutte antiterroriste et le tournant préventif de la justice," *Esprit* (March–April 2008): 151–54.
39. Delmas-Marty, *Libertés et sûreté*, 188.
40. Annette Wieviorka, *L'ère du témoin* (Paris: Plon, 1998).
41. Daniel Mendelsohn, *The Lost: A Search for Six of Six Million* (New York: HarperCollins, 2006), 391.
42. Pierre Nora, "General Introduction: Between Memory and History," in *Realms of Memory: Rethinking the French Past*, vol. 1: *Conflicts and Divisions*, trans. Arthur Goldhammer (New York: Columbia University Press, 1996), 1–20.
43. Nikolay Koposov, *Memory Laws, Memory Wars: The Politics of the Past in Europe and Russia* (Cambridge: Cambridge University Press, 2018).
44. François Hartog, *Croire en l'histoire* (Paris: Flammarion, 2016), 9–36.
45. Olivier Roy, *Is Europe Christian?*, trans. Cynthia Schoch (Oxford: Oxford University Press, 2020), 87.
46. Jean-Louis Comolli, *Daech, le cinéma et la mort* (Lagrasse: Verdier, 2016), 36, 72.
47. Phil. 3:13. See also "Past/Present, Old/New" in chapter 1.
48. Edward T. Hall, *The Silent Language*, cited in Hartmut Rosa, *Alienation and Acceleration: Towards a Critical Theory of Late-Modern Temporality* (Malmö: NSU Press, 2010), 77.
49. Hartmut Rosa, "Social Acceleration: Ethical and Political Consequences of a Desynchronized High-Speed Society," in *Alienation and Acceleration: Social*

Acceleration, Power, and Modernity, ed. Hartmut Rosa and William E. Scheuerman (University Park: Pennsylvania State University Press, 2009), 104.
50. See chapter 2, note 77.
51. Bouton, *Temps de l'urgence*, 261–63.
52. "Un horloge pour 10 000 ans," *Le Monde*, blog of Frédéric Joignot, February 22, 2018. The website of the Long Now Foundation, which is based in San Francisco, declares that the clock is under construction and that others are planned. Yet the name of the foundation seems ambiguous. Why "Long Now," which is very presentist, for a cultural project directed toward a long ten-thousand-year future?
53. François Hartog, "L'histoire à venir?," in *L'histoire à venir*, by Patrick Boucheron and François Hartog (Toulouse: Anacharsis, 2018).
54. According to a survey carried out in March 2019 by the market research company OpinionWay, 48 percent of French people think it is too late to reverse global warming. A range of survivalist reactions has sprung up, and permaculture is on the rise.
55. Isabelle Stengers, *In Catastrophic Times: Resisting the Coming Barbarism*, trans. Andrew Goffey (N.p.: Open Humanities, 2015).
56. Michaël Foessel, *Après la fin du monde: critique de la raison apocalyptique* (Paris: Seuil, 2012).
57. Olivier Rey, *Leurre et malheur du transhumanisme* (Paris: Desclée de Brouwer, 2018).
58. Daniel Cohen, *Les gènes de l'espoir à la découverte du génome humain* (Paris: Robert Laffont, 1993), 261.
59. Armin Grunwald, "What Does the Debate on (Post)human Futures Tell Us?," in *Perfecting Human Futures: Transhuman Visions and Technological Imaginations*, ed. J. Benjamin Hurlbut and Hava Tirosh-Samuelson (Wiesbaden: Springer Fachmedien, 2016), 35–50.
60. Nikolai Vassev, "Artificial Intelligence and the Future of Humans," *Forbes*, May 6, 2021, https://futurism.com/kurzweil-claims-that-the-singularity-will-happen-by-2045. See also Ray Kurzweil, *The Singularity Is Near: When Humans Transcend Biology* (New York: Penguin, 2005), 136 and passim.
61. See the sections "'Indefinite Progress'" and "The Case of Ernest Renan" in chapter 5.
62. Henri de Lubac, *La Postérité spirituelle de Joachim de Flore* (Paris: Lethielleux, 1979). See also "The Abbot of Fiore: Temporalized Accommodation" in chapter 3.
63. "La légende des siècles," in *The Poems of Victor Hugo* (New York: Atheneum Society, 1909), 435.
64. See "From the Greeks to the Christians" in the introduction.
65. For a brief history of the word *Anthropocene*, see Christophe Bonneuil and Jean-Baptiste Fressoz, *The Shock of the Anthropocene: The Earth, History and Us*, trans. David Fernbach (London: Verso, 2016), 3–18.

66. "Welcome to the Anthropocene," *Economist*, May 26, 2011, https://www.econo mist.com/leaders/2011/05/26/welcome-to-the-anthropocene. Readers of the *New York Times* and *Le Monde* frequently come across worrying news about the Anthropocene.
67. The term *Earth system* refers to the body of physical, geological, and biological processes as they interact with one another, operating at different scales, each with its own temporality, involving living things and inanimate things, life in general.
68. Jan Zalasiewicz, "The Extraordinary Strata of the Anthropocene," in *Environmental Humanities: Voices from the Anthropocene*, ed. Serpil Oppermann and Serenella Iovino (London: Rowman and Littlefield, 2017), 115–31. Zalasiewicz is a geologist at the University of Leicester and chair of the Anthropocene Working Group of the International Commission on Stratigraphy.
69. Zalasiewicz, 123, 124.
70. Zalasiewicz, 126–27, 129. [*TN*: For the mid-twentieth century as the boundary line, see 127.]
71. Zalasiewicz, 115.
72. Lucretius, *The Nature of Things*, trans. A. E. Stallings (London: Penguin, 2007), 36 (2. 1–2).
73. Dipesh Chakrabarty, "The Human Condition in the Anthropocene," Tanner Lectures in Human Values, delivered at Yale University, February 18–19, 2015, https://tannerlectures.utah.edu/_resources/documents/a-to-z/c/Chakrabarty %20manuscript.pdf. The summation of the thoughts presented in his lectures appears in Chakrabarty, *The Climate of History in a Planetary Age* (Chicago: University of Chicago Press, 2021).
74. Dipesh Chakrabarty, *Provincializing Europe: Postcolonial Thought and Historical Difference* (Princeton, NJ: Princeton University Press, 2000).
75. Karl Jaspers, *La situation spirituelle de notre époque*, trans. Jean Ladrière (Paris: Desclée de Brouwer, 1952), 11, 20. Jaspers also relies on the concept of "situation" (30ff.).
76. Zoltàn Boldizsár Simon, *History in Times of Unprecedented Change: A Theory for the Twenty-First Century* (London: Bloomsbury Academic, 2019).
77. Bonneuil and Fressoz, *Shock of the Anthropocene*.
78. J. R. McNeill and Peter Engelke, *The Great Acceleration: An Environmental History of the Anthropocene Since 1945* (Cambridge, Mass.: Belknap, 2014), 6.
79. Clive Hamilton, "Utopias in the Anthropocene," quoted in Dipesh Chakrabarty, "Lecture I. Climate Change as Epochal Consciousness," in "The Human Condition in the Anthropocene," 141.
80. Andrew Shyrock and Daniel Lord Smail, *Deep History: The Architecture of Past and Present* (Berkeley: University of California Press, 2011).
81. See "Apotheosized Humanity" in chapter 5.
82. Dipesh Chakrabarty, "Lecture II. Decentering the Human? Or, What Remains of Gaia," in "The Human Condition in the Anthropocene," 181.

83. The Atomic Clock, since 1947 the gauge of how much time separates us from nuclear Armageddon, was advanced in 2018 to two minutes to midnight. It has seen its brief enlarged to encompass all the threats facing mankind and the planet. Nick Bostrom has reviewed that various outcomes mankind is facing—extinction, recurrent collapse and recovery, some sort of intermediate state, posthumanity. He concluded that the last is the most likely. See Nick Bostrom, "The Future of Humanity," https://nickbostrom.com/papers/future.pdf, accessed November 5, 2021.
84. David Archer, *The Long Thaw: How Humans Are Changing the Next 100,000 Years of Earth's Climate* (Princeton, N.J.: Princeton University Press, 2009), 9.
85. Bruno Latour, *Facing Gaia: Eight Lectures on the New Climatic Regime*, trans. Catherine Porter (Cambridge: Polity, 2017), 245.
86. Denis Diderot, "Encyclopedia," Encyclopedia of Diderot & d'Alembert Collaborative Translation Project, trans. Jeremy Caradonna (Ann Arbor: Michigan Publishing, University of Michigan Library, 2006), http://hdl.handle.net/2027/spo.did2222.0000.004.
87. Latour, *Facing Gaia*, 247–48.
88. Fredric Jameson, "Future City," *New Left Review* 21 (May–June 2003): 76, cited in Latour, *Facing Gaia*, 108.
89. Land-use planning belongs to the government's futuristic logic, devised at a time when the civil engineers of France's Corps of Bridges and Roadways and its elite bureaucrats boldly blazed ahead with plans to build the future.
90. See the beginning of chapter 5.
91. John Sutter and Lawrence Davidson, "Teen Tells Climate Negotiators They Aren't Mature Enough," CNN website, December 17, 2018, https://www.cnn.com/2018/12/16/world/greta-thunberg-cop24/index.html.
92. Greta Thunberg (@gretathunberg), "Today is #AutismAwarenessDay," *Instagram*, April 1, 2019, https://www.instagram.com/p/BvviCzVhKpk/.
93. Masha Gessen, "The Fifteen-Year-Old Climate Activist Who Is Demanding a New Kind of Politics," *New Yorker*, October 2, 2018.
94. Hans Jonas, "Toward an Ontological Grounding of an Ethics for the Future," trans. Hildgarde and Hunter Hannum, in *Mortality and Morality: A Search for the Good After Auschwitz*, ed. Lawrence Vogel (Evanston, Ill.: Northwestern University Press, 1996), 99–100.
95. Jean-Pierre Dupuy, *Pour un catastrophisme éclairé: quand l'impossible est certain* (Paris: Seuil, 2002). In *Après la fin du monde*, Michaël Foessel attacks what he calls "the logic of the worst." He writes, "When we presume that catastrophe is already certain, we hand over from the outset all of the world's transformations to processes out of human control. We then picture the world's future as destiny, a rejection of the countless efforts made in modern times to think it an undecided horizon" (18–19).
96. Pierre-Henri Castel opens *Le mal qui vient: Essai hâtif sur la fin des temps* (Paris: Cerf, 2018) by declaring, "Less time will elapse between me and the last man

than between me and, say, Christopher Columbus" (11). The remainder of the book explores this idea. In *Devant l'effondrement: essai de collapsologie* (Paris: Les liens que libèrent, 2019), Yves Cochet, who had served as minister of the environment, announced that our way of life would end sometime between 2020 and 2035.

97. In an opinion piece on southern Australia's devastating months-long wildfires, published in *Le Monde* on January 11, 2020, Clive Hamilton, a professor at the University of Canberra, opened as follows: "You would think it was the apocalypse. A national catastrophe is unfurling; there are new shocks daily." He concluded by noting that a "harder to define" act of mourning was now necessary: grieving "the death of the future."

98. See "Kairos and Revolution" in chapter 5. Latour is never at a loss for a metaphor. In a passage that does not address the apocalypse, he is describing our current moment. Just as the sixteenth century was destabilized by "the shock of the discovery of *new lands* . . . it is the shock of discovering *new ways* of being on Earth that destabilizes us." See Latour, *Facing Gaia*, 190.

99. Latour, *Facing Gaia*, 195; Bruno Latour, *We Have Never Been Modern*, trans. Catherine Porter (Cambridge, Mass.: Harvard University Press, 1993).

100. Latour, *Facing Gaia*, 219. Inasmuch as the first characteristic of modern times is the erasure of limits, entailing the opening of an indefinite future, namely eternity, apocalypse must be removed from the horizon, to be replaced by a futuristic, temporalized utopia.

101. Latour, 212, 219, 285.

102. Taking his lead from Henri Bergson's reflections, Péguy expatiates on the present at length in *A Joint Note on Mr. Descartes*. He writes, "A man [Bergson] saw that the present was not the very edge of the recent past but instead the very edge of the near future. . . . And that it was imperative to seize the present in the present. . . . That the present possessed a certain unique way of being." See Charles Péguy, *Note conjointe sur M. Descartes*, in *Œuvres en prose complètes*, Bibliothèque de la Pléiade (Paris: Gallimard, 1992), 3:1440.

103. Latour, *Facing Gaia*, 176, 177.

104. Latour, 289.

105. Latour, 177.

106. Latour, 285–86, 218, 289, 251, 290.

CONCLUSION

1. Bruno Latour, *Facing Gaia: Eight Lectures on the New Climatic Regime*, trans. Catherine Porter (Cambridge: Polity, 2017), 217, 109, 117, 140–41.

2. In an interview in *Le Monde* in August 2019, Philippe Descola applied a similar sense of commonality to Brazil's Xingu River and France's Loire. He added, "This may be utopian, but it's urgent." Even utopias experience emergencies.

See Philippe Descola, "En Amazonie, c'est d'abord le milieu de vie des Amérindiens qui est détruit," *Le Monde*, August 27, 2019, https://www.lemonde.fr/idees/article/2019/08/27/philippe-descola-en-amazonie-c-est-d-abord-le-milieu-de-vie-des-amerindiens-qui-est-detruit_5503139_3232.html.

3. Dipesh Chakrabarty, "The Climate of History: Four Theses," *Critical Inquiry* 35 no. 2 (2009): 220.
4. Chakrabarty has proposed and unearthed a series of oppositions between the world and the globe, between the globe and the planet, between *anthropos* and *homo*, between susatinable and survivable or livable, between power and force. This suggests the range of approaches he brings to the new human condition that he examines in his forthcoming book.
5. Dipesh Chakrabarty, *The Climate of History in a Planetary Age* (Chicago: University of Chicago Press, 2021), 222. On Benjamin, see the section "A Singular Kairos" in chapter 5 of the present book.
6. Karl Jaspers, *Man in the Modern Age*, trans. Eden Paul and Cedar Paul (Garden City, N.Y.: Anchor, 1957), 5, 14. Jaspers also uses the concept of "situation": the emergence of a certain consciousness implies specific behaviors. He relied on the same concept in his study of the atomic bomb, published in 1958.
7. See "The Paschal Tables, the Years of the Incarnation, End of Times" in chapter 2 and "Renovatio Deflected: The Humanists" in chapter 4.
8. See "The Epistles of Paul" in chapter 1.
9. The Supreme Pontiff Francis, *Encyclical Letter: Praise Be to You, Laudato Si,' On Care for Our Common Home* (San Francisco: Ignatius, 2015), 16, 21, 113, 144–48.
10. Pope Francis, 97, 107, quoting Pope Benedict XVI, "Address to the German Bundestag," Berlin, September 22, 2011, AAS 103 (2011), 668.
11. Pope Francis, 50–51.
12. Pope Francis, 156. He adds, "The Eucharist joins heaven and earth; it embraces and penetrates all creation. . . . The Eucharist . . . direct[s] us to be stewards of all creation." He is practically repeating the words of Paul in Col. 1:20.
13. This is one of the book's leitmotivs.
14. In the conclusion of a forthcoming book, Dipesh Chakrabarty will address this topic.
15. *The Memoirs of François René, Vicomte de Chateaubriand, Sometime Ambassador to England*, trans. Alexander Teixeira de Mattos (London: Freemantle, 1902), 6:209. The solution he proposes, on which we shall not linger, consists in a combination of Christianity and progress. A "free and mighty" (220) future was inconceivable outside of Christian hope.
16. This is a chronos previously devastated by presentism.
17. Michel Guérin, *Le cimetière marin au boléro: Un commentaire du poème de Paul Valéry* (Paris: Belles Lettres, 2017), 146. Guérin notes, "Once the wind rises . . . the space that opens up and that of action, which divides itself, begin all over, breaking so as to begin anew." To confront these contemporary anxieties, see the reflections of Frédéric Worms on the most pressing problems of our time

and how to respond, in *Pour un humanisme vital: Lettres sur la vie, la mort et le moment présent* (Paris: Odile Jacob, 2019).

18. Jules Michelet, *Journal*, ed. Paul Viallaneix (Paris: Gallimard, 1962), 2:126.
19. François Hartog, *Regimes of Historicity: Presentism and Experience of Time*, trans. Saskia Brown (New York: Columbia University Press, 2015), 80, citing Chateaubriand, *Essai historique, politique et moral sur les révolutions anciennes et modernes, considérées dans leurs rapports avec la Révolution Française* (1797; 1826) (Paris: Gallimard, 1978), 15.

INDEX

Abraham, 19, 62–64, 70–71, 78
Abrahamic religions, viii
acceleration, 157–59, 195–97
accommodatio (accommodation of divine to human nature), 84, 85–92, 122–25
Advent, 54–56
Aeschylus, 6
Africanus, Julius, 58–61, 95
Against Apion (Josephus), 58, 251n29
Agamben, Giorgio, 101
al-Baghdadi, Abu Bakr, xiii
Allen, William, 175
American Metrological Society, 175
Anaximander, 2
Anders, Günther, 187–89, 190, 224
Anno Domini dating system, 52, 75, 82, 176
Anno Mundi dating system, 75, 78
Anselm of Havelberg, 87–89, 104, 106, 111–12
Anthropocene era, xii, xvi, xix, 209–34
Antichrist, 73, 79, 97, 99, 133
Antiochus IV (Epiphanes, Antiochus), 16, 21, 22, 25, 37, 93–94, 97, 99, 226

Apocalypse of John, 19, 35–44
Apocalypse of Weeks, 23
apocalyptic presentism, xix, 97, 151, 219
apocalypticism/apocalyptists: acceleration of time in, 12; Apocalypse of John, 35–41; calendars and eras, 53; epistles of Paul, 28–35; futurology of, 222–225; history and, 226; introduction to, xi–xiii; Jesus as, 25–26, 48; New Testament and, 25–47; prophets and, 19–25; as unending, 79
Apollo, 15
apotheosized humanity, 170–72
arcana imperii, 123
Arendt, Hannah, xviii
Aristotle, 1, 3, 156, 232
as though not (*hôs mê*), 46–47
Ascension of Jesus, 56
Assyrian Empire, 70, 243n25
atomic bombs, 185–89, 216
Augustine: accommodation and, 86–87; Apocalypse of John, 36; Christian regime of historicity, 109–10, 137–38; *The City of God*, 65–66, 68–74, 86, 100,

Augustine, *The City of God* (*continued*) 139–40; meditation on time, 1, 3–5; plenitudo temporis, 28; Revelation, 43; simultaneity of the nonsimultaneous, 229–30; structure of universal history, 47; unfaithfulness to, 104
Auschwitz, 155, 182, 183, 185, 203

Bacon, Francis, 158
Beckett, Samuel, 180, 190–92
Bede, Venerable, 60, 76, 78–81
before the Law (*ante legem*), 98
Benjamin, Walter, 181–82, 227–28
Benveniste, Émile, 51
Bernard of Chartres, 106
Bible, the: chronology of, 125–32, 141–50; Gospels, 13–19, 25–31, 37, 76, 84, 173; New Testament, 8, 15, 16, 25–47, 45, 56–57, 75, 90, 112; Old Testament, 15, 17, 30, 46, 56–57, 90, 112, 120, 135–36
Birks, John, 190
Bloy, Léon, 179
Blumenberg, Hans, 13–14
Bodin, Jean, 115–17, 152
Bonaparte, Napoléon, 162–63, 167
Boniface VIII, Pope, 56
Book of Daniel: Christian Daniel, 96–98; Christian order of time, 70, 72; Christian regime of historicity, 16, 19–23, 25; kairos and, 56–57; Newton on, 136, 139; *translatio* and, 115–22; uniqueness of, 93–96
Book of Jubilees, 23
Bossuet, Jacques-Bénigne, 11, 115, 121–23, 132–37, 139, 214
Buffon, Count, 141–45, 211–12, 214–15, 226–27
Bush, George W., xi

Caesar, Julius, 54, 129
calendars and eras, 51–56
Calvinism, 127

Camus, Albert, 181, 185
capitalism, 194, 218, 227
Carter, Jimmy, xi
catastrophe, 16, 20, 24, 45, 93, 97, 150, 186–87, 196–97, 210
Catholic Church, 36–37, 108, 114, 126, 133, 206, 231
Certeau, Michel de, xviii, 45
Chakrabarty, Dipesh, viii, 216, 219, 227–28
character of a year, 129–30
Charlemagne, 100–1, 106, 121
Chateaubriand, 163–65, 233, 235
Chenu, Marie-Dominique, 88
Christian *felicitas*, 68
Christian order of time: calendars and eras, 51–56; chronologers of, 56–74, 79–82; defined, 3–4; introduction to, viii–ix, 49–51; Paschal tables, 74–75, 76–79
Christian presentism, xix, 108, 118, 125, 141, 156, 205–7, 217, 220
Christian regime of historicity: *accommodatio* perverted, 122–25; Augustine on, 109–10, 137–38; champions of, 132–37; chronology of the Bible, 125–32; commitment to, 109–11; defined, 49; extension into present, 104–5; Gospels, 13–14; humanists, 111–15; introduction to, viii–xi, xvi, 10–13; La Peyrère, Isaac on, 126–28; modern time and modern regime of, 155–57; new covenant and, 14–19, 109; old covenant and, 109; overview of, 44–48; Pétau, Denis on, 131–32; prophets and apocalyptists, 19–25; *renovatio* deflected, 84, 111–15; Revelation, 41–44; Scaliger, Joseph on, 128–31; *translatio* recused and transformed, 115–22
Christly Kairos: Apocalypse of John, 37; apocalyptic present of, 230; Christian order of time, 60, 75, 77; Christian regime of historicity, 31–32, 48;

chronos and, 83–84, 92, 100; city of God, 151; expanded power over chronos time, 147; French Revolution and, 168; as hypothesis by Pétau, 132; temporal "plenitude" of, 110
Chronicle or History of the Two Cities (Otto of Freising), 102–4
chronologers: Africanus, Julius, 58–61; Augustine, 65–66, 68–74; challenges of, 56–58; of Christian order of time, 56–65; Eusebius of Caesarea, 26–27, 36, 58–65; Exiguus, Dionysius, 79–82; Orosius, 65, 66–68, 70
chronophagous chronos, 212
Chronophores, x
chronos: acceleration and, 157–59, 195–97; apotheosized humanity, 170–72; atomic bombs ending World War II, 185–89; changes in nineteen seventies, 189–90; changes to, 183–84; Christian regime of historicity, 11; chronology of the Bible, 125–32, 141–50; chronophagous chronos, 212; COVID-19 epidemic and, 235–37; defined, viii–ix, xv–xviii, 151; doubled chronos, 3–5; efforts to capture, 8–9; enriches through humanizing, 166; French Revolution and, 165–66, 171; Greek understanding of, xix, 2, 5; kairos and, 5–7, 8, 75, 139–41, 152; krisis and, 7–8, 139–41; modern time and modern regime, 155–57; new split within, 184–90; perfection and perfectibility, 152–55; planetary age, viii; presentism and, 190–211; progress and, 151–60, 170–72, 178–81; *reformatio* (reform), 84, 105–8, 159–60; Renan, Ernest on, 170–75; restoration (*restitutio*), 112, 211–12; solar cycles, 76; *status* in, 90; synchronizing clocks, 175–77; temporalized creation, 148–50. *See also* negotiating with chronos; time

City of God, The (Augustine), 65–66, 68–74, 86, 100, 139–40
civil history, 227
Cohen, David, 210
Cold War, 184, 189
Commentary on Daniel (Jerome), 96–97
Comolli, Jean-Louis, 206–7
Condorcet, Marquis of, 141, 145–47, 154, 180, 182, 211, 215
Constantine, 50, 102–3
Constitutional Festival (1793), 157
Convention Concerning the Protection of the World Cultural and Natural Heritage, 202, 227
cosmological time, 1
Council of Nicaea, 77
COVID-19 epidemic, 235–37
Creation, 71, 131–32
creative repetition, 24
crimes against humanity, 185
crisis and krisis, 167–70, 236
Crucifixion, 75, 76–77
Crutzen, Paul, 190, 212–13
cultural patrimony, 204
Cuvier, Georges, 150
Cuvillier, Elian, 36–37, 247n112
Cyril of Alexandria, 80
Cyrus, 16

Daniel, 19, 38–39, 72–73. *See also* Book of Daniel
Dante, 90
Darwin, Charles, 148–49
Day of Judgment, 11–13, 21, 23, 44–46
day of the Lord (*dies Domini*), 50, 54
day of the sun (Sunday), 50, 54
days of Zeus, 51–52
Declercq, Georges, 80
De Gaulle, Charles, 188
De Lubac, Henri, 211
De Martino, Ernesto, 83, 180–81
delayed Parousia, 34, 43, 47
Delmas-Marty, Mireille, 203

Democracy in America (Tocqueville), 156
democracy in real time, 198
destiny (*fatum*), 14
diathekê, defined, 15
digital condition, 212
Discourse on the Origin of Inequality (Rousseau), 153–54
Discourse on Universal History (Bossuet), 58, 89, 115, 121–23
Discourses on the First Ten of Titus Levy (Machiavelli), 112
Divine Comedy, The (Dante), 90
divisions of the seasons, 52
dominate (*libido dominandi*), 69
Don Pedro II, 176
Dupront, Alphonse, 197, 202
Dupuy, Jean-Pierre, 222
Durand, Guillaume, 55–56

Earthbound, 225
Earth's order of time, 215, 216–22
Easter, 52, 54–55, 74–78
Ecclesiastes, xviii, 13, 110
Ecclesiastical History (Eusebius of Caesarea), 26–27, 113
Ecclesiastical History of the English People (Bede), 81
ecology of man, 230
Edict of Milan, 50
Einstein, Albert, 176
Eleazar, 10
Elijah, 17, 19, 27
Enoch, 19, 24
epistles of Paul, 28–35
epoch divisions and Jesus, 49
epochs, defined, 142
Epochs of Nature (Buffon), 142–45
Esprit (magazine), 186–87
Eucharist, 37, 41, 230–31
Eusebius of Caesarea, 26–27, 36, 58–65, 113, 128–31, 136
Exiguus, Dionysius, 79–80, 129
Ezra, Fourth Book of, 21–22

Falwell, Jerry, xi
fasti days, 53–54
Feast of the Nativity, 54
Febvre, Lucien, 180
Final Judgment, 11–12, 23, 26, 35, 68, 79, 223
First Discourse (Buffon), 144
first Latin day (*feria prima*), 54
Foucault, Michel, 192
Fourth Book of Ezra, 21–22
Francis, Pope, 230–31
Franco-Prussian War, 178
French Constitution, 202–3
French Revolution, ix, 145, 147, 157, 162–68, 171, 224, 236
Future of Science, The (Renan), 170–71
futurism, 141, 190, 193, 199, 204, 210–11, 219
futurology, 222–25

Gaia, 2, 225–26
Galison, Peter, 176
Gandhi, Mahatma, x
Gauchet, Marcel, 201
General Assembly of UNESCO, 202, 227
Genius of Christianity, The (Chateaubriand), 165
"getting back to the land" movement, 209
globalization, vii, x, 194, 207–8, 216, 233
God: Apocalypse of John and, 40–41; chronos time and, 171–72; as creator of heaven and earth, 130; as ruler of times, 12, 20
God is dead, 179
godly perfection vs. human coarseness, 85–86
Gospels, 13–19, 25–31, 37, 46, 75–76, 84, 173, 245n62
Gould, Stephen Jay, 149
Graf von Moltke, Helmuth, 176
Grafton, Anthony, 129
Great Leap Forward, 176
Greek history and the Bible, 59
Greek Orthodox church, 36
Greek understanding of chronos, xix, 2, 5

Greenwich Mean Time (GMT), x, 176
Gregory I, 105
Gregory VII, 105

Hamilton, Clive, 218
Hebrew history and the Bible, 59
Hecataeus of Miletus, 57–58
Hegel, G. W. F., 162, 167
Hellenism, 19
Heloise, 106
Herodotus, 94, 99
Hertz, Joseph, x–xi
Hesiod, 51–52
Hippocratic crisis, 167
Hippocratic school, 7–8
Hippolytus of Rome, 58
Hiroshima bombing, 185–89
historia magistra, 113
Historical Picture of the Progress of the Human Spirit, A (Marquis of Condorcet), 145–46
Histories Against the Pagans (Orosius), 65, 66–68
history as guide (*historia magistra*), 14
History of France (Michelet), 165–66
History of the Future (Vieira), 118
Hollande, François, 195
Holocene era, 213, 220
holy men (*theios anêr*), 14
Holy Roman Empire, 101, 103–4, 111, 115–17
Holy Spirit, 26, 36, 90–91, 172
Homo faber, 215
Homo sapiens, 215, 227
homocentric history, 216
hope, 199
Hugo, Victor, 154–55, 212
human time, xvi–xvii
humanists, 111–15
Hutton, James, 149

Immaculate Conception, 140
in-between time (*media aetas*), 112

Incarnation, 79–82, 99, 131–32, 158
industrial revolution, 218
innovation, 62, 74–75, 88, 129, 196
Inquisition, 117–18
intermediate time, 162, 205
International Commission on Stratigraphy, 213
International Meridian Conference, 176
International Union of Geological Sciences, 213
Islamic State, xiii, 206–7

Jameson, Fredric, 220
Jaspers, Karl, 187, 216, 228
Jaurès, Jean, 197
Jerusalem, destruction of, 16
Jesus: as apocalyptist, 25–26, 48; Ascension of, 56; birth of, 60, 66, 129–30; as *Christos*, 56; coming of the kingdom of God, 16–17; Crucifixion, 75, 76–77; death of, 15, 76; epoch divisions and, 49; Gospels and, 13–14, 16–19; Incarnation, 79–82, 83, 85, 99; Last Supper, 15, 37; as a man, 174; as messiah, 230; new time inaugurated by, 28; regeneration of, 163; resurrection of, 29, 37, 44, 76, 79; as truth of the Old Testament, 120
Jewish Antiquities (Josephus), 58
Jewish millenarianism, 128
Joachim of Fiore, 84, 89–92, 99, 104, 111, 118, 121, 152, 172, 211, 260n42
John, 35–44, 139
John of Patmos, 37
John Paul II, Pope, 206
John the Baptist, 17, 27, 75, 118
John XXIII, Pope, 206
Josephus, Flavius, 58
Judgment Day (Krisis), ix, 11, 24–27, 33, 46–48, 61, 162
judicial time, 185
Julian period, 129–30
just-about nothing—memory, 203–5

kairoi (suitable moments), 8, 182
kairos: apocalypticism and, 13, 27; Christian regime of historicity, 11, 48; chronos and, 5–7, 8, 75, 139–41, 152; defined, viii–ix, 5, 11–12; modern time and, 178; revival of, 160–62, 166–67; revolution and, 162–65. *See also* Christly Kairos
kairos of now (*ho nun kairos*), 31, 46
katechon, 34, 35, 47, 73, 101
Koran, xiii
Koselleck, Reinhart, 156–57, 195
krisis: apocalypticism and, 13, 27, 225; Christian regime of historicity, 11, 48; chronos and, 7–8, 139–41; crisis and, 167–70, 236; defined, viii–ix, 7–8, 12; revival of, 160–62, 166–67
Kronos, 2, 149
Kurzweil, Ray, 210–11

Labrousse, Ernest, 167, 169
Landes, Richard, 72
Lanzmann, Claude, 204
La Peyrère, Isaac, 126–28
Larousse, Paul, 160
Last Day (*ultimus dies*), 72
last period of time (*novissimum tempus*), 72
Last Supper, 15, 37
Latour, Bruno, 220, 224–27, 273n98
Law, the, 98–99
laws of time, 52
Legend of the Ages, The (Hugo), 154–55, 212
Le Goff, Jacques, 55
Lent, 55
Les lieux de mémoire (Nora), 204
Les temps modernes, 186
Liebknecht, Karl, 161–62
Life of Jesus, The (Renan), 170, 174
liturgical calendars, 53–56, 83
Long Now Foundation, 208
Louis XVI, 169

Lucretia, 114
Luke, 18, 25–26, 75
lunar cycles, 76
Luther, Martin, 107–8, 114
Lyell, Charles, 149–50
Lysippos, 5–6

Machiavelli, Niccolò, 112
Maistre, Joseph de, 163–64
Make America Great Again, 209
Mallarmé, Stéphane, xviii–xix
man of *anomia,* 73
Manetho, 130
Manuel, Frank, 134–36
Mao Zedong, 176, 193
Map, Gautier, 111
Maranhão state, 119–20
Marcellinus, 86–87
Mark, 25–26, 28
Marshall Plan, 184
Martyr, Justin, 45
Marxism, 160
Matthew, 25–26, 75
McCarthy, Cormac, xii
Meirieu, Philippe, 200–1
Memoirs from Beyond the Grave (Chateaubriand), 233
memory and presentism, 203–5
Mendelsohn, Daniel, 203–4
Method for the Easy Comprehension of History (Bodin), 115–17
Michelet, Jules, 165–66, 171, 234
Middle Ages, 108, 160
millenarianism, 36, 128
modern regime of historicity, 155–57, 177–79
Momigliano, Arnaldo, 94
montanism, 36
Mosaic covenant, 15
Mosaic Law, 85, 86
Mosaic time, 31
Moses, 23, 57, 78, 118, 119
Mounier, Emmanuel, 186–87

Nagasaki bombing, 185–89
Natural History (Buffon), 142
Natural History of the Epochs of Nature, The (Buffon), 142
natural time, xvi–xvii, 161
nearly all—memory, 203–5
nefasti days, 53–54
negotiating with *chronos*: *accommodatio*/accommodation, 84, 85–92; Anselm of Havelberg, 87–89; Book of Daniel and, 93–98; introduction to, 83–85; Joachim of Fiore, 89–92; Otto of Freising, 102–4; *reformatio*, 84, 105–8; temporalized accommodation, 89–92; *translatio*, 84, 92–105
Nehru, Jawaharlal, 176
Neoplatonism, 5, 50
new covenant, 14–19, 109
new presentism, 192–95
New Testament, 8, 15, 16, 25–47, 45, 56–57, 75, 90, 112
Newton, Isaac, 132–37, 175
Nietzsche, Frederic, 178–79
Nora, Pierre, 204
novelty/novelties, 111, 178
now of presentism, 199–201
Nuremberg trials, 184–85

Observations Upon the Prophecies (Newton), 136
Obsolescence of Human Beings, The (Anders), 187
old covenant, 109
Old Testament, 15, 17, 30, 46, 56–57, 90, 112, 120, 135–36
On the Reckoning of Time (*De temporum ratione*) (Bede), 79, 81
On the Threshold of the Apocalypse (Bloy), 179
On Time (Bede), 80–81
Opus de doctrina temporum (Pétau), 131
oracle of chronology, 131
oracles, 14–15

Order of Time, The (Pomian), xvii–xviii
order of time (*taxis*), 2
Origin of Species, The (Darwin), 148
Orosius, 65, 66–68, 70
Otto III, 106
Otto of Freising, 102–4, 111, 121
over time (*processu temporis*), 87
Ozouf, Mona, 163

pagans/paganism, 19–20, 50, 65, 66–68, 113–14
Papon, Maurice, 185
Parallel of the Ancients and the Moderns, The (Perrault), 153
Parousia, xiii, 33–34, 40–48, 84, 110, 158, 171
Pascal, Blaise, 107, 123–25
Paschal tables, 74–75, 76–79, 129
Passion, 75–76, 80
Passover, 75–76
Passover meal, 52
pastism, 197–98
Paul, 18–19, 28–35, 57, 85–86
pax augusta, 66
pax christiana, 66
Péguy, Charles, 24, 160
Pentateuch, 10
Pentecost, 55
perfection and perfectibility, 152–55
Perrault, Charles, 153
Pétau, Denis, 131–32
Peter, 28
Philosophical Dialogues (Renan), 172
physical truths, 144
Pius IX, Pope, 140
planetary age, viii
Plato, 3, 5
plenitude of time, 44
Poincaré, Henri, 176
political religiosity, xi
politics of presentism, 197–99
Pomian, Krzysztof, xvii
Poseidippos of Pella, 5–6
posthumanists, 146, 210

Potestà, Gian Luca, 89
Praise Be to You (*Laudato Si'*) (Pope Francis), 230–31
pre-Adamites, 126–28
precautions, 202–3
presentism: acceleration/urgency and, 195–97; apocalyptic presentism, xix, 97, 151, 219; Christian presentism, xix, 108, 118, 125, 141, 156, 205–7, 217, 220; chronos and, 190–211; introduction to, vii, xix; memory and, 203–5; new presentism, 192–95; now of, 199–201; politics of, 197–99; protection, precautions, and prevention, 202–3; *reformatio* (reform), 201–2; short glossary of, 195–207; summary of, 207–11
prevention, 202–3
Principles of Geology (Lyell), 149
processus time, 161
progress and chronos, 151–60, 170–72, 178–81
Promethean gap, 188
prophets, 19–23, 19–25
protection, 202–3
Protestants, 108, 114, 133
Provincial Letters (Pascal), 107, 123–25

Rationale divinorum officiorum (Manual of divine offices) (Durand), 55–56
Rationarium temporum (Pétau), 131
real time, 194, 198
reformatio (reform), 84, 105–8, 159–60, 201–2
Reformation, 85, 108
regeneration (*regeneratio*), 178
relativity, theory of, 176
Renan, Ernest, 13, 151, 160, 170–75, 211, 219
renovatio (renewal), 84, 100–1, 111–15, 152, 230
restoration (*restitutio*), 112, 211–12
Revelation of John, 41–44, 91, 139
revolution and kairos, 162–65

Richard the Lionheart, 90, 119
Ricoeur, Paul, 4, 24, 51
right to memory, 204
Roger, Jacques, 142
Roman church, 36
Roman Empire, 34–35, 50, 98–102
Romme, Gilbert, 162–63
Rosa, Hartmut, 195
Rousseau, Jean-Jacques, 153–54
Rovelli, Carlo, xvii–xviii
Royer, Clémence, 148
ruler of seasons (*kairous*), 20
ruler of times (*chronous*), 12, 20

Sabbath, 71
SAMU (Service d'aide médicale urgente), 196
Sartre, Jean-Paul, 186, 187
saving time, 198
Scaliger, Joseph, 58, 128–31
Schmitt, Carl, 34–35, 101, 103–4
Schmitt, Jean-Claude, 54
scholasticism, 113
secret power of wickedness, 73
seers, 14–15
sempiternity (*aiôn*), 8
sensorium Dei, 175
Sermon on Providence (Bossuet), 11
Serres, Michel, 189
Seven Against Thebes (Aeschylus), 6
Shoah (Lanzmann), 204
short-termism, 209
Sibylline Oracles, 95
silent language of time, 207
simultaneity of the nonsimultaneous, 229–30
Singularity, the, 211
six days of Creation, 71
six spans of time, 144
Slow Food movement, 208
socialized time, 51
solar cycles, 76
Soubirous, Bernadette, 140, 221–22

spiritual age, 91–92
spiritual intelligence, 91
Spiritual Posterity of Joachim of Fiore, The (de Lubac), 211
Stalin, Joseph, 176
status in chronos time, 90
Strabo, Walafrid, 87
Stranger, The (Camus), 181
Streeck, Wolfgang, 194
suitable moments (*kairoi*), 8, 182
sustellein, defined, 31
synchronizing clocks, 175–77
synoptic Gospels, 25–26

Taubes, Jacob, 36
tempora christiana, 66–67
temporalities of the Anthropocene, 212–16, 226–34
temporalized accommodation, 89–92
temporalized creation, 148–50
Tertullian, 34–35, 53, 85
theory of relativity, 176
Theory of the Earth (Hutton), 149
Thesaurus temporum (Manetho), 130
Third Age of the Spirituals, 111
Thunberg, Greta, 221, 222
time: absolute time, 131–34, 175–76, 181; acceleration of, 12; cosmological time, 1; defined by Aristotle, 1; defined by Augustine, 1, 3–5; of deviation, 55; Earth's order of time, 215, 216–22; Greenwich time, x, 176; human time, xvi–xvii; in-between time (*media aetas*), 112; intermediate time, 162, 205; judicial time, 185; last period of time (*novissimum tempus*), 72; laws of time, 52; Mosaic time, 31; natural time, xvi–xvii, 161; order of time (*taxis*), 2; over time (*processu temporis*), 87; plenitude of, 44; *processus* time, 161; real time, 194, 198; of renewal, 55–56; saving time, 198; silent language of, 207; socialized time, 51; world time (Universal Time), 176. *See also* Christian order of time; chronos; kairos
timely (*en kairô*) intervention, 8
Titus, 16
Tocqueveille, Alexis de, 156
tota simul (all at once), 22
transhumanists, 146, 172, 210–11
transitional justice, 204
translatio studii, 113
translatio (succession of empires), 84, 92–105, 115–22
Trinity, 91, 92, 172
Trojan War, 95

under the Law (*sub lege*), 98
United Nations Conference on the Human Environment, 202
Universal Expositions, 155
Uranus, 2
urgency, 195–97
Ussher, James, 130

Valéry, Paul, xv, xix, 66, 180, 234
Vernant, Jean-Pierre, 2
Vieira, António, 117–22, 152
Virgil, 69
Virgin Mary, 140
Voltaire, 145

Waiting for Godot (Beckett), 190–92
week of years, 96
Wieviorka, Annette, 203
Works and Days, The (Hesiod), 51–52
world calendar, x
world time (Universal Time), 176
World War I, 179, 180, 207, 223
World War II, 184–89

ZAD (*zones à défendre*), 221
Zalasiewicz, Jan, 213–14, 219, 271n68
Zeus, 2, 6, 7
zoecentric history, 216

EUROPEAN PERSPECTIVES

A SERIES IN SOCIAL THOUGHT AND CULTURAL CRITICISM

Lawrence D. Kritzman, Editor

Gilles Deleuze, *Nietzsche and Philosophy*

David Carroll, *The States of "Theory"*

Gilles Deleuze, *The Logic of Sense*

Julia Kristeva, *Strangers to Ourselves*

Alain Finkielkraut, *Remembering in Vain: The Klaus Barbie Trial and Crimes Against Humanity*

Pierre Vidal-Naquet, *Assassins of Memory: Essays on the Denial of the Holocaust*

Julia Kristeva, *Nations Without Nationalism*

Theodor W. Adorno, *Notes to Literature*, vols. 1 and 2

Richard Wolin, ed., *The Heidegger Controversy*

Hugo Ball, *Critique of the German Intelligentsia*

Pierre Bourdieu, *The Field of Cultural Production*

Karl Heinz Bohrer, *Suddenness: On the Moment of Aesthetic Appearance*

Gilles Deleuze, *Difference and Repetition*

Gilles Deleuze and Félix Guattari, *What Is Philosophy?*

Alain Finkielkraut, *The Defeat of the Mind*

Jacques LeGoff, *History and Memory*

Antonio Gramsci, *Prison Notebooks*, vols. 1, 2, and 3

Ross Mitchell Guberman, *Julia Kristeva Interviews*

Julia Kristeva, *Time and Sense: Proust and the Experience of Literature*

Elisabeth Badinter, *XY: On Masculine Identity*

Gilles Deleuze, *Negotiations, 1972–1990*

Julia Kristeva, *New Maladies of the Soul*

Norbert Elias, *The Germans*

Elisabeth Roudinesco, *Jacques Lacan: His Life and Work*

Paul Ricoeur, *Critique and Conviction: Conversations with François Azouvi and Marc de Launay*

Pierre Vidal-Naquet, *The Jews: History, Memory, and the Present*

Karl Löwith, *Martin Heidegger and European Nihilism*

Pierre Nora, *Realms of Memory: The Construction of the French Past*

Vol. 1: *Conflicts and Divisions*

Vol. 2: *Traditions*

Vol. 3: *Symbols*

Alain Corbin, *Village Bells: Sound and Meaning in the Nineteenth-Century French Countryside*

Louis Althusser, *Writings on Psychoanalysis: Freud and Lacan*

Claudine Fabre-Vassas, *The Singular Beast: Jews, Christians, and the Pig*

Tahar Ben Jelloun, *French Hospitality: Racism and North African Immigrants*

Alain Finkielkraut, *In the Name of Humanity: Reflections on the Twentieth Century*

Emmanuel Levinas, *Entre Nous: Essays on Thinking-of-the-Other*

Zygmunt Bauman, *Globalization: The Human Consequences*

Emmanuel Levinas, *Alterity and Transcendence*

Alain Corbin, *The Life of an Unknown: The Rediscovered World of a Clog Maker in Nineteenth-Century France*

Carlo Ginzburg, *Wooden Eyes: Nine Reflections on Distance*

Sylviane Agacinski, *Parity of the Sexes*

Michel Pastoureau, *The Devil's Cloth: A History of Stripes and Striped Fabric*

Alain Cabantous, *Blasphemy: Impious Speech in the West from the Seventeenth to the Nineteenth Century*

Julia Kristeva, *The Sense and Non-Sense of Revolt: The Powers and Limits of Psychoanalysis*

Kelly Oliver, *The Portable Kristeva*

Gilles Deleuze, *Dialogues II*

Catherine Clément and Julia Kristeva, *The Feminine and the Sacred*

Sylviane Agacinski, *Time Passing: Modernity and Nostalgia*

Luce Irigaray, *Between East and West: From Singularity to Community*

Julia Kristeva, *Hannah Arendt*

Julia Kristeva, *Intimate Revolt: The Powers and Limits of Psychoanalysis*, vol. 2

Elisabeth Roudinesco, *Why Psychoanalysis?*

Régis Debray, *Transmitting Culture*

Steve Redhead, ed., *The Paul Virilio Reader*

Claudia Benthien, *Skin: On the Cultural Border Between Self and the World*

Julia Kristeva, *Melanie Klein*

Roland Barthes, *The Neutral: Lecture Course at the Collège de France (1977–1978)*

Hélène Cixous, *Portrait of Jacques Derrida as a Young Jewish Saint*

Theodor W. Adorno, *Critical Models: Interventions and Catchwords*

Julia Kristeva, *Colette*

Gianni Vattimo, *Dialogue with Nietzsche*

Emmanuel Todd, *After the Empire: The Breakdown of the American Order*

Gianni Vattimo, *Nihilism and Emancipation: Ethics, Politics, and Law*

Hélène Cixous, *Dream I Tell You*

Steve Redhead, *The Jean Baudrillard Reader*

Jean Starobinski, *Enchantment: The Seductress in Opera*

Jacques Derrida, *Geneses, Genealogies, Genres, and Genius: The Secrets of the Archive*

Hélène Cixous, *White Ink: Interviews on Sex, Text, and Politics*

Marta Segarra, ed., *The Portable Cixous*

François Dosse, *Gilles Deleuze and Félix Guattari: Intersecting Lives*

Julia Kristeva, *This Incredible Need to Believe*

François Noudelmann, *The Philosopher's Touch: Sartre, Nietzsche, and Barthes at the Piano*

Antoine de Baecque, *Camera Historica: The Century in Cinema*

Julia Kristeva, *Hatred and Forgiveness*

Roland Barthes, *How to Live Together: Novelistic Simulations of Some Everyday Spaces*

Jean-Louis Flandrin and Massimo Montanari, *Food: A Culinary History*

Georges Vigarello, *The Metamorphoses of Fat: A History of Obesity*

Julia Kristeva, *The Severed Head: Capital Visions*

Eelco Runia, *Moved by the Past: Discontinuity and Historical Mutation*

François Hartog, *Regimes of Historicity: Presentism and Experiences of Time*

Jacques Le Goff, *Must We Divide History Into Periods?*

Claude Lévi-Strauss, *We Are All Cannibals: And Other Essays*

Marc Augé, *Everyone Dies Young: Time Without Age*

Roland Barthes: *Album: Unpublished Correspondence and Texts*

Étienne Balibar, *Secularism and Cosmopolitanism: Critical Hypotheses on Religion and Politics*

Ernst Jünger, *A German Officer in Occupied Paris: The War Journals, 1941–1945*

Dominique Kalifa, *Vice, Crime, and Poverty: How the Western Imagination Invented the Underworld*

Dominique Kalifa, *The Belle Époque: A Cultural History, Paris and Beyond*

Antonio Gramsci, *Subaltern Social Groups: A Critical Edition of Prison Notebook 25*

Julia Kristeva, *Dostoyevsky, or The Flood of Language*